The Barnum & Bailey Greatest Show on Earth

GENERAL VIEW OF THE PRINCIPAL COLOSSAL WATERPROOF EXHIBITION PAVILIONS EXACTLY THE SAME AS WILL BE ERECTED, TOGETHER WITH A REALISTIC PICTURE of the ARRIVAL OF OUR 4 TRAINS OF 67 SPECIALLY CONSTRUCTED RAILWAY CARS, WITH THE HORSES, TWO MENAGERIES AND VAST SHOW MATERIAL

THE CIRCUS MOVES BY RAIL

Front Endsheets:

Baggage horses wend their way between cuts of cars as the Ringling Bros. and Barnum & Bailey Circus prepares to unload at Brooklyn, New York, the first under-canvas stand of the 1936 season — *R. E. Trexler.*

Beyond a Ringling baggage wagon and Flatcar 141, a circus dowager peers from the door of her Al G. Barnes-Sells Floto Circus elephant car at the start of another day on the 1938 tour — *Authors' Photo.*

Back Endsheets:

A pullover team of the Cole Bros.-Clyde Beatty Circus leans into the harness to roll Wagon 29, dining department, over the deck of a Mt. Vernon flatcar — *Gene Baxter.*

A railroad coach, Percherons, flatcars, and heavy baggage wagons make up the scene as the first section of the Ringling circus train awaits unloading at Brooklyn, New York, in 1936 — *R. E. Trexler.*

THE CIRCUS MOVES BY RAIL

By

Tom Parkinson and Charles Philip Fox

PRUETT **P**PUBLISHING COMPANY

Boulder, Colorado 80301

Library of Congress Cataloging in Publication Data

Parkinson, Tom.
  The circus moves by rail.

  Includes index.
  1. Circus trains.   I. Fox, Charles Philip,
1904-   joint author. II. Title.
GV1822.P37   791.3'028   78-23457
ISBN 0-87108-515-1

First Edition

1 2 3 4 5 6 7 8 9

Printed in the United States of America

Acknowledgements

The authors wish to thank and acknowledge the assistance of the many circus and railroad historians, photographers and enthusiasts, as well as both railroaders and circus people who have helped them in the preparation of this book. In particular, they wish to thank the Circus World Museum and its Chief Librarian and Historian, Robert L. Parkinson. The authors thank Ringling Bros. and Barnum & Bailey Combined Shows, Inc., for permission to reproduce material involving circus names it owns, among them Ringling Bros. and Barnum & Bailey Circus, Barnum & Bailey Greatest Show on Earth, Ringling Bros. World's Greatest Shows, Sells Floto Circus, Hagenbeck-Wallace Circus, Sparks Circus, John Robinson Circus, Al G. Barnes Circus, Buffalo Bill's Wild West and Forepaugh-Sells Bros. Circus.

Contents

Prologue

First attempts at moving by rail
Circus experiments, 1830s–1870s — 1

Origin

The Barnum show of 1872
W. C. Coup — 15

Development

Show train growth, numbers, 1873–1978
"Railroad Show" as a status symbol — 21
Heyday

Operations

How shows function by rail
Routing, contracting, the New York Central Week,
    exclusive contracts — 39
Railroad influence on routes
Rates, tariffs, show script

Advance Cars

Advertising departments aboard special cars
Box brigades
Country routes, "Railroad work" — 75
Opposition
Billing

Flatcars

Car lengths and designs
Makers
Loading orders — 97
Steel and wooden cars

Stockcars

Car designs
Makers — 115
Baggage stock, ring stock, ponies, lead stock,
    elephants

Coaches

Living aboard a show train
Assignment of space; berths, compartments, three-high
Private cars
Ballet girls' car — 129
Side show car
Riding the flats
Pie cars

Show Moves

Runs and jumps
Switching, consists, car rosters, circus train
    crews, loading orders — 159
Railroad operations
Winter maintenance and circus car shops

Excursions

Special trains, lower rates for circus day   235

Unusual Moves

Dukie runs, Sunday runs, sleeper jumps
Famous long and short moves
Feed and water stops   245
Floating
Reaching New York

Disasters

Show trains in wrecks, floods, and fires   259

Two-Car Shows

Amazing miniatures
Tunnel cars
Baggage car moves   277
Passenger service
Gilly shows

Modern Moves

Ringling-Barnum's new era
Tunnel car procedures
Piggybacks, rack cars   287
New system, new units
Consists
Aboard a circus train in 1977

Outgrowths

Car shows
Chautauqua
Uncle Tom's Cabin
The Rabbit Foot Show   323
Holiday on Ice
Ice Capades
Carnivals
Circus World Museum's circus parade train

Appendix   368

Index   387

This book is dedicated to the general agents, advance car managers, twenty-four-hour men and train masters of the railroad circuses. On big shows and little, they were experts in operations, heroes in crisis, and above all, troupers, with it and for it. Among them were some of the greatest circus stars.

Prologue

On grade crossings or curves, on bridges or branches, at sidings and junctions and depots and yards, the circus train was an attraction that marked the day, elated the senses, and engraved the memory.

If heralds on boxcars aroused imagination about distant places on ordinary days, then a circus train—ornately lettered, carrying strange cargo, holding mysterious promise—created great new excitement on circus days.

Railroading, of course, was so intriguing as to warrant day-after-day fascination with cars and locomotives and schedules and all the rest. Circuses were captivating for their posters, parades, and, above all, their performances. So the combination of circusing and railroading was about as much as one pair of eyes could encompass, one intellect could comprehend. In an age when men went down to the depot daily to see the train come in, routine was utterly shattered if a white-flagged engine rounded the bend to reveal that it had a red and gold circus train in tow.

And things haven't changed much in more than a hundred years.

Ordinary crossings and sidings became places of wonder as locomotives chugged the strange and brilliant consist into view. The scene fairly burst into action. Engines spotted cars. Men set the runs. Horses clomped down the ramps. Wagons rolled off the flats. Eight-horse teams appeared. Crews gathered. Crowds formed. Boys gaped. A midget hopped down from a coach, and a camel peered from a stockcar. Huge wagons, more cages, a calliope, and a span of zebras materialized. Then a dozen elephants surprised you from behind.

The posters said "train after train" and "a thousand men and horses" and "three herds of elephants" and "wild animals from every clime." Surely, they underestimated what the circus train gave forth!

There were circuses before there were railroads, and there were trains before there were tracks. A concept of a circus performance took form in England and was transplanted intact to early America. But changes soon became apparent. American showmen gave this form of entertainment the mobility for which it is famous. The idea of a travelling show, specifically the playing of one-day stands, was a development of American circuses. European circuses constructed buildings; Americans built wagons.

By the 1830s, numerous circuses and menageries were playing up and down the Eastern Seaboard and venturing across the Alleghenies. These were wagon shows, drawn from town to town by teams of horses in a continual battle against the miserable roadways of the time.

Showmen, like armies, referred to their fleets of wagons as trains even before western pioneers turned their kind of wagon train into circles for the night. Circus men had cage trains—the convoys of light cage wagons and omnibuses moving rapidly along the lanes and trails. And they had baggage trains—slower wagons loaded down with tents and poles and seats and trunks. So early circus records are peppered with references to trains that meant caravans of wagons moving overland.

In the middle third of the nineteenth century, wagon circuses multiplied and grew. Dozens of them crisscrossed the limited road network. And there were big ones—some with a hundred wagons and four hundred horses, scores of employees, and tons of wonders. They transported rhinos and hippos and huge tents with forty-foot poles and 6,000 seats. If anything approached the railroad circus as a wonderment, it was the wagon circus. Often it was a huge affair and always it was a huge event, perhaps the town's principal entertainment of the year.

Major wagon outfits like the Adam Forepaugh Circus, the Howes Great London Show, the Van Amburgh Menagerie, or the Spalding & Rogers Circus toured the little eastern nation and stretched westward with it to the Mississippi and even a little beyond.

As soon as the iron horse made its appearance, these horse operas quickly gravitated to the railroads—just as they also utilized canals and riverboats, just as later they would turn to motor trucks. Circuses tried every form of transportation, but it was with the railroads that they assembled the greatest system for success.

There were occasional minor attempts at railroading by a few earlier shows, but in the 1850s circus men settled down to the task at hand. It was practically a family affair at first, with the shadow of Dr. Gilbert Spalding cast over nearly all of the experiments. Spalding, a guiding light of circus business at this time, was perhaps the most innovative circus manager of all.

The Stone & Madigan Circus reportedly made many railroad jumps as it played Mississippi Valley territory in 1851. This is hard to fathom, since there were so few miles of railway operable in that area at the time. It probably made some jumps by rail but more by the standard wagon methods.

This show was named for Den Stone, a leading clown

and Henry Madigan, an established rider, both straight off of the Spalding & Rogers Circus. On their staff was a brother-in-law of Spalding, Wessell T. B. Van Orden, Jr., who had served on Spalding & Rogers as a partner, press agent, and caretaker for cantankerous clowns. It wouldn't be surprising if Spalding money backed this show.

New in 1853 was the Railroad Circus & Crystal Amphitheater, apparently a spin-off from Spalding & Rogers. The manager was Van Orden. With it were Den Stone, Henry Madigan, and several other Spalding graduates, including H. F. Nichols and Le Jeune Burte.

Each of the pioneer railroad shows in this series operated only a single season and was replaced by another. But for 1854 there were two such shows. One was Madigan, Myers & Barton's Railroad Circus & Amphitheater of the Republic. The other was Den Stone's Original Railroad Circus. Not surprisingly, familiar Spalding names were involved.

The Stone show set the tone that rail circuses would follow for some years to come when it declared, "The great facility afforded by railroad transit gives preeminence to this troupe in every respect over the worn-out, behind-the-age, slow, perambulating baggage wagon system of the old fogey managements."

Following in this procession of annual railroad extravaganzas was the Great Western Railroad Circus of 1855. The sequence and timing suggest that each of these shows might have been the prior year's edition in a new guise. The Great Western was secretive about its origins—no one's name was listed in its title—but it included Spalding veterans such as Wash Chambers, scenic rider, and Madame Olinza, rope walker. And the Stone show's manager became the Great Western's advance agent.

Seemingly, this outfit kept a low profile so as not to draw undue attention to its experimentation just yet, probably out of deference to its manager. And who was he? Dr. Gilbert Spalding.

All of these were small shows, nothing to compare with

the big ten-elephant outfit that Seth B. Howes operated then, for example. In fact, none of these had even one elephant. Nor did any of them have a menagerie or trained wild animals. The exception was a Russian bear named Nicholas on the Den Stone Circus, and Nicholas probably trouped in chain and muzzle rather than in a cage wagon.

Moreover, none of these forerunners had a street parade. The Den Stone show made it quite clear in advertising that it had "No money wasted in outside show to allure and deceive the inexperienced. No chariots or montebank processions." Translated, that means no parade, and, extended, it adds to the suspicion that these several railroad outfits had no wagons at all. The Railroad Circus & Crystal Amphitheater boasted of a chariot race, but a pair of such two-wheeled carts hardly constituted a convoy of circus wagons. Consequently, it may well be that these few early shows utilized no flatcars—only stockcars for their horses and boxcars into which all other show property was loaded. Nor is it at all certain that they used any passenger cars; the people could ride over in one of the numerous local passenger trains, and they lived in hotels, just as they did with wagon shows. At most, a single day coach transported the personnel.

Locally rented drays could have been used to shuttle the show equipment between train and showgrounds. If this were the case, these early circuses operated in the same way that baggage car shows of a later time would function. To the immediate point, they were not faced with the question of how heavy circus wagons in number could be loaded and unloaded efficiently from railroad equipment.

These were not long trains, only six or eight cars, and therefore they might sometimes have been moved in regular freights and sometimes as specials. The so-called western roads of the time were fairly well standardized as to the gauge of track, but there appears to have been little exchange of cars between lines. And since some different gauges still existed, it may be likely that different cars were hired at each town or each time they changed railroads.

With benefit of experience from his own show and those in which he may have had an interest, Spalding came forth with a new show for 1856—the highly publicized Spalding & Rogers Railroad Circus.

He ordered nine custom-built railroad cars from the established firm of James Goold & Sons of Spalding's old hometown, Albany, New York. Nine cars did not comprise a very large circus; it was no larger than its few predecessors. This show also was devoid of menagerie and parade equipment. Its street procession was limited to a mounted band of eighteen pieces. The performance, however, was very strong, particularly with its imposing array of leading bareback riders.

The show declared that its cars were built to be taken from the railroad track to the showgrounds each day. That is the way the ads read, but it seems most unlikely. Moreover, at the opening stand, Washington, D. C., there was some ambiguity in the wording which suggests the possibility that it was merely the show property and not the railroad cars which were transferred daily from track to lot. There are accounts which speak of some type of containerized units which were moved on railroad cars and then rolled through the streets on very small wheels, a system sure to collapse on the first muddy lot. If, as the show said, those cars were taken from the track to the lot, they must have reassembled the Road-Railer units, which had both steel and rubber wheels and which Ringling Bros. and Barnum & Bailey in 1977 was studying for possible future use. Operation of the Spalding & Rogers Circus train long has been a mystery for circus historians, but the possibility exists that it, too, lacked wagons and flatcars; that it, too, shuttled show property from ordinary boxcars to the day's showgrounds.

This circus made an impressive route through Pennsylvania, New York, Massachusetts, Maine, the British provinces, and into Michigan. Adjustable axles on the cars compensated for any change in gauge between railroads. At the end of the season, the personnel took a steamboat south to join those on other Spalding & Rogers units, one travelling by wagon and one by riverboat. But those nine custom cars were "switched off at Cincinnati," and Spalding & Rogers made no further attempt at railroading. A true railroad circus still did not exist.

Others, however, were to pick up the banner. Among them were the Hyatt Railroad Circus, Whitby's Metropolitan Railroad Circus, Haight & Chambers, and the Dan Rice show. Howes & Robinson rode leased cars down through the Middle West during the Civil War—a trip marked by a jarring halt when a center pole overhanging a boxcar roof jammed into a railside embankment.

For 1866, Lewis B. Lent loaded up the circus that normally performed in his "iron building" in New York City and went on a tour "per railway." His show included a fancy bandwagon for street processions, necessitating a flatcar on the train. He played eastern territory for three years with that set-up, then sold the bandwagon and continued with his railroading. It is possible that Lent used no flats other than the one for the bandwagon. He apparently did keep the same train all season, speaking of "cars leased for the purpose."

So, after as much as eighteen years of experimentation, circusdom still had not developed the real railroad circus. They billed themselves as railroad circuses without yet realizing just what that ultimately would come to mean. But they tried.

Meanwhile, in the 1860s a number of ordinary wagon circuses, making most of their moves overland, were trying some special jumps by train. In these cases, they remained as wagon circuses. An occasional railroad move didn't change the fact that they had enough horses to move everything overland at once and that they carried omnibuses to transport the people. There was a major difference between a wagon show that rode a train on occasion and those railroad outfits that were unable to operate away from the tracks.

The Hemmings, Cooper & Whitby Circus was a good-sized overland show. It trouped for eight and one-half

4

months in 1869, playing some 204 cities and towns and making all but twelve or fifteen of those jumps by wagon, a grueling contest as it turned out.

It opened in Philadelphia and immediately shipped by rail to Altoona. After several regular wagon moves, it left Cincinnati by steamboat. Next came several difficult moves through the mud to villages in Indiana and Illinois. Richard Hemmings wrote that it was "cold and miserable." Getting to Greencastle was a "hard drive on the stock." En route to Brazil involved a "very bad muddy road all the way," so he "shipped some of the stuff through in the cars." Four of the next five jumps were made by rail, but Shelbyville, Sullivan, and Arcola, Illinois, lacked rail connections. As a result, the baggage stock had to drag the show wagons through the muddy roads. While the bulk of his circus was moving overland, sometimes Hemmings himself would slip away from the struggle and "go through on the cars;" he'd find the depot and take a local to the next town rather than ride the show wagons through the night.

Out of Lewiston, Illinois, Hemmings went to Canton by train, while the show equipment was shipped loose in boxcars. The show's teams pulled the empty wagons overland—thirty miles of mud including a detour because a bridge had been washed out.

That was the easy part. Leaving Iowa City in July for Richmond, the show sloshed around in muddy roads, found that bridges were washed out, and finally turned back. It just couldn't get to Richmond. Nor did it make any of the next three towns. The show was flooded out. In desperation, they found a railroad and loaded everything on system cars that took it to Muscatine, Iowa. That town wasn't on the schedule, but they hastily passed out some bills and gave a show. Then they moved on to Fort Madison, partly by train and partly by steamboat. The Hemmings, Cooper & Whitby experience was better than most in that season. Of twenty-eight major circuses that opened, only six completed the season because of the bad business resulting from endless rains.

In a dozen boom years railroads had been built almost

everywhere in the eastern half of the continent. And work was being completed on a landmark line—the railroad that would link the eastern half with distant California! Circus men had their eye on that route to the West. One show that might have acted was the C. S. Noyes Crescent City Circus. It switched to rails in late 1869 and never stopped, winter or summer, for five years, but Texas was west enough for them.

Instead, it was the Dan Castello Circus that made the breakthrough first railroad trip to the West Coast, a saga that actually began in April 1868 when it opened in Maryland. It travelled coast to coast but was still a marginal operation, as much a wagon show riding a train as a rail show in the later sense of the words. It usually moved by train, but it also could leave the trackage to reach more remote towns. When it left the rails, it had horses enough for overland moves. And those wagons were of light design, including high, spindly wheels. There were omnibuses and buggies for taking the people over the roads. And its train was a string of system cars, not show property.

As the last spikes were driven at Promontory Point, the Castello Circus already was on its way West. The whole American population was agog about the transcontinental railroad, but none was more alert to its prospects than the Castello troupe. Its advance man rode the first through train after the completion of the tracks. The show worked its way toward Omaha to set forth upon the new Union Pacific. In a few more days it would play places like Grand Island, North Platte, and Cheyenne by train.

It left the rails to go overland some 110 miles to become the first circus to play Denver; rails had not yet reached that city. The show pushed up mountain roads to reach Central City, and it played Golden, Georgetown, and Boulder before returning to the Cheyenne side-track for its cars.

Then the circus continued westward by rail. In some ways it was like those trial railroad runs in the 1850s; it, too, had only eight cars. In some ways it was like Hemmings—it went off on wagons. But it also represented new departures beyond the matter of its route: the Castello Circus carried an elephant by rail. There were ten cage wagons with menagerie animals in residence. Show gear was packed in baggage wagons on flats, not boxcars. In this evolution, the Castello show was closer than the others to the final goal.

Continuing by rail to a string of Utah towns, the Castello troupers were shocked to find that a rival Great Railroad Combination Circus, eastbound, had played in Ogden; others were also eager to reach new towns and try new trains for circusing.

From Reno, the Castello Circus again went to wagons. It played a string of desert-mountain hamlets before picking up its cars at Truckee, California.

Triumphantly, the circus exhibited in San Francisco for four summer weeks. Then it toured other California cities to complete the season. It turned in its train to the Central Pacific and sold most of its own equipment to a California circus, then disbanded. Dan Castello himself kept some of his trick horses and perhaps the bandwagon. Aboard a regular passenger train, he deadheaded back to the central states, destined to take part in even greater circus railroad events.

The railroad circus was an enormous and powerful combination of two energetic and enterprising institutions, epitomized by these views. A Norfolk & Western locomotive brings a Ringling section along as it pounds through Virginia. Pittsburghers turn out in force to watch the first wagon come off the flats; next in line is a Mack truck and then a giraffe den. In a painting-like scene, the Al G. Barnes Circus train of 1924 graces Union Pacific tracks — *Author's Collection.*

A mighty institution, the circus reached unbelievable zeniths in size, efficiency, and self-sufficiency, due in great measure to its marriage with railroads — *Circus World Museum.*

Americans knew circuses earlier as overland affairs — horse-drawn outfits that expended most of their energy battling the horrendous roads of the time. That was the normal way to operate until the advent of the railroad show. Not until there was something with which to compare did showmen know to nickname wagon circuses as "mud shows." But the reason always was clear. That the mire remained when mud shows motorized is demonstrated by the Seils-Sterling Circus in Iowa during the 1920s — *Norman Wilbert.*

DEN STONE'S GREAT ORIGINAL

RAILROAD CIRCUS!

will exhibit at Detroit

Friday and Saturday, June 9th and 10th.

This superb Equestrian Troupe is organized and equipped upon an entirely new principle, and conducted in conformity with the times in which we live. This Company will introduce for the first time in any country, a Troupe of

FLYING ARTISTES,

comprising the most prominent Riders, Gymnasts, Acrobats, Comic Geniuses and Pantomimic Performers, that ever traveled in any previous concern.

NO MONEY WASTED IN OUTSIDE PARADE,

to allure and deceive the inexperienced. No chariots or other mountebank processions. But, instead thereof, the Proprietors have made an

IMMENSE INVESTMENT IN TALENT,

American, English, German and French. The great facilities afforded by railroad transit, gives pre-eminence to this Troupe in every respect, over the worn out, behind the age, slow, perambulating baggage wagon system of the old fogy managements. The features in Den Stone's Circus are

Fast Horses--Fast Riders--Fast Novelties.

Magnitude, Splendor, Grandeur, a full Circus Performance, in strict conformity with the bills, liberality to all in his employ, and the highest order of talent in his profession. In this exhibition will be given all the great points of the Hippodrome, as well as those graceful and athletic sports belonging the time-honored Arena.

Grotesque or Trick Clown, MR. BURTE.
Master of the Circle, FRANK WHITTAKER.
Leader of the German Band, HERR ELLSINHAMER.
Equestrian Director, W. AYMAR.
Manager of the Troupe, S. O. BUTTS.
The principal Riders are—

MLL'E MARIETTA,	MR. WATERMAN,
LE JEUNE BURTE,	DEN STONE,
J. WARD,	W. AYMAR,
F. WHITTAKER,	MLL'E MARIK,
ALBERT AYMAR,	L. LIPMAN.

Together with the extraordinary performances of the

RUSSIAN BEAR, NICHOLAS,

in several acts of Horsemanship.

THE CLOWN, DEN STONE,

will open his inexhaustible Budget of Fun, dispensing a profusion of laughing philosophy, bon mots, hits at the times, fresh jokes, comical sayings, repartees, sympathy, satire, sentiment and stump speeches, galvanized grins, fantastic grotesques, love ditties and soft yarn, which he will distribute to the laughter loving multitude with prodigal liberality.

☞ Price of admission 25 cents. Performance commences at 2 and 7 P. M. je2dtd

---

Left: Den Stone's Circus was prominent among the pioneers in railroading, but it was only a small outfit and hardly a match for the biggest wagon shows of the era. It would be another twenty years before "railroad show" implied "big show" — *Detroit Public Library. Right:* One of the earliest attempts at circus railroading, the Railroad Circus & Crystal Amphitheater of 1853, probably was a Spalding operation in thin disguise — *Detroit Public Library.*

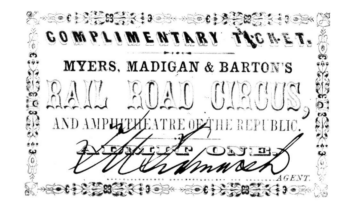

As soon as there were either circuses or railroads, there were passes. So it is little wonder that when Myers, Madigan & Barton's Rail Road Circus & Amphitheater of the Republic first tried railroad travel, its agent provided complimentary tickets for the conductors who handled his cars. The reverse side is franked by the agent as a "Conductor's Ticket, good any time in the season." That was in 1854, and such passes have been in circulation every season since — *Authors' Collection.*

RAILROAD CIRCUS

AND

CRYSTAL AMPHITHEATRE,

Seating 5000 Persons!

With a selection of Performers from the European and American Circuses and Hippodromes, expressly for this colossal enterprise, with

MORE NOVELTIES AND TALENT

Than has ever been offered by a Traveling Company, will exhibit at Detroit on

THURSDAY, FRIDAY AND SATURDAY,

September 8th, 9th and 10th.

ADMISSION TWENTY-FIVE CENTS ONLY.

Positively no half-price.

Among the distinguished Artists are the following, who now first make a Tour of this country: M'LLE ROSA, the most beautiful and expert Female Equestrian the profession has ever produced. DONNA ISABELLA, the celebrated Spanish Mistress of the Horse, with her beautiful thorough-bred Pyrenean Mares, Countess Montejo and Queen Christiana. LE JEUNE BURTE, the Boy-Hero, confessedly the most extraordinary Equestrian on the Continent. HERR CUIST, MAITRE VALENTINI, and MONS. GULIEME, the famous European Hippodrome Performers, in those three most exciting feats of the Hippodrome—

La Perch Equipoise, La Trapaze, and a Spirited Chariot Contest.

DEN. STONE, the celebrated NEW ORLEANS CLOWN—the accomplished Gentlemen, skillful Rider, and piquant Wit, with his Ballet and Pantomime Troupe, producing every night the thrilling Equestrian Pantomime entitled

THE BRIGAND.

Besides these, there are Messrs. H. P. MADIGAN, WILLIAMS, H. F. NICHOLS, SAM. BURTE, DURR, LOVETT, Misses MARY, PAULINE and MARGUERETTA, and Maitres JAMES and CHARLES, etc. etc.

MYERS' celebrated Brass, Reed and String Band constitutes the Orchestra.

The Stud of trained, Pad, Trick, and Manege Horses are the most beautiful and obedient that have ever been seen in this country. aug29dtd

9

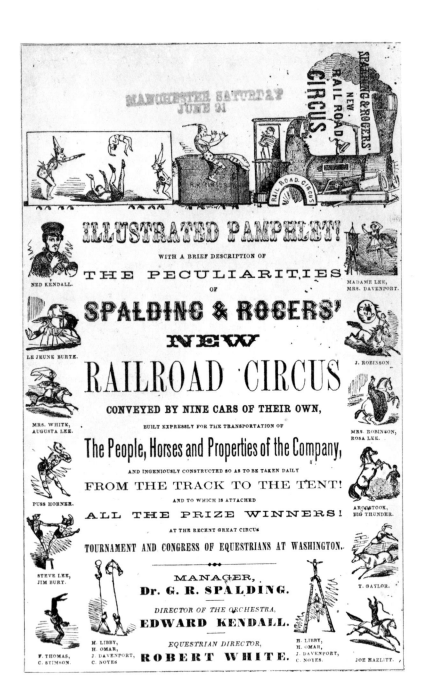

In order to furnish to their Eastern and Northern Patrons the same degree of Novelty, originality and perfection that Messrs. SPALDING & ROGERS have afforded to the citizens of the South and West, on their three Exhibition Steamers, on the Mississippi, (the FLOATING PALACE, JAMES RAYMOND, and BANJO,) after experimenting at great expense, they have at length projected

A NEW RAILROAD CIRCUS!

FOR WHICH THEY HAVE BUILT NINE CARS OF THEIR OWN!

Expressly for the transportation of the establishment, and so ingeniously constructed as to be taken daily, with their contents,

FROM THE TRACK TO THE EXHIBITION GROUNDS!

Thus obviating the great and inseparable drawbacks of the old fashioned Wagon Circus, — Skeleton Team Horses, fagged out Ring Horses, tired Performers, sleepy Clowns, dilapidated Harness and Wagons, and tarnished Trappings—the natural consequence of twenty miles a day of night travel over rough roads.

Under the old regime, the Company are always fatigued and querulous; the Ring Horses leg-weary, and anything but the flashy animals they are pictured on the bills; the Clown loses his mother wit, if he ever had any, and is too sleepy to nourish any he may have acquired; the performers wade through a dull and vapid performance with the least possible labor; the musicians scarcely open their eyes until they give the long wished for blast for the afterpiece; the ticket seller gruffly makes the change for the ticket, in receiving which the door-keeper rudely thrusts you aside in his dreamy listlessness; the ushers follow you at a snail's pace while you hunt up a seat for yourself; the landlord works all night to wake up the company to breakfast at three in the morning, and for his pains often has his bill disputed for a few pennies by the worn out manager.

2

Opposite page, left: A wonder well before its time, the Spalding & Rogers Railroad Circus held out the dream for a year before reverting to standard wagon operation. Details of Spalding & Rogers' railroading methods are a mystery still not uncovered by historians — *Authors' Collection. Opposite page, right:* Spalding & Rogers clearly believed that their railroad experiment was second to steamboating, with which they scored their greatest success. But their description of wagon show life revealed a full understanding of the need for railroad transportation — *New York Historical Society. Above:* Beginning in 1866, Lewis B. Lent moved his circus by chartered cars and was among the first to carry a circus wagon regularly on a flatcar. His artist could draw locomotives but didn't understand at all that circus musicians would ride in a coach — not pinned to their bandwagon seats by a cloud of smoke and soot — *Authors' Collection.*

COMING ON WHEELS!

MAGINLEY & CO.'S
ROYAL CIRCUS, BRITISH MUSEUM,
MAMMOTH MENAGERIE,
And Wonderful School of Educated Animals

IMPORTANT ANNOUNCEMENT to the entire press and populace of New Brunswick and Nova Scotia.

The above Grand Establishment will positively appear in the Provinces as Announced on their Programmes that were distributed months ago, presenting the largest array of Arenic Artists, and Zoological attractions ever offered the public, employing more men, more horses, cages, carriages, chariots, and animal dens, and spreading more canvas by thousands of yards than any organization ever in the Provinces.

It costs no more to visit this immense Establishment than is demanded by a small and inferior *Rail Road Circus*, which only presents stale attractions, and dissatisfy the public after witnessing them. Save your money for the BIG SHOW, and receive five times the amount in amusement and instruction. Recollect that all reports circulated against this Mammoth Show is caused through *fear and jealousy* of our approach. Also recollect that inferior concerns try to poison the minds against a GREAT ENTERPRISE thereby endeavoring to hold their ground in public patronage; but people are staying away from small shows, and only patronizing the larger ones.

Be prepared for the *large Elephants, the huge Rhinoceros*, and the forty horse team driven by one man.

Recollect, Maginley's Big Show is coming.

CLAUDE De HAVEN, Agent

GOD SAVE THE QUEEN.

MAGINLEY & CARROLL'S
GREAT
RAILROAD SHOW

THOROUGHLY REORGANIZED & EQUIPPED
In the City of New York, for the Season of 1868.

PARAGONS OF EQUESTRIAN ART.

The Great Aim of the Managers is
ORIGINALITY AND EXCELLENCE
AND WITH THIS VIEW THEY HAVE CONGREGATED AN
ASSEMBLAGE OF ARTISTES,
From the MOST CELEBRATED SCHOOLS OF EQUESTRIAN & GYMNASTIC ART
Both in Europe and America.

RAILROAD SHOW!
THE FACILITIES FOR SPEED AND CERTAIN TRANSIT ARE UNEQUALLED.
No Jaded Horses and Wearied, Travel-Worn Performers.
EVERYTHING FRESH, NOVEL AND BRILLIANT.
THIS NE PLUS ULTRA EXHIBITION WILL BE AT

Indianapolis, Monday, April 20,
WHERE THEY WILL GIVE
2 GRAND EXHIBITIONS, AT 2 AND 6½ O'CLOCK P. M.
Admission, Cents. Children under 10, Half Price.

Prominent in the BRILLIANT ARRAY OF TALENT will be found

M'LLE MARIE ELIZE
ON HER BARE-BACK STEED, "ESMERALDA."

MAD. CARROLL,	Mr. W. B. CARROLL
M'LLE GERTRUDE & M'LLE KATIE	Mr. W. ROLLANDE,
THE BELMONT BROTHERS.	FLYING IN THE AIR. Mr. J. G. ADAMS,
BILLY DUCROW.	Mr. JOHN NAYLOR
ROBT. JOHNSON,	Mr. JAS. ESSLER,
	MAST. WILLIE,

The Famous Thorough-Bred
TRICK AND RACE HORSE "ROSEWOOD,"

Equestrians, Voltigeurs, Athletes, Danseuses and Hippo-Dramatists

THE DEPARTMENT OF MOMUS
MR. BEN. MAGINLEY

CHAS. MYER'S SUPERB CORNET & G. W. PEARSON'S STRING BAND

Opposite page: When Ben Maginley took a wagon circus to the Maritime Provinces in the 1860s, he howled mightily that it was superior to "a small and inferior Rail Road Circus" also in the neighborhood. But by 1868 he had a new partner and a new stance. Now Maginley & Carroll's was a railroad circus, boasting that it was free of those "jaded horses and wearied travel-worn performers" such as afflicted wagon shows. Maginley's was typical of dozens of shows that touted their transport of the moment to the full capacity of their press agent — and with no concern for contradictory claims of prior seasons — *Authors' Collection.*

Dan Castello's Circus made it all the way to California on brand new rails in 1869; however, it still was more of a standard wagon circus than a full railroad show. It left the tracks from time to time to reach such remote cities as Denver by wagon. Here, "overland" did not carry the circus connotation of wagon operation, but rather the same usage that gave Union Pacific its "Overland Route" slogan — the concept of coming to San Francisco by land instead of by ship and Panama — *Barkin-Herman, Milwaukee.*

DAN CASTELLO'S MENAGERIE AND CIRCUS!

Overland from the Atlantic to the Pacific.

NIXON, HOWES & CASTELLO......Proprietors
JAMES M. NIXON......Director
CHAS. C. PELL......General Business Agent

This establishment, after travelling throughout the East, North and South, has at length reached the Pacific Coast. During the past nine months it has doubled the Southern States, and travelled through portions of Kentucky, Indiana, Illinois, Missouri, Kansas, Iowa and Nebraska, making thousands of miles over the various railroads, and reaching this city without injury to a single person or animal, will open for

A SHORT SEASON IN SAN FRANCISCO,
ON THE
Old Circus Lot on Jackson street,
COMMENCING ON
MONDAY......JULY 26

Both Exhibitions under one Canvas, and one price of admission.
THE MENAGERIE contains many rare and beautiful Animals.
The Equestrian and Gymnastic Troupe comprises artists from all quarters of the globe, who are unequalled in their special roles.
The Grand and Imposing Street Pageant will take place from the Pavilion at 11 o'clock A. M., when all the resources of this vast establishment will be brought into requisition; when may be seen, in an open carriage, the Cheetah, or Hunting Leopard, saved from the burning of Barnum's Museum by the person who has it in charge.
The Procession will be headed by the Golden Chariot, containing Clerenshaw's Cornet Band.

ADMISSION......ONE DOLLAR
Children under 10 years......Fifty Cents
Doors open at 7. Performance commences at 8.

MATINEES Wednesdays and Saturdays

ADMISSION TO MATINEES......FIFTY CENTS
No half-price.

William Cameron Coup battled lethargy and opposition from both railroad people and circus troupers to perfect the system for transporting big circuses by rail — *W. Gordon Yadon.*

14

Origins

William Cameron Coup grew up on overland wagon circuses—the mud shows—so he knew there had to be a better way. He had made all of those miserable rides through mire or dust. He had seen worthy circuses lose money and time by playing crossroad villages simply because the next sizable town was too far for the horses to walk in a single morning. He wanted to change all of that. Coup had lots of ideas about circus operation, and the new railroads figured in more than one of them.

At the age of sixteen he had run away from a father, stepmother, and double family to cast his lot with show business. By chance, the outfit departing his Indiana town that night belonged to Seth B. Howes, one of the great showmen in American circus history. Other partners in the show were Sherwood Stratton, father of the famous Tom Thumb, and Lewis B. Lent, an equally prominent pioneer circus man. So Coup was to have skilled teachers; he couldn't have done better had he known what he was doing.

Howes had rented the name of a great celebrity of the time, an impresario and museum director. Although the celebrity had no more to do with the show than that, the outfit was called by this man's renowned name: P. T. Barnum's Colossal Museum & Menagerie. Later, Coup was sideshow manager for the Mabie Circus, which toured frontier territory of Illinois, Iowa, and Missouri. Then he joined the famous Yankee Robinson, learning from still another

master in the circus profession, and he became assistant manager of Yankee's big wagon circus.

Completing the 1869 campaign with the Robinson show, Coup heard his wife urge that they settle down, quit the road. And he was about to agree. But upon returning to their home in the circus colony of Delavan, Wisconsin, Coup soon was in touch with Dan Castello, himself recently back from the exciting railroad trip to California. Predictably, Coup and Castello devoted the winter to planning a new show, not their ultimate, but an interim operation. They chartered a Great Lakes steamer, the *Benton,* and played booming lumber camps along the shores of Lake Michigan. Then came another winter spent as circus people always spend them—planning yet another circus.

This time it would be the biggest wagon show in the business. It would play New England, where the towns were larger and the jumps were shorter. Most important, it would duplicate a step that Coup had learned from Seth B. Howes nineteen years earlier. Now Barnum was rich and retired. There was little assurance that the eccentric old gent would listen seriously to the thirty-five-year-old showman. But Coup wrote his proposal, and in time Barnum responded. This letter of October 8, 1870 stated that he would join with Coup in putting out a show the following spring, that he would charge three percent of the gross for the use of his name, and that he would pull together a collection of exhibits such as he featured at his New York museum—stuffed fish and birds, automatons, and perhaps Siamese twins or a Cardiff giant.

Dan Castello came to the partnership with strong credentials as well. He, too, had rented the Barnum name for short-term use on an earlier circus. His own name was widely known. The pair now assembled ten carloads of trained animals and circus gear, shipping them from Delavan to New York as the nucleus for their new P. T. Barnum's Museum, Menagerie, Caravan and Hippodrome. It opened in Brooklyn in April 10, and indeed it was a gigantic affair, claiming 600 horses and featuring Admiral Dot, the El Dorado Elf; Colonel Goshen, the Palestine Giant; Fiji cannibals; and a giraffe.

For that tour, Coup developed the first of his railroad ideas—the circus excursion system. Under it, circus agents working in advance arranged for railroads at each town to run special trains from surrounding villages on circus day. The plan worked beautifully. Added throngs came to the circus. The railroads enjoyed the surge of extra passenger business on show days. Often they sold both rail tickets and circus tickets to buyers who lined up at depot windows throughout the territory. Everybody won.

During the next winter, Coup set about to create the railroad circus he had been dreaming of. It would differ from the other attempts, and Coup's active mind held all of the answers. The Barnum wagon show had played towns of all sizes, and daily receipts had ranged from $1,000 to $7,000. Larger towns meant larger receipts, so Coup determined that by his system a railroad circus could skip the small spots and exhibit only in the profitable cities.

Over the winter he badgered and pleaded with railroad people, sending telegrams to superintendents, asking them if they could move the circus on schedule. Some were puzzled, some cited limitations and doubts, some said no. Coup refused to accept such answers. He would accept only the affirmative. Then he zeroed in on the Pennsylvania Railroad offices at Philadelphia in early 1872. The Barnum Circus was opening for an extended stay in New York and

then would function in its standard wagon-show fashion for the first three one-day stands.

At the fourth stand, New Brunswick, New Jersey, on April 18, 1872, with cars from the Pennsylvania, he would convert the Barnum Circus to railroad operation. Reluctantly, the Pennsy supplied the cars.

It was not easy, although Coup had made advance preparations. He had envisioned the system for pulling wagons up a ramp and onto flatcars. The method involved bridging from car to car with crossover plates and chocking wagons into place aboard the train. Most important, he had devised the system for loading from the end of the train and along its length, whereas others had manhandled wagons over the sides of each car.

"We were new at the work and so commenced loading at 8 p.m. and finished the job at 8 a.m.," Coup recalled of New Brunswick. The only complication was the loss of a camel that had fallen off of a ramp. Even so, twelve hours was far too long. Since the show had only a short run to Trenton for the next performances, it kept to its schedule. Equally short jumps to Camden and Philadelphia allowed additional time in experimentation and practice in loading the second and third times. At Trenton, Coup rented sleepers for performers and musicians and coaches for circus working men.

"It was quite laughable during the earlier portion of the season," Coup related, "to watch the expressions on the faces of our performers when they came on to join us and were shown the sleeping cars, which were to be their homes for the next six months."

"It's too good to last; the expense will break the show," they figured. But it did last, and the difficulties of wagon trouping were behind them.

Coup had constant trouble with the cars. He was mystified that the railroads did not settle upon a uniform height and width for cars. Brake wheels mounted at the end sill were in the way of wagons that rolled from car to car; they had to be remounted. Not the least of Coup's problems was

P. T. BARNUM'S GREAT SHOW.

The first circus train, as developed by William Cameron Coup for the Barnum show in 1872, stands on a siding near the show grounds at Kalamazoo, Michigan, October 24. The stark flats have no hand brakes mounted on ends of cars to interfere with wagons rolling along the flats, but neither are the cars littered with the chocks that would be necessary to stabilize the wagons while en route. Beyond the train is the big top, its two poles signifying a one-ring layout — *Albert Conover Collection.*

P. T. Barnum, who voiced strong objection to the railroad idea and to the all-night efforts in making the costly system work. Eventually, Barnum was to claim it as his own idea, but first he tried to prevent the change.

The show went on to Camden and Wilmington, where Coup told the railroad superintendent that if they could manage to load by 2 A.M. and reach Baltimore by 5 A.M., the project could be termed a success. The superintendent ordered the road cleared, and the show arrived in Baltimore just short of the difficult schedule. The move to Washington was easy, but there the yardmaster refused to remove the brake wheels and insisted that the show be loaded one car at a time. That would have taken twenty-four hours—time that the show did not have to spare. In that much time it was scheduled to make the jump, unload, set up the show, give the parade, present the performances, and start to reload, all in another town. So Coup invited the yardmaster to a restaurant and distracted him until the circus crew could dismount the brake wheels and load their train. Coup had set himself a schedule even tougher than normal circus operation. In this season the Barnum show was scheduling not only a morning street parade, but also a third daily performance. Yet, Coup's perfection of circus railroading methods and his persistence with both circus and railroad personnel proved successful.

Up to a point, Coup was doing much the same as earlier showmen had tried with trains. Now he would take the final steps in the creation of a true railroad circus. Difficulty with the Pennsylvania cars convinced him that he must build his own. A series of car builders whom he contacted could not meet his exacting time schedule, but finally an Ohio builder agreed to deliver the custom-designed flatcars by the time the circus reached Columbus for performances thirty days hence. At Cleveland, Coup purchased several Palace horse cars. When the circus pulled into Columbus on June 28, the crew found waiting for it a new and brightly painted train with uniform platform cars for wagons, chariots, cages, and carriages; a Wagner sleeping car for the artists; plainer sleeping cars for the laborers; boxcars for the extra items; and Palace cars for the horses and other large animals. With several weeks' practice and with flatcars of uniform height, the loading and unloading were made simple. "Thus," Coup wrote, "the Herculean task of putting the first railroad show of any magnitude on its own cars was successfully accomplished. Finally, system and good order came out of chaos."

The system was a success. Now the show could travel 100 miles a night and still have time to put up tents and seats, give a street parade, and present two, even three, performances per day. It could skip undesirable towns and villages and instead play only the sizable cities, running Coup-styled excursions from the feeder towns.

Initially, Coup and company made little publicity hay out of their new-found methods. During the experimental period they dared not advertise a system that might have been abandoned at any time. After success was assured, they still played out the route with little reference to railroading in the ads. They could not yet be expected to realize the extra status that would be enjoyed by a railroad circus. Nor could they know at the outset that railroading itself, especially the unloading of the train, was destined to prove such an attraction that hundreds of people would crowd the yards each day to see it done. They couldn't see then that this gratis performance would both rival the one under the tent and help to sell tickets to that main event.

At Quincy, Illinois, in August 1872, no mention was made of railroading, and more attention was given to Dan Castello than to Barnum's name. The show was billed as P. T. Barnum's Great World's Fair and Dan Castello's Chaste and Refined Circus, with the latter name in the largest type. Similarly, at Chicago the show stressed the museum aspect out of deference to religious objections to circuses. The advertising there read: "P. T. Barnum's Great Travelling Museum, Menagerie, Caravan, Hippodrome, Polytechnic Institute and International Zoological Gardens with Free Admission to Dan Castello's Mammoth Circus."

The only reference to railroading applied to excursion trains that would run on all the railroads for a distance of seventy-five miles "to bring in the multitudes." The parade included the Revolving Temple of Juno with a twenty-camel hitch. There were mechanical lady bell ringers, telescopic golden chariots made in London, a giraffe, the Fiji Islanders, sea lions, a mechanical Dying Zouave, and a whale's jawbone.

If at first the recently entrained Barnum show failed to advertise the new railroading capabilities, it did not take long for the show to make up for that shortcoming and proceed directly to the circus privilege of exaggeration. By September the advertising had decided that the amazing facts were not amazing enough, and it had arrived at unbridled, if unnecessary, exaggeration. Now the ads declared that the new show was "transported on three trains of forty cars each." In fact, there were 65 cars, not 120. This exaggeration was a rather constant claim for the rest of the season. But the press agents couldn't seem to agree about the number of engines. At Galesburg, Illinois, they neglected to mention the locomotives. At Clinton, Iowa, and Watertown, Wisconsin, they said to expect four locomotives per train, for a total of sixteen. For Milwaukee, Racine, and Fond du Lac, they declared that the show traveled on three trains of thirty-eight cars each and six locomotives. At Chicago in October they made no reference to trains. This was the first anniversary of the Chicago fire, and the city was preoccupied by its recollections. Nevertheless, P. T. Barnum's World's Fair scheduled four shows daily to accommodate the throngs that came to the tents at State Street and Twenty-Second Street.

In this season, as earlier, other circuses also were experimenting with railroading. L. B. Lent still made some moves by rail. Loudest was the Great Eastern Circus, which made a number of moves by rail. But none equalled Barnum; none matched Coup's system.

The memorable first season for a true railroad circus ended September 30 at Detroit. Most of the show went at once to New York. Because horses were ill, the opening of a winter engagement at the Hippotheatron was postponed one week to November 18. Then at 4 A.M. Wednesday, December 24, the Hippotheatron caught fire and P. T. Barnum's Great Travelling Exposition & World's Fair went up in smoke. The train, however, was elsewhere and survived to transport the rebuilt Barnum show of 1873.

After that Detroit closing, Barnum rented his name to a second showman, Pardon A. Older, and delivered to him at Cincinnati a consignment of Barnum features and major animals for a tour of the South under Barnum's name.

This enraged Coup. Barnum's insistence on putting his name out to several showmen simultaneously, despite the great success of the principal circus, was to be their undoing. P. T. Barnum came into a greater share of the circus. Castello departed. Coup became restless and irritable about Barnum. And P. T. was ever the egotistical celebrity. He leased his name to still another showman, Pogey O'Brien, an asthmatic con artist, for yet another Barnum show that would compete directly with Coup's organization. As a result, the first partnership blew up. Coup sold out in disgust.

Even so, Coup left Barnum with a going concern, a truly operable railroad circus with four seasons of experience. They had escaped the muddy roads. They had managed new ease and comparative comfort never before known to trouping land circuses. But most of all, they had gained mobility. And as Coup would note later, "It also greatly advertised us; vast crowds assembled at the depot to watch us load and unload."

Coup's persistence had created the railroad circus, proved its worth, and set it forth on a course that would require no change for a hundred years. And after that century, it still would inspire new developments in railroading itself.

It was near this depot and perhaps even at this crossing in New Brunswick, New Jersey, that W. C. Coup first put the Barnum circus on a train. Work began at 8 p.m., April 18, 1872 and required twelve hours. This was the New Brunswick depot in the mid-1870s. The profile of a locomotive is at the left and the silhouette of a turntable is beyond the gaslight. Extra planking for the crossing lies between the tracks — *Rutgers University Library*.

Development

The immediate result of Coup's sensation was a schism in the circus business. There were those who rushed to copy the Barnum show's successful system—and among them were a number of showmen who cited their rent-a-train moves as evidence that they were the true harbingers of this new salvation. But for each one that embraced the railroad concept there was another circus that looked upon the idea with scorn.

Coup and Barnum pointed to their 1873 show as the epitome of "what steam, electricity, and a million dollars can do"—although there was precious little electricity around the outfit, and no million dollars. Their press agents boasted of "150 railroad cars in requisition" and declared that the Barnum show had surveyed the field and found that railroads could not supply enough cars. Therefore, the show was buying up a whole fleet. They even stated that in addition to its own trains, the circus would use whatever extra cars the railroad could supply from time to time. That was a pretty big yarn to swallow. But it did mean that the railroad show was continuing.

The 1873 payroll included a master of transportation, who was in charge of the train, plus one "conductor" in charge of the Wagner sleeping car and another "conductor"—perhaps more accurately a porter—in charge of the other sleepers. The show also had a car inspector, as well as a crew to load and unload wagons. At Salem, Massachu-setts, the show experienced a risk common in railroading; a man was killed while coupling cars.

The 1873 show inaugurated two new features; one, the second ring for the performance; the other, a so-called "flying squadron" of twenty men who traveled one day ahead of the show to pound the tent stakes. Consequently, the show gained that extra time on circus day.

The Great Eastern's claims of the prior year were no longer high enough. Now it professed to have 100 cars, six passenger coaches, and four locomotives. It had less than half that many cars, but it was traveling by rail. L. B. Lent's Circus was still navigating on a train "chartered for the purpose." Many important shows continued as wagon outfits but used rented cars part of the time. Among them was the pioneer John Robinson Circus.

The powerhouse of the circus business at this time was not the new Barnum show, but rather the giant enterprise of a rough and coarse Philadelphia horse and meat dealer, Adam Forepaugh. As Coup's railroad innovations set the Barnum show apart, Forepaugh snorted a typical response: he had tried it and didn't like it.

"The Great Forepaugh Show was shipped by railroad from Baltimore to Pittsburgh," he advertised in 1872, "and it required 129 freight cars and six passenger coaches, occupying an army of 200 men three days and nights in loading."

Of course, Coup would say that this illustrated the novelty and necessity for his new system of loading, but Forepaugh figured that it emphasized the enormity of his circus.

"Since then," he continued, "the Immensely Huge and Colossal Proportions of the Concern have compelled us to
Abandon Railroads Forever
and now the Great Forepaugh Show presents the wonderful and magnificent spectacle of a
City Moving Overland."

The gruff Mr. Forepaugh continued about his big show, "Don't confound it with any of the railroad frauds skipping over the state and skimming the public!" Then he turned to other matters. He heralded a mechanical Dolly Vardon from Paris and recalled that it was he who had introduced the idea of presenting both circus and menagerie as a single show but under separate tents.

Forepaugh's ads invited newspaper editors from other cities to visit the show as his guest in Milwaukee or Chicago, since it would be playing all towns in the area that could "accommodate 525 men and horses, 1,500 animals, etc."

So the mighty Forepaugh was casting his lot with the wagon showmen. Who needs the railroads?

But as Forepaugh's own bravado betrayed, all the talk of railroad shows began to spook the traditional overland showmen. Robbins & Co.'s Circus in 1873 put it this way: "Special Notice: This stupendous organization is not a railroad establishment but travels by wagons. 168 horses are used to transport it through the country, also quite an army of men, about 125 in number."

The J. W. Warner & Co. Great Pacific Combination said that it "would require, if traveling by railroad, 100 cars and five locomotives."

"Be particular," it declared, "not to confuse this wonderful organization with light-wasted railroad, steamboat, and paper balloon shows that are using from 10 to 30 cars, notwithstanding the exaggerated statements of their using more [that] are widely published."

The wagon shows all faced the crisis by pointing out that they were simply too big to travel by railroad. And the railroad outfits countered that only they could perform under ideal conditions. "No more tired horses, sleepy people, dirty costumes," they said. And all thanks to the railroads.

William Washington Cole, destined to be one of the gentlemen greats of circus business, but a mere youngster at this time, was among the first to duplicate the Coup-Barnum system and its success. The W. W. Cole New York & New Orleans Circus, only about a year beyond being a fifty-horse mud show, trouped forth in 1873 as a thirty-five-car railroad marvel.

"Remember this is no worn-out wagon show with worn-out horses dragging it over the road," Cole declared.

The new Cole show played towns along the Union Pacific and Central Pacific route to the West. In mid-June 1873 it became the first circus to give both afternoon and night performances in San Francisco. Moving south along the new Southern Pacific, the Cole advance advertising car had to wait for construction crews to drive spikes in new trackage as it reached Tucson and moved on to El Paso. Backtracking to the Central Pacific, the eastbound Cole circus took giant strides, touching down for performances in only four cities in all the miles between San Francisco and Omaha. On October 11 it closed into winter quarters at Quincy, Illinois. In a twenty-six-week season it had touched Galveston on the Gulf, south San Francisco on the Pacific, and Marquette on Lake Superior. It had 9,387 miles to its score. The wonders of railroading were realized.

The first to play to and from the West Coast entirely by rail, the W. W. Cole Circus later was the first to reach Puget Sound. Chilly Billy Cole's geographical accomplishments were great, but they were only typical of the widespread efforts by showmen to reach new territory. The first circus in a town was sure to reap a bonanza.

Coup's accomplishment and Cole's further development were but some manifestations of the continuing national emphasis on railroads. The matter of standardizing track gauge was nearly complete. Mergers forged larger lines out of uncounted short lines. New construction added greatly to the ballooning mileage available to railroad cars. The rush to build lines through the Southwest and Northwest was a major factor.

For circuses there suddenly were many more reachable places in which to exhibit in the established sections of the country. Moreover, towns were popping up all along the new railroads. Circuses, of course, were but one expression of the way railroads affected American life. The jokes, the music, the fashions—all followed the railroad theme. It was even more concentrated than the Tin Lizzie craze of the 1920s or the television rage of the 1950s.

Circuses took a lead in the rush to rails and in the parallel fad for railroading. The differences were phenomenal. Nearly overnight, showmen could look differently upon the question of territory. Much wider areas became available, and individual jumps from town to town could be a great deal longer than before. Circus horizons were far expanded. The Mississippi Valley no longer was "the West," and railroading circus men were among the first to take advantage of the new transportation to California, Washington, Oregon, and Arizona. The railroad circus was thriving, and it would continue to do so as long as railroads dominated American life.

The age of steam centered upon the Cole circus with enthusiasm in 1875. In heavy advertising against the Adam Forepaugh Circus in Iowa, Cole proclaimed that his train was up to sixty cars. He advertised a steam calliope as the noisy if not too melodious feature of his street parade. And more, the Cole circus had a steam man—a puffing, smoking sheet metal automaton that looked like the Tin Woodman of Oz.

The venerable Howes Great London Circus took to the rails in 1875 with fifty-two cars leased from the United States Rolling Stock Company. The Cooper & Bailey Circus, a highly professional outfit, caught the railway bug and bought forty-two standard length cars for the 1876 season. Then, like the others, it highballed for the West Coast via the Union Pacific and Central Pacific. It pulled into Peta-

luma, California, on the SF&NP, then moved by wagons overland thirty miles to Napa before resuming with the CP Railroad at Fairfield; at this time such a wagon move was the great exception and only served to point out the completeness of the conversion to railroading.

The Cooper & Bailey show of 1872 had made it quite clear that it was a proper wagon circus. "World's Fair on Wheels," they said, and "Not a railroad or boat show . . . Traveling on their own conveyances. 350 men and horses."

But four seasons later the same circus had this to say:

"Coming on 42 cars (our own property), no more, no less, this number being from 12 to 24 more cars than will be regularly run by any other circus or menagerie company traveling in the West. Ask the station agent . . . Facts tell for themselves. Then judge as to the magnitude. This fact decides the great show question."

Similarly, the Barnum show—just four years into the rail show era—was offering to sell a holdover advertising wagon from its mud show days, and already it was disposing of replaced rail equipment—"nine long flatcars, one sideshow car, one elephant car, two Palace stockcars."

Forepaugh, of course, could not keep to that wagon persuasion. He made the switchover in 1877, when he paid $40,000 for a train of thirty-seven cars built by the Barney & Smith firm at Dayton, Ohio. And Forepaugh, like a teenager with his first automobile, took off at once for California! By the late 1870s he was not only roaring along with his own show train, but also had become a busy dealer in surplus circus gear, including flats and stockcars.

James A. Bailey, commandant of the Cooper & Bailey Circus, acquired the Howes Great London Show in 1879 and combined the lot with the P. T. Barnum Show in 1880. This not only set him up as the new saviour of old Phineas, but also gave them a glut of surplus circus gear. At the resulting sale the big purchaser was the John Robinson Circus, which acquired a train of its own to replace the twenty system cars it had been using. Predictably, it then raced for the Omaha jumping-off place and scooted for

California via the Union Pacific and Central Pacific. Billed as the Old John Robinson World Exposition & Electric Light Show, it, too, made history in San Francisco. It was the first three-ring circus in that city, and it placed the first big display ads ever seen in San Francisco newspapers. By this time the Southern Pacific and the Santa Fe had linked up in the Southwest, so the John Robinson Circus in 1882 could return by a different route of fresh towns.

The first fully coordinated combine of railroad cars and circus wagons built for each other was waiting for the W. W. Cole Circus when it returned from Australia in 1881. Wagons were dimensioned both for their own loads and for loading on the flats. Lengths of seat planks, for example, determined the length of the wagon that would carry them. And wagons were grouped so as to utilize the full length of each flatcar. Use of cross-cages gave the show a maximum number of animals in a minimum of train space. In all, the show was eminently well designed, and it gave an impression of immensity far beyond its twenty-five-car size.

W. W. Cole spoke up:

"I own every car in my train, built expressly for my use. My train cost me more money than it requires to equip, entire, many of the exhibitions now traveling. With a single exception, I am the only man in the United States that owns the cars that carries [sic] his show. When my train is made up, it is a magnificent sight. See my railroad cars."

The Cole train boasted of the newly perfected Westinghouse automatic air brakes plus Potter three-link drawbar couplers, features few railroads yet could claim. The train was built by the Missouri Car & Foundry Company of St. Louis. Included were five sixty-foot flats, six fifty-foot flats, seven fifty-foot stockcars, one fifty-foot elephant car, three show sleepers, one private car with kitchen and staterooms, and two advertising cars. Straight from Down-Under, Cole moved onto his new outfit at San Francisco and promptly put it to the test by routing the show to Halifax, Nova Scotia.

Under Bailey's aegis, the new Barnum & London combination was moving on seventy-seven cars in 1881. They detailed it as nine Palace cars totaling 540 feet, five elephant cars totaling 270 feet, twenty stockcars totaling 1,000 feet, forty gondolas and flatcars totaling 2,000 feet, and three advertising cars totaling 195 feet—close enough to a mile of show train for circus advertising purposes!

Sells Bros. Circus, on thirty-eight cars in 1883, boasted of three Wagner Palace sleeping cars. Already the Sells train crewmen were being called the "Raise Yer Backs." When the show played Allegheny City, Pennsylvania in May it had to leave its sleepers behind because of a narrow tunnel, but the cars were picked up again en route to New Brighton. It really didn't make much difference, because the Sells people still were stopping at hotels daily, just as they had with the wagon shows.

In fact, performers on rail shows often still used hotels. On the Barnum show of 1886, performers among the 520 employees used 255 hotels in the season. The show traveled 10,447 miles on seventy railroads and two ferryboats, played 177 days, and used fifty-two cars to carry such features as the skeleton of the late, departed Jumbo.

Two memorable names were added to the circus roster in 1884, both wagon outfits. At Peru, Indiana, the Great Wallace Circus took to the road with fifty-five wagons and 185 horses. At Baraboo, Wisconsin, five young brothers named Ringling launched their circus with nine wagons and rented horses. They were in respectable company. The pioneer Van Amburgh Circus & Menagerie continued on wagons as the principal holdout eschewing railroads. Like many others, the new Wallace show was not long in converting. For its second season it traveled by wagon and boat, but for the third it became a fifteen-car railroad circus. It took the Ringlings slightly longer, but in 1890 they bought eleven surplus cars from the Forepaugh Circus and continued their rapid climb toward the top of the circus heap by turning to railroad operation.

One man bucked that great westward current among

circuses and came East to establish his show—William F. Cody, whose Buffalo Bill's Wild West began in 1883 with nine cars (some said it was eight cars of show and one of firewater). For lack of troupers' know-how, its existence continued wobbly until Cody worked out a deal by which James A. Bailey took over the show's routing and rail-roading.

Bailey's main interest was his own principal attraction—Barnum & Bailey Greatest Show on Earth. But upon the death of Adam Forepaugh, Bailey acquired that major circus and combined it in a new partnership as the Adam Forepaugh & Sells Bros. United Circus, using the Sells rail equipment. It was the surplus Forepaugh cars that Bailey put under the Buffalo Bill show in 1894 to systematize that operation.

By this time it was clear that the best circuses moved by rails. The term "railroad show" was more than a transportation factor. Now it was a status symbol and an expression of size. Anything called a "railroad show" carried with it an implied assurance of quality and immenseness. A small rail show had it all over a big wagon operation, in the public's eye.

And circuses, like railroads, popped up, merged, and collapsed in profusion. The best ones held a steady course; others came and went. The leaders now were clearly identified as the Barnum & Bailey Greatest Show on Earth and the newer Ringling Bros. World's Greatest Shows.

In 1890, Ringling Bros. had eighteen cars, Barnum & Bailey had fifty-four. In successive years Ringling grew to twenty-two crs, thirty-two cars, thirty-eight cars, forty-two cars, forty-seven cars, fifty cars, and finally, fifty-six cars by 1897. By then, Barnum & Bailey was moving in a nineteen-car section, a seventeen-car section, a nineteen-car section, and the advance car, but that rig was soon side-tracked while Bailey took his outfit to a new train in Europe. For five years Barnum & Bailey toured Europe aboard sixty-seven cars which had been custom-built in England. In the United States the Ringlings were campaigning for top recognition, exploiting Barnum & Bailey's absence.

Barnum & Bailey celebrated its return to the States with a 1903 train of eighty-two cars, each sixty feet long. Ringling Bros. met the competition with a gigantic eighty-five-car show.

Meanwhile, Bailey left the Barnum train in Europe and sent the Buffalo Bill Show to the Continent to utilize fifty of the cars. Each was fifty-four feet long and eight feet wide (compared to a nine-foot width on the W. W. Cole train). The Cody show moved in three sections. At both ends of each section was a show car that had US couplers on one end and British couplers at the other. With this arrangement, the cars could be coupled to the third-class brake carriage used by the British railroads at each end of the show car sections; a locomotive picked up the head end.

When Bailey died, the Ringlings bought the Barnum & Bailey Circus but continued to operate it as a separate organization. During the same period, Cody came home and had to scrounge for cars. He obtained six from circuses at Peru, Indiana, purchased two sleepers from the Cummins Wild West, and bought eight flats and two boxcars from Walter L. Main. In all, Buffalo Bill accumulated forty cars. After Pawnee Bill became a partner, the outfit invested in new sixty-five-foot steel cars and claimed an all-steel train by 1912. But when the Two Bill's show went broke the next season, the auction inventory revealed that there were still twenty wooden flats and stocks in the forty-five-car consist. Still, steel show cars had come on the scene.

These first years of the twentieth century were the heyday of the railroad circus. Never were more to be found. Never were they bigger or better. A high point came in 1911, when the roster of flatcar railroad circuses included thirty-two shows.

Railroad Circuses of 1911

Show	Total Cars	Advance	Flats	Stocks	Coaches
Ringling Bros.	84	3	40	26	15
Barnum & Bailey	84	4	39	27	14
Forepaugh-Sells	50	3	25	13	9
Buffalo Bill-Pawnee Bill	48	2	20	14	12
101 Ranch	27	2	10	9	6
John Robinson	42	2	20	10	10
Hagenbeck-Wallace	48	2	23	13	10
Sells Floto	30	1	13	9	7
Al G. Barnes	17	1	7	5	4
Sparks	10	1	4	3	2
Yankee Robinson	20	2	8	5	5
Campbell Bros.	28	2	11	7	8
Young Buffalo	22	2	6	6	8
Gentry Bros.	15	1	7	4	3
Sanger Great European	10	1	4	3	2
Sun Bros.	9	1	4	2	2
Mighty Haag	13	1	6	3	3
Kit Carson (at opening)	12	1	5	3	3
Gollmar Bros.	24	2	10	6	6
Howes Great London	16	1	6	5	4
Famous Robinson	18	1	8	4	5
Frank A. Robbins	15	1	7	3	4
Cole & Rice	8	1			
W. H. Coulter (before mid-season)	13	1	5	4	3
Indian Pete's (combination)	12	1	5	3	3
Downie & Wheeler	10	1	5	2	2
Sig Sautelle (late in year)	11	1	4	3	3
California Frank's	11	1	4	3	3
Bulgar & Cheney	5	—	3	1	1
Tiger Bill's	11	1	4	3	3
Welsh Bros.	9	1	3	2	3

In addition, there were numerous two-car shows, including Mollie Bailey, Buckskin Ben, Christy, Cole & Johnson, Cole & Rogers, King & Tucker, Jones Bros., Montgomery Queen, James Masterson, etc.

All data represents the best available information. In several cases, the make-up of a train was changed during the season and only one version is reflected here. In some instances, conflicting information exists and one version has been selected on a judgemental basis.

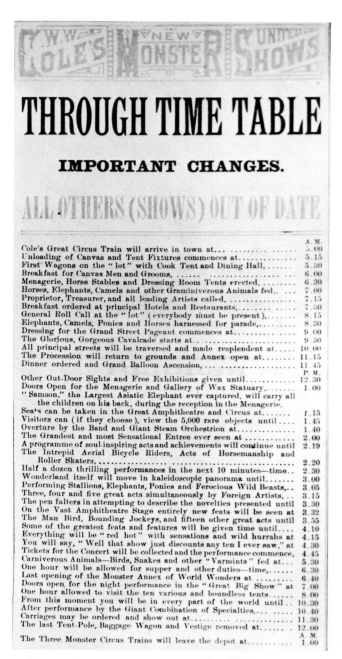

Courier for W. W. Cole's Circus, 1882 — *Circus World Museum.*

While many sought the status of a railroad circus, and boosters wished such success for others, the rail show was not for everyone. Some big wagon shows of late years tried railroading and found it not to their liking. The rugged old M. L. Clark Circus tried a train in 1909. Another southern perennial, The Mighty Haag Shows, took to the high iron from 1909 to 1914. And the Orton family, which had circuses from 1854 onward and tried rails from time to time, had a final railroading fling in 1916. All three turned it in as a poor second and returned to the security of their wagon shows.

Some show people would travel only with railroad circuses, while others were identified as wagon show people. Within the business, circuses were categorized by the number of railroad cars they used. It was this railroad scale that usually served to measure a circus' size, rather than the number of people, the dimension of the tents, the quality of acts, or the population of the elephant herd. Showmen spoke of a ten-car show, a thirty-car show, or whatever, using this as a generic term to signify the outfit's spot in the hierarchy of circusdom. The number of cars on a show carried with it a whole array of assumptions about costs, routing, equipment, and personnel.

A major milestone came in 1919, when the Ringling family concluded that it should combine its two huge units into one circus as Ringling Bros. and Barnum & Bailey Combined Shows. It got underway as a ninety-five-car monster, with forty-two flats, twenty-six stockcars, twenty-four coaches, and three advertising cars.

Then in 1923 it reached 100 cars—forty-six flats, twenty-seven stocks, twenty-two coaches, one dining car, one private car, and three advertising cars. It continued on 100 cars through 1928.

In that postwar period there was a great scurry to get into the circus business, and all available equipment was snapped up. Many showmen calculated that a railroad circus would transport them right to the end of the rainbow and that this was the moment to try their hand. In the minor leagues, Rhoda Royal Circus and the Campbell, Bailey & Hutchinson outfit got into action soon enough to find cars. But they had a nondescript array of old oil drays and ice wagons mixed in with their true circus wagons. Several other would-be showmen gave up for lack of cars. The Venice Transportation Co. raised the price of rental cars by five dollars to forty dollars monthly for flatcars and fifty dollars for stockcars, reflecting the demand.

But the 1920s had no dearth of small shows to participate in the endless to-and-fro that always marked the circus business. Howes Great London became Golden Bros. and then Lee Bros. The old Gollmar title was revived and replaced with the Heritage Bros. title. A new World Bros. Circus became Robbins Bros. The veteran Gentry Bros. Dog & Pony Show was renamed the Gentry-Patterson Circus. The Walter L. Main Circus of the early 1920s sold its equipment to the revived 101 Ranch Wild West, and the Main title was leased to the King brothers' growing operation. The sturdier independents of the time included the Al G. Barnes Circus on the West Coast, the Sparks Circus in the East, and the Christy Bros. Circus out of Texas.

But the greatest momentum in the business originated with the rowdy American Circus Corporation. It operated the Hagenbeck-Wallace, the Sells Floto, and the John Robinson circuses. From time to time its principals had fielded the Howes Great London, the Yankee Robinson, the Sanger Great European, and the Famous Robinson shows. By the late 1920s it had acquired the Barnes and Sparks circuses as well.

In a showdown between the American Circus Corporation and Ringling-Barnum, it was John Ringling who paid. He bought the Corporation in 1929, which put him in command of six principal railroad circuses. Included were Ringling Bros. and Barnum & Bailey on ninety cars; the Floto show with forty; Hagenbeck-Wallace and Barnes, each on thirty cars; John Robinson with twenty-five; and Sparks with twenty. In all, he captained a fleet of 235 circus railroad cars and all of the accompanying show equipment.

Several independents also operated at the time: 101 Ranch Wild West, thirty cars; Christy Bros., twenty; Gentry Bros., fifteen; Cole Bros., ten; Robbins Bros., thirty; and Buck Jones Wild West, thirteen.

They all were at the countdown.

With the Great Depression at hand, the whole set was in for trouble. For some, it came quick and proved fatal. Buck Jones and Gentry Bros. did not complete the '29 tour. Christy, Cole, Robbins, and Robinson saw 1930 but no more. Sparks and 101 Ranch folded in 1931. Sells Floto disappeared after 1932, cutting the railroad circus roster to three in 1933.

A new Cole Bros. started up in 1935 and did well, so it launched a new Robbins Bros. in 1938. That was also the year when Col. Tim McCoy's Real Wild West made its brief flare. With those, plus Ringling, Hagenbeck, and Barnes, six were on the road in 1938—a season that proved to be disastrous. By 1939 only two remained.

In that era there was frequent talk of one or more of the principal motorized circuses converting to rails. It was a standard, logical goal to hope that your truck show could become a ten-car circus. And there were continuous, standard, logical rumors to declare that one truck show or another intended to do just that.

A good number of show people felt that it was just a matter of time before the Tom Mix Circus converted from Fords to flats in the late 1930s. The Wallace Bros. Circus of 1944 actually gave basis to such rumors by announcing that it would move at least its elephants by rail. Circus observers believed that Charlie Sparks surely would have his Downie Bros. on rail before long. When the Parker & Watts Circus was to be organized, its owners debated about whether to begin with trains or trucks. They decided on the latter, but clearly planned to take the big step in a year or two. When the King Bros. & Cristiani Circus of the 1950s enjoyed success, it made inquiry about renting the Hagenbeck-Wallace name and going out on rails. In the 1960s good thought was given to changing the Kelly-Miller Circus into a railroad outfit. But none of these ever made it.

On the other hand, some shows did graduate from highways to railways. The movement came about as part of the great rush to get into the circus business during and after World War II. The nefarious Dailey Bros. Circus bought carnival cars and made wagons out of semi-trailers for 1944. The Russell Bros.' motorized outfit made the switch in 1945. In 1947 a new truck show with the old Sparks name changed to rails and boasted new custom-built wagons on Warren flats leased from Ringling. Arthur Bros. put its new paint over old Hagenbeck wagons and traveled aboard fifteen cars. Skipping the truck phase, Austin Bros. appeared as a new railroad circus. The high-water mark for this rush to rails occurred in 1945, when six such circuses were in operation. But the roster began to decline almost at once.

Dailey Bros. thrived for most of its seven seasons as a railroad outfit. Russell Bros. Pan-Pacific Circus soon became the Clyde Beatty Railroad Circus and did well. But Austin, Arthur, and Sparks each lasted only a season in the rail category. Ringling zoomed up to a record 108 cars and quickly cut back to eighty.

While the 1930s had wiped out most of the famous old railroad circuses and the 1940s had brought new optimism, the 1950s cleared the picture—and nearly cleared the tracks of rail shows.

Dailey folded in 1950. Cole Bros. Circus eased out of the scene during the same season. The last pair of traditional railroad circuses continued into 1956. Ringling Bros. and Barnum & Bailey had found the going increasingly tough for a few years, and it finally shuddered to a halt at Pittsburgh in mid-season. It would rise again but in different form.

The fifteen-car Clyde Beatty Circus had closed even earlier because of poor business in the unbelievably rugged season of 1956. Then it came under new management, reopened, and made a highly profitable tour late in the same year. Fittingly, it was operated by a concentration of veteran troupers with credits that read like an encyclopedia of circus accomplishment. But that was the last of it—last of the traditional circus with both train and tents.

Until these final gasps, the railroad circus had held its high status. But the challenge of truck shows was ever greater, and the star of indoor circuses continued to rise. By an almost imperceptible switch, it was no longer a comparison between railroad shows and motorized circuses. Now the distinction was between tented circuses and those that played indoor arenas, without regard to how they traveled.

Ringling substituted a few railroad cars to reach engagements at Madison Square Garden and Boston Gardens in 1957, but thereafter it used mostly motor trucks and a scant three baggage cars to keep any railroad rating at all. No flats, no stockcars, no coaches or bill cars, and for that matter, no tent. By 1957 the Beatty show was all differentials and steering wheels, which means that the last traditional tented railroad circus was the Clyde Beatty Circus of 1956.

Then, happily, a revitalized Ringling reversed the field. It climbed from the doldrums to new prosperity, and did it on trains.

Any railroad circus worth its salt had a lithograph showing an exciting view of its train's arrival. Whether it be Cole Bros. or any of another dozen shows, these lithographs invariably depicted the streets full of elephants, camels, and horses and the yards jammed with untold numbers of railroad cars — *William White Collection.*

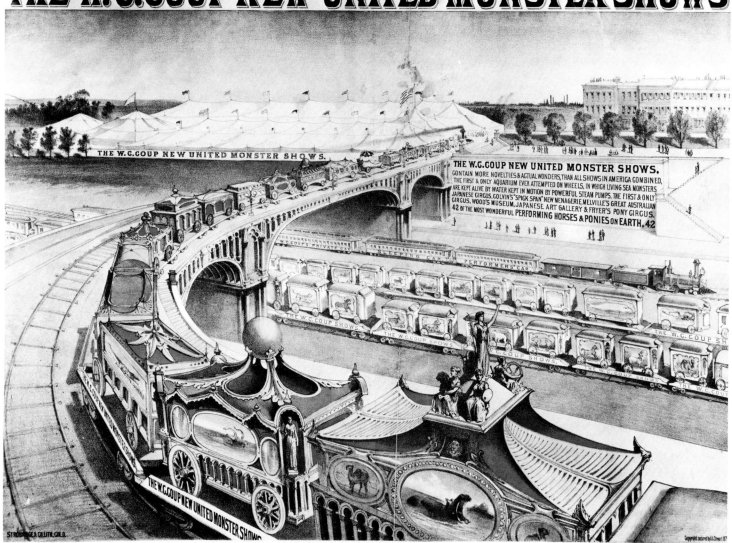

W. C. Coup came back into the game under his own name and tried railroading a show once again. In reality, his twenty-five-car outfit did not look much like this, but the posters left no doubt that Coup's was a railroad show — *Harold Dunn Collection*.

The Barnum show continued to thrive on rails, but while circus advertising featured the railroad theme, poster artists regularly came up with more imagination than historical accuracy. This 1876 poster would have you believe that the tents already were up while two sections still were moving into town and the coaches already were leaving. If indeed any American locomotive was named "P. T. Barnum," it was by decision of the railroad; the circus never owned any locomotive power. However, perhaps the artist knew what he was drawing when he indicated that the cars were built by the LaMothe Manufacturing Company and patented in 1875. In that era the terms "platform car" and "gondola" were used for what is known today as a flatcar, except that platform cars had no sides or gunnels, and the gondolas had low, removable sides of stakes and slats instead of permanent sides — *Harold Dunn Collection.*

After Forepaugh crossed over to the railroad way, he, too, went all out in his poster art. Here four sections of the circus train steam mightily for the distant showgrounds where, unrealistically, the tents have already been erected. If the artist made other mistakes (such as depicting elephants in an open-top kraal-style car), at least he was consistent in facing all the wagons the same way on the various trains — *Harold Dunn Collection.*

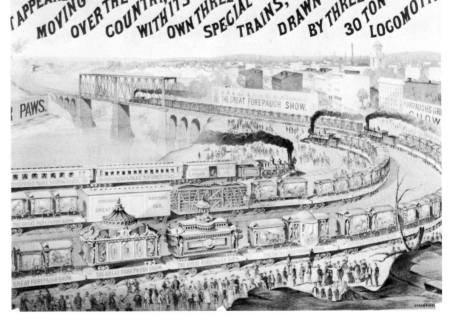

32

During the 1880s and thereafter, dozens of shows boasted of their railroad status. The Burr Robbins poster of 1883 indicates how the word "railroad" became part of the show's name — *Authors' Collection*.

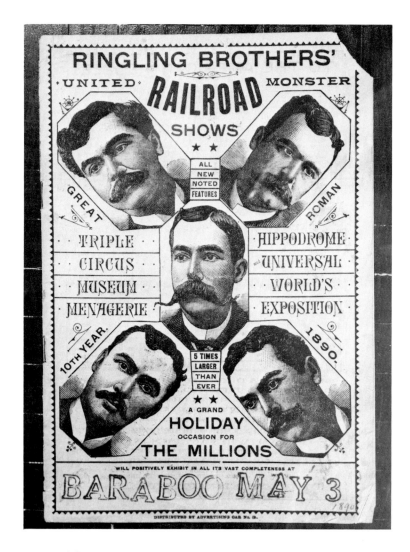

Railroaders' kids and dogs stand alongside this Canadian 4-4-0 locomotive in the belief that it was the one which had killed Jumbo the elephant on September 15, 1885 at St. Thomas, Ontario. In commemoration, Engine 297 is fitted with the silhouette of a running elephant affixed to its headlight, giving it even more prominence than the royal crest mounted between the two drive wheels. But that roundhouse version of history is questionable since other accounts of the collision between Jumbo and a Canadian National train indicate that a different engine made that scene. Some photographs of the dead elephant alongside the tracks show a different locomotive. There is no assurance that the engine on the scene the next morning was party to the accident. And it is likely that the first engine — maybe 297 — proceeded with its cars and attempted to make up lost time as soon as the dead elephant was cleared from the tracks — *Authors' Collection*.

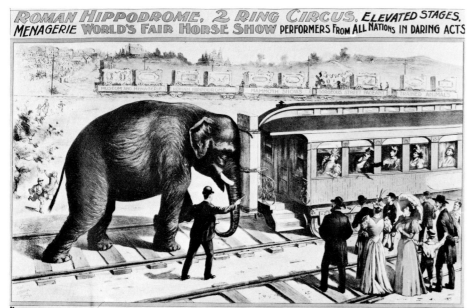

ROMAN HIPPODROME, 2 RING CIRCUS. ELEVATED STAGES. MENAGERIE WORLD'S FAIR HORSE SHOW PERFORMERS FROM ALL NATIONS IN DARING ACTS

"WHAT DO YOU THINK OF AN ELEPHANT PUSHING A WHOLE TRAIN OF CARS"

Opposite: In 1890 Ringling Bros. Circus switched from wagon operation and amended its title to read "United Monster Railroad Shows." But this courier was used to advertise the one town in which the circus did not function fully as a railroad outfit. Baraboo, Wisconsin, was the show's winter quarters, so the train already was unloaded. That night, however, the show would have been loaded for the first time as a railroad outfit. May 3 was a Saturday, allowing for a Sunday off as protection in case a delay occurred in the unaccustomed railroad operation — *Authors' Collection. Left:* Even stock paper — that printed in blank for any circus to add its own name — stressed the railroad operation. And what about an elephant pushing a train of cars? There's more concern for the fact that the artist drew the elephant out of scale. At that size it wouldn't fit in any circus railroad car — *Authors' Collection. Above:* Catching some of the romance of circus railroading, this view shows the second section of Gollmar Bros. twenty-five-car circus train rattling through Wisconsin hill country in 1912. All of the stockcars were among the 15 cars that preceded this train. Here, the three-flat cut of canvas-covered cages is loaded poles to the engine. And the first four flats of the train are loaded poles to caboose. So to unload, the train will be split to straddle the crossing — *Bernard G. Corbin Collection.*

Just as early railroad shows derided wagon circuses, so the newfangled truck circuses thumbed their noses at the railroads. In this 1928 courier, Andrew Downie recalls that his career included several railroad circuses, but now he's operating on seventy-five trucks. "Most of us have got circuses and railroads mixed up together in our minds . . . they seem to be inseparably tied up with one another," says the Downie courier. But now he can "tell the Interstate Commerce Commission that they needn't bother about adjusting mileage rates so far as he is concerned." Actually railroading figured hugely in the circus business for another thirty years after Downie changed to trucks. But then it would be touch and go — *Circus World Museum*

Al G. Barnes Circus and Hagenbeck-Wallace shared the same artwork depicting twin steam locomotives rushing "through the dawn" with a circus train in tow. The shows were under the same management when these lithographs were used in 1933 and 1934. Fourteen years later the competing Cole Bros. Circus borrowed the same art but altered the train and added a flag for the cover of its advertising courier. Circuses found it just as important to be railroad shows as to have elephants or clowns — *Below: Joseph Fleming; Right, Author's Collection.*

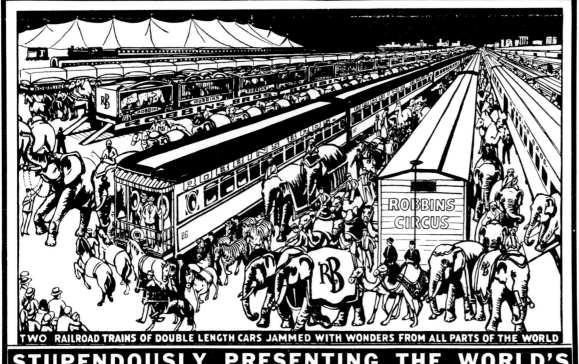

TWO RAILROAD TRAINS OF DOUBLE LENGTH CARS JAMMED WITH WONDERS FROM ALL PARTS OF THE WORLD

STUPENDOUSLY PRESENTING THE WORLD'S FAMOUS, BIGGEST AND GREATEST FEATURES

This Robbins Brothers herald of 1938 is typical of the emphasis that was placed on railroad shows — if it was a railroad show, it had to be the biggest and the best — *Authors' Collection.*

GALA, GOLDEN, FREE
Street Parade
WILL BE GIVEN IN THE FORENOON
LONGEST, COSTLIEST, MOST MAGNIFICENT EVER PRESENTED IN THIS OR IN ANY OTHER COUNTRY—AND ALL NEW! A VAST
ROBBINS DAY GIFT
A Colossal Marvel of Rainbow Gorgeousness, so Long That it Takes the Mammoth Pageant Almost 30 Minutes to Pass a Given Point. A Solid Block of Elephants, Camel and Zebra Teams. Six Bands of Music. Automatic Pipe Organs. Two Steam Calliopes.

Enough Horses to Equip an Army.

A Mile of Elaborately Carved and Gilded Allegorical Floats, Tableau Wagons.

ROBBINS BROS. CIRCUS
is the One and Only Railroad Show Mindful Enough of the Public to Give A Free Street Parade.

Operations

John Ringling said, "We can relax now; we're on the Santa Fe." It was the circus king's way of stating that the railroads, so vital to circus operation, varied tremendously in their attitudes about circuses and consequently in their service and the price they charged for it. If it were circuses that designated Class I railroads, there would be some additions and subtractions for the list now compiled on ground rules set by the Association of American Railroads.

Basic to the whole relationship between circuses and railroads is the fact that when they engage in moving a show, the railroads are no longer common carriers. Instead, their legal position is that of private carriers. Thus, the roads are not obligated to carry circuses, and the Interstate Commerce Commission's interjection is substantially less. For show moves, the railroad rents the use of its trackage and supplies a train crew as well as locomotive and caboose. But the cars in the train belong to the circus, and with that go both greater liability and the prospects for additional charges.

Rulings by the Interstate Commerce Commission have put it quite clearly:

"A railroad company, although a common carrier, when acting outside the performance of its legal duties, may contract as a private carrier."

"A railroad has the right to refuse to transport cars owned by a circus company except on its own terms."

"A railroad is not required, as a common carrier, to transport a circus train, a part of which is loaded with wild animals, over its line, but may refuse to transport such train, except under a special contract limiting its liability to that assumed by a private carrier."

"A carrier is under no common-law obligation to furnish motive power and servants to move a circus company's train over its road at reduced rates."

"A special contract between a carrier and a circus company for reduced rates and exemption from liability for claims and damages on account of accident or injury from the carrier's negligence is not contrary to public policy."

At the outset, each railroad set show rates as it chose; much bidding, bargaining, and negotiation occurred. When government regulation began in 1887, those old conditions continued. However, during World War I when the government took over operation of the railroads, the administration decreed that rates would be set by region. Thus, the southern roads established one table of rates, eastern roads another, western roads a third. On August 26, 1920, these rates were increased thirty-five percent. As a result, an association of rail show owners, representing four circuses and seventy-one carnivals, took action against the roads.

They presented a complaint before the Interstate Commerce Commission, charging that the Katy, Rock Island, and Frisco rates were unreasonable and unjustly discriminatory.

The ICC noted that the roads acted as private carriers,

citing a Frisco contract which stipulated that the railroad merely supplied the motive power, tracks, and personnel to shows. It even stated that the train crew, the dispatchers, and others involved in the operation of these moves acted as employees of the circus, not the railroad, although operation had to be according to Frisco rules, regulations, and time cards. Direction and management stayed with the railroad.

The hearing officers ruled that the roads had not been unreasonable and that rates were not out of line with others. The showmen even had asked that the ICC take jurisdiction and set the rates, but the agency declined.

While a special affinity often existed between circuses and railroaders, the attitudes and options taken by the lines varied substantially. Just as John Ringling commented about the Santa Fe, the Chicago and North Western Railway generally has been among those railroads soliciting circus business via their traffic departments. On the other hand, if William Cameron Coup thought the Pennsylvania Railroad disinterested in 1872, his successors found the Penn Central's performance uninspired a century later. Circuses also recognized that even when a line's traffic department was cooperative, its operating department might bring another story.

Too often railroads discouraged circuses, sometimes for valid reasons and sometimes for what showmen suspected was the reluctance to interrupt a routine by adding an extra train, scheduling an extra crew, providing an extra locomotive, and disrupting the usual pattern of activity in the offices and yards.

In addition to the options were the actual problems. Both the railroad and the circus had to be concerned about the quality of the roadbed, particularly on branch lines; the availability of sufficient motive power; and the existence of adequate side trackage.

Sometimes individual railroads and circuses have worked out sweetheart deals giving the circus an exclusive privilege for traveling the line. This had a second side, of course; it meant that other circuses would be denied the privilege of traveling on that road. The W. W. Cole Circus often arranged exclusive privileges when it played the newly opened lines of the pioneer West. While it was reported in 1935 that Ringling-Barnum held an exclusive pact with the New York Central that season, the probability is that shutout contracts long since had been discontinued.

Representing the circus in all of its dealings with the main offices and executives of the railroads was the show's general agent. He was a circus executive with a strange mix of skills and expertness, and he called upon all of them when he dealt with both the railroads and the municipal governments that were so vital to the success of his show. One of the general agent's duties was to improve the show's relationships with the railroads and cultivate friendships with the appropriate railroad officers. John Ringling, himself the president and owner of several short-line railroads, was a member of the inner circle of railroad presidents and board chairmen. A true tycoon, he met with them on his own terms. His successful contacts with railroad brass and lesser lights benefited not only his own circuses, but also all of the other railroad shows in business at the time. Benefits that he won for Ringling Bros. and Barnum & Bailey came also to apply to rival circuses and their general agents.

The business side of moving a circus train started with the general agent's winter work of mapping the coming season's route for the show. In hotel rooms or an office full of economic data and *Railway Guides* plus the personal knowledge that comes from seeing show trains over the rails for many seasons, the general agent put together his plans. He wanted to get his outfit to the towns where it would make the most money, yet he must route it so that cities fell into logical sequence for reasonable mileage and economical moves. It took time and money to transfer from one railroad to another, and neither was to be wasted by a circus. Consequently, the agent took careful note of general geography and of specific towns on a given railroad's trackage. The agent needed to know about motive power, roadbeds, and side trackage, likely train speeds, and even the attitude of a railroad and its operating personnel toward circuses.

Most veteran circus agents were well acquainted with the general freight agents and other pertinent officials of the railroads with which they did business. As the route took shape, the show agent called at the various railroad offices and set the contracts. Since rival agents were eager to know where the competition would be, railroad executives were cautioned to keep the show's routing plans secret. The route might be played exactly as planned, but often late changes became necessary. These might be brought about by crop conditions, strikes, or other adverse economic situations that make a town less desirable. The agent then might want to strike that town from the route and alter his railroading plans. Prior appearance in the city by a rival circus might also induce the agent to back away. Sometimes it entailed a hasty trip back to the city where the railroad brass was headquartered, but crafty circus agents soon learned that it was easier and faster to leave contracts signed in blank during their first visit of the year. Then by telegraph or telephone they could instruct the railroad official about how to fill in the contract forms for the new routing plans.

Most likely the show would play substantially the same general territory in which it had exhibited before. While some circuses have consistently played a national route, more of them have established a regional territory and stuck to it. Showmen placed great importance on the relationship between show titles and territories. A circus whose name was a household word in one state might be totally unknown in the adjacent state. Norris & Rowe was famous in the Far West, Frank A. Robbins Circus stayed strictly to the East, and never the twain shall meet. The Sparks Circus, with winter quarters at Macon, Georgia, generally played through the eastern states, sometimes including eastern Canada, and then toured the South. The Al G. Barnes Circus early each season exhibited in Los Angeles and sub-sequently made its way northward along the coast before making a giant swoop through the Great Plains and mountain states. Indiana circuses such as Cole Bros. and Hagenbeck-Wallace began their season in the Middle West, turned east, and doubled back to the Great Plains before heading south. Ringling Bros. and Barnum & Bailey always opened in New York and then played the East, Middle West, and South, in that order. Sometimes it played the West.

Each year a typical general agent faced up to the question of whether he should change territory or expand it on a one-time basis to invade Texas, California, or Canada. These were optional adventures taken only occasionally by most shows.

Sometimes there was territory to be avoided. Many of the major circuses steered clear of the South for a surprisingly long time after the Civil War because of lower economic conditions. For some early years of its existence, the Barnum Circus avoided the South because of the bad reputation incurred by another circus which had rented the Barnum name for a southern tour. For many seasons the John Robinson Circus cut a wide arc to avoid Texas, since it had experienced a battle with the townspeople there and feared attachment and other legal action if it should cross the border.

General agents also were affected by routing pacts developed between circuses. Several such agreements existed between Barnum & Bailey and its chief rivals. It and the Forepaugh Circus agreed to alternate territory for several years in the 1880s, with each playing eastern cities one year and the central states the next. The Barnum show and Ringling Bros. agreed to similar routing pacts before their combination.

Within his territory the general agent selected the cities his circus would play. There were about 6,000 cities, towns, and villages of sufficient size to interest one circus or another in a given year. Territory and population requirements peculiar to circuses of various sizes served to limit the field immensely. The general agent then trimmed the list further to the 180 or 200 towns that he might play in a typical season of one-day stands. Cities were included or skipped on the basis of their crop condition, industrial payrolls, business volume, and other economic measurements. Further, a city worth playing at one time of the year might be totally worthless to a circus a few weeks earlier or later. The agent might have decided that it was advisable to play a maximum number of industrial cities or he may have opted for including towns in the coalfields of West Virginia or the steel mill area of Northern Ohio, depending on prevailing conditions. A show might play western wheatland at harvest time, move on to the corn belt, and then reach the tobacco markets just before playing the cotton country.

Affecting his decisions also was the matter of opposition from other circuses. Each agent attempted to learn the confidential route plans of his rivals. If a big circus was playing a given city, a smaller competitor probably would skip the town. Being the second circus of the season was not a good gamble. But if a city was several years fresh, if it had not had a circus for some time, it would be particularly attractive to the general agent.

Looming large in the whole matter of laying out the route was the influence exerted by railroads on the general agent's plans. The simple matter of which towns were served by a single line might well determine those that the circus could play. It may be too costly or time consuming to leave one railroad and use another to reach a given town, particularly if an alternate city existed on the first line. Transfer charges, the cost of extra switching, and compulsory car inspections were incurred each time the circus left one railroad and arrived on another. It was necessary also to consider junctions, wyes, and connecting points with other lines. To decide on one city sometimes implied that several others along a given railroad must be played as well. Ringling advance people referred to the "New York Central week," and a study of old routes confirms that sometimes the show played Albany, Schenectady, Syracuse, Rochester, and Buffalo, and sometimes it didn't; but if it played one it probably played them all. Similar factors of railroading and allied geography affected every circus route.

Once a tentative route was mapped out, perhaps with some alternative cities designated in advance, the general agent acted to contract the railroad moves and make the local arrangements for lots and licenses in each city. He was assisted in this by contracting agents who traveled well in advance of the circus to prepare the way.

Contract forms prepared by the railroads and offered to the circus agents specified that the railroad would pick up the show train from a given connecting line and move it to one or more towns served by this railroad. Usually the standard contract stated that sidings, motive power, crews, and other factors were included in the basic price. In most cases the speedy schedule of a circus playing one-night stands meant that the demurrage clause did not apply.

There were some tough provisions regarding liabilities. Although the show was moving on a given railroad, behind the road's locomotives, and in the hands of the road's crew, the circus was liable for any basic damage claims and was required to indemnify the railroad. If an accident tore up a stretch of track, the circus was required to pay for repairs. If the railroad caused damage to circus-owned cars, it retained the privilege of repairing them in its own shops. In the event that the railroad was found responsible for loss of animals, the contract specified low amounts of money to be paid as damages. For example, the road would be required to pay only $500 for a $5,000 trained elephant or a giraffe worth $10,000; or $100 for a zebra worth $3,500 or $50 for a leopard worth $3,000. The circus had no recourse if trains were late and it lost the income from a matinee.

While one phase of the contract stated the railroad's agreement to move the show, the other part covered the amount that the circus would pay for this service. Rates for moving show trains were determined largely by the regional freight rate organizations, primarily the eastern, western, and southern groups of railroads. Rates were tabulated in five-car increments for shows ranging from ten to thirty-five cars and in ten-car increments for forty through 110 cars. Thus, it cost the same to move, say, thirty-one cars as to move thirty-five cars, and as a consequence nearly all show trains in modern times have been made up of cars in multiples of five or ten. Circuses of five or fewer cars usually moved in passenger service, but if it became necessary to move in freight, a four-car show paid the ten-car rate. Rate tables also indicated different charges according to the mileage traveled, and the circus paid a lower rate if it were moving from its final exhibition of the season to winter quarters. The following are typical shows' moves and charges:

Hagenbeck-Wallace Circus, 35 cars, 1932, Russellville to Conway, Arkansas, MoPac Railroad, $562.

John Robinson's 10 Big Shows, 45 cars, 1904, Jellico, Tennessee, to London, Kentucky, L&N Railroad, $675.

Gollmar Bros. Circus, 24 cars, 1911, Seymour to Green Bay, Wisconsin, GB&W Railroad, $100.

Ringling Bros. and Barnum & Bailey Circus, 100 cars, 1927, Little Rock to Memphis, MoPac Railroad, $2,475.

Sells Floto Circus, 40 cars, 1930, Aurora to Waukegan, Illinois, C&NW Railway, $602.

Ringling Bros. and Barnum & Bailey, 79 cars, 1956, Worcester to Springfield, Massachusetts, NYC Railroad, $2,364.88.

Arthur Bros. Circus, 14 cars, 1945, Iron Mountain to Escanaba, Michigan, C&NW Railway, $377.

La Tena Circus, 15 cars, 1917, Superior to Cumberland, Wisconsin, Omaha Railway, $250.

Mighty Haag Shows, 15 cars, 1913, Rice Lake to Spooner, Wisconsin, Omaha Railway, $225.

Wheeler Bros. Circus, 27 cars, 1916, Mankato to Shakopee, Minnesota, Omaha Railway, $225.

Sun Bros. Circus, 9 cars, 1915, St. Ignace to Sault Ste. Marie, Michigan, DSS&A Railway, $200.

Heritage Bros. Circus, 15 cars, 1926, Des Plaines to Woodstock, Illinois, C&NW Railway, $308.

Al G. Barnes-Sells Floto with RBBB, 50 cars, 1938, Watertown to Huron, South Dakota, C&NW Railway, $1,023.

Norris & Rowe Circus, 20 cars, 1905, Janesville to Madison, Wisconsin, C&NW Railway, $150.

A fifty-mile move for a twenty-car circus typically cost $327.50 in 1930 and $682.59 in 1950. Similarly, a series of rate increases meant that a move which cost $1,000 in 1935 cost $1,841 in 1947, $2,633 in 1950, and $3,028 after 1952.

In 1942 Ringling Bros. and Barnum & Bailey paid $201,303 to move ninety cars along 13,008 miles. In 1947 it cost $318,300 to take 108 cars 13,346 miles. In 1950, with eighty cars, the circus traveled 15,932 miles and paid $466,958 in freight bills. In 1953 the circus was reduced to seventy cars but traveled 19,078 miles and paid $515,943.

In 1971 the Ringling-Barnum Blue unit* played forty-five cities and used thirty cars on twenty railroads to cover 23,627 miles under seventy-five contracts for $445,000.

The 1971 Red unit of Ringling-Barnum covered 16,922 miles to play forty-five cities at a cost of $324,625.

Included in all such circus moves was a provision for

* * * * *

*Distinguishing between its two shows raised problems for the Ringling organization. They were both of the same size and it was of great value to use the powerful Ringling Bros. and Barnum & Bailey title on each. There could be no "second unit" connotation, since it implies that one is smaller. So management tagged one the Blue unit and the other the Red unit.

prepaid passenger fares to cover the transportation of advance agents and bill posters. The contract was with the railroad's freight department even though it provided for the transportation of circus employees in the show-owned coaches. The amount also paid for the transportation of the advertising car in passenger service and for those bill posters and other advance men who might be traveling on regular passenger trains. For these purposes railroads issued show scrip, which consisted of books of coupons worth a total of fifteen dollars each. An advance agent presented books of scrip to a conductor, who removed the amount required to cover the cost of the agent's trip. The circus was entitled to draw out show scrip valued at an amount equal to twenty percent of the total contract. Unused scrip could be cashed in.

While some railroads charged exactly the amounts specified in rate tabulations, others interpreted the rules differently and added such extra charges as they desired. At one particularly irksome time the Ringling Circus was billed for services of railroad detectives and again for a substantial number of extra engines that had reportedly been stationed along the way "in case they were needed"—a circumstance that had not arisen. The charges for switching and transfers grew larger. While standard contracts had included the use of sidetracks in the basic amount, some railroads charged extra for the trackage. A few others interpreted the rules to mean they could charge extra when a show train moved in more than one section, although the rate tables implied that this was covered and everyone knew that an eighty-car circus would be moved in two or three sections.

In all, the increase in railroad costs by 1954 prompted Henry Ringling North to meet with the eastern railroads to seek a reduction. They agreed to eliminate show scrip and reduce the total contract cost by twenty percent. This was both helpful and practical since there were fewer passenger trains on which to use the scrip; besides, agents were beginning to use other forms of transportation anyway.

Rule 63 of the Interstate Commerce Commission's Tariff Circular 20 provides that "rates for specified movements of circuses and other show outfits may be established on not less than one day's notice to the commission. Such tariffs must bear reference to this rule and must publish the charges specifically, showing the number and kinds of cars moved . . . ." Consequently, upon completion of a contract with a circus, the railroad would establish a new tariff and publish it accordingly. It would detail the number and types of cars that a show was using, note the dates of exhibitions along the line, and establish the amount to be charged for each daily move. Tariffs would often include the number of people to be transported on the bill car and the number included on the show train itself. Since tariffs were to be published for individual moves, each specified that it would expire upon completion of the show moves involved, and when the same show made the same move a year later, another tariff would be issued.

After that would follow additional paper work. Billing orders would be issued to the agent at each town in which the circus intended to exhibit, and the agent would be instructed to collect the amount due. Waybills, train orders, and receipts required signatures and changed hands as the business of managing a circus move transpired. The purpose of the paper work was to transfer the responsibility for the circus from the railroad's traffic department, or general offices, to the local freight agents and operating personnel.

Suddenly, the circus advertising car was transferred from a connecting line, awaiting its next move. The line's paper work had been completed, the prices had been set, and then there were actual cars to handle and motive power to assign.

Above: These blocky, seventy-four-inch wheels drove the Milwaukee Road's locomotive #220, a 4-8-4 Northern built by the American Locomotive Company, the type of motive power often used by the Milwaukee for moving circus trains over its lines. The engine developed a tractive effort of 62,119 pounds and weighed 824,100 pounds — *Authors' Photo. Right:* Locomotive 376 is nestled in the roundhouse for inspection in 1951. This 2-8-2 Mikado was classified by the Chicago Milwaukee St. Paul & Pacific as an L-3. Because of its tractive effort of 62,949 pounds, this class of locomotive frequently was assigned to circus trains — *Authors' Photo.*

Left: A J-A class 2-8-2 Mikado, #2600, moves slowly through the Butler yards north of Milwaukee in 1949. This is the type of locomotive that the Chicago and North Western Railway generally assigned to the heavy circus trains of Ringling Bros. and Barnum & Bailey — *Authors' Photo. Below:* The Pacific Electric Railway used motive power like this 300 horsepower Electric Baldwin for switching circus trains or moving to connecting lines in southern California — *Southern Pacific-Pacific Electric Railway Photo; F. W. DeSautelle Collection.*

When circus trains weighing 1,500 to 2,000 tons hit the Wyoming division or mountain territory on the Union Pacific, operating personnel favored the 4-8-4 Northerns like this one seen in 1956. Its tractive force was 63,000 pounds — *Union Pacific Railroad Photo; F. W. DeSautelle Collection.*

The CB&Q rolled circus trains over its line with EMD 6,000-horsepower freight diesels like #135 seen here in 1955 — *Chicago, Burlington & Quincy Railroad; F. W. DeSautelle Collection.*

47

Left, above: The Santa Fe used a Mikado 2-8-2 like #4060 to pull circus trains many times. Here, it rolls a more prosaic train of cattle cars in 1952 — *Santa Fe Railway; F. W. DeSautelle Collection. Left, below:* The Erie Railroad preferred this type of freight motive power for hauling heavy circus trains. The 1960 photograph shows a four-unit A-B-B-A — *Erie-Lackawanna Railway; F. W. DeSautelle Collection. Above:* L&N locomotive 1537 in the J-3 class, a 2-8-2, was built by the American Locomotive Company at Schenectady, New York, in 1922 and was the type of motive power used by the line to haul circus trains — *Louisville & Nashville Railroad; F. W. DeSautelle Collection.*

AL. G. BARNES & SELLS-FLOTO OFFICIAL ROUTE --- 1937

Date	City	State	Railroad	Ms.
SEASON 1937				
Mar. 20	San Diego	Cal.	P.E.-A.T. & S.F.	143
Mar. 21	San Diego	Cal.		
FIRST WEEK				
Mar. 22	Santa Ana	Cal.	A.T. & S. F.	92
Mar. 23	Riverside	Cal.	S. P.	99
Mar. 24	Alhambra	Cal.	S. P.	59
Mar. 25	Pasadena	Cal.	S. P.	9
Mar. 26	Los Angeles	Cal.	S. P.	10
Mar. 27	Los Angeles	Cal.		
Mar. 28	Los Angeles	Cal.		
SECOND WEEK				
Mar. 29	Los Angeles	Cal.	Hill and	
Mar. 30	Los Angeles	Cal.	Washington Sts.)	
Mar. 31	Los Angeles	Cal.		
Apr. 1	Los Angeles	Cal.		
Apr. 2	Glendale	Cal.	S. P.	7
Apr. 3	Long Beach	Cal.	S. P.	32
Apr. 4	Long Beach	Cal.		
THIRD WEEK				
Apr. 5	Hollywood	Cal.	S. P. P. E.	29
Apr. 6	Hollywood	Cal.	(Fairfax near	
Apr. 7	Hollywood	Cal.	Wilshire)	
Apr. 8	Santa Monica	Cal.	P. E.	20
Apr. 9	Ventura	Cal.	P.E.-S.P.	87
Apr. 10	San. Barbara	Cal.	S. P.	28
Apr. 11	S. Lu Obispo	Cal.	S. P.	119
FOURTH WEEK				
Apr. 12	Salinas	Cal.	S. P.	134
Apr. 13	Santa Cruz	Cal.	S. P.	38
Apr. 14	Modesto	Cal.	S. P.	125
Apr. 15	Fresno	Cal.	S. P.	92
Apr. 16	Bakersfield	Cal.	S. P.	107
Apr. 17	Taft	Cal.	Sunset	45
Apr. 18	Visalia	Cal.	Sunset-S. P.	126
FIFTH WEEK				
Apr. 19	Merced	Cal.	S. P.	96
Apr. 20	Napa	Cal.	S. P.	154
Apr. 21	San Rafael	Cal.	N. W. P.	40
Apr. 22	Alameda	Cal.	N.W.P.-S.P.	101
Apr. 23	Oakland	Cal.	S. P.	5
Apr. 24	Oakland	Cal.		
Apr. 25	Oakland	Cal.		
SIXTH WEEK				
Apr. 26	San Jose	Cal.	S. P.	41
Apr. 27	Redw'd City	Cal.	S. P.	22
Apr. 28	San Mateo	Cal.	S. P.	8
Apr. 29	San Francisco	Cal.	S. P.	18
Apr. 30	San Francisco	Cal.		
May 1	San Francisco	Cal.		
May 2	San Francisco	Cal.		
SEVENTH WEEK				
May 3	Vallejo	Cal.	S. P.	73
May 4	Santa Rosa	Cal.	S.P.-N.W.P.	63
May 5	Eureka	Cal.	N. W. P.	230
(Night Only)				
May 6	Eureka	Cal.		
May 7	Petaluma	Cal.	N. W. P.	246
(Night Only)				
May 8	Stockton	Cal.	N.W.P.-S.P.	138
May 9	Willows	Cal.	S. P.	135
EIGHTH WEEK				
May 10	Chico	Cal.	S. P.	62
May 11	Marysville	Cal.	S. P.	43
May 12	Sacramento	Cal.	S. P.	52
May 13	Reno	Nev.	S. P.	151
May 14	Alturas	Cal.	S. P.	214
(Night Only)				
May 15	Klamath Falls	Ore.	S. P.	98
May 16	Montague	Cal.	S. P.	115
(Afternoon Only)				
NINTH WEEK				
May 17	Ashland	Ore.	S. P.	54
May 18	Medford	Ore.	S. P.	13
May 19	Eugene	Ore.	S. P.	205
May 20	Marshfield	Ore.	S. P.	121
May 21	Corvalis	Ore.	S. P.	177
May 22	Salem	Ore.	S. P.	36
May 23	Portland	Ore.	S. P.	52
TENTH WEEK				
May 24	Portland	Ore.		
May 25	Portland	Ore.		
May 26	Longview	Wash.	U. P.	49
May 27	Aberdeen	Wash.	U. P.	97
May 28	Seattle	Wash.	U. P.	145
May 29	Seattle	Wash.		
May 30	Seattle	Wash.		
ELEVENTH WEEK				
May 31	Bellingham	Wash.	G. N.	118
June 1	Vancouver	B. C.	G. N.	
June 2	Vancouver	B. C.		
June 3	Mt. Vernon	Wash.	G. N.	86
June 4	Everett	Wash.	G. N.	36
June 5	Tacoma	Wash.	G. N.	89
June 6	Tacoma	Wash.		
(Afternoon Only)				
TWELFTH WEEK				
June 7	Yakima	Wash.	N. P.	131
June 8	Walla Walla	Wash.	U. P.	128
June 9	Lewiston	Ida.	U. P.	128
June 10	Moscow	Ida.	N. P.	51
June 11	Co. d'Alene	Ida.	N. P.	129
June 12	Spokane	Wash.	N. P.	34
June 13	Spokane	Wash.		
(Afternoon Only)				
THIRTEENTH WEEK				
June 14	Missoula	Mont.	N. P.	237
June 15	Butte	Mont.	N. P.	120
June 16	Dillon	Mont.	U. P.	69
June 17	Idaho Falls	Ida.	U. P.	143
June 18	Twin Falls	Ida.	U. P.	163
June 19	Pocatello	Ida.	U. P.	118
June 20	Salt Lake City	Utah	U. P.	170
FOURTEENTH WEEK				
June 21	Salt Lake City	Utah	U. P.	170
June 22	Logan	Utah	U. P.	108
June 23	Park City	Utah	U. P.	68
June 24	Evanston	Wyo.	U. P.	96
June 25	Ogden	Utah	U. P.	76
June 26	Provo	Utah	U. P.	83
June 27	Price	Utah	D. & R. G.	85
(Afternoon Only)				
FIFTEENTH WEEK				
June 28	G. Junction	Colo.	D. & R. G.	170
June 29	Salida	Colo.	D. & R. G.	234
(Night Only)				
June 30	Pueblo	Colo.	D. & R. G.	96
July 1	Alamosa	Colo.	D. & R. G.	127
July 2	Trinidad	Colo.	D. & R. G.	124
July 3	Las Vegas	N. M.	A. T. & S. F.	33
July 4	Santa Fe	N. M.	A. T. & S. F.	82
SIXTEENTH WEEK				
July 5	Raton	N. M.	A. T. & S. F.	192
July 6	La Junta	Colo.	A. T. & S. F.	101
July 7	Col. Springs	Colo.	A. T. & S. F.	109
July 8	Loveland	Colo.	C. & S.	99
July 9	Denver	Colo.	C. & S.	43
July 10	Denver	Colo.		
July 11	Ft. Morgan	Colo.	C. B. & Q.	78
SEVENTEETH WEEK				
July 12	Sterling	Colo.	U. P.	41
July 13	Boulder	Colo.	U. P.	117
July 14	Ft. Collins	Colo.	U. P.	59
July 15	Greeley	Colo.	U. P.	104
July 16	Laramie	Wyo.	U. P.	110
July 17	Rock Springs	Wyo.	U. P.	236
July 18	Rawlings	Wyo.	U. P.	119
(Afternoon Only)				
EIGHTEENTH WEEK				
July 19	Sidney	Nebr.	U. P.	276
July 20	Scotts Bluff	Nebr.	C. B. & Q.	104
July 21	Casper	Wyo.	C. B. & Q.	171
July 22	Thermopolis	Wyo.	C. B. & Q.	135
July 23	Billings	Mont.	C. B. & Q.	195
July 24	Lewistown	Mont.	G. N.	136
NINETEENTH WEEK				
July 26	Great Falls	Mont.	G. N.	137
July 27	Havre	Mont.	G. N.	123
July 28	Glasgow	Mont.	G. N.	153
July 29	Williston	N. D.	G. N.	157
July 30	Minot	N. D.	G. N.	120
July 31	Fargo	N. D.	G. N.	233
Aug. 1	Grand Forks	N. D.	G. N.	79
TWENTIETH WEEK				
Aug. 2	Bemidji	Minn.	G. N.	117
Aug. 3	Hibbing	Minn.	G. N.	150
Aug. 4	Duluth	Minn.	N. P.	74
Aug. 5	Brainerd	Minn.	N. P.	118
Aug. 6	St. Cloud	Minn.	N. P.	63
Aug. 7	Willmar	Minn.	G. N.	58
Aug. 8	Pipestone	Minn.	G. N.	106
TWENTY-FIRST WEEK				
Aug. 9	Estherville	Ia.	R. I.	101
Aug. 10	Albert Lea	Minn.	R. I.	84
Aug. 11	Austin	Minn.	C.M.St.P. & P.	19
Aug. 12	Fairmont	Minn.	C.M.St.P. & P.	77
Aug. 13	Mankato	Minn.	C.M.St.P. & P.	77
Aug. 14	Clear Lake	Ia.	C.M.St.P. & P.	116
TWENTY-SECOND WEEK				
Aug. 16	Coun. Bluffs	Ia.	CMSt.P&P-R.I.	272
Aug. 17	O'Neill	Nebr.	C. & N. W.	197
(No Show)				
Aug. 18	Chedron	Nebr.	C. & N. W.	250
Aug. 19	Alliance	Nebr.	C&NW-CB&Q	73
Aug. 20	Broken Bow	Nebr.	C. B. & Q.	190
Aug. 21	Hastings	Nebr.	C. B. & Q.	121
TWENTY-THIRD WEEK				
Aug. 23	North Platte	Nebr.	U. P.	136
Aug. 24	Kearney	Nebr.	U. P.	95
Aug. 25	Fairbury	Nebr.	U. P.	115
Aug. 26	Manhattan	Kans.	U. P.	95
Aug. 27	Concordia	Kans.	U. P.	94
Aug. 28	Superior	Nebr.	A. T. & S. F.	41
Aug. 29	Abilene	Kans.	A. T. & S. F.	96
TWENTY-FOURTH WEEK				
Aug. 30	McPherson	Kans.	U. P.	91
Aug. 31	Eldorado	Kans.	M. P.	62
Sept. 1	Fort Scott	Kans.	M. P.	147
Sept. 2	Springfield	Mo.	S. L.-S. F.	104
Sept. 3	Joplin	Mo.	M. P.	84
Sept. 4	Miami	Okla.	S. L.-S. F.	56
TWENTY-FIFTH WEEK				
Sept. 6	Tulsa	Okla.	S. L.-S. F.	89
Sept. 7	Enid	Okla.	S. L.-S. F.	121
Sept. 8	Clinton	Okla.	A. T. & S. F.	142
Sept. 9	Pampa	Tex.	A. T. & S. F.	140
Sept. 10	Woodward	Okla.	A. T. & S. F.	116
Sept. 11	Alva	Okla.	A. T. & S. F.	57
Sept. 12	Anthony	Kans.	A. T. & S. F.	60
TWENTY-SIX WEEK				
Sept. 13	Wellington	Kans.	A. T. & S. F.	45
Sept. 14	Great Bend	Kans.	A. T. & S. F.	147
Sept. 15	Garden City	Kans.	A. T. & S. F.	119
Sept. 16	Dodge City	Kans.	A. T. & S. F.	50
Sept. 17	Pratt	Kans.	R. I.	77
Sept. 18	Liberal	Kans.	R. I.	136
TWENTY-SEVENTH WEEK				
Sept. 20	Amarillo	Tex.	R. I.	153
Sept. 21	Amarillo	Tex.		
Sept. 22	Amarillo	Tex.		
Sept. 23	Amarillo	Tex.	"Tri-State	
Sept. 24	Amarillo	Tex.	Fair'	
Sept. 25	Amarillo	Tex.		
Sept. 26	Childres	Tex.	Ft. W. & D. C.	116
TWENTY-EIGHTH WEEK				
Sept. 27	Wichita Falls	Tex.	Ft. W. & D. C.	107
Sept. 28	Duncan	Okla.	FtW & DC-RI	60
Sept. 29	Chickasha	Okla.	R. I.	39
Sept. 30	Hobart	Okla.	R. I.	72
Oct. 1	Lawton	Okla.	R. I.	95
Oct. 2	Altus	Okla.	S. L.-S. F.	57
TWENTY-NINTH WEEK				
Oct. 4	San Angelo	Tex.	A. T. & S. F.	250
Oct. 5	Brownwood	Tex.	A. T. & S. F.	98
Oct. 6	Weatherford	Tex.	A. T. & S. F.	148
Oct. 7	Bonham	Tex.	T. & P.	147
Oct. 8	Denton	Tex.	T. & P.	81
Oct. 9	Waxahachie	Tex.	M. K. T.	68
Oct. 10	Hillsboro	Tex.	M. K. T.	42
THIRTIETH WEEK				
Oct. 11	Bryan	Tex.	M. K. T. I.-G. N.	130
Oct. 12	Palestine	Tex.	I. G. N.	117
Oct. 13	Henderson	Tex.	I. G. N.	75
Oct. 14	Tyler	Tex.	I. G. N.	33
Oct. 15	Terrell	Tex.	T. & P.	106
Oct. 16	Ranger	Tex.	T. & P.	160
Oct. 17	Breckenridge	Tex.	T. & P.	26
THIRTY-FIRST WEEK				
Oct. 18	Cisco	Tex.	T. & P.	28
Oct. 19	Abilene	Tex.	T. & P.	74
Oct. 20	Colorado	Tex.	T. & P.	69
Oct. 21	Big Spring	Tex.	T. & P.	35
Oct. 22	Midland	Tex.	T. & P.	40
Oct. 23	Pecos	Tex.	T. & P.	93
THIRTY-SECOND WEEK				
Oct. 25	El Paso	Tex.	T. & P.	214
Oct. 26	Lordsburg	N. M.	S. P.	147
Oct. 27	Tucson	Ariz.	S. P.	165
Oct. 28	Phoenix	Ariz.	S. P.	87
SEASON ENDS				
Home run to Baldwin Park, Calif.			S. P.	440
TOTAL SEASON MILEAGE				20,016

To launch his season's work, the circus' general agent maps out a route for the show to follow through the year's tour. This is the final route as played by the Barnes-Sells Floto Circus in 1937; the agent would have produced many editions and changes through the season to arrive at this — *Authors' Collection.*

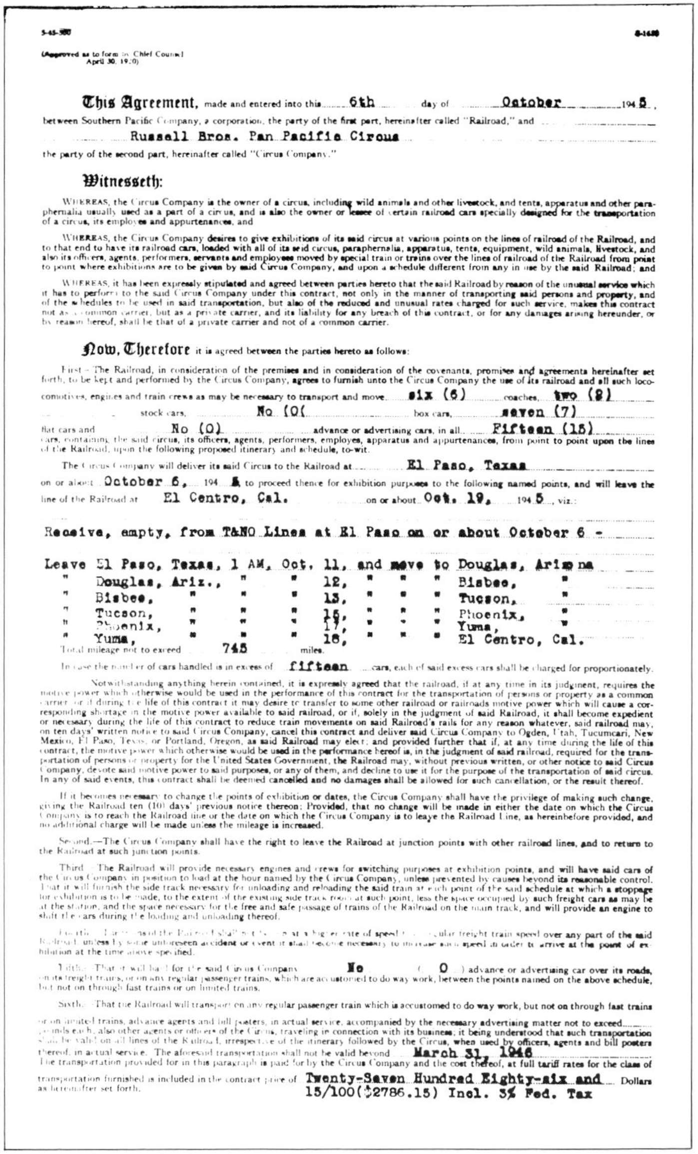

5-45-500 | 8-1680

(Approved as to form by Chief Counsel April 30, 1920)

This Agreement, made and entered into this 6th day of October 1945, between Southern Pacific Company, a corporation, the party of the first part, hereinafter called "Railroad," and Russell Bros. Pan Pacific Circus the party of the second part, hereinafter called "Circus Company."

Witnesseth:

WHEREAS, the Circus Company is the owner of a circus, including wild animals and other livestock, and tents, apparatus and other paraphernalia usually used as a part of a circus, and is also the owner or lessee of certain railroad cars specially designed for the transportation of a circus, its employes and appurtenances, and

WHEREAS, the Circus Company desires to give exhibitions of its said circus at various points on the lines of railroad of the Railroad, and to that end to have its railroad cars, loaded with all of its said circus, paraphernalia, apparatus, tents, equipment, wild animals, livestock, and also its officers, agents, performers, servants and employees moved by special train or trains over the lines of railroad of the Railroad from point to point where exhibitions are to be given by said Circus Company, and upon a schedule different from any in use by the said Railroad; and

WHEREAS, it has been expressly stipulated and agreed between parties hereto that the said Railroad by reason of the unusual service which it has to perform to the said Circus Company under this contract, not only in the manner of transporting said persons and property, and of the schedules to be used in said transportation, but also of the reduced and unusual rates charged for such service, makes this contract not as a common carrier, but as a private carrier, and its liability for any breach of this contract, or for any damages arising hereunder, or by reason hereof, shall be that of a private carrier and not of a common carrier.

Now, Therefore it is agreed between the parties hereto as follows:

First.—The Railroad, in consideration of the premises and in consideration of the covenants, promises and agreements hereinafter set forth, to be kept and performed by the Circus Company, agrees to furnish unto the Circus Company the use of its railroad and all such locomotives, engines and train crews as may be necessary to transport and move six (6) coaches, two (2) stock cars, No (0(box cars, seven (7) flat cars and No (0) advance or advertising cars, in all Fifteen (15) cars, containing the said circus, its officers, agents, performers, employes, apparatus and appurtenances, from point to point upon the lines of the Railroad, upon the following proposed itinerary and schedule, to-wit.

The Circus Company will deliver its said Circus to the Railroad at El Paso, Texas on or about October 6, 1945 to proceed thence for exhibition purposes to the following named points, and will leave the line of the Railroad at El Centro, Cal. on or about Oct. 19, 1945, viz.:

Receive, empty, from T&NO Lines at El Paso on or about October 6 -

Leave El Paso, Texas, 1 AM, Oct. 11, and move to Douglas, Arizona
" Douglas, Ariz., " " 12, " " " Bisbee, "
" Bisbee, " " " 13, " " " Tucson, "
" Tucson, " " " 15, " " " Phoenix, "
" Phoenix, " " " 17, " " " Yuma, "
" Yuma, " " " 18, " " " El Centro, Cal.

Total mileage not to exceed 745 miles.

In case the number of cars handled is in excess of fifteen cars, each of said excess cars shall be charged for proportionately.

Notwithstanding anything herein contained, it is expressly agreed that the railroad, if at any time in its judgment, requires the motive power which otherwise would be used in the performance of this contract for the transportation of persons or property as a common carrier, or if during the life of this contract it may desire to transfer to some other railroad or railroads motive power which will cause a corresponding shortage in the motive power available to said railroad, or if, solely in the judgment of said Railroad, it shall become expedient or necessary during the life of this contract to reduce train movements on said Railroad's rails for any reason whatever, said railroad may, on ten days' written notice to said Circus Company, cancel this contract and deliver said Circus Company to Ogden, Utah, Tucumcari, New Mexico, El Paso, Texas, or Portland, Oregon, as said Railroad may elect; and provided further that if, at any time during the life of this contract, the motive power which otherwise would be used in the performance hereof is, in the judgment of said railroad, required for the transportation of persons or property for the United States Government, the Railroad may, without previous written, or other notice to said Circus Company, devote said motive power to said purposes, or any of them, and decline to use it for the purpose of the transportation of said circus. In any of said events, this contract shall be deemed cancelled and no damages shall be allowed for such cancellation, or the result thereof.

If it becomes necessary to change the points of exhibition or dates, the Circus Company shall have the privilege of making such change, giving the Railroad ten (10) days' previous notice thereon; Provided, that no change will be made in either the date on which the Circus Company is to reach the Railroad line or the date on which the Circus Company is to leave the Railroad Line, as hereinbefore provided, and no additional charge will be made unless the mileage is increased.

Second.—The Circus Company shall have the right to leave the Railroad at junction points with other railroad lines, and to return to the Railroad at such junction points.

Third.—The Railroad will provide necessary engines and crews for switching purposes at exhibition points, and will have said cars of the Circus Company in position to load at the hour named by the Circus Company, unless prevented by causes beyond its reasonable control. That it will furnish the side track necessary for unloading and reloading the said train at each point of the said schedule at which a stoppage for exhibition is to be made, to the extent of the existing side track room at such point, less the space occupied by such freight cars as may be at the station, and the space necessary for the free and safe passage of trains of the Railroad on the main track, and will provide an engine to shift the cars during the loading and unloading thereof.

Fourth.—[illegible] of the Railroad shall not [illegible] at a higher rate of speed [illegible] regular freight train speed over any part of the said Railroad, unless by some unforeseen accident or event it shall become necessary to increase such speed in order to arrive at the point of exhibition at the time above specified.

Fifth.—That it will haul for the said Circus Company No (0) advance or advertising car over its roads, on its freight trains, or on any regular passenger trains, which are accustomed to do way work, between the points named on the above schedule, but not on through fast trains or on limited trains.

Sixth.—That the Railroad will transport on any regular passenger train which is accustomed to do way work, but not on through fast trains or on limited trains, advance agents and bill posters, in actual service, accompanied by the necessary advertising matter not to exceed ______ pounds each, also other agents or officers of the Circus, traveling in connection with its business; it being understood that such transportation shall be valid on all lines of the Railroad, irrespective of the itinerary followed by the Circus, when used by officers, agents and bill posters thereof, in actual service. The aforesaid transportation shall not be valid beyond March 31, 1946. The transportation provided for in this paragraph is paid for by the Circus Company and the cost thereof, at full tariff rates for the class of transportation furnished is included in the contract price of Twenty-Seven Hundred Eighty-six and 15/100($2786.15) Incl. 3% Fed. Tax Dollars as hereinafter set forth.

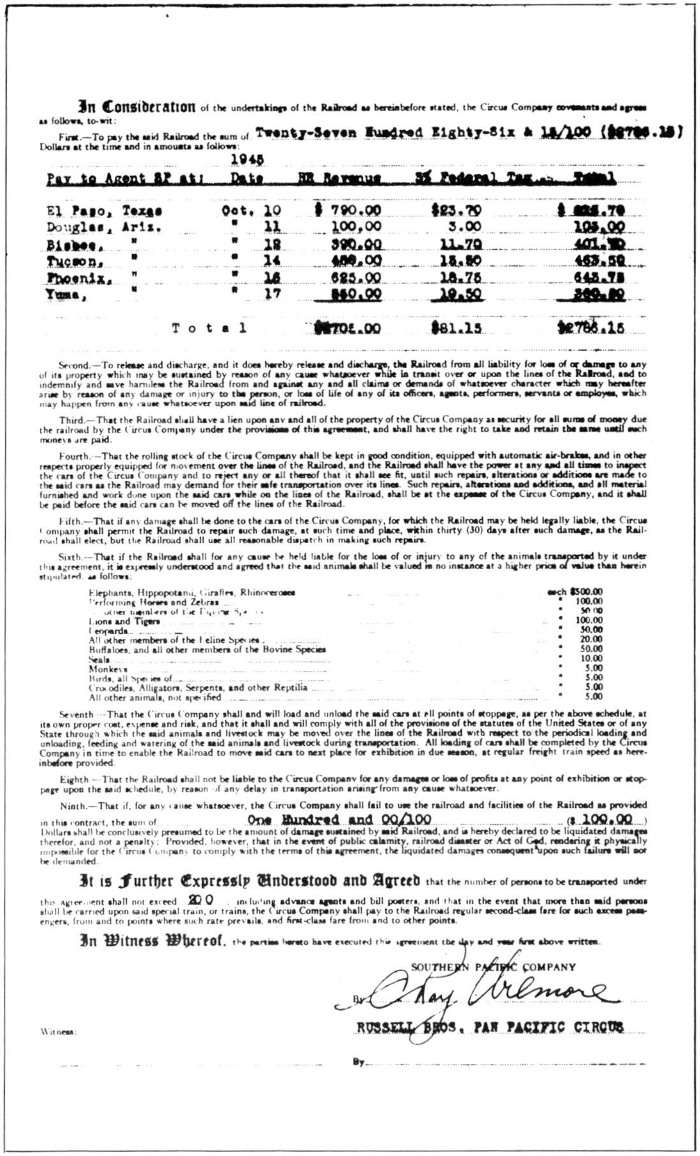

In Consideration of the undertakings of the Railroad as hereinbefore stated, the Circus Company covenants and agrees as follows, to-wit:

First.—To pay the said Railroad the sum of Twenty-Seven Hundred Eighty-Six & 15/100 ($2786.15) Dollars at the time and in amounts as follows:

Pay to Agent SP at:	1945 Date	RR Revenue	3% Federal Tax	Total
El Paso, Texas	Oct. 10	$ 790.00	$23.70	$ [illegible].70
Douglas, Ariz.	" 11	100.00	3.00	103.00
Bisbee, "	" 12	390.00	11.70	401.[illegible]
Tucson, "	" 14	[illegible].00	13.[illegible]	463.50
Phoenix, "	" 16	625.00	18.75	643.75
Yuma, "	" 17	[illegible].00	19.50	[illegible]
Total		$2705.00	$81.15	$2786.15

Second.—To release and discharge, and it does hereby release and discharge, the Railroad from all liability for loss of or damage to any of its property which may be sustained by reason of any cause whatsoever while in transit over or upon the lines of the Railroad, and to indemnify and save harmless the Railroad from and against any and all claims or demands of whatsoever character which may hereafter arise by reason of any damage or injury to the person, or loss of life of any of its officers, agents, performers, servants or employes, which may happen from any cause whatsoever upon said line of railroad.

Third.—That the Railroad shall have a lien upon any and all of the property of the Circus Company as security for all sums of money due the railroad by the Circus Company under the provisions of this agreement, and shall have the right to take and retain the same until such moneys are paid.

Fourth.—That the rolling stock of the Circus Company shall be kept in good condition, equipped with automatic air-brakes, and in other respects properly equipped for movement over the lines of the Railroad, and the Railroad shall have the power at any and all times to inspect the cars of the Circus Company and to reject any or all thereof that it shall see fit, until such repairs, alterations or additions are made to the said cars as the Railroad may demand for their safe transportation over its lines. Such repairs, alterations and additions, and all material furnished and work done upon the said cars while on the lines of the Railroad, shall be at the expense of the Circus Company, and it shall be paid before the said cars can be moved off the lines of the Railroad.

Fifth.—That if any damage shall be done to the cars of the Circus Company, for which the Railroad may be held legally liable, the Circus Company shall permit the Railroad to repair such damage, at such time and place, within thirty (30) days after such damage, as the Railroad shall elect, but the Railroad shall use all reasonable dispatch in making such repairs.

Sixth.—That if the Railroad shall for any cause be held liable for the loss of or injury to any of the animals transported by it under this agreement, it is expressly understood and agreed that the said animals shall be valued in no instance at a higher price of value than herein stipulated, as follows:

Elephants, Hippopotami, Giraffes, Rhinoceroses	each $500.00
Performing Horses and Zebras	" 100.00
All other members of the Equine Species	" 50.00
Lions and Tigers	" 100.00
Leopards	" 50.00
All other members of the Feline Species	" 20.00
Buffaloes, and all other members of the Bovine Species	" 50.00
Seals	" 10.00
Monkeys	" 5.00
Birds, all Species of	" 5.00
Crocodiles, Alligators, Serpents, and other Reptilia	" 5.00
All other animals, not specified	" 5.00

Seventh.—That the Circus Company shall and will load and unload the said cars at all points of stoppage, as per the above schedule, at its own proper cost, expense and risk, and that it shall and will comply with all of the provisions of the statutes of the United States or of any State through which the said animals and livestock may be moved over the lines of the Railroad with respect to the periodical loading and unloading, feeding and watering of the said animals and livestock during transportation. All loading of cars shall be completed by the Circus Company in time to enable the Railroad to move said cars to next place for exhibition in due season, at regular freight train speed as hereinbefore provided.

Eighth.—That the Railroad shall not be liable to the Circus Company for any damages or loss of profits at any point of exhibition or stoppage upon the said schedule, by reason of any delay in transportation arising from any cause whatsoever.

Ninth.—That if, for any cause whatsoever, the Circus Company shall fail to use the railroad and facilities of the Railroad as provided in this contract, the sum of One Hundred and 00/100 ($ 100.00) Dollars shall be conclusively presumed to be the amount of damage sustained by said Railroad, and is hereby declared to be liquidated damages therefor, and not a penalty; Provided, however, that in the event of public calamity, railroad disaster or Act of God, rendering it physically impossible for the Circus Company to comply with the terms of this agreement, the liquidated damages consequent upon such failure will not be demanded.

It is Further Expressly Understood and Agreed that the number of persons to be transported under this agreement shall not exceed 200 including advance agents and bill posters, and that in the event that more than said persons shall be carried upon said special train, or trains, the Circus Company shall pay to the Railroad regular second-class fare for such excess passengers, from and to points where such rate prevails, and first-class fare from and to other points.

In Witness Whereof, the parties hereto have executed this agreement the day and year first above written.

SOUTHERN PACIFIC COMPANY

By Ray Welmore

Witness:

RUSSELL BROS. PAN PACIFIC CIRCUS

By

The agreement between Southern Pacific and the Russell Bros. Circus in 1945 was typical of most contracts between shows and railroads. The line agrees to move the show at stated prices. The circus accepts virtually all liability. Many other details and responsibilities are accounted for — *Authors' Collection.*

File 15081-Sub.7

CIRCUS AND CARNIVAL RATES

CIRCUS AND CARNIVAL RUNS UP TO 200 MILES ARE SHOWN IN DOLLARS AND CENTS PER RUN
CIRCUS AND CARNIVAL RUNS OVER 200 MILES ARE SHOWN IN DOLLARS AND CENTS PER MILE
DEAD HEAD OR HOME RUNS ARE SHOWN IN DOLLARS AND CENTS PER MILE

Miles	6 to 10 cars	11 to 15 cars	16 to 20 cars	21 to 25 cars	26 to 30 cars	31 to 35 cars	36 to 40 cars	41 to 50 cars	51 to 60 cars	61 to 70 cars	71 to 80 cars	81 to 90 cars	91 to 100 cars	101 to 110 cars
50 and under	476.00	583.00	688.00	769.00	847.00	953.00	953.00	1173.00	1290.00	1407.00	1525.00	1642.00	1759.00	1935.00
51 to 60	543.00	648.00	755.00	847.00	927.00	1045.00	1045.00	1290.00	1422.00	1539.00	1671.00	1789.00	1906.00	2097.00
61 to 70	609.00	715.00	820.00	927.00	1005.00	1139.00	1139.00	1407.00	1539.00	1671.00	1802.00	1934.00	2082.00	2289.00
71 to 80	661.00	781.00	887.00	994.00	1085.00	1217.00	1217.00	1510.00	1657.00	1802.00	1934.00	2082.00	2228.00	2451.00
81 to 90	702.00	834.00	953.00	1059.00	1153.00	1298.00	1298.00	1613.00	1774.00	1934.00	2067.00	2212.00	2360.00	2596.00
91 to 100	741.00	873.00	1005.00	1112.00	1217.00	1376.00	1376.00	1700.00	1876.00	2053.00	2199.00	2344.00	2493.00	2742.00
101 to 120	847.00	994.00	1153.00	1271.00	1390.00	1574.00	1574.00	1934.00	2140.00	2344.00	2507.00	2668.00	2830.00	3113.00
121 to 140	941.00	1099.00	1271.00	1403.00	1535.00	1734.00	1734.00	2140.00	2360.00	2578.00	2771.00	2962.00	3150.00	3465.00
141 to 160	1005.00	1191.00	1363.00	1510.00	1656.00	1868.00	1868.00	2317.00	2551.00	2784.00	2990.00	3196.00	3400.00	3740.00
161 to 180	1073.00	1258.00	1442.00	1602.00	1747.00	1986.00	1986.00	2446.00	2696.00	2962.00	3164.00	3370.00	3575.00	3933.00
181 to 200	1112.00	1310.00	1510.00	1668.00	1827.00	2064.00	2064.00	2551.00	2814.00	3079.00	3298.00	3518.00	3738.00	4112.00
Over 200 miles Exhibition Runs Rate per mile	5.56	6.55	7.55	8.34	9.13	10.33	10.33	12.76	14.07	15.39	16.49	17.59	18.69	20.56
Home Run or Dead head Rate per Mile	4.46	5.21	6.05	6.72	7.29	8.24	8.24	10.22	11.26	12.30	13.24	14.07	14.94	16.43

Effective October 1, 1949

Rates for moving circuses were set by regional committees, such as the Western Trunk Line Committee, which issued this table of rates in 1949 to include a ten percent increase. Movements were priced according to mileage and the number of cars — as a result, circuses were among the first to use extra-long cars. Prices are quoted for increments of five or ten cars. Since it cost as much to move thirty cars as it did for twenty-six, circuses tended to add or subtract cars in blocks of five or ten — *Authors' Collection*.

16. IT IS CLEARLY KNOWN AND UNDERSTOOD AND SPECIALLY CONTEMPLATED BY THE PARTIES THERETO:

(a)   That the character of the services to be performed involves hazard;

(b)   That the place of performance changes from day to day with constantly changing conditions of premises, with attendant varying degrees of safety.

(c)   That the times, manner and means of transportation offered and furnished by the EMPLOYERS increase the risk of travel beyond the ordinary.

(d)   That the circus trains of the EMPLOYERS, with all persons and property thereon, are transported, not as common carrier, but by private arrangement whereby the EMPLOYERS agree to hold and save transporting railway or railroad harmless and free from claim or liability for injury to the person or property of the ARTIST, his servants and troupe, whether occasioned through the negligence of said railroad, its officers or employees; said railroad assuming no liability for injury to the ARTIST by its negligence or otherwise in any manner.

(e)   That all said contracts now or during the course of employment entered into between the EMPLOYERS and transporting railroads, the ARTIST hereby ratifies and agrees thereby to be bound, the same being the means of furnishing opportunity for this employment.

(f)   The ARTIST renounces his rights as "passenger." That no relations of common carrier exist either between the ARTIST and the EMPLOYERS or the ARTIST and any railroad while traveling in or occupying cars of the EMPLOYERS, or while on railroad tracks in going to or from said cars;

(g)   That the ARTIST at all times is free to elect whether he or she will accept traveling accommodations offered by the EMPLOYERS and usual in the circus business thereby effectually and unconditionally releasing from liability for all negligence the transporting railroad and the EMPLOYERS as herein provided, or, to choose and obtain at the ARTIST'S personal expense regular railroad transportation between exhibition stands;

(h)   It is recognized and understood that the peculiar nature of the circus business requires these similar extraordinary covenants and conditions of release and assumption of risks elsewhere contained in this contract, all of which are hereby mutually entered into and accepted with binding effect, and for which in the salary paid herein there is included a particular allowance as express consideration supporting same.

NOW, THEREFORE, in consideration of the salary paid and acknowledging that said release from the EMPLOYERS to transporting railroads is a material consideration herein, and recognizing special but not exclusive consideration from the extensive travel, widened opportunity to present acts and advertise same, benefits of board and traveling accommodations on circus cars, benefits in securing other engagements gained by connection with the EMPLOYER'S institution, and benefits beyond the scope of employment—THE ARTIST DOES HEREBY RELEASE and forever discharge to the EMPLOYERS from all claims, demands, liability and cause of action for personal injury to the ARTIST and loss or injury to property, and for sickness, and death, whether sustained or received while in the performance of his duty or otherwise or while occupying or traveling in circus trains, or on railroad tracks or yards, whether due to the fault or negligence in any degree of the EMPLOYERS, their agents or employees or any transporting railroad, its officers or servants in any manner; and

THE ARTIST FURTHER does hereby and upon the consideration and conditions hereinabove recited, release and forever discharge each and every railroad company, its officers and servants engaged in transporting the EMPLOYER'S circus of and form all claims, demands, liabilities and causes of action for injury to the person or property of the ARTIST while on its tracks or yards or while occupying or being transported in said circus cars and in any manner, place or time received, whether due to the fault of negligence of said railroad, its officers, agents or servants, or the EMPLOYERS or their servants, acting separately or combined. and

THE ARTIST FURTHER agrees to protect, indemnify, and save the EMPLOYERS harmless with respect to any money the EMPLOYERS may be compelled to pay or surrender or liability to which EMPLOYERS may be subject in consequence of any accident or injury or death to the ARTIST or to any servant in the employ of the ARTIST while occupying circus cars or while upon the tracks or yards of any said railroad company; and the ARTIST does hereby give the right at any time to the EMPLOYERS to assign this contract to any such railroad to be used in its defense.

IN WITNESS WHEREOF, the above named parties have hereunto set their hands and seals, by these presents firmly binding themselves, their heirs and executors.

ROBBINS BROS. BIG 4-RING CIRCUS

In presence of

BY _____ _____ (Seal)

_____   Employers

_____   _____ _____ (Seal)

Repercussions of railroad contracts are felt by the performers of the circus when they sign on for the season. Robbins Bros. employees waived any rights as railroad passengers and released the show from any future claims arising out of railroad moves — *Circus World Museum.*

This Memorandum of Agreement, made LOUISVILLE, KY.

this **Eleventh** day of **October** 1893., between the Louisville & Nashville Railroad Company, hereinafter known as the Railroad Company, and **REYNOLDS' GREAT RAILROAD SHOWS** hereinafter known as the Circus Company.

Witnesseth: The Railroad Company agrees to furnish the necessary motive power to move, and the necessary crews to man, the following cars, viz:

```
        Five (5) flat cars
        Four (4) stock cars
        Two  (2) coaches
        One  (1) combination car
and one (1) advertising car in advance of the circus
```

The cars indicated above to be delivered to the Louisville & Nashville R.R. at Memphis, Tenn., and the movements over this Company's lines to be as follows; viz:

Leave Memphis, Tenn. about midnight, Oct.23rd, and run to Brownsville, Tenn.
Leave Brownsville, Tenn. about midnight, Oct.24th, and run to Milan, Tenn.
Leave Milan, Tenn., Texx about midnight, Oct.25th, and run to McKenzie, Tenn.
Leave McKenzie, Tenn. about midnight, Oct.26th, and run to Paris, Tenn.
Leave Paris, Tenn. about nidnight, Oct. 27th, and run to Erin, Tenn.
Leave Erin, Tenn. about nidnight, Oct. 28th, and run to Clarksville, Tenn.
Leave Clarksville, Tenn., about midnight, Oct.30th, and run to Guthrie, Ky.
Leave Guthrie, Ky., about midnight, Oct.31st, and run to Springfield, Tenn.
Leave Springfield, Tenn. about nidmight, November 1st, and run to Nashville, Tenn.

The Railroad Company will charge of the above service, the following amounts, which are to be paid to the agents of the Railroad Company at the points named below, before the movement of the Circus train from that point, viz:

```
To the agent at Memphis, Tenn.----------------------- $150.00
To the agent at Brownsville, Tenn.------------------    131.25
To the agent at Milan, Tenn. ----------------------     131.25
To the agent at McKenzie, Tenn.-------------------      131.25
To the agent at Paris, Tenn.-----------------------     131.25
To the agent at Erin, Tenn.------------------------     131.25
To the agent at Clarksville, Tenn.----------------      131.25
To the agent at Guthrie, Ky.,---------------------      131.25
To the agent at Springfield, Tenn.---------------       131.25
```

In earlier times, agreements between railroads and shows were more simple. In this 1893 pact, the Louisville & Nashville agreed to transport the Reynolds Great Railroad Show to a series of Tennessee stands — and with little qualification or complication — *Circus World Museum.*

I.C.C. A-10496

MISSOURI PACIFIC RAILROAD COMPANY

(Guy A. Thompson, Trustee)

FREIGHT TARIFF C-480

LOCAL RATES

ON

RINGLING BROS. AND BARNUM & BAILEY
COMBINED SHOWS, INC.

CONSISTING OF EIGHTY (80) CARS, VIZ.: FORTY-SIX
(46) FLAT CARS, TWENTY-SIX (26) COACHES AND EIGHT (8) STOCK CARS

RATES IN DOLLARS AND CENTS PER RUN

FROM	DATE	TO	RATE
TEXARKANA . . . . ARK.-TEX. (SEE ITEM 7)	OCTOBER 29, 1955.	HOT SPRINGS . . . . .ARK.	$3,389.00
HOT SPRINGS . . . . .ARK.	OCTOBER 30, 1955.	PINE BLUFF. . . . . .ARK. (SEE ITEM 8)	$2,324.00

THIS TARIFF IS ALSO APPLICABLE ON INTRASTATE TRAFFIC

ISSUED OCTOBER 20, 1955.　　　　　# EFFECTIVE OCTOBER 29, 1955.

(EXPIRES WITH MOVEMENT)

ISSUED UNDER AUTHORITY OF RULE 63 OF INTERSTATE COMMERCE COMMISSION TARIFF
CIRCULAR 20.

ISSUED BY
J. S. SMITH, FREIGHT TRAFFIC MANAGER
MISSOURI PACIFIC BUILDING
13TH AND OLIVE STREETS
ST. LOUIS 3, MO.

(PRINTED IN U.S.A.)　　　　　(125 - AUTHY. 21298)

TARIFF C-480

ITEM 1.

EXCEPT AS OTHERWISE PROVIDED, THE AMOUNTS SHOWN IN RATE COLUMN ARE TO BE COLLECTED BY
AGENT BEFORE SHOW LEAVES HIS STATION. (SEE ITEMS 4 AND 5.)

ITEM 2.

THE TRANSPORTATION OF RINGLING BROS. AND BARNUM & BAILEY COMBINED SHOWS, INC. IS PER-
FORMED UNDER SPECIAL CONTRACT NO. 5, ENTERED INTO BETWEEN RINGLING BROS. AND BARNUM & BAILEY
COMBINED SHOWS, INC. AND GUY A. THOMPSON, TRUSTEE, MISSOURI PACIFIC RAILROAD COMPANY, DEBTOR,
OCTOBER 5, 1955.

ITEM 3.

FULL PASSENGER FARE TO BE PAID FOR ALL PERSONS IN EXCESS OF FIFTEEN HUNDRED (1500) BONA
FIDE EMPLOYES OF THE SHOW PROPER.

ITEM 4.

IN ADDITION TO THE CHARGES SHOWN HEREIN, THE RINGLING BROS. AND BARNUM & BAILEY COMBINED
SHOWS, INC. AGREES TO ALSO PAY THE COST OF INSTALLATION AND REMOVAL OF CROSSING PLANKS AT ALL
EXHIBITION POINTS WHERE IT IS NECESSARY TO INSTALL PLANKS TO TAKE CARE OF LOADING AND UNLOAD-
ING.

ITEM 5.

IN ADDITION TO THE OTHER CHARGES PROVIDED HEREIN, THE RINGLING BROS. AND BARNUM & BAILEY
COMBINED SHOWS, INC. AGREES TO ALSO PAY THE MISSOURI PACIFIC RAILROAD COMPANY $1.21 PER CAR
PER DAY FOR TRACK RENTAL AFTER FIRST SEVEN (7) DAYS UPON ARRIVAL ON ALL CARS STORED ON THE
RAILS OF THE MISSOURI PACIFIC RAILROAD COMPANY.

ITEM 6.

CARS TO BE HANDLED IN THREE (3) SECTIONS.

ITEM 7.

RECEIVE EMPTY CARS FROM THE TEXAS AND PACIFIC RAILWAY COMPANY AT TEXARKANA, ARK.-TEX., ON
OCTOBER 29, 1955.

ITEM 8.

DELIVER EMPTY CARS TO THE ST. LOUIS SOUTHWESTERN RAILWAY COMPANY AT PINE BLUFF, ARK., ON
OCTOBER 31, 1955.

(THE END)

ICC's limited interest in circus movements does include a require-
ment that a tariff be posted, as Missouri Pacific did for a Ringling
move between Texarkana and Hot Springs in 1955. Circus tariffs
cover a single move only, and for another circus or another season's
move between the same towns, a new tariff would be posted —
Authors' Collection.

MISSOURI PACIFIC RAILROAD COMPANY

125

AUTHORITY No.H-4873

IN CONNECTION WITH
UNION RAILWAY COMPANY FX 5 No.4

F R E I G H T   T A R I F F

O F

L O C A L   A N D   J O I N T   R A T E S
NO. 7 5 4 3

O N

GOLDEN BROTHERS CIRCUS

CONSISTING OF FIFTEEN (15) CARS, VIZ. SEVEN (7) FLAT, THREE (3) SLEEPING,
THREE (3) STOCK, ONE (1) DINING AND ONE (1) ADVERTISING (SEE ITEM No.9).

RATES IN DOLLARS AND CENTS PER RUN

| FROM | DATE | TO | RATE | |
			COLUMN 1 SEE ITEM No.1	COLUMN 2 SEE ITEMS Nos.2 & 6
MEMPHIS, TENN. (SEE ITEM No.7)	SEPTEMBER 30, 1923	EARLE, ARK.	$570.00	$585.00
EARLE, ARK.	OCTOBER 1, 1923 (ABOUT MIDNIGHT)	NEW AUGUSTA, ARK.	435.00	450.00
NEW AUGUSTA, ARK.	OCTOBER 2, 1923 (ABOUT MIDNIGHT)	BEEBE, ARK.	435.00	450.00
BEEBE, ARK.	OCTOBER 3, 1923 (ABOUT MIDNIGHT)	MORRILLTON, ARK.	450.00	450.00
MORRILLTON, ARK.	OCTOBER 4, 1923 (ABOUT MIDNIGHT)	CLARKSVILLE, ARK.	450.00	450.00
CLARKSVILLE, ARK.	OCTOBER 5, 1923 (ABOUT MIDNIGHT)	OZARK, ARK.	450.00	450.00
OZARK, ARK.	OCTOBER 6, 1923 (ABOUT MIDNIGHT)	VAN BUREN, ARK. (SEE ITEM No.8)	450.00	450.00

ISSUED SEPTEMBER 24,1923.

+EFFECTIVE SEPTEMBER 30,1923.
EXPIRES WITH NOVEMBER 8,1923.

+ISSUED UNDER AUTHORITY OF RULE 63 OF INTERSTATE COMMERCE COMMISSION'S TARIFF
CIRCULAR No 18-A: ALSO ISSUED UNDER AUTHORITY OF ARKANSAS RAILROAD COMMISSION
GENERAL ORDER No.330, DATED SEPTEMBER 18,1923.

ISSUED BY
D. E. LINCOLN,
Asst. Freight Traffic Manager
ST. LOUIS, MO

(PRINTED IN U.S.A.)

ITEM No.1. THE AMOUNTS SHOWN IN COLUMN 1 ARE TO BE COLLECTED BY THE AG.
BEFORE THE SHOW LEAVES HIS STATION, PLUS ANY CHARGES ACCRUING UNDER ITEM No.6.

ITEM No.2. THE AMOUNTS SHOWN IN COLUMN 2 INCLUDE ALL CHARGES TO BE PAID BY
THE SHOW COMPANY (EXCLUSIVE OF ANY CHARGES ACCRUING UNDER ITEM No.6). THE DIFFERENCE
BETWEEN THE RATES IN COLUMN 1 AND COLUMN 2 REPRESENTS THE COST OF TRANSPORTATION
WHICH HAS BEEN PURCHASED AND PAID FOR IN ADVANCE BY THE SHOW COMPANY FOR THE USE OF
ITS ADVERTISING AGENTS OR BILL POSTERS (SEE ITEM No.5).

ITEM No.3. THE TRANSPORTATION OF GOLDEN BROTHERS CIRCUS IS PERFORMED UNDER
SPECIAL CONTRACT No. 32, ENTERED INTO BETWEEN GOLDEN BROTHERS CIRCUS AND THE
MISSOURI PACIFIC RAILROAD CO., SEPTEMBER 24,1923.

ITEM No.4. FULL PASSENGER FARE TO BE PAID FOR ALL PERSONS IN EXCESS OF THREE
HUNDRED (300) BONA FIDE EMPLOYES OF THE SHOW PROPER, AND TWENTY-ONE (21) MEN WITH
THE ADVERTISING CAR.

ITEM No.5. NOT TO EXCEED TWENTY PER CENT (20%) OF THE CHARGES SHOWN IN COLUMN
2 IS FOR TRANSPORTATION OF ADVERTISING AGENTS OR BILL POSTERS IN THE EMPLOY OF THE
SHOW COMPANY, AND HAS BEEN FURNISHED IN THE FORM OF FIFTEEN DOLLARS ($15.00) SHOW
SCRIP BOOK COUPONS, WHICH ARE HONORED ON ALL TRAINS OF THE MISSOURI PACIFIC RAILROAD
COMPANY CARRYING PASSENGERS IN ACCORDANCE WITH PASSENGER DEPARTMENT CIRCULAR No.A-
16-1919, ISSUED BY PASSENGER TRAFFIC MANAGER.

ITEM No.6. IN ADDITION TO THE CHARGES PROVIDED HEREIN, GOLDEN BROTHERS CIRCUS
AGREES TO PAY TO UNION RAILWAY COMPANY OR MISSOURI PACIFIC RAILROAD COMPANY, TRACK
RENTAL CHARGE OF ONE DOLLAR ($1.00) PER CAR, PER DAY, OR FRACTION THEREOF, ON ALL
CARS REMAINING ON THEIR TRACKS AT MEMPHIS, TENN., EARLE, NEW AUGUSTA, BEEBE,
MORRILLTON, CLARKSVILLE, OZARK, OR VAN BUREN, ARK., LONGER THAN FORTY-EIGHT (48)
HOURS FOLLOWING THE FIRST 7:00 A.M. AFTER ARRIVAL, SUNDAYS EXCLUDED; SUCH CHARGES
ARE TO BE COLLECTED BY AGENT OF UNION RAILWAY COMPANY OR MISSOURI PACIFIC RAILROAD
COMPANY AT EACH POINT WHERE SUCH CHARGES ACCRUE.

ITEM No.7. RECEIVE LOADED CARS FROM ILLINOIS CENTRAL R.R., AT MEMPHIS, TENN.,
SEPTEMBER 30,1923.

ITEM No.8. DELIVER EMPTY CARS TO ST.LOUIS-SAN FRANCISCO RY., AT VAN BUREN,
ARK., OCTOBER 8, 1923.

ITEM No.9. GOLDEN BROTHERS CIRCUS HAS THE PRIVILEGE OF HAVING ITS ADVERTISING
CAR TRANSPORTED IN ADVANCE OF THE CARS CONTAINING THE SHOW PROPER, UPON DUE NOTICE
TO THE OFFICERS AND AGENTS OF THE MISSOURI PACIFIC RAILROAD COMPANY, THE ADVERTISING
CAR TO BE ATTACHED TO THE REGULAR TRAINS OF MISSOURI PACIFIC RAILROAD COMPANY,
OR OTHERWISE, AS MAY BE DETERMINED BY ITS OFFICERS AND AGENTS.

Similar tariffs were issued by the L&N for the Rhoda Royal Circus in
1921 (page 57), by the Missouri Pacific for the Golden Bros. Circus
in 1923, and for most other circus contracts since the ICC set up the
procedure — *Authors' Collection.*

LOUISVILLE AND NASHVILLE RAILROAD COMPANY
General Freight Office.

Form 589.

Billing Order No. A-6657
(Cancels B.O. No. A-6647)

Louisville,Ky. October 11,1921.
File 580676

RHODA ROYAL CIRCUS.

To Agents:-

You are authorized to bill from points shown below the above Circus Company composed of four coaches, three stock, seven flats and one advertising car in advance of the Circus, total fifteen cars, to be furnished by the Circus Company with not to exceed 200 persons who will travel with the Circus. All in excess of 200 persons to pay regular passenger fare.

When cars used by the Circus Company occupy the Railroad Company's tracks at any point for a longer period than forty-eight (48) hours, a track rental charge will be assessed at the rate of one dollar ($1.00) per car per day or fraction thereof, plus 3 percent war tax on all cars remaining at an exhibition point longer than forty-eight (48) hours following the first seven (7) A.M. after arrival, Sunday excluded. When rental charges accrue no further movement will be made until such charges are paid. Rental charges thus accruing should be reported to the Auditor of Receipts and not to the Car Service Association. No mileage or per diem will be allowed on these cars. These storage charges to apply on the advance car as well as the cars of the Circus proper.

The movement to be made as follows:-

To be received loaded from the C.N.O.& T.P. Ry. at Junction City,Ky., early morning October 19th,1921 and run to Lebanon,Ky.
Leave Lebanon about midnight October 19th,1921 and run to Elizabethtown,Ky.
" Elizabethtown about " " 20th, " " " " Munfordsville,Ky.
" Munfordsville " " " 21st, " " " " Glasgow,Ky.
" Glasgow, " " " 22nd, " " " " Russellville,Ky.
" Russellville, " " " 24th, " " " " Springfield,Tenn.
" Springfield, " " " 25th, " " " " Columbia, "
" Columbia " " " 26th, " " " " Lawrenceburg,"
" Lawrenceburg " " " 27th, " " " " Sheffield, Ala.
There to be delivered empty to connection with connecting line for the Southern Railway.

For this service the Railroad Company will charge the following amounts, payment to be made to the Agent of the Railroad Company at points named below before movement, during regular week day working hours.

To the Agent at Junction City,Ky. $331.50 plus $ 9.95 war tax.
" " " " Lebanon, Ky. $331.50 " 9.95 " "
" " " " Elizabethtown,Ky. $331.50 " 9.95 " "
" " " " Munfordsville,Ky. $331.50 " 9.95 " "
" " " " Glasgow, Ky. $406.50 " 12.20 " "
" " " " Russellville,Ky. $356.50 " 10.70 " "
" " " " Springfield,Tenn. $444.00 " 13.32 " "
" " " " Columbia, Tenn. $331.50 " 9.95 " "
" " " " Lawrenceburg, Tenn. $331.50 " 9.95 " "

(Continued on Sheet 2)

Billing Order No. A-6657.

Sheet 2.

Form 589.

The above charges include transportation of not exceeding 200 persons.
This billing order expires with movement.
Please be governed accordingly.

Issued by
E.A.deFuniak, General Freight Agent,
Louisville,Ky.

A.M.H.

57

No Supplement to this tariff will be issued except for the purpose of cancelling the tariff.

I. C. C. No. B- 406

SEABOARD AIR LINE RAILROAD COMPANY

Local Freight Tariff

—OF—

RATES AND CHARGES FOR TRANSPORTATION AND HANDLING OF

RINGLING BROS. AND BARNUM & BAILEY COMBINED SHOWS, INC.

Consisting of 70 Privately owned cars as follows:

First Section	Second Section	Third Section
3 Stock cars	2 Stock cars	-
15 Flat cars	18 Flat cars	8 Flat cars
4 Coaches	8 Coaches	11 Coaches
22 Cars Total	28 Cars Total	19 Cars Total

1 Advertising Car

Leave	Time	Date	To Be Hauled To	Special Rate
Miami, Fla.	11:59 PM	11-23-52	Sarasota, Fla.	$4,399.00

ISSUED: October 31, 1952

Issued on one (1) day's notice under authority of Rule 63—I. C. C. Tariff Circular 20.

EFFECTIVE: November 4, 1952

EXPIRES December 31, 1952 unless sooner cancelled, changed or extended.

SHOW SCRIP BOOKS: As a part of the consideration of the contract executed by the Carrier and the Circus or Show Company, in the form set forth in Tariff I. C. C. B-1, Carrier will, except in connection with movement from last exhibition point to winter quarters, issue to the Circus or Show Company, for use exclusively by bona fide bill posters and advertising agents of the Circus or Show Company, Show Scrip Books, at the rate of $15.00 per book.

Not exceeding 150 pounds of personal baggage will be checked on each book, and in addition, the holder will be allowed to carry, without charge, in baggage cars, advertising matter, material and tools, but the combined weight of such personal baggage, advertising matter, materials and tools shall not in any case exceed 300 pounds.

These books, which must be paid for in advance by the Circus or Show Company, will be issued to the extent of value amounting to not more than ten (10) per cent of the gross transportation revenue accruing to the Carrier, as shown herein, and will be good for said travel for the period therein limited.

Amount paid by the Circus or Show Company for Show Scrip Books will be deducted by Carrier from the contract charge for the last run or runs.

TRACK RENTAL CHARGES: The rate of transportation shown will include track rental charge of outfit (does not include any charge for occupancy by employees of said cars while so parked) at point of exhibition or point of interchange on rails of this company for a period of not more than 48 hours, exclusive of Sundays. On all cars remaining at point of exhibition or point of interchange longer than 48 hours, following the first 7 A. M. after arrival, Sundays excluded, a track rental charge of $1.00 per car per day or fraction thereof will be made.

RENTAL OF EQUIPMENT: The Special Rates shown herein include transportation of paraphernalia and bona fide employees of the show, traveling with it or in advance cars, but do not include rental for equipment furnished by Carrier.

For all other than its privately owned cars, used by the Circus or Show Company while on the rails of this Company, charges for rental will be, for each twenty-four (24) hour period, or fractional part thereof:

On Box Cars	$18.75 per car	On Baggage Cars	$37.50 per car
On Flat Cars	18.75 per car	On Coaches	37.50 each

These charges are to be collected by agents in advance and will be in addition to all other charges herein provided for.

Issued by
J. P. DERHAM, Jr., Assistant Vice-President,
S. A. L. Railroad Building, Norfolk 10, Va.

SARGENT

Seaboard Air Line's local freight tariff itemizes the agreement for moving seventy Ringling cars in 1952 and spells out the terms for advance men using show scrip. It covers a move from Miami to the show's winter quarters in Sarasota, Florida. Rate tables provided for lower prices when the show was headed for home rather than to another exhibition stand — *Authors' Collection.*

As plans take shape, portions of the route are released for public information. Colorful route cards are available in advance of the time period so that employees and associates will know where the circus will be and where it can be reached by mail or by visit — *Authors' Collection.*

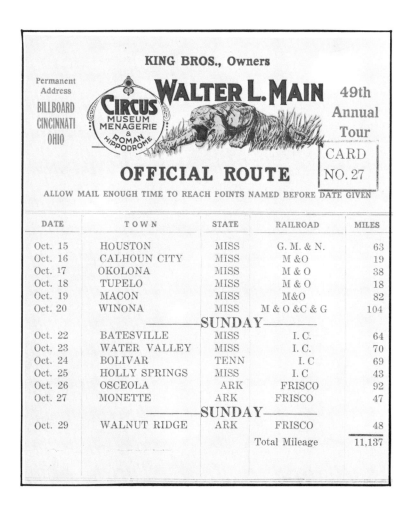

DATE	TOWN	STATE	RAILROAD	MILES
Oct. 15	HOUSTON	MISS	G. M. & N.	63
Oct. 16	CALHOUN CITY	MISS	M & O	19
Oct. 17	OKOLONA	MISS	M & O	38
Oct. 18	TUPELO	MISS	M & O	18
Oct. 19	MACON	MISS	M & O	82
Oct. 20	WINONA	MISS	M & O & C & G	104
SUNDAY				
Oct. 22	BATESVILLE	MISS	I. C.	64
Oct. 23	WATER VALLEY	MISS	I. C.	70
Oct. 24	BOLIVAR	TENN	I. C	69
Oct. 25	HOLLY SPRINGS	MISS	I. C	43
Oct. 26	OSCEOLA	ARK	FRISCO	92
Oct. 27	MONETTE	ARK	FRISCO	47
SUNDAY				
Oct. 29	WALNUT RIDGE	ARK	FRISCO	48
			Total Mileage	11,137

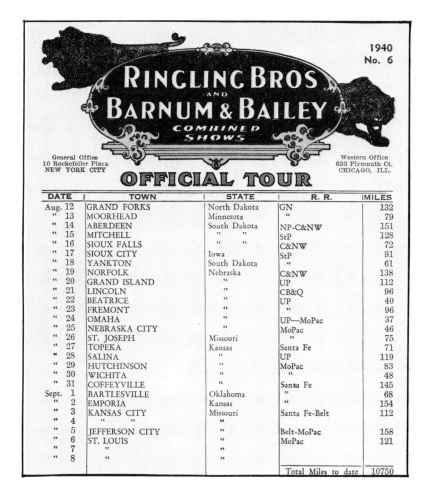

DATE	TOWN	STATE	R. R.	MILES
Aug. 12	GRAND FORKS	North Dakota	GN	132
" 13	MOORHEAD	Minnesota	"	79
" 14	ABERDEEN	South Dakota	NP-C&NW	151
" 15	MITCHELL	" "	StP	128
" 16	SIOUX FALLS	" "	C&NW	72
" 17	SIOUX CITY	Iowa	StP	91
" 18	YANKTON	South Dakota	"	61
" 19	NORFOLK	Nebraska	C&NW	138
" 20	GRAND ISLAND	"	UP	112
" 21	LINCOLN	"	CB&Q	96
" 22	BEATRICE	"	UP	40
" 23	FREMONT	"	"	96
" 24	OMAHA	"	UP—MoPac	37
" 25	NEBRASKA CITY	"	MoPac	46
" 26	ST. JOSEPH	Missouri	"	75
" 27	TOPEKA	Kansas	Santa Fe	71
" 28	SALINA	"	UP	119
" 29	HUTCHINSON	"	MoPac	83
" 30	WICHITA	"	"	48
" 31	COFFEYVILLE	"	Santa Fe	145
Sept. 1	BARTLESVILLE	Oklahoma	"	68
" 2	EMPORIA	Kansas	"	154
" 3	KANSAS CITY	Missouri	Santa Fe-Belt	112
" 4	" "	"		
" 5	JEFFERSON CITY	"	Belt-MoPac	158
" 6	ST. LOUIS	"	MoPac	121
" 7	"	"		
" 8	"	"		
			Total Miles to date	10750

59

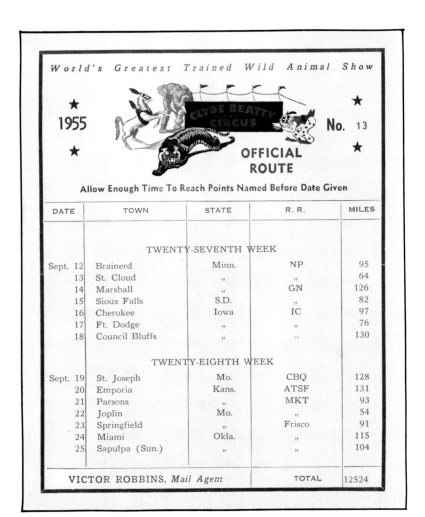

1955 ★ **No. 13**

CLYDE BEATTY CIRCUS

★ ★

OFFICIAL ROUTE

Allow Enough Time To Reach Points Named Before Date Given

DATE	TOWN	STATE	R. R.	MILES
	TWENTY-SEVENTH WEEK			
Sept. 12	Brainerd	Minn.	NP	95
13	St. Cloud	„	„	64
14	Marshall	„	GN	126
15	Sioux Falls	S.D.	„	82
16	Cherokee	Iowa	IC	97
17	Ft. Dodge	„	„	76
18	Council Bluffs	„	„	130
	TWENTY-EIGHTH WEEK			
Sept. 19	St. Joseph	Mo.	CBQ	128
20	Emporia	Kans.	ATSF	131
21	Parsons	„	MKT	93
22	Joplin	Mo.	„	54
23	Springfield	„	Frisco	91
24	Miami	Okla.	„	115
25	Sapulpa (Sun.)	„	„	104
VICTOR ROBBINS, *Mail Agent*			**TOTAL**	**12524**

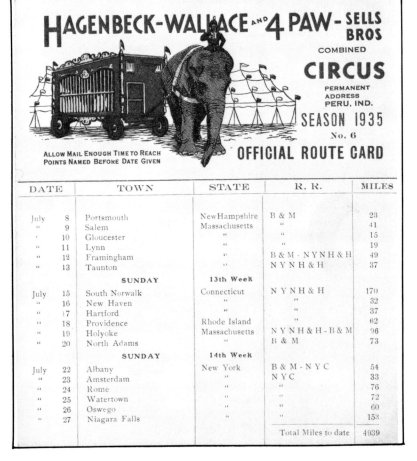

HAGENBECK-WALLACE AND **4 PAW-SELLS BROS**

COMBINED

CIRCUS

PERMANENT ADDRESS PERU, IND.

SEASON 1935 No. 6

OFFICIAL ROUTE CARD

ALLOW MAIL ENOUGH TIME TO REACH POINTS NAMED BEFORE DATE GIVEN

DATE		TOWN	STATE	R. R.	MILES
July	8	Portsmouth	New Hampshire	B & M	23
"	9	Salem	Massachusetts	"	41
"	10	Gloucester	"	"	15
"	11	Lynn	"	"	19
"	12	Framingham	"	B & M - N Y N H & H	49
"	13	Taunton	"	N Y N H & H	37
		SUNDAY	13th Week		
July	15	South Norwalk	Connecticut	N Y N H & H	170
"	16	New Haven	"	"	32
"	17	Hartford	"	"	37
"	18	Providence	Rhode Island	"	62
"	19	Holyoke	Massachusetts	N Y N H & H - B & M	96
"	20	North Adams	"	B & M	73
		SUNDAY	14th Week		
July	22	Albany	New York	B & M - N Y C	54
"	23	Amsterdam	"	N Y C	33
"	24	Rome	"	"	76
"	25	Watertown	"	"	72
"	26	Oswego	"	"	60
"	27	Niagara Falls	"	"	153
			Total Miles to date		4939

Barnum & Bailey
Greatest Show on Earth

GENERAL OFFICES and WINTERQUARTERS
BRIDGEPORT, CONN.

· SEASON 1913 ·

· OFFICIAL ROUTE ·

DATE	TOWN	STATE	R.R.	MILES
May 5	Altoona	Penn.	P. R. R.	131
" 6	Johnstown	"	"	37
" 7	Pittsburgh	"	"	77
" 8	"	"	"	
" 9	Wooster	Ohio	Pennsylvania Lines	135
" 10	Marion	"	"	84
SUNDAY				
May 12	St. Louis	Missouri	New York Central Lines	447
" 13	"	"	"	
" 14	"	"	"	
" 15	"	"	"	
" 16	"	"	"	
" 17	"	"	"	
SUNDAY				
May 19	Terre Haute	Indiana	New York Central Lines	192
" 20	Danville	Illinois	"	57
" 21	Indianapolis	Indiana	"	85
" 22	Cincinnati, Cumminsville	Ohio	B. & O. Ry System	118
" 23	Norwood	"	"	6
" 24	Springfield	"	Pennsylvania Lines	84
SUNDAY				
May 26	Columbus	Ohio	New York Central Lines	45
" 27	Uhrichsville	"	Pennsylvania Lines	99
" 28	Wheeling	W. Virginia	"	70
" 29	Alliance	Ohio	"	87
" 30	Cleveland	"	"	55
" 31				

PERMANENT ADDRESS AND WINTER QUARTERS, BRIDGEPORT, CONN.

Permanent Address
BILLBOARD
CINCINNATI
OHIO

GENTRY BROS. CIRCUS
FOUNDED IN 1887

41st Annual Tour

OFFICIAL ROUTE   CARD NO. 20

ALLOW MAIL ENOUGH TIME TO REACH POINTS NAMED BEFORE DATE GIVEN

DATE	TOWN	STATE	RAILROAD	MILES
Sept. 10	Circleville	Ohio	Penn.	30
11	Wilmington	Ohio	Penn. and B. & O.	49
12	Hillsboro	Ohio	B. & O.	36
13	Hamilton	Ohio	B. & O.	86
14	Troy	Ohio	B. & O.	54
15	Union City	Ind.	Big Four	70
SUNDAY				
17	Shelbyville	Ind.	Big Four	84
18	Seymour	Ind.	Penn.	41
19	Madison	Ind.	Penn.	62
20	Columbus	Ind.	Penn.	41
21	Franklin	Ind.	Penn.	20
22	Martinsville	Ind.	Big Four	26
SUNDAY				
24	Princeton	Ind.	Penn. and C. & E. I.	112
			Total Mileage to date - - - - -	6,838

Issued by John Griffin

61

RINGLING BROS
WORLD'S GREATEST SHOWS

OFFICIAL ROUTE

ALLOW MAIL ENOUGH TIME TO REACH POINTS NAMED BEFORE DATE GIVEN.
GENERAL OFFICES No. 221 INSTITUTE PLACE. CHICAGO. ILL.

DATE	TOWN	STATE	R. R.	MILES
Oct. 15	Cleburne	Texas	G. C. & S. F. Ry.	99
" 16	Gainesville	"		93
" 17	Wichita Falls	"	M. K. & T. Ry.	89
" 18	Lawton	Oklahoma	M. K. & T. and Frisco Rys.	134
" 19	Clinton	"	C. R. I. & P. Ry.	128
" 20	Enid	"		124
	SUNDAY			
Oct. 22	Chickasha	Oklahoma	C. R. I. & P. Ry.	97
" 23	Ardmore	"	Santa Fe	119
" 24	Ada	"	St. L. S. F. Ry.	80
" 25	Okmulgee	"		79
" 26	Muskogee	"		39
" 27	Fort Smith	Arkansas	M. V. R. R.	105
	SUNDAY			
Oct. 29	Paris	Texas	St. L. S. F. Ry.	168
" 30	Terrell	"	T. M. R. R.	84
" 31	Corsicana	"	T. M. and H. & T. C. R. Rs.	81
Nov. 1	Tyler	"	St. L. S. W. Ry.	75
" 2	Texarkana	Arkansas		128
" 3	Little Rock	"	Mo. Pac. Ry.	145
	SUNDAY			
Nov. 5	Memphis	Tennessee	Mo. Pac. Ry.	148
	END OF SEASON			
	Baraboo	Wisconsin	I. C. and C. & N. W. Rys.	687

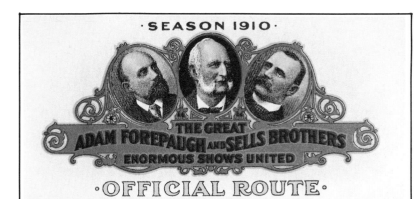

THE GREAT
ADAM FOREPAUGH AND SELLS BROTHERS
ENORMOUS SHOWS UNITED

·OFFICIAL ROUTE·

DATE	TOWN	STATE	R. R.	MILES
May 23	Shamokin	Pennsylvania	Penna. R. R.	59
May 24	Mahanoy City	Pennsylvania	P. & R. R. R.	29
May 25	Lebanon	Pennsylvania	P. & R. R. R.	80
May 26	Lancaster	Pennsylvania	P. & R. R. R.	28
May 27	West Chester	Pennsylvania	Penna. R. R.	29
May 28	Chester	Pennsylvania	Penna. R. R.	18
	SUNDAY			
May 30	Philadelphia — Week of	Pennsylvania	Penna. R. R.	14
	SUNDAY			
June 6	Camden	New Jersey	Penna. R. R.	
June 7	Atlantic City	New Jersey	Penna. R. R.	65
June 8	Bridgeton	New Jersey	Penna. R. R.	68
June 9	Long Branch	New Jersey	C. R. R. of N. J.	84
June 10	Perth Amboy	New Jersey	C. R. R. of N. J.	29
June 11	Elizabeth	New Jersey	C. R. R. of N. J.	12
	SUNDAY			
June 13	New York — Week of	N. Y.	C. R. R. of N. J. and Bush Terminal Co.	12

PERMANENT ADDRESS AND WINTER QUARTERS, BARABOO, WIS.

HAGENBECK-WALLACE CIRCUS

PERMANENT ADDRESS PERU, IND.

SEASON 1934

DATE CITY	STATE	RR IN	RR OUT	MILES
			NS	51
Oct. 1 Raleigh	NC	NS	ACL	63
Oct. 2, Fayetteville	NC	NS	ACL	99
Oct. 3, Goldsboro	NC	ACL	ACL	84
Oct. 4, Wilmington	NC	ACL	ACL	110
Oct. 5, Florence	SC	ACL	ACL	39
Oct. 6, Sumter	SC	ACL		94
SUNDAY			SOU	
Oct. 8, Charleston	SC	ACL	SOU	128
Oct. 9, Columbia	SC	SOU	C&WC	83
Oct. 10, Augusta	Ga.	SOU	SOU	101
Oct. 11, Anderson	SC	C&WC	SAL	43
Oct. 12, Greenwood	SC	SOU	SOU	84
Oct. 13, Athens	Ga	SAL		
SUNDAY			SOU	148
Oct. 15, Rome	Ga	SOU	SOU	63
Oct. 16, Anniston	Ala	SOU	SOU	65
Oct. 17, Birmingham	Ala	SOU	SOU	55
Oct. 18, Tuscaloosa	Ala	SOU	WofA	90
Oct. 19, Selma	Ala	SOU	L&N	50
Oct. 20, Montgomery	Ala	WofA		
SUNDAY		L&N	L&N	163
Oct. 22, Pensacola	Fla	L&N		

Total Miles to Date.................10,171

EDDIE WOECKENER, Mail Agent

AL. G. BARNES SELLS-FLOTO COMBINED CIRCUS

PERMANENT ADDRESS
331 MADISON AVENUE —— NEW YORK, N. Y.

No. 17
SEASON 1938

Date	City	R.R.	Miles
	SEVENTEENTH WEEK		
July 18	Portage, Wis.	StP	103
July 19	Janesville, Wis.	StP	77
July 20	Davenport, Iowa	StP	142
July 21	Peoria, Ill.	CRIP	94
July 22	Decatur, Ill.	ICRR	77
July 23	Springfield, Ill.	ICRR	46
	EIGHTEENTH WEEK		
July 24	Joliet, Ill.	C&A	148
July 25	Kalamazoo, Mich.	MC	151
July 26	Lansing, Mich.	GT	74
July 27	Battle Creek, Mich.	GT	45
July 28	South Bend, Ind.	GT	121
July 29	Racine, Wis.	GT-CNW	162
July 30	Milwaukee, Wis.	CNW	24
	NINETEENTH WEEK		
July 31	Milwaukee, Wis.		
Aug. 1	Rockford, Ill.	CNW	103
Aug. 2	Madison, Wis.	CNW	64
Aug. 3	Fon du Lac, Wis.	CNW	90
Aug. 4	Appleton, Wis.	CNW	37
Aug. 5	Green Bay, Wis.	CNW	32
Aug. 6	Wausau, Wis.	CNW	94

Miles to Date........11,562

OFFICIAL ROUTE CARD

SPARKS CIRCUS

THE 20TH CENTURY WONDER SHOW

SEASON 1931

Permanent Address

221 INSTITUTE PLACE   CHICAGO

TENTH WEEK

Date	City	RR	Miles
July 13	Millinocket, Me.	B. & A.	140
July 14	Bangor, Me.	M. C.	71
July 15	Ellsworth, Me.	M. C.	28
July 16	Calais, Me.	C. P. R.	104
July 17	St. John, N. B.	C. N. R.	118
July 18	Moncton, N. B.	C. N. R.	90

ELEVENTH WEEK

July 20	Charlottetown, P. E. I.	C. N. R.	116
July 21	Summerside, P. E. I.	C. N. R.	48
July 22	Amherst, N. S.	C. N. R.	75
July 23	Truro, N. S.	C. N. R.	77
July 24	Windsor, N. S.	D. & A.	57
July 25	Kentville, N. S.	D. & A.	25

TWELFTH WEEK

July 27	Digby, N. S.	D. & A.	79
July 28	Yarmouth, N. S.	D. & A.	60
July 29	Bridgewater, N. S.	C. N. R.	168
July 30	Halifax, N. S.	C. N. R.	83
July 31	North Sydney, N. S. (Night Only) C.N.R.		274
Aug. 1	Sydney, N. S.	C. N. R.	20

THIRTEENTH WEEK

Aug. 3	New Glasgow, N. S.	C. N. R.	182

Mileage to date   4987

Card No. 10

OFFICIAL ROUTE CARD   1929

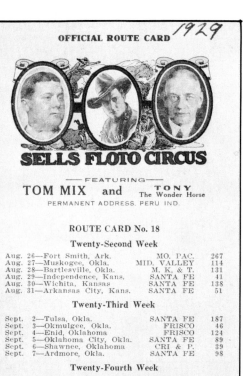

SELLS FLOTO CIRCUS

— FEATURING —

TOM MIX and **TONY** The Wonder Horse

PERMANENT ADDRESS. PERU IND.

ROUTE CARD No. 18

Twenty-Second Week

Aug. 26	Fort Smith, Ark.	MO. PAC.	267
Aug. 27	Muskogee, Okla.	MID. VALLEY	114
Aug. 28	Bartlesville, Okla.	M. K. & T.	131
Aug. 29	Independence, Kans.	SANTA FE	41
Aug. 30	Wichita, Kansas	SANTA FE	138
Aug. 31	Arkansas City, Kans.	SANTA FE	51

Twenty-Third Week

Sept. 2	Tulsa, Okla.	SANTA FE	187
Sept. 3	Okmulgee, Okla.	FRISCO	46
Sept. 4	Enid, Oklahoma	FRISCO	124
Sept. 5	Oklahoma City, Okla.	SANTA FE	89
Sept. 6	Shawnee, Oklahoma	CRI & P.	39
Sept. 7	Ardmore, Okla.	SANTA FE	98

Twenty-Fourth Week

Sept. 8	Dallas, Texas	SANTA FE and T P	136
Sept. 9	Dallas, Texas		
Sept. 10	Forth Worth, Texas	TEX-PAC	32
Sept. 11	Waco, Texas	SANTA FE	122
Sept. 12	Temple, Texas	SANTA FE	44
Sept. 13	Austin, Texas	M. K. & T.	71
Sept. 14	San Antonio, Texas	I. G. & N.	80

Total Mileage To Date 9548 Miles

JAMES McCOY, Mail Agent.

OFFICIAL ROUTE CARD

JOHN ROBINSON'S CIRCUS

THE PIONEER CIRCUS OF THE WORLD

PERMANENT ADDRESS, PERU. IND.

No. 21   **SEASON 1929**

TWENTY-FIRST WEEK

Date	City	State	R.R. In	R.R. Out	Miles
Sept. 16	Columbia,	S. C.	So.	So.	128
Sept. 17	Greenville,	S. C.	So.	So.	145
Sept. 18	Charlotte,	N. C.	So.	So.	107
Sept. 19	Concord,	N. C.	So.	So.	21
Sept. 20	High Point,	N. C.	So.	So.	58
Sept. 21	Statesville,	N. C.	So.	So.	60

TWENTY-SECOND WEEK

Sept. 23	Salisbury,	N. C.	So.	Yadkin RR	25
Sept. 24	Albermarle,	N. C.	Yadkin RR	Yadkin RR	30
Sept. 25	Burlington,	N. C.	Yadkin-So.	So.	101
Sept. 26	Raleigh,	N. C.	So.	SAL RR	60
Sept. 27	Henderson,	N. C.	SAL RR	SAL RR	48
Sept. 28	Weldon,	N. C.	SAL RR	ACL-RF&P PENN	52

TWENTY-THIRD WEEK

Sept. 30	Trenton,	N. J.	ACL-RF&D-PENN		367

Total Mileage to date, 11,978

LAWRENCE ANDERSON, Mail Agent

The Great Northern Railway's bill of lading documented the consist of Ringling's 1953 train, including car numbers. No explanation has surfaced on what the Great Northern meant by cookhouse cars or why they were singled out. Actually, the numbers represent flatcars carrying wagons that contained the circus' cookhouse equipment, but that many flats also would carry a great deal of other circus gear — *Authors' Collection.*

825—WABASH RAILWAY COMPANY—825
NORMAN B. PITCAIRN and FRANK C. NICODEMUS, Jr., Receivers

PREPAID FREIGHT BILL

FREIGHT BILL NO.

CAR INITIALS AND NUMBER	DATE	WAYBILL No.
SEE BELOW	MAY 12TH 1940	5394

TO	STATION	STATE	FROM	STATION	STATE
LAFAYETTE INDIANA				Decatur, Ill.	

SHIPPER

COLE BROS CIRCUS

ROUTE

WABASH

To WABASH RAILWAY COMPANY, Debtor.

CONSIGNEE AND ADDRESS

COLE BROS CIRCUS

For Charges on articles to be transported

INSTRUCTIONS (Regarding Icing, Ventilation, Heating, Milling, Weighing, Etc. If Iced, Specify to whom Icing Should be Charged)

DESCRIPTION OF ARTICLES AND MARKS	WEIGHT	RATE	FREIGHT	ADVANCES	PREPAID
11 FLATS VIZ 41 44 45 43 47 42 46 48 40 39 49	220000		530 00		
6 STOCK VIZ 30 32 34 61 60 35	120000		135 00		
7 COACHES VIZ 57 56 55 54 53 52 51	140000				
	480000		665 00		665 00
ESTIMATED WEIGHT 20000 LBS PER CAR					
COPY COPY COPY	COPY COPY	COPY COPY COPY			

| | | | | TOTAL | |

RECEIVED PAYMENT FOR THE COMPANY_____19____

_____AGENT

PER_____

Draw checks to order of WABASH RAILWAY COMPANY

The Wabash Railway's 1940 prepaid freight bill itemized the car numbers and estimated weight for the Cole Bros. Circus — *Authors' Collection.*

Union Pacific's freight receipt for a 1955 move in Oregon listed eighty carloads of circus plunder in the same casual way it would itemize a single crate of more prosaic freight — *Authors' Collection.*

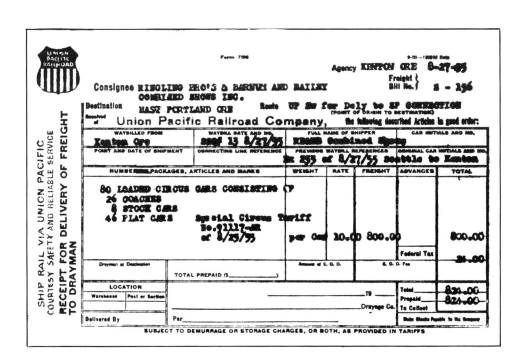

FORM 1415

I. C. C. No. x **674**

WABASH RAILWAY COMPANY.

cancels
ICC X-673

TRAFFIC DEPARTMENT

LOCAL TARIFF FOR TRANSPORTATION OF

HAGENBECK-WALLACE CIRCUS

IN CARS: **12** ....Flat ......—......Box ......**6**......Stock ......—......Sleeping

......**6**......Passenger Coach ......—......Baggage ......**1**......Advertising ......**25**......Total

with privilege of stopping for exhibition at stations named, as follows:

1938 Date	FROM	TO	Miles	Total Charges to collect	DIVISIONS Freight	Passenger	War Tax Freight	War Tax Passenger	
About									
4 11	Decatur, Ill.	Springfield, Ill.		(This is to serve as notice					
4 12	Springfield, Ill.	LaFayette, Ind.		(of advance movement of (Advertising Car in charge					
4 13	LaFayette, Ind.	Ft. Wayne, Ind.		(of Mr. V. C. Williams and (28 Men.					
	cc s:								
	1 C.Clark			1 C.C.Miller					
	1 A.V.Burwell			1 M.Lonindele					
	1 Agt., LaFayette, Ind.			6 W.M.Garvin					
	1 J L Craig			2 G.S.Ward					
	1 J.B.Dooley			1 R.A.Jessmore					
	1 D.L.Gilbert								

......Cars to be received from the......**Illinois Central**......at......**Decatur, Ill.**

and delivered......to the......**Pennsylvania R.R.**......at......**Ft. Wayne, Ind.**

The cars to be received from and delivered to connecting lines as above, without switching charges, transfer, or other expense to the Wabash Ry.

The Advertising Car, with Manager and Bill Posters, will precede the show ten to fifteen days and will be hauled in such trains as may be designated by the Superintendent of the Wabash Ry. Charges for this service are included in the amounts given above.

Total charges to collect as above must be prepaid for each run.

Each forwarding agent will waybill prepaid, at amount shown above, to the next station where stop is to be made. In arriving at the total weight, estimate at twenty thousand (20,000) pounds each car hauled, passenger or freight The numbers and initials of all the cars must be noted on the waybill.

Agents will acknowledge receipt hereof **PROMPTLY** and advise if fully understood.

St. Louis, Mo.,......**April 9, 1938**......192x......**C. J. Sayles**

Effective......**April 9, 1938**......x192......**Freight Traffic Manager**

The Wabash Railway used a local tariff form, detailing the 1938 Hagenbeck-Wallace Circus train, to alert railroad operating personnel to the approaching movement of the advance advertising car — *Authors' Collection.*

More paper work documented the movement of the show's advertising car. It was covered by the same contract as the main part of the show. The railroad asked the conductor to report which of its trains moved the bill car, the date, and the number of billposters it carried — *Circus World Museum.*

THE PENNSYLVANIA RAILROAD COMPANY

Philadelphia, Pa., January 11th, 1917.

CIRCUS CAR ORDER No. 428

TO CONDUCTORS:
When instructed move BARNUM & BAILEY SHOW advertising car No. 3
in regular passenger train service, containing not in excess of twenty five persons
with necessary baggage and billing material, from and to the following points:

FROM	TO	TRAIN NUMBER	DATE	Number of Persons	CONDUCTOR
		To be filled in by Conductor			
Jersey CITY, N.J.	West Philadelphia, Pa.				
West Philadelphia	Chester, Pa.	5238	4/30	17	
Sunbury	York, Pa.	568	5/17	21	
York	Harrisburg, Pa.	Extra			
Harrisburg	Lewistown, Pa.	3	5/17	20	
Lewistown	Altoona, Pa.	669	5/17	20	
Altoona	Johnstown, Pa.	7063	5/16	17	
Johnstown	Greensburg, Pa.	7303	5/18	20	
Greensburg	Charleroi, Pa.	685	5/19	14	
Charleroi	Pittsburgh, Pa.	7873	5/24	17	
Pittsburgh	McKeesport, Pa.				
McKeesport	Uniontown, Pa.	7804	5/25	20	

Compensation therefor being covered by Special Contract No. 2 between

Good until June 1st, 1917, and only when signed and countersigned by the parties indicated, and certified by Manager in charge of the car.

COUNTERSIGNED:

General Freight Agent.   General Supt. Transportation.

I, Wm. Delly Manager of Advertising Car No. 3
do hereby certify that all persons carried on this order are regular bona fide employes of
BARNUM & BAILEY SHOW, and entitled to passage under the terms
and conditions of Special Contract above referred to

Conductors honoring this order will make proper note on cash reports, referring to the number of this order. Conductor honoring on final run will lift order, and return to Auditor of Passenger Traffic attached to cash report. Manager of advance car will be required to give local agent ample notice of desired movement, so that necessary instructions may be issued.

69

ISSUED BY

New York Central System

$15.00
SHOW SCRIP BOOK

Form N.Y.C.-S.S. No. **17225**

1. ISSUED ON ACCOUNT OF SHOW CONTRACT.
   No. *H 2.* DATED *5/5/48*
   (PAYMENT FOR THIS BOOK BEING INCLUDED IN SAID CONTRACT).

2. GOOD FOR THE EXCLUSIVE USE OF AN ADVERTISING AGENT OR BILL POSTER IN THE EMPLOY OF

   Darley Bros Circus

   SHOW

   WHO MUST PRESENT LETTER OF IDENTIFICATION SIGNED BY

   R. M. Harvey

   THE AUTHORIZED REPRESENTATIVE OF SAID SHOW. (SEE SECTION 8.)

3. VALID ONLY BETWEEN STATIONS ON ABOVE NAMED RAILROAD AS FOLLOWS:

   NEW YORK CENTRAL SYSTEM
   B/O P & L E RR
   AND I. H. B. RR

4. NOT GOOD ON TRAINS NUMBERS 1, 12, 25, 26, 30, 31 or electric

5. VOID AFTER DATE CANCELLED BY PUNCH IN MARGIN. NOT GOOD PRIOR TO *5/5/48*

VOID AFTER	
Jan	Feb
Mar	Apr
May	Jun
July	Aug
Sep	Oct
Nov	Dec
Day	1
2	3
4	5
6	7
8	9
10	11
12	13
14	15
16	17
18	19
20	21
22	23
24	25
26	27
28	29
30	31
1900	
47	48
49	50
51	52
53	54
55	56

(Continued on Inside Cover)

Show scrip resulted from the circus' need to transport billposters ahead of the show as individuals on regular passenger trains. Each book of scrip was worth fifteen dollars toward the cost of a passenger's railroad ticket. People traveling on the show train were covered by the contract and price, but agents and billposters moving separately utilized scrip. Shows were allowed to purchase scrip in an amount equal to ten percent of the freight contract — *Authors' Collection.*

(Continued from Outside Cover.)

CONDITIONS.

6. The coupons contained herein each having a value of one cent, will be accepted at the authorized tariff fares and charges under the following conditions.

7. THIS BOOK IS ONLY GOOD FOR TRANSPORTATION WHEN PRESENTED TO CONDUCTOR ON TRAIN AND IS NOT EXCHANGEABLE FOR TICKETS AT TICKET OFFICES.

8. Holder shall submit such identification, in addition to that required in Section 2, in form of billposting contracts, show tickets or other satisfactory evidence, as may be requested by conductor.

9. If other than the person whose name is shown in credentials, with which this book must be presented, as provided herein, attempts to use this book it will thereby become void and will be confiscated by any agent or conductor to whom presented, who will collect lawful tariff fare.

10. The holder of this ticket is entitled to transportation of not to exceed 150 pounds of personal baggage, and in addition will be allowed to carry free in baggage cars advertising matter, material and tools, but the combined weight of personal baggage and advertising matter, material and tools, shall not in any case exceed 300 pounds.

11. Good for excess baggage charges (excess weight, excess size, excess valuation) as authorized in baggage tariffs.

12. The person by whom this book is used assumes all risk of accident, injury or damage to person, baggage or property and by accepting and using this book expressly agrees that the New York Central Railroad shall not be liable, under any circumstances, for injury to the person, or for loss or damage to the baggage or other property of the passenger using it, whether such injury, loss or damage be caused by the negligence of the agents or employees of the New York Central Railroad, or otherwise, howsoever.

13. If book contains insufficient coupons, the difference will be collected in cash.

14. Coupons will not be accepted unless detached by conductor, baggage agent or other authorized employee.

15. Coupons not bearing same number as this cover, or detached coupons, presented without a cover, will not be honored.

16. The cover of this book must be surrendered to conductor or train collector when the last coupons are detached.

J H Baird
Gen. Pass. Traffic Mgr.
NEW YORK, N. Y.

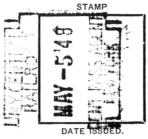

STAMP

MAY-5'48

DATE ISSUED.

Since John Ringling was the president of several short-line railroads and knew something of the circus business, railroads went to this friend for aid in writing the conditions for using show scrip. Mr. John provided, under Paragraph 10, that such a passenger was entitled to the transportation of 300 pounds of baggage, advertising matter, and tools, meaning that a billposter could carry a day's supply of posters plus necessary ladders, paste, buckets, and brushes. If the weight of his gear was too much, he could pay the excess charges with more scrip. Almost all railroads but the Erie used the same scrip form — *Authors' Collection.*

RINGLING BROS. AND BARNUM & BAILEY COMBINED SHOWS, INC.
Consist for the 1977 Tour of the:

RED UNIT

Robert A. Maio
Director of Transportation
Ringling Bros. - Barnum &
Bailey Combined Shows, Inc.
1015 Eighteenth St., NW
Washington, DC 20036

The Red Unit Trainmaster is Charles "Smitty" Smith. He can be found in coach #40.

The Red Unit Train consists of a total of 36 cars. Twenty-eight cars each 85'6"
long and eight piggy-back flat cars each 95'6" long. One of the flat cars is a
bi-level. Distance from top of rail to car bed is 54" on the 85' cars and 42"
on the flat cars. Weight averages at 100 tons per car. All cars are within the
dimensions of National Clearance. All cars are company owned equipment.

PREFERRED RUNNING ORDER & STORAGE SPACE

Engine		
5 Stocks (Side Loading Animal Cars)	427 feet	
21 Coaches (Occupied Sleepers)	1,795	"
8 Flats (1-bilevel included)	765	"
2 Tunnels (End Loading Baggage Cars)	171	"
TOTAL STORAGE SPACE REQUIRED	3,158 feet	

To properly handle the Red Unit, consider the train in three sections:

I.   COACHES: The 21 coaches are car numbers #40 through #60. Our own generators
     provide electrical power. Cuts can be made in several places provided that a
     generator car remains with each section. Generator cars are #46 and #54. Cars
     #45 and #46 can never be separated. Please consult with Trainmaster or Electrician
     before making any cuts. All coaches are equipped with septic holding tanks. There
     must be an access road alongside the storage tracks for sanitation service and fuel
     oil delivery. The coaches must be stored within easy access to a water supply. We
     carry 650 ft. of garden type hose which attaches to a 3/4" faucet or fire hydrant
     with reducer.

II. STOCK CARS: The five stock cars are #30 through #34. The stocks may be spotted
     on straight or slightly curved ground level track (no built up ballast) and may
     be unloaded from either side by our own 8 foot ramps. There must be an adequate
     clearing adjacent clearing adjacent to the track so that the animals can descend
     and assemble safely. After unloading the stock cars must be stored with the
     coaches from which they draw power and water. Note: Car #34 does not contain
     animals and may be spotted with coaches during unloading operation if space is
     not adequate.

III. UNLOADING EQUIPMENT CARS: The ten equipment cars are #20 through #29: eight
     piggy back flat cars (1 bi-level included) and two tunnel cars. These cars may
     be unloaded in several ways but must be from straight track. We have three ramps
     sets of our own 36 ft. ramps. We prefer to use three ramps whenever possible,
     but unloading can be accomplished from two. Whenever possible we will prefer
     to use three unloading ramps even if the cars are not all in the same area.
        Unloading can be accomplished by various means among them, side by side.
     split crossing, piggy back ramps, and opposite ends of the same track. These
     unloading methods can be used in combination with the three sections. The best
     combination will be determined by the advance coordinator and operation staff
     of the railroad. We require a 50 foot minimum crossing.
        After unloaded, cars are to be removed to store elsewhere. Equipment consists:
     Flats: #20 (ramp flat), #21,#22,#23,#29 (ramp flat), #24,#28,#25 (bi-level car);
     Tunnels: #26 (ramp tunnel) and #27.

NOTE: The direction in which the poles (tongues on the circus wagons) are facing
      upon arrival in your city is critical since the equipment can only be
      unloaded from the ramp cars and in only one direction. This direction will
      be determined by you and the Advance Coordinator upon inspection of the
      unloading site.

      The air brakes are set for direct release. Do not use over 90 pounds of
      train line pressure.

      Please consult with Trainmaster or Electrician before making any cuts.

We are looking forward to having you serve THE GREATEST SHOW ON EARTH!

A refinement of modern show train operation
is this informational sheet provided by the
circus for the railroad operations people who
will be handling the train — *Ringling Bros.
and Barnum & Bailey.*

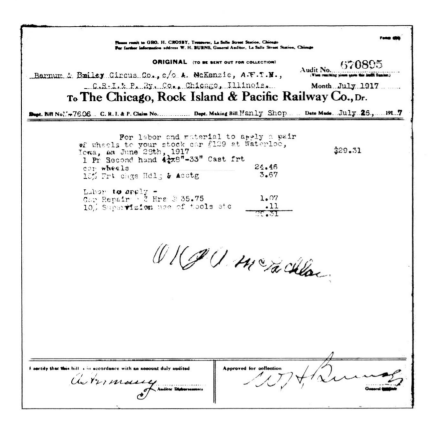

ORIGINAL (TO BE SENT OUT FOR COLLECTION)

Audit No. 670895

Barnum & Bailey Circus Co., c/o A. McKenzie, A.F.T.M.,
C.R.I.& P. Ry. Co., Chicago, Illinois.

Month July 1917

To The Chicago, Rock Island & Pacific Railway Co., Dr.

Dept. Bill No. 7606   C. R. I. & P. Claim No. ....   Dept. Making Bill Manly Shop   Date Made July 26, 1917

For labor and material to apply a pair
of wheels to your stock car #129 at Waterloo,
Iowa, on June 29th, 1917 $29.31
1 Pr Second hand 4½x8"-33" Cast frt
car wheels   24.46
15% Frt chgs Hdlg & Acctg   3.67

Labor to apply -
Car Repair 3 Hrs @ 35.75   1.07
10% Supervision use of tools etc   .11
                                                    ─────
                                                    29.31

OK P U McFaddlen

I certify that this bill is in accordance with an account duly audited

A Hemmausy
Auditor Disbursements

Approved for collection

W H Burns
General Auditor

Northern Pacific billed Barnum & Bailey
$7.81 for wood and iron parts, plus labor —
Circus World Museum.

When the show train makes the move, it
probably incurs added costs for switching, repairs, or other services from the railroad. In
1917 the CRI&P billed Barnum & Bailey Circus $29.31 for a pair of replacement wheels
on a stockcar. That included labor at about
thirty-five cents an hour — *Authors' Collection; Circus World Museum.*

Form 3434 Sh.

St. Paul, Minn., ... 191....

Barnum & Bailey Circus Co.,

221 Institute Place, Chicago, Ill.

7-58 T. **Northern Pacific Railway Company,** *Dr.*

191 7   Mem. No. ....   Mechanical Department.

For Repairs to Cars, per

DATE 1917	CAR Initials	CAR Numbers	MISC. Description	MISC. Value	Cart Lbs.	Wrought Lbs.	Mall. Lbs.	LUMBER Feet	SPRINGS Lbs.	LABOR Hours
7-14	B&B	103		08						
14		102		08						
14		154								1¼
14		115		09						
14		104		60						
14		108		1 32		6		52		5
		Quantity,				6		52		6¼
		Price,				.03		4		.28
		Value,		2 17		18		2,08		1,82

Total Debit, $6.25   Plus 25% $1.56   Amount Due, $7.81

I certify that the above is correct:

G. H. Gilman
Master Car Builder

A.R.R.C.No.245   I.C.C.No.A-7556
cancels   cancels
A.R.R.C.No.242   I.C.C.No.A-7545

MISSOURI PACIFIC RAILROAD COMPANY

FREIGHT TARIFF

OF
LOCAL RATES
No. C-117-A
Cancels No. C-117

ON

SPARKS CIRCUS

Consisting of Twenty (20) Cars, viz: Nine (9) Flat Cars, Five (5) Coaches, Five (5) Stock Cars and One(1)Advertising Car,(See Item No.9)

RATES IN DOLLARS AND CENTS PER RUN

FROM	DATE	TO	RATE Column 1 See Item No. 1	RATE Column 2 See Items Nos.2 & 6
Walnut Ridge,Ark. (See Item No. 7)	October 6, 1929 (About Midnight)	Batesville, Ark.	$360.00	$450.00
Batesville, Ark.	October 7, 1929 (About Midnight)	Conway, Ark.	$560.50	$695.50
Conway, Ark.	October 8, 1929 (About Midnight)	Russellville,Ark.	$360.00	$450.00
Russellville,Ark.	October 9, 1929 (About Midnight)	Morrilton, Ark.	$360.00	$450.00
Morrilton, Ark.	October 10, 1929 (About Midnight)	Hot Springs,Ark.	$482.50	$587.50
Hot Springs, Ark.	October 11, 1929 (About Midnight)	Pine Bluff, Ark.	$362.50	$452.50
Pine Bluff, Ark.	October 12, 1929 (About Midnight)	Tallulah, La. (See Item No. 8)	$575.00	$695.50

Issued September 28, 1929.

#Effective October 5, 1929.
Expires with November 12, 1929 unless sooner cancelled, changed or extended.

Issued under authority of Rule 63 of Interstate Commerce Commission Tariff Circular No. 20; also issued under authority of Arkansas Railroad Commission General Order No. 330 dated September 19, 1923.

Issued by:-
D. R. L I N C O L N
Freight Traffic Manager,
Missouri Pacific Building,
210 North 13th Street,
St. Louis, Missouri.
(150 - H-6702)

(Printed in U.S.A.)

Item No. 1. The amounts shown in Column 1 are to be collected by the agent before the show leaves his station, plus any charges accruing under Item No. 6.

Item No. 2. The amounts shown in Column 2 include all charges to be paid by the Show Company (exclusive of any charges accruing under Item No. 6). The difference between the rates in Column 1 and Column 2 represents the cost of transportation which has been purchased and paid for by the Show Company for the use of its Advertising Agents and Bill Posters (See Item No. 5).

Item No. 3. The transportation of Sparks Circus is performed under Special Contract No. 48, entered into between Sparks Circus, and Missouri Pacific Railroad Company, September 27, 1929.

Item No. 4. Full passenger fare to be paid for all persons in excess of Four Hundred (400) bona fide employees of the Show proper and Twenty-four (24) men with Advertising Car.

Item No. 5. Not to exceed twenty percent (20%) of the charges shown herein is for transportation of Advertising Agents or Bill Posters in the employ of the Show Company, and has been furnished in the form of Fifteen Dollar ($15.00) Show Scrip Book Coupons, which are honored on all trains of the Missouri Pacific Railroad carrying passengers in accordance with Passenger Department Circular No. A-16-1919, issued by Passenger Traffic Manager.

Item No. 6. In addition to the other charges shown herein Sparks Circus agree to pay the Missouri Pacific Railroad track rental charge of One Dollar ($1.00) per car, per day or fraction thereof, on all cars remaining on its tracks at Walnut Ridge, Batesville, Conway, Russellville, Morrilton, Hot Springs, Pine Bluff, Ark. or Tallulah, La., longer than forty-eight (48) hours following the first 7:00 A.M. after arrival, Sundays excluded; such charges to be collected at each point where charges accrue.

Item No. 7. Receive empty cars from St.Louis-San Francisco Railway at Hoxie, Ark., and switch to Walnut Ridge, Ark., before five (5:00) O'Clock P.M., October 5, 1929.

Item No. 8. Deliver loaded cars to Illinois Central Railroad at Tallulah, Louisiana.

Item No. 9. Sparks Circus has the privilege of having its Advertising Car and contents, property and employees therein, transported in advance of the cars containing the show proper, and upon due notice to the officers and agents of Missouri Pacific Railroad Company said Advertising Car to be attached to the regular trains of Missouri Pacific Railroad Company, or otherwise as may be determined by its officers and agents.

Freight tariffs covering circus moves cite the authority of Rule 63 of Interstate Commerce Commission Tariff Circular 20. It provides that rates for specified movements of circuses and other show outfits may be established on not less than one day's notice to the commission and must bear reference to this rule. While notice of the rates must be forwarded to the ICC, establishment of the rates is up to the railroads — *Authors' Collection.*

SWITCHING BILL

Form 1879 Regular

Sheet No. 2

Temple Texas October 28, 1953 19 ___

Ringling Bros & Barnum &
Bailey- Combined Shows

FREIGHT BILL No.	SW 2 Contd.

Car Numbers only- See Below

SWITCH ORDER No.	

To Gulf, Colorado and Santa Fe Railway Company, Dr.

For Switching Service as follows:

SWITCH WAYBILL		DESTINATION OR POINT OF ORIGIN		REVENUE WAYBILL		CAR	
DATE	NUMBER			DATE	NUMBER	INITIAL	NUMBER

ROAD, TRACK OR INDUSTRY			CONTENTS	WEIGHT	RATE	CHARGES	
FROM		TO				THIS LINE	OTHER LINES
RB & BB Platform cars Viz				RB&BB Stock Cars Viz			
112	108	234	356		101		
113	109	235	357		102		
114	110	236	358		103		
115	111	237	359		225		
117	227	238	360		226		
117	228	239	361				
11?	???	2?0	362				
104	230	241	?63				
1?5		2?2					
1?7	??1	2?3					
	???	?4?					
	???	?55					

Received Payment _____ 19 ___

_____ Agent Total to Collect

The Gulf Colorado & Santa Fe still referred to "platform cars" when it prepared to bill Ringling for switching its stockcars and flatcars at Temple, Texas, in 1953. Basic rates for movements often were augmented by a multiplicity of extra charges — *Authors' Collection.*

Advance Cars

They were called advertising cars for their role with the circus, or advance cars because they traveled a couple of weeks ahead of the show, or bill cars because they were loaded with the circus bills and billposters. Eventually every showman just referred to the "car" and knew it as the rolling home and work base of that bellicose bunch called "billers," whose aggressive ways managed to paste circus lithographs and date sheets on nearly every flat surface that came within their range.

Up to twenty-five or thirty men lived on and worked out of a typical advertising car, and the biggest shows operated two, three, and even four cars in advance of their show dates. The usual circus, however, utilized a single advance car. Since the circus played most towns for only one day, the bill car, too, had to complete its work in a single day for each town in order to maintain its lead ahead of the circus. Despite the killing pace of the route, billing crews posted enormous quantities of paper in every city. Typically, good-sized circuses would post 6,000 or even 10,000 sheets per day.

Advance cars often were combination cars, sometimes converted baggage or postal cars. Their configuration of windows, side doors, and decorations was enough to make a master car builder's head swim. The sides were painted up as rolling billboards for the circus they heralded. Enameled lions leaped over the truss rods, and huge gilded clowns grinned alongside the open vestibules.

Inside, the bill cars had great long work tables over storage lockers jammed with circus posters in a multitude of varieties and sizes. Above the long table tops were standard Pullman upper berths where the crew slept when the day's work was done. There was an office for the advance car manager and possibly another for the contracting press agent. At one end was an upright boiler to produce steam for cooking flour-based paste. About half of the bill cars tied that boiler to a galley where the paste maker doubled as cook and fed the crew. A few bill cars over the years attached a calliope to that same boiler, thus adding even another way for the bill car to call attention to the advent of the circus.

On the worktables the crews made up their loads, or "hods," of paper for the next day's work. Lithographers handled the one-sheets and half-sheets that would find the way to shop windows. They affixed date strips with localized show information to the pictorial lithographs of assorted designs and interspersed these with larger date sheets that named the city, day, and date of performances. Billposters arranged their supplies of bigger posters that would be pasted on the sides of sheds, fences, and barns. A sheet was a printer's unit of measure, forty-four by twenty-eight inches. Typical circus paper came in three-, six-, eight-, and sixteen-sheet sizes. Several of these—some giant pictorials, some oversized dates—were combined to make spectacular billing displays whenever space permitted. On the car, too, were those specialists called banner men who climbed tall ladders or dangled from roofs to reach the high walls where they tacked muslin circus advertising.

The car manager mapped out their work for the town at hand, assigning some men to certain streets or neighborhoods and others to the country routes. Lithographers usually walked the city streets with their sticks and hods under their arms. Billposters generally worked with horses and wagons rented from those pre-Hertz establishments called livery stables. Later, they had a fleet of pick-up trucks or station wagons that fanned out from the bill car each day.

Other billers were assigned "railroad work" in which they rode local passenger trains out of the main city and posted bills at each of the whistle-stops. Working alone or in pairs, they carried hods of paper, buckets of paste, and their long-handled brushes, all checked as baggage under terms of the show scrip with which they paid their fares.

Near the bill car's sidetrack they could catch their assigned train out of the city. Upon arrival at the initial town on their day's list, the billers hopped off, pulled their gear after them, and set about to decorate the fences, coal sheds, barns, and grain elevators with circus posters. One or two men could post a little town by the time the next train was due. Then they rode over to the next village to duplicate the procedure.

In 1894 the Barnum & Bailey show was especially proud of the volume of work turned out by its billers. Between Indianapolis, where the show would play July 30, and LaPorte, Indiana, where it was scheduled for August 18, the show's three advance cars billed for eighteen one-day stands, most of them in Michigan. Scheduled about one week apart, the various bill cars stopped over in each of those cities.

Car Two's men did the massive city work and wagon routes, reaching 434 towns on ninety-two city and country routes and posting 60,100 sheets of posters in that span. Car Six hit the same spots and posted another 35,173 sheets in its assignment of repairing and augmenting the billing done a couple of weeks earlier by Car Two.

In between came Car Four to handle the railroad work. Its men made 118 railroad routes of twenty-five to forty-five miles each. These routes took them to 588 territorial towns, where they posted 38,792 sheets.

This means that, on an average, the billers split into six or seven pairs, each pair going out from that day's city to work an assigned area of four or five small towns. At each stop they posted two or three stands of paper, usually in three-, four-, and six-sheet combinations. Then they hustled to catch the train again.

The system was continued by circuses as long as there were local trains, and after that they continued to bill the surrounding territory by motor truck. In this way the area people knew that the circus was coming, and they would be present in great numbers when the show arrived and the ticket wagon opened for business.

In the event that a circus crossed routes with a rival, activities were geared even higher. The biggest shows carried so-called opposition crews composed of billers available at a moment's notice for assignment in towns where opposition with another circus flared. In highly competitive times, the largest circuses had a separate car for opposition work; more often there was an opposition brigade. In circus parlance, a brigade was any group of perhaps three or four billers assigned some special task away from the normal range of the bill car. They might take an extra trunk of bills and be gone from the car for a week, while jumping out to post another town in opposition to a rival circus. Sometimes other brigades followed the bill car to replace damaged stands of paper, and still others took on similar special assignments that were issued by the circus general agent.

On completion of a day's work, the billing crew reassembled at the advertising car, dined on the paste maker's latest recipes, and fell asleep in the bill car bunks. Sometime during the night the car was added to a regular passenger train that would take it to the next town on the circus' route. By morning the crew would find itself on a siding or team track in still another town where all the walls were devoid of circus art, and all of the windows awaited these men with posters that said "the circus is coming."

The Adam Forepaugh show of 1877 was one of the first circuses with a railroad advertising department. In 1878 the Barnum show described its advertising Palace car as "the most brilliant, dazzling, and superbly magnificent specimen of vehicular architecture which American skill has ever contrived or native art has ever beautified." In the 1890s several shows used three and four advertising cars each. The 101 Ranch Wild West Show of 1916 may have been the first to use its own trucks for country routes in conjunction with the advance car. The Sparks Circus once carried a Model T pick-up truck aboard the bill car; end doors were opened and runs set so that the truck could be loaded or unloaded. Depression times caused such shows as Robbins Bros. Circus to eliminate the railroad bill car and substitute trucks. By 1955 even the mighty Ringling Bros. and Barnum & Bailey Circus had eliminated its bill car and was handling its then limited posting with motor trucks.

Advertising cars were mobile and effective operations. In 1891 the Adam Forepaugh Circus found opposition in thirty-nine western towns. Its opposition car, the *Cyclone,* left Omaha on May 26 to combat the rivals on those thirty-nine fronts. Forty-seven days later, on July 2, the car was at Portland, Oregon. It had traveled 5,000 miles and posted 300,000 sheets of lithographs. That evening it headed east out of Portland to resume its usual routing routine. Three days and 2,200 miles later the car was spotted at Marysville, Missouri, and the crew was ready to post the town for the show's appearance three weeks hence.

The life of a show agent and his crew was seldom serene. Arthur Hopper, the agent for the John Robinson Circus, reported to show owner Jerry Mugivan in July 1927 that Norfolk and Roanoke had been brigaded to protect against Ringling. They also had brigaded Bristol and tacked some banners in Johnson City as John Robinson sought to win the customers and deter the competition.

A problem had arisen concerning the circus' use of a wooden advertising car. Hopper reported that the railroads and the Interstate Commerce Commission were concerned about cars similar to those used by the John Robinson Circus. "The owners of private wooden cars will find that there are plenty of ways that the railroads can make it disagreeable for them, even if they will handle the wooden cars. Local trains are few and far between now, and it is next to impossible to make any time unless you have a car that can be handled on steel trains. Even now our advertising car is moved on steel trains almost every day, which is against the rules of some roads."

The show's aged wooden car was about to be replaced by a spanking new steel model. Hopper said, "We will not be bad off by having the new car. As a matter of appearance and neatness I believe that it will help keep the standard of the show and help business, as quite a number of people see the advertising car. Of course people like to see and talk about things that look nice and up-to-date. We often hear natives crack jokes about the appearance of our advertising car and I believe that with our new car, they will talk about the good appearance."

Hopper also complained about local billposting companies that sought to charge the circus even though they performed no work for it; and, failing in that, they sought to have the city require the circus to buy an extra license for bill posting.

Hopper's crew, he reported, had taken some extra precautions in Altoona to counteract competition from the 101 Ranch Wild West. And Hopper was staying with the car until it reached Roanoke, one of the cities to which he had dispatched an early brigade in opposition with Ringling.

If the circus advertising car was unique in railroading as a mobile, self-sufficient operation, then close on its heels was an even more amazing development in the annals of show business and railroading—the circus train itself.

A circus advance car, carrying the billposters who advertised the show, moved about two weeks ahead of the circus itself. The lone car moved on passenger trains when possible, freights when necessary. Photos of bill cars en route are rare. In this one, a C&NW train heads out of Milwaukee, bound for Madison, with the silver Ringling bill car on the end. It's July 9, 1951, and the circus will play Madison on July 25 — *Authors' Photo.*

A typical circus advance car, this one for Ringling Bros. and Barnum & Bailey poses for its first picture at the Pullman-Standard shops in 1923 — *Edwin B. Luce Collection.*

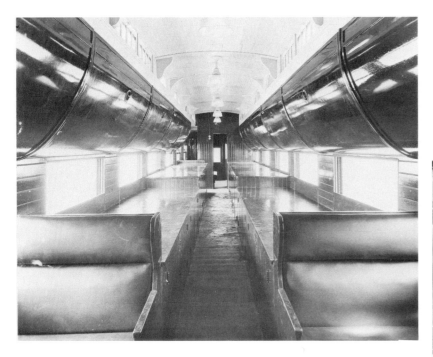

Left: Interior photos of bill cars are a rarity, and this one, a builder's photo taken by Pullman-Standard in 1923, shows the new Ringling-Barnum Number 2 Car. Most of the car space is given over to work tables, poster lockers, and standard upper berths. Billposters assembled their hods of paper on the work tables and pasted localized date strips on each piece. After a long day of posting circus paper around town, the billers returned to the car, opened the upper berths, and slept while the car was hauled to the next town — *Edwin B. Luce Collection.*

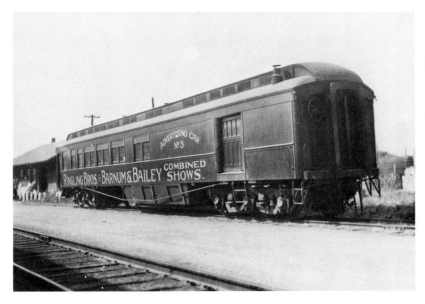

Ringling Bros. and Barnum & Bailey Circus had three advance advertising cars until 1927, used two in most seasons through 1940, but then cut back to one. It has had none since 1955. Few other modern shows had more than one. Depending upon the number, duties were divided among the cars. The first might carry mostly lithographers and billposters. The second might bring a few billers to augment the initial work and repair any damaged stands, but this car might also bring the bannermen, who scaled high walls to tack huge canvas banners. A third car might bring more of the same, or it might have a crew that specialized in "opposition," the fight against competing shows' similar advance crews wherever their routes crossed. Regular cars stayed to a strict schedule, maintaining their lead time ahead of the train that trailed it. But opposition cars were highly mobile and might hop in a widely erratic route back and forth across the show's territory as enemy shows turned up. These two photographs depict Ringling Number 3 car in 1922 and the Number 2 car in 1937 — *Circus World Museum, left; Authors' Photo, above.*

79

Above, left: Windows in the center, workrooms at each end, and the absence of vestibules or end doors mark this advance car. The Cole Bros. title has been painted on a whole retinue of different circuses. This is probably the 1916 model — *Circus World Museum. Above, right:* The Orton bill car heralded a losing cause. Although the Orton family has been prominent in circuses for about 120 years, this 1916 attempt at railroading was a financial disaster, and the tour was aborted. Then the family returned to the trouping it knew best — overland wagon shows — *Circus World Museum. Left:* Conservatism was the word for this paint job. But vivid color still would set the car apart on any team track where it might stop for the day. The Gollmars were first cousins of the Ringlings — *Circus World Museum.*

Left: This was the cozy abode where Mrs. L. C. Gillette kept house for her husband, the car manager for the John H. Sparks Circus in 1902. Like certain other small shows, Sparks chose not to decorate the bill car, and the only identification is the word "Private." But for picture-taking purposes, the paste-and-brushes crew posted a streamer on the side of the car. It promised balloon ascensions and parachute jumps when the show got to town — *Authors' Collection. Below, left;* Unusual lettering marked this 1903 advance car of the Gollmar Bros. Circus — *Authors' Collection. Below, right:* The Norris & Rowe tour of 1906 took the outfit into Mexico and to western Canada as well as to the United States. They shuffled some railroad cars after a wreck at Saskatoon in July, but this probably is the bill car used prior to that incident — *Authors' Collection.*

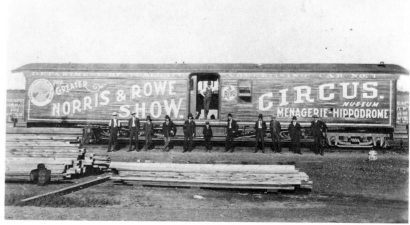

Left: Sells-Floto was still a new combination of circus names when this Number 1 Car rolled ahead of the show in 1907. It was then owned by the publishers of the *Denver Post — Circus World Museum. Below:* Billers and their badge of office — the long-handled paste brush — swarm over Engine 17 of the Detroit & Mackinaw Railroad at Rose City, Michigan, in 1911 to declare that they are with the Frank A. Robbins Circus — *Milt Robbins Collection.*

82

Above: The Rentz show of the 1890s conducted its advertising from a boxy wooden advance car — *Authors' Collection. Left:* The car manager sits in the open side door as the crew for the Forepaugh-Sells bill car poses beside its elaborate paintings — *Authors' Collection.*

Snow was on the ground when the car builder snapped this picture, but spring would find itself heralding the advent of Buffalo Bill's Wild West — *Denver Public Library.*

"Savage Crees" and "famous frontier women" were not enough to keep Beveridge's Montana Wildest West in action. The show that followed this advertising car lasted only three days in 1895 — *Authors' Collection.*

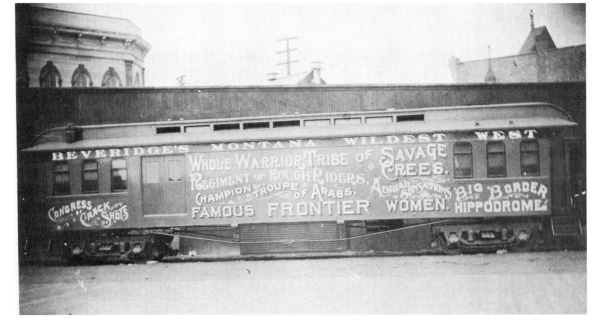

Above: This Sparks bill car cut a fine figure in 1916 — *Authors' Collection. Left:* This advertising car is the last of its breed. Ringling-Barnum used it from 1947 through 1955. It was left in quarters for the 1956 season, when few posters were used, and since then the circus has utilized other advertising crews. The last Ringling bill car now stands at the Circus World Museum. This is a 1949 view. A veteran of forty years around Ringling bill cars, F. A. (Babe) Boudinot was general agent in the last years of the car's use — *Authors' Photo.*

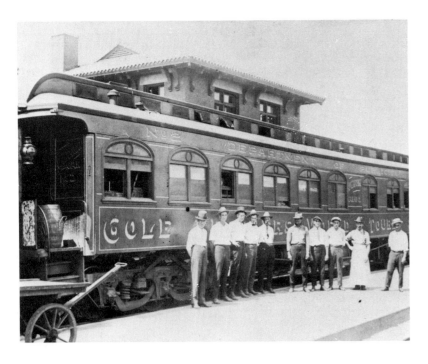

Above: Billers for the Adam Forepaugh show exhibited a giant poster of old Adam himself, but by this 1891 stop in Lincoln, Nebraska, the founder had died and James A. Bailey was a secret stockholder — *Authors' Collection. Left:* Typical depot architecture rises behind the Cole Bros. Number 2 car of 1916 — *Joseph T. Bradbury Collection.*

Right: Robbins Bros. Circus called it advertising car no. 2, but it was the only one they had. The show was one of few to make money in the difficult season of 1938, thanks in part to work done by the crew on this car — *Gene Baxter Photo. Below:* The proud title of the Hagenbeck-Wallace Circus graced a fleet of bill cars over the years. Pictured is the 1935 version for Hagenbeck-Wallace & Forepaugh-Sells Combined Circus — *Circus World Museum.*

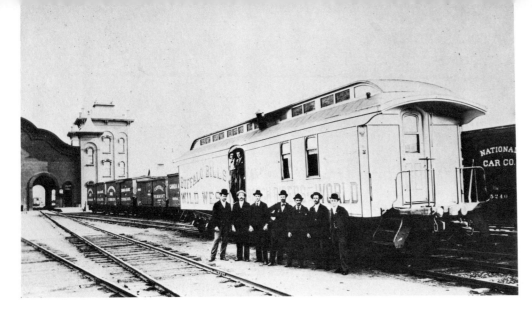

Buffalo Bill's skills were in the saddle rather than in the business operation of shows, so he struck a deal for James A. Bailey to handle his railroading and advertising. This is Bailey's crew on the Buffalo Bill advance car — *Authors' Collection.*

The big Adam Forepaugh Circus utilized its advertising car (as well as its cargo of posters) to publicize its patriotic spectacle of the year, "The American Revolution." Once an arch rival of the Barnum & Bailey outfit, the Forepaugh show became a Bailey property and was managed by Bailey's brother-in-law — *F. Beverly Kelley Collection.*

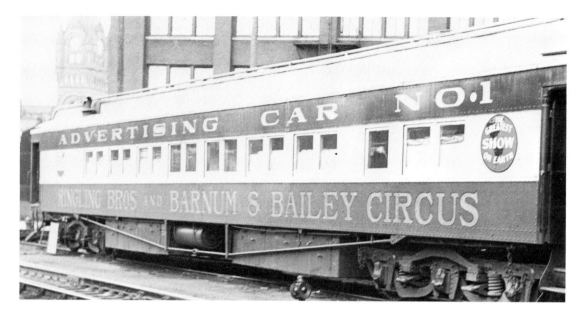

John Robinson's Circus billers ran up the United States flag on their bill car to mark July 4, 1924, but three years later the show's agent was telling the owner that railroads didn't want to handle the old wooden car. At that time the circus was expecting to take delivery soon on a spanking new all-steel car. The 1927 John Robinson advance car was assigned to the Al G. Barnes Circus in 1932, then the Al G. Barnes & Sells-Floto Combined Shows in 1937 and 1938. With new paint it became this Ringling Bros. and Barnum & Bailey Number 1 Advance Car of 1938-1946. Demoted, the car carried the circus laundry equipment for several years. Then it was placed on display at the Circus World Museum in Baraboo, Wisconsin. When the car was refurbished, excited workmen found a hoard of old John Robinson posters stuffed into the roofing, undetected by its inhabitants for thirty years! — *Authors' Collection.*

RAILROAD ROUTE REPORT.

Tickets Issued — Michigan Central

The Ringling Bros. and Barnum & Bailey Combined Shows

Advance Car No. 2, at Detroit, 1923. Made by W. O'Brien

Miles	Population	Place Where Posted	Owner's Name	On What Posted	Sheets Posted	No. Sheets Posted	Tickets	Tickets Numb
		Warren	Warren Furn.	Grain shed	37	2	11	
			P. Wolf	Implement shed	81	6		
		Utica	Utica Mill Co.	fence + shed	75	6	28	
			" "	feed shed	40	2	18	
			J. Fochs	coal shed	30	2	18	
		Orien	M. Letz	Lumber shed	422	8	32	
		Rochester	S. A.	Hay shed	51			
		Oxford	A. Carroll	Barn	56	3	18	
					812	29		

INSTRUCTIONS: Bill Poster must in every case get permission of owner or person in charge for each daub and have them sign contract for same. Carefully write down on report sheet each daub, owner's name, number of sheets, tickets, etc., at time of posting.

Bill Poster.

Typical of a railroad's instructions for handling a circus advertising car, this Chicago and North Western car order tells conductors and agents to move the Ringling-Barnum Number 1 car from Chicago to Evanston and Milwaukee in 1934 — *Authors' Collection.*

The age of local passenger trains permitted circus billers to leave their home-base bill car in the morning and ride into the feeder towns to post bills. They would slap up their big lithographs and date sheets on sheds and fences near the depot, then jump aboard the next train to make the next little town. According to this report, two Ringling billers rode the Michigan Central out of Detroit and put up 812 sheets of circus posters (at a cost of only twenty-nine free tickets!) at the five stops in forty miles. That 422-sheet stand of paper on the lumber shed at Orien would have been a beauty. In late afternoon they would catch a southbound train for the return to their bill car in Detroit. That night the car went to Indianapolis, next stand of the oncoming circus — *Authors' Collection.*

CHICAGO AND NORTH WESTERN RAILWAY COMPANY
OFFICE OF PRESIDENT
CHICAGO

FRED W. SARGENT
PRESIDENT

July 17th, 1934

File 2000-SHG

ICC No. A-1470
Ill. C.C. A-51

Contract No. 757

RINGLING BROS. & BARNUM BAILEY
COMBINED SHOWS
ADVERTISING CAR NO. 1

CAR ORDER

TO CONDUCTORS AND AGENTS: C.& N.W. RY.

    A contract has been executed under Authority of Rule 63, Tariff Circular 20 of the Interstate Commerce Commission, covering the haul over our line of Advertising Car No. 1 of the RINGLING BROS. & BARNUM BAILEY COMBINED SHOWS, as follows:

    On or about July 19th, to be received from the New York Central Railroad at Chicago, Ill.

    Thence: Chicago, Ill. to Evanston, Ill.
    Evanston, Ill. to Milwaukee, Wis.

    To be delivered to the Chicago, Milwaukee, St. Paul & Pacific Railroad at Milwaukee, Wis.

    This car will be occupied by Mr. Walter Gilby in charge, and 28 men, who are to be transported with the car account of circus contract on file with the General Freight Department.

    Car is NOT to be handled on Limited trains, and this contract expires August 3rd, 1934.

Fred W. Sargent
PRESIDENT

Above: For all the ballyhoo about two great shows being consolidated, this outfit misspelled its own name on its advertising car. The year was 1896, and two long-established titles — Sells Bros. Circus and Adam Forepaugh Circus — were linked for the first time. It was mainly the Sells show property with the expanded name painted over it, so perhaps it is understandable that the Sells painter didn't know about that "E" in "Forepaugh." Ladders, slung under the car, are for the billers and bannermen to reach the high walls with their posters — *Authors' Collection. Below:* Graphic arts people might quarrel with the title layout and the prominence given to the word "world's" over the Ringling name. But then this was 1890, the first year the Ringling Bros. Circus had any railroad cars to paint. And no one could deny that the car would catch your eye — *Authors' Collection.*

Above: More than any other category of circus people, it seems, the billposters loved to pose for photographs. Here is the annual "class picture" of the advance crew of Miller Bros. 101 Ranch Real Wild West in 1927 — *Authors' Collection. Right:* This bill car seems to roll and yaw even when standing still. It was ahead of the John Robinson Circus in 1899 — *Authors' Collection.*

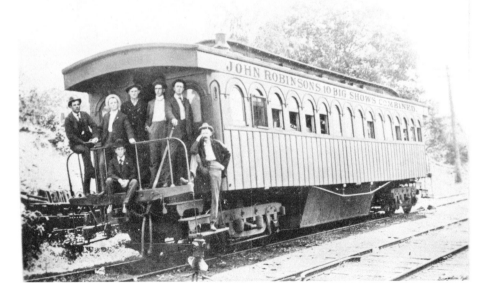

Right: "Coming Soon!" turned the 1949 Cole Bros. Circus advance car into an effective rolling billboard wherever it went. Here it is parked at the Louisville station — *F. Beverly Kelley Collection. Below:* The whole Sun Bros. Circus used just nine cars, so its advance was a substantial part of the rolling stock. The Sun outfit played the Southeast for nearly fifty years; this was the bill car of about 1909 — *Authors' Collection.*

93

Above: Circuses were so linked with railroading that fences and sheds near the tracks were especially likely spots for the billers to decorate — *Authors' Photo. Right:* The pattern was the same for this latter-day Ringling-Barnum advertising car as it had been for other circus advance cars over seven or eight decades. The lockers below and berths above were a convenient way to make the car serve its dual purpose as work space and living quarters — *Authors' Photo.*

COLE BROS. CIRCUS

WEATHER Good

At Des Moines, Ia. Show Date July 18th Car Date July 5th

R. R. Rock Island Arrive July 4th Depart 11:30 PM

	Sheets	Price	CHECKS ISSUED	Amount
Town Bill Poster	Sheets	Price		
Sniper H. E. Peterson	565	7¢		$39.55
	Route	Price		
Livery				

PAPER POSTED	Sheets	Tickets		Sheets	Tickets
Town Bill Boards			Town Lithographs	1693	934
Country Posting no routes			Town Banners Murphy		
Country Lithos.	321	180	Cards		
Town Daubs	565	49	Programs		
			Total	2579	1163

COUNTRY ROUTES	Sheets	Tkts.	COUNTRY ROUTES	Sheets	Tkts.
Ringling had about 40 banner walls squared and some empties.					
Lithoe Route - Talley					
Urbandale	6	6			
Johnston	13	10			
Herald	12	4			
Granger	25	20			
Polk City	9	6			
Crooker	10	4			
Ankeny	17	10			
Saylorville	3	2			
Saylor	2	2			
Carney	6	6			
Bonderant	28	12			
Altoona	11	8			
	142	90			
Lithoe Route- Rhodes					
Clover Hill	2	2			
West Des Moines	50	24			
Commerce	3	2			
Boonville	16	8			
Van Meter	18	12			
Fort Des Moines	12	6			
Norwalk	24	8			
Carlisle	6	6			
Avon	2	2			
Levey	2	2			
Youngstown	4	2			
Ivry	15	2			
Rising Sun	2	2			
Adelphi	4	2			
Runnells	22	8			
	179	90			

12 men on the car

Car Manager V. A. Williams

F. 28—1500—3/38—C. B.

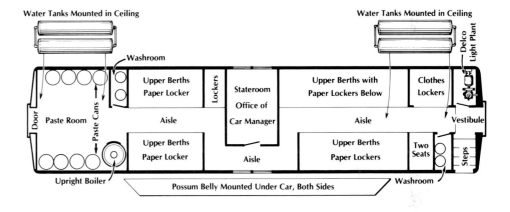

Left: Daily reports from circus bill cars indicated the railroad and departure time along with detailed statistics about the number of posters put up and the number of tickets issued in payment — *Authors' Collection. Above:* Billposter Frank Larkin recalled the details from which this drawing was made. It depicts the Ringling Number 1 Car prior to 1940. A focal point on the car was the paste room, where flour and water were cooked together with steam heat to make paste for the billers. Lockers or "possum bellies" under the car carried ladders and brush handles. Part of one vestibule was given over to a Delco light plant, since the car often sat by itself in yards and had to supply its own utilities — *Frank Larkin.*

The Number 1 Car for Wallace & Company's Great All Feature
Show not only displayed gladiator and jungle decorations painted by
one Harry Temple, but also exhibited a dressy curtain on the car's
single window amidships — *Authors' Collection.*

Flatcars

The mainstay of the railroad circus was the custom-built circus flatcar, the double-length platform car. Just as the rails provided a solid path for trains, so, too, the flatcars amounted to a steel and plank highway on which circus wagons moved.

Flats usually approximated half of the circus consist, a little less on a Wild West show. From Coup's first efforts, circus flats necessarily had no obstructions to traffic over the end sills; show wagons had to roll from flat to flat. Consequently, brake wheels or levers were on the sides of the cars. The beds of the flats were wooden and therefore had to be redecked from time to time. Precut oak decking fit between two steel beams and readily slid into place. This lateral surface was topped with longitudinal pine planking that gave a running surface for wagon wheels and was soft enough for the chock spikes to grab a purchase.

In each cut of flats were two runs cars—one at each end. These were fitted with the hardware used in loading and unloading—the snubbing post and the slots in which the runs were hooked into place as ramps. "Possum bellies" provided storage space for transporting the blocks, timbers, ropes, hooks, and allied gear for the loading process. The runs themselves—thirty-foot steel and hardwood ramps—were manhandled onto the decks for travelling, straddled by the wagons.

The first flats for circus purposes were thirty and forty feet in length, but soon showmen shifted to longer cars.

They had discovered that the lines moved circus cars at rates calculated by number, not length. It cost the same to move ten forty-foot cars as it did to move ten sixty-footers. The difference of two hundred lineal car feet—the equivalent of five shorter flats—was a free bonus. Because the latter gave fifty percent greater loading space for wagons, circuses used sixty-foot cars for many years and ultimately converted to seventy- and seventy-two-foot cars long before the railroads began to use any significant number of longer flats of their own.

The final lengths came almost concurrently with the advent of steel cars. The first show flats of steel were the nine sixty-foot units with Buffalo Bill's Wild West in 1911, 1912, and 1913. It also was using eleven wooden flats at the same time. Cole Bros. World Toured Shows of 1916 claimed an all-steel train including seven steel flats, which might have been new or might have been purchased from the Buffalo Bill consist.

Two car-building firms were responsible for nearly all of the circus flats. One was the Warren Tank Car Company of Warren, Pennsylvania; the other was the Mt. Vernon Car Manufacturing Company of Mt. Vernon, Illinois. In the 1920s the American Circus Corporation bought Mt. Vernon cars for its units—Hagenbeck-Wallace, John Robinson, and Sells-Floto. The Al G. Barnes show also bought Mt. Vernons, as did Christy Bros., Robbins Bros., and Sparks.

By 1926 both Warren and Mt. Vernon were advertising heavily for shows to switch from sixty-foot cars to the new seventies, and from wood to steel. The largest order—the forty flats for the new trains of Ringling Bros. and Barnum & Bailey—went to Warren and was delivered part in 1927 and part in '28. The last order for an all-new show train was placed with Warren in 1938 by Col. Tim McCoy's Real Wild West Show.

Flats were resold many times, so a car could hide many old show titles under its multiple coats of paint. Cars from Sells-Floto and Hagenbeck-Wallace could have been assigned to the Al G. Barnes Circus in the 1930s and then found their way to the Ringling train. Flats that began with Gentry or Walter L. Main in the 1920s went to Christy Bros. Circus and then to Cole Bros. for fifteen years before being scrapped in 1951 by the Luria Steel and Trading Company.

On a few rare occasions other firms built circus flats. The Hagenbeck-Wallace and Sells-Floto shows bought Keith cars, built in Chicago in the 1920s. With so many shows collapsing during the Depression, flats became a drug on the circus market for a while, but by 1947 Ringling needed more and bought five from the Thrall Car Company of Chicago.

Both Mt. Vernon and Warren cars display distinctive profiles. Mt. Vernons have a straight top edge and straight angular lines for the lower edge of the drop-frame sides. In contrast, Warren car sides have gently arcing lines, top and bottom. Keith cars looked very similar to Warren's. Thrall cars were more boxy and straight lined than the others; Ringling trainmen called them the "slick sides."

Circuses usually owned their flatcars, but almost never have these been identified as private property by the usual "X" serial code system. While other private owners labelled their cars as REX or GATX, circuses used simple digit numbers, perhaps 38 through 52 or 40 through 48. On the Ringling-Barnum show, cars carried three-digit numbers, the first number designating the section in which the car was operated. As an example, flats 132, 232, and 332 would represent cars in the first, second, and third sections respectively. When the Venice Transportation Company leased flats and stockcars to circuses, its rolling stock was designated with the initials of that company and possibly with a show title as well.

As new equipment became available or was required, circus cars were upgraded; thus, wooden flatcars disappeared. During the 1920s, all show trains upgraded their brake systems. Cast iron wheels were replaced. More recently, shows have bought new equipment to upgrade the trucks and bearings. W. A. Settlemire, treasurer of the Mt. Vernon Company, reported that while their engineers had the basic designs for show cars, each circus had its own specs built into the cars it ordered. The Tim McCoy order with Mt. Vernon's rival, for example, called for twelve cars, each seventy-two feet long, empty weight, 56,500 pounds, loaded weight, 100,000 pounds.

Perhaps the last wooden flats were a pair originating with the 101 Ranch Wild West Show and used last with the Bill Hames Carnival in the 1940s. When Ringling Bros. and Barnum & Bailey Circus discontinued the use of flatcars after 1956, most of them were sold in 1961 to the Royal American Shows. Two more Ringling flats, numbers 235 and 355, came to the Circus World Museum in Baraboo, Wisconsin. A third, 244, was used to take Ringling wagons to New York in 1957. Somehow it reached a Chicago railway salvage company, which sold it to the Circus World Museum. A Warren car like 244 measures seventy-three feet over the couplers, seventy feet for the bed, and nine feet, nine and one-fourth inches in width.

Specialized circus flatcars were the heart of show trains but were freaks in general railroading. Throughout two world wars, the roads and the government said that they were good for nothing but shows. Only a few hundred steel flats ever were built, and they were of interest only to showmen. Until about the time they disappeared from show trains, everyone else overlooked the particular advantages of circus flatcars. But ultimately this renegade rolling stock gave rise to some of the most modern equipment in up-to-date railroading—long piggyback and rack cars.

Flatcars were the bulk and the heart of circus trains. Ringling's long trains of long cars eased through the big-city yards with heavy cargo of show wagons and trucks in 1950 — *Authors' Photo.*

Above: Forty years earlier, the principles were the same. The Ringlings' first cousins, the Gollmar Bros., had wooden flats on a small-town sidetrack, but the basics of show train operation were unchanged — *Circus World Museum. Right:* Poised above the end sill of a Warren flatcar, the America steam calliope is shrouded in canvas to protect its elaborate wood carvings. Chocks under the wheels steady the wagon during its rail ride — *Bill Backstein Photo.*

Left: A Mount Vernon car is mixed in with a string of Warren flats on the Cole Bros. Circus. An AC Bull-dog Mack grinds along with a solid-tired baggage wagon in tow — *Gene Baxter Photo. Above:* The back end gang of the 1937 Hagenbeck-Wallace train crew clusters around 19 Cage to await a pull-over team. A string of still-loaded flats stretches down the siding — *Eddie Jackson Collection.*

101

Right: From the time of Coup's first custom-built cars, hand brakes on circus flatcars have been mounted at the side. Grab irons and steps conform to ICC regulations and railroad standards. The cross-over plate is in position to carry the wagon between flats — *Circus World Museum. Above:* Barnum & Bailey baggage wagons are loaded tightly on the Barnum & Bailey wooden flats at Utica, New York, in 1908. Empty cars at the far right bow upward because of truss rod pressure, but loaded cars straighten out under the weight — *Gene Baxter Collection.*

102

Canvas-shrouded cages of the Ringling show await unloading from a string of wooden flats — *Jim McRoberts Collection.*

Two styles of wooden flats mark the 1906 Great Wallace train — *William Woodcock Collection.*

Bracing from the tie rods built an arch into the profile of wooden flats. Heavy wagons tended to eliminate the arch, and aging flats sometimes sagged in the middle. These well-kept cars belonged to Ringling Bros. Circus about 1915. In the foreground, the snubber and his rope man await another wagon to unload — *Circus World Museum.*

Initials on these Sells-Floto flats reveal that they are leased from the Venice Transportation Company, an Illinois outfit which rented cars to many circuses in the decades prior to the Great Depression — *Circus World Museum.*

Right: Ringling Bros. and Barnum & Bailey stayed the longest with wooden flatcars and used these sturdy units into the late 1920s — *Circus World Museum. Below:* The catalogue of the Mount Vernon Manufacturing Company circa the 1920s offered thirty-ton wooden flats like this sixty-foot job they built for Howe's Great London Shows — *Authors' Collection.*

MOUNT VERNON CAR MANUFACTURING COMPANY . MOUNT VERNON, ILLINOIS, U. S. A.

1681. 30-Ton Wood Circus Flat Car. Length, 60' 0"; width, over sills, 8' 9"; inside of side plank, 8' 5"; gauge, 4' 8½". Couplers, automatic; draft gear, spring type; brakes, automatic air; double floor for wheel runs; trucks, Diamond arch bar type; all metal; inside hung brakes; O. H. steel axles; 33" A. R. A. cast iron wheels; U. S. safety appliances; painted and lettered as desired.

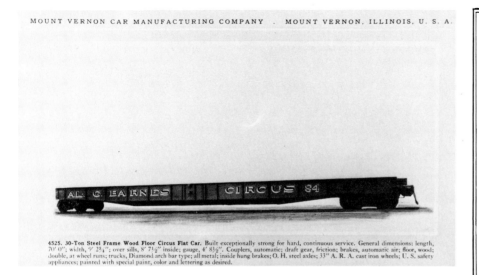

4525. 30-Ton Steel Frame Wood Floor Circus Flat Car. Built exceptionally strong for hard, continuous service. General dimensions: length, 70' 0"; width, 9' 2¾"; over sills, 8' 7½" inside; gauge, 4' 8½". Couplers, automatic; draft gear, friction; brakes, automatic air; floor, wood; double, at wheel runs; trucks, Diamond arch bar type; all metal; inside hung brakes; O. H. steel axles; 33" A. R. A. cast iron wheels; U. S. safety appliances; painted with special paint, color and lettering as desired.

Above: The Mount Vernon catalogue circa the 1920s also listed its model 4525, a thirty-ton steel-framed circus flat seventy feet long. Mount Vernon was one of the two principal brands of circus steel flat-cars — *Authors' Collection. Right:* The other principal builder of circus flats was the Warren Tank Car Company. It won the biggest order of all when Ringling Bros. and Barnum & Bailey converted to steel cars starting in 1928 — *Circus World Museum.*

FOR SALE

On account of standardizing with steel equipment, we have for sale our 1928 Train, consisting of Flat, Stock and Elephant Cars, 60 feet in length, wooden construction and practically all 80,000 pounds capacity. These cars are just out of service, having been used by us last season and are in good repair. They can be inspected at our Sarasota, Fla., Winter Quarters. As we will need the track room the prices on these cars will be right for a quick sale.

RINGLING BROS. AND BARNUM & BAILEY,

SARASOTA, FLA.

Above: Ringling-Barnum offered its older cars for sale. There always has been considerable exchange of railroad equipment among circuses — *Circus World Museum. Left:* Clyde Beatty's wild animals and the Cole Bros.' menagerie ride Mount Vernon flats in 1935 at Guelph, Ontario — *Walter Tyson Collection.*

Left: Towers sat on a string of system flats loaded with rails to watch the unloading of the Sells-Floto Show in the 1920s — *Circus World Museum. Below:* The Clyde Beatty Circus acquired Warren flats from the Beckmann & Gerity Carnival to convert from truck-show operation. Here, a Chevy tractor rolls over the flats with its semi-trailer loaded with canvas and big top poles — *Gene Baxter Photo.*

The Robbins Bros. Calliope sits in the middle of flat #43, a Warren model with lots of lettering — *Robert Good Photo*.

Bold letters proclaim the Cole Bros. Circus title on the side of Warren flat #41 in 1941 — *William White Collection*.

The Warren flats on the Ringling-Barnum show were seventy feet long. By the late 1930s, a few rubber-tired wagons were mixed in with the wooden-wheeled baggage wagons — *Jim McRoberts Photo*.

Whenever possible, the circus trainmaster put the heaviest wagons over the trucks of the flatcar; thus, the 1928 Sparks stringer wagon is at the end of flat 26 — *Eddie Jackson Photo*.

Showmen often prided themselves on loading their flatcars tightly to maximize the use of space. None was loaded more tightly than the Hagenbeck-Wallace show in 1922, with both the cage and parade wagon out over the couplers — *Circus World Museum*.

Even steel flats had wooden decks. These Ringling cars at the Sarasota winter quarters are cluttered with cross-over plates and chocks. The hardware at the center is to keep the cross-over plates from falling off. Chains are used to tie down the end wagons — *Paul Tharp Photo.*

Corners of cross-over plates were tipped down to give them a grip in the wooden deck. The chock block had two spurs on the bottom side, also to dig into the decking and keep wagons in place — *Authors' Photograph.*

Unusual in circus railroading was this Cole Bros. flatcar fashioned by cutting down a stockcar. The truss rods were added to build strength back into the car after the superstructure was removed — *William White Collection.*

These 1944 Arthur Bros. flatcars were fashioned out of whale show cars. The Warren Tank Car Co. had built several custom units for exhibitors of stuffed whales during the 1930s — *Circus World Museum.*

112

Above: Just as Keith flats resembled Warrens, so Thrall cars were similar to Mount Vernons in profile. This builder's photograph of a Thrall car shows why showmen nicknamed them "slick sides." The RBX numbering system was a rare exception to the normal designation of circus cars — *Francis W. DeSautelle Collection. Left:* Here, the Thrall cars are in operation on the Ringling train. Warren and Mount Vernon were out of business by the time Ringling bought several of these cars, including RBX 10 in May 1949. Its capacity was 100,000 pounds and load limit 104,200 pounds. Its light weight was 64,800 pounds. This car was equipped with AB brakes — *Francis W. DeSautelle Collection.*

113

Brackets on the side identify this Al G. Barnes Circus flat as a runs car. The snubbing post will fit into the brackets for the unloading process. Rugged show wagons increase their efficiency and load by adding side racks to carry tent poles — *Joseph Fleming.*

Mount Vernon flats took the Miller Bros. 101 Ranch Wild West Show into Portsmouth, New Hampshire, during 1927 — *Authors' Collection.*

Stockcars

Usually they all are lumped together as stockcars, but the railroad equipment that transported uncaged animals of a circus involved several modifications to accommodate different species. There were cars for the broad-backed baggage stock that pulled the circus wagons. There were others for the trim performing horses, more for ponies or camels and zebras. And there were still others fitted out differently for the most popular circus animals of all—the elephants.

Like the circus flats, these stockcars were seventy to seventy-two feet long, twice the length of the first circus stockcars and nearly twice the length of other stockcars in regular freight service. Like the flats, too, they were built mostly by the Warren Tank Car Company and the Mt. Vernon Car Manufacturing Company. When circuses used baggage stock before the tractor era, stockcars made up about one quarter of a circus train, a greater portion of a Wild West show train.

As with a railroad's ordinary cattle cars, the standard circus stockcar had slatted sides; the lower half was solid, but the upper half was slatted for ventilation.

Into the 1920s most such cars were wooden, and at that time even the ends were slatted. But with the advent of steel cars, the ends became of solid design.

A car for ring stock had individual stalls for thirty-two head of horses. The sides were hinged, and all stalls were swung open for loading. When each horse had been placed in its lateral stall, the wooden side was swung into place alongside of it. Each horse was loaded into the same stall every time.

In the case of baggage stock, each car carried up to twenty-seven horses; they were placed side by side, crosswise in the car, and in the same spot each night. One end of the car and then the other was loaded from the center door. Last aboard was the wedge horse, trained to wedge itself between the two groups of horses already on board. Thus loaded tightly, the stock was able to withstand the jolting, stopping, and starting of the train without falling.

From the roof a chain was suspended over each horse. An S-hook at the end was attached to the horse collar to take up that weight for the night. Harness was removed from a circus horse only at the stable tents on the lot during the day. Each stockcar was equipped with covered troughs. At the appropriate time a teamster's helper would walk along the roofs of the moving show train. Atop each car he would pull the chains that opened the inside mangers and exposed the grain to the horses.

Elephant cars constituted the greatest variation from the norm in stockcars. Camels, zebras, and certain other animals were called lead stock because they could be led from place to place. They rode in stockcars just like those for horses. Ponies were loaded in the same fashion except that they often were double-decked. But elephant cars were different. The big "rubber mules" were loaded three pairs in each half, all facing the center doors. Each animal was chained in place. One main difference was that car sides were not slatted. Sometimes they were solid, and sometimes they included windows or small ventilators, due to the fact that an elephant's health is more vulnerable. Because elephants are susceptible to pneumonia, precautions needed to be taken against cold and drafts. Elephant cars usually had a greater load capacity than horse cars, and sometimes they were higher or had more clearance at the doors—all to accommodate their hefty tenants. An elephant car could carry up to twelve or thirteen adult animals. Often that practical limitation determined how large a herd of elephants a show would troupe.

If the herd was smaller, unneeded car space was used efficiently anyway. Often bunks were built in the cars for the elephant handlers. Sometimes the rest of the car would be used for lead stock, perhaps camels. Or this might be where the show loaded a spare big top, wholesale stocks of program booklets, or concession supplies. An extra center pole for the big top might be lashed to the roof of a stockcar.

The Warren Tank Car Company turned out a few special cars for the Depression-era shows that exhibited mummified whales. During World War II, when circus cars were in great demand and short supply, some old whale show cars were resurrected to serve as circus stockcars. In several cases, damaged or excess stockcars were stripped down to serve as flatcars.

When Tom Mix had a private car on the Sells-Floto Circus, his horses were accorded equivalent treatment and space in a stockcar. But perhaps the most unusual usage of a circus stockcar involved Goliath and Pawah. As a featured white elephant on the Ringling show, Pawah could not associate with the ordinary grey elephants. So in 1927 Warren built a stockcar with a special configuration for transporting a white elephant in proper style. An off-center wall divided the interior into a long end and a short end. The latter was home for Pawah. But after the '27 tour, the white elephant was replaced as a feature attraction by a different kind of elephant. This was Goliath, the sea elephant, tons of blubber with a powerful tail and flippers. The show installed a huge water tank in the short end of the stockcar for Goliath, and the monster moved in.

Each day they took Goliath from the car to the showgrounds for his starring role under the big top. Returning, his flatbed wagon was backed up to the extra door on the custom stockcar, and Goliath was coaxed to transfer. Regularly he flopped into his rolling pool for the night's trip. The other portion of the car was filled with ordinary land elephants. But the sea elephant brought a slight problem. En route, Goliath's movements and the sloshing of the water caused the car to sway, and sometimes it derailed. Even so, no serious damage resulted, and the unusual stockcar with its unusual passenger made four seasons with Ringling and a final tour in 1932 with Sells-Floto.

Stockcars came at the head end of most circus consists to minimize the jolts taken by animals as engineers took up the slack in their trains. In this Ringling-Barnum move, Northern Pacific 1835 is tied on to elephant cars, marking it as the show's second section — *Gene Baxter*.

CIRCUS CARS

FOR LEASE AND SALE

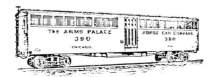

We have Palace Horse Cars 50 feet long; most desirable
for safe transportation of circus horses also

Advance, Privilege, Baggage, "Living" and Box Cars
equipped for passenger and freight service
leased on liberal terms

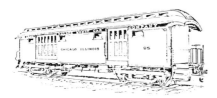

WRITE FOR PARTICULARS

ARMS PALACE HORSE CAR CO.

1220 MONADNOCK BLOCK, CHICAGO, ILL.

While the Arms Palace Horse Car Company was
best known for leasing stockcars for general use,
they also gave special attention to circus railroad
needs. This advertisement appeared in the 1906
route book of the Sells-Floto Circus — *Authors'
Collection.*

In teams of six and eight horses, the baggage stock of the Hagenbeck-Wallace Circus in 1931 prepares to quit the stockcars and begin the day's work of hauling circus wagons — *Authors' Collection.*

A sure-footed Percheron clomps down the ramp of a Hagenbeck-Wallace stockcar. The door is held out to keep the horse from getting too close to the edge of the ramp. Many shows had sides on the ramps for this purpose. The ramps were carried in racks under the cars — *Authors' Collection.*

In addition to heavy baggage horses, the stockcars also bring the circus ring horses. Here grooms unload the Barnum & Bailey ring stock in 1914. At the right, other circus hands prepare to back a new-fangled automobile out of its garage wagon — *H. H. Conley Collection*.

On smaller shows it was the same story. Here baggage stock of the Sanger's Great European Shows is unloaded from wooden stock cars in 1911 — *Circus World Museum*.

Three stockcars of the 1922 Gentry Bros. Circus head up the fourteen-car consist at Goldfield, Nevada, now a ghost town — *Authors' Collection.*

Stockcar 352 carried performing horses for Ringling-Barnum. To the left of the sliding door is the unloading ramp. Also slung under the car are two side panels for the ramp. I-bolts and rings fastened along the side of the car are used for tethering horses as they are unloaded. On the roof of the car are the protruding pipes through which chains reach down to covers on the mangers. Early in the morning a man pulls the chains to expose oats to the horses — *Edwin B. Luce Collection.*

121

Inside of Ringling's stockcar 349, the names of ring horses are chalked on the upright posts — Nellie, Blush, Susan, Twinkle, Geneva, Rusty, and an unnamed black horse. Each horse was loaded in the same position each night, and they were kept in the same order at the stable tents every day. The horses' heads faced to the left. As each horse was loaded into the car, a panel was swung alongside to create an individual stall. In the photograph, panels are stacked in the open position at the left. Near the roof line at the right is a roll of canvas which could be lowered to keep out the draft on cold nights — *Paul Tharp Photo.*

Seven stockcars comprise about one-quarter of the Hagenbeck-Wallace train in 1921 — *Walker Morris Collection.*

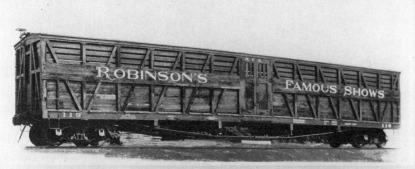

2297. 30-Ton Wood Circus Stock Car. Inside dimensions: length, 59' 2½"; width, 8' 4¾"; height, 7' 5¾"; gauge, 4' 8½". Couplers, automatic; draft gear; spring type; brakes, automatic air; roof, double board; trucks, Diamond arch bar type; all metal; inside hung brakes; O. H. steel axles; 33" A. R. A. cast iron wheels; U. S. safety appliances; painted and lettered as desired.

Above: The Mount Vernon Car Manufacturing Company built stock-cars. Model 2297 was 59 feet, 2½ inches long — *Authors' Collection. Right:* When the John Robinson Circus bought new cars in 1928, the Mount Vernon Car Company published this full-page ad in *The Billboard.* The endorsement from show owner Jerry Mugivan was in partial response to Ringling's buying cars from the competition. Stockcars usually were slatted, and elephant cars generally had solid sides with some windows or ventilators — *Authors' Collection.*

123

Below: The Barnes and Sells-Floto titles were combined for 1937 and '38. Here, the show's Mount Vernon stockcars stand idle after all the action has moved from sidetrack to show-grounds — *Gene Baxter Photo. Right:* Loaded flats wait in the distance as Sells-Floto baggage stock is unloaded in 1918 — *Jules Bourquin.*

Camels were stockcar passengers. Here a Bactrian camel comes down the ramp. Notice the hooks on the bottom end of the ramp. If unloading were to take place on the opposite side of the stockcar, this ramp would have been pulled out on the other side, and these hooks now on the ground would have been hooked to the sill of the car — *Circus World Museum.*

Long-horned steers come bounding off of a stockcar in a blur. It's the Tim McCoy Real Wild West Show of 1938, where cowboys figured it was better to rope the critters than try to lead them off of the car individually. The McCoy train comprised the last sizable circus order for custom railroad equipment — *Circus World Museum.*

Zebras were carried in the stockcars along with the dromedaries and camels to comprise the circus lead stock — those animals that could be led from train to showgrounds without cages. This was the scene as Ringling Bros. and Barnum & Bailey Combined Circus unloaded at Albany, New York, in the 1930s — *Gene Baxter Photo.*

4229. 30-Ton Steel Underframe and Steel Superframe Elephant Car. In the building of this type of car particular attention is given to the severe service they are to perform, as well as providing ample room for the lading. General dimensions: length, 70′ 0″ inside; width, 8′ 4½″ inside; height, rail to top of running board, 12′ 8″; gauge, 4′ 8½″. Couplers, automatic; draft gear, friction; brakes, automatic air; roof, canvas-covered; one end partition off, providing sleeping accommodations for the attendants; trucks, Diamond arch bar type; all metal; inside hung brakes; O. H. steel axles; 33″ A. R. A. cast iron wheels; U. S. safety appliances; painted with special paint, color and lettering as desired.

The off-center door on the stockcar that Mount Vernon built for the Sparks Circus hints of custom design. This was primarily an elephant car; the main center section would carry the Sparks herd. But slatted sides at the short end suggest that camels were stabled here. And, like many elephant cars, this one had bunks at the other end for the elephant handlers. The seventy-foot car had a canvas-covered roof — *Authors' Collection.*

Elephant cars are identified by having vents rather than slats in the sides. When the last of these Cole Bros. elephants is off the car, they'll tail up and walk to the lot — *Gene Baxter Photo.*

Apparently eager to get its show on the road, this elephant watches as the crew places a ramp to the stockcar door on Cole Bros. Circus in 1947 — *William White Collection.*

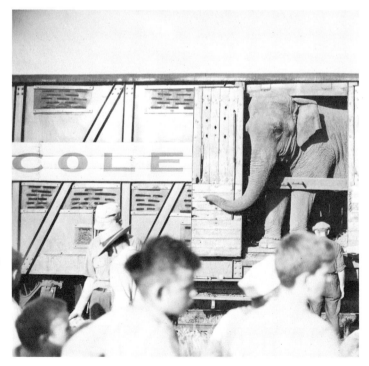

Coaches

While many people have spent great portions of their lives on trains, no one outdid circus troupers in this respect.

Train crews might live in dormitory cars for the few days of a long run, but then they would have time off and would return to a family.

Maintenance-of-way crews might live in bunk cars for a while. Travelling salesmen spent a lot of weeknights in Pullman accommodations and days in coaches, but after a week they returned to the house and yard.

For circus people, however, those coaches were home itself for twenty to thirty weeks at a go. As Tuffy Genders, a Ringling unit manager, said in 1969, "It's when I get off of the train that I feel that I'm away from home and travelling."

Circus people worked at the showgrounds all day and evening. Then they went home to the cars for the jump to the next town. Those cars were the one great constant in their lives. The towns, the lots, the weather all changed, but the cars remained the same and comprised a home.

When Coup first supplied cars for circus people, they looked on in wonder, accepted the luxury, and blinked in disbelief at trouping in such comfort. What an improvement over living in wagons! In the century that followed, some continued in luxury, and other show people found the cars a little crowded. The caste system of circus life was especially pronounced when it came to assigning train space. But whatever one's station in the society, a high point in trouping was the experience of life on the show train.

"Just out of Pullman service" is the way show owners described their coaches. Indeed, a few shows bought brand new cars for circus use, but more often the cars were aging by the time they traded Pullman green for circus red. In any case, any car coming into circus ownership usually was gutted at once to make room for the bunks that were needed in show operation. True, there were private cars for the top brass, or portions of a car would be set aside for the private use of bosses or stars. Key personnel was assigned a half or third of a car, or a section. But that kind of space was the exception. Usually it was a matter of a bunk framed of lumber and fitted with storage space for a suitcase at most. The big question was not merely between upper and lower berths: more than a few circus coaches had three-high bunks.

A married couple doing an act in the performance might share a lower on the train. A newcomer might draw an upper and have to spend a couple of seasons or more with the show to have a chance at a lower berth. The working men—canvasmen, train crew, and teamsters, for example—might be assigned two to a bunk. Little wonder that it was popular to sleep under a wagon on the flats on hot July nights.

Cars were assigned by department. Performers and staff personnel lived in one or more of the cars. Single girls were congregated in what was inevitably nicknamed the "virgin car." Clowns were segregated in another car, bandsmen elsewhere. Ticket sellers, candy butchers, sideshow attractions—all were quartered by department in the same section of the train. On the Clyde Beatty Railroad Circus of the 1950s, for example, there were four coaches: one for the use of the staff, one for the performers, one for the working men, and one for the band, candy butchers, ticket sellers, and others.

Once allotted such space, troupers often redecorated to suit their personal tastes. Girls stitched distinctive window curtains. Wall space was repainted and picture frames went up. There might be space for a flower vase. Performers with a whole section could have even more amenities of home. The stars and brass in greater space boasted of fancy paneling, comfortable furniture, rugs, dinettes, and Pullman kitchens—cozy homes on rails. Owners of sufficiently large and prosperous shows occupied an entire private car and lived in luxury paralleling that of railroad presidents. The apogee of luxurious hospitality on a big circus was to accept the owner's invitation to join him and his family for dinner on "the car"—his private car where a porter and maid assisted the chef.

Elsewhere on the show train a porter was assigned to each car. He was the boss in that domain. As housekeeper he kept the car neat and liveable, but he also enforced rules, solved differences, and cooled tempers. He was the mailman and errand boy. He picked up laundry and provided sandwiches. While other circus employees were busy with performances and the show itself, the porter had the day free for cleaning the cars and running the downtown errands. For all these services, circus porters received handsome tips from their tenants.

Circus coaches often were given names after the pattern of Pullman cars. On the Ringling Bros. and Barnum & Bailey Circus the cars for working men generally carried the names of states, and those for performers and executives usually were named for cities. Often the names had a special meaning in a show's history or the owner's background. Thus, cars carried the names of the Ringlings' home state of Wisconsin and Barnum's home state of Connecticut. The *Florida* and *Sarasota* were coach names. Car 84 was the *Cleveland* in the 1930s, but its name was changed to *Evanston* when it became the rolling home of Robert Ringling, who lived in that Illinois city. Car 40, the *Connecticut,* lost out to *Montana* in the mid 1940s because the show's connection with the eastern state had faded into history and a second generation of Ringlings had obtained huge ranch holdings in Montana.

The Buffalo Bill Wild West Show named its cars for Indian tribes. Sells-Floto used city names, and later, when its manager built up a new show as Cole Bros., it also carried city names on the cars, including owner Zack Terrell's private car, the *Owensboro.* On the Downie & Wheeler Circus of 1912 the cars were called *Dixie, Georgia,* and *LaTena,* the latter named for Andrew Downie's wife. With the Mighty Haag Railroad Shows of 1909-1914 the cars were named *Shreveport, Caddo,* and *Louisiana,* all for the site of the show's winter quarters. With Dailey Bros. in 1945 the coaches carried family names. The 18 Car was *Ben,* for Ben Davenport; the 19 Car was called *Eva,* for Mrs. Davenport; and the 100 Car was called *Norma,* for their daughter. The fourth car, 52, was named *Butch,* for the show treasurer. When Col. Tim McCoy was featured with Ringling Bros. and Barnum & Bailey for 1936 and 1937, he lived on the *Cheyenne.* In the next season he built his own Colonel Tim McCoy Real Wild West Show and, like Buffalo Bill, named his cars for Indian tribes.

Number 40, a new *Cheyenne,* had two staterooms, a bedroom, living room, dining room, kitchen, and three shower baths. The 41, *Arapaho,* boasted two bedrooms, living room, dining room, kitchen, bath, plus several double berths. Car 42, the *Navajo,* had three staterooms plus double berths; 43, the *Comanche,* was all double berths; 44, the *Osage,* was half pie car and half double berths; 45, the *Dakota,* was half double berths and half three-high berths; 46, the *Blackfoot*, was one-quarter pie car and three-quarters three-high berths; 47, the *Pawnee*, had two-high and three-high berths; and 48, the *Apache*, contained three-high berths.

Naturally, the owner of the show, Tim McCoy, lived on the new *Cheyenne*. Meanwhile, his place with Ringling-Barnum had been taken by "Bring 'Em Back Alive" Frank Buck, and as a result, the name of the old *Cheyenne* had been changed to the *Malaya*, in deference to its new tenant. After the McCoy show closed, the *Cheyenne* became the *Owensboro* on Cole Bros. Circus.

John Ringling's private car was called the *Jomar*, a contraction of the names of John and Mable Ringling. Charles Ringling's private car was the *Caledonia*. In 1941, when Jack Dempsey toured with Cole Bros. Circus, he lived on the *Loretto*, a private car formerly owned by business tycoon Charles M. Schwab.

While some shows used names, nearly all of them used numbers on their cars. Usually the cars were numbered in sequence with one set for flatcars, one set for stockcars, another set for coaches, and plenty of unused numbers between each series. With the big Ringling Bros. and Barnum & Bailey Circus, numbers of coaches, as with flats and stocks, took on additional significance: all 100 series cars were in the first section, 200 series in the second section, 300 series in the third section, and 400 series in the fourth section.

In 1920 the Ringling-Barnum circus carried twenty-four coaches in its consist of ninety-five cars. During 1923 there were twenty-two sleeping cars, one dining car, and one private car. In 1929 the first Ringling section included four coaches, the second had six such cars, the third section comprised three sleepers and one storage car, while the fourth included ten sleepers and one office car. In 1932 twenty-five coaches were used. There were twenty-seven coaches in 1936, twenty-three in 1941, and the all-time high occurred in 1947, with forty-one sleepers in a train of 108 cars. By 1950, seventeen coaches were on the Ringling train.

Just after World War I, Ringling Bros. and Barnum & Bailey Circus had obtained an all-new string of twenty-four war surplus hospital cars from the United States government. In 1923, therefore, the show had a fully new and modern train. By 1947, however, those same cars were due for replacement. So once again the circus went to war surplus stocks and purchased hospital cars, this time twenty-five all-steel, eighty-five-foot cars. The old train was grounded at Sarasota where it served as motel space for circus people during the winter. The new World War II hospital cars provided luxurious quarters in 1948. They even were air-conditioned until mid-season. At that time the Middle West was seized in a heat wave, and the circus found it impossible to buy sufficient quantities of ice to keep the air-conditioning system up to par. The troupers' patience gave way to demands for comfort while the show was at Decatur, Illinois, and no ice could be had. That night circus people broke out all the glass windows, and thereafter the management made no further effort to obtain ice and operate the cooling system.

While virtually all coaches on show trains are used for living space, there have been a few exceptions. One was the *Florence Nightengale*, a former Hagenbeck-Wallace coach converted for use on the Ringling Bros. and Barnum & Bailey show train of 1936 as a hospital car. The show's doctor and his staff used it for their headquarters. Ailing employees could be treated readily; injured performers and working men could stay with the show while recuperating. It was a good idea, but the *Nightengale* proved to be too great a luxury for circus life and it was discontinued. Another step toward self-sufficiency was the Ringling circus laundry car. It carried commercial-sized laundry equipment and provided cleaning services for all of the show's wardrobe and costumes as well as for train linens, cookhouse tablecloths, and employee uniforms. More recently, the circus established a business office on the train. Personnel would function there throughout the day rather than move its office equipment to the arena where performances were currently being given.

Often circus coaches saw service on numerous shows and switched from one to another, subject only to a new paint job. In 1948, for example, the Clyde Beatty circus bought coaches from Ringling-Barnum.

Life aboard a show train gave a dimension to trouping that was absent in wagon shows and was lost again in the age of motor homes. Most circus people of the era recalled the coaches as satisfactory, perhaps even fondly. After all, whether one had a private car or shared a three-high bunk with another trouper, for about eight months of the season, year after year, one's place in the coaches was home.

Circus man J. Augustus Jones (center) stands alongside one of his circus coaches in 1915. The combination car number 60 bears the initials of his Jones Bros. shows — *Joseph Bradbury Collection.*

The Central Vermont Railroad's 474 wheels along with a half dozen sleepers of the Dailey Bros. Circus at Burlington, Vermont, in 1949. Irregular alignment of windows attests to the lack of air conditioning — *Gene Baxter Photo*.

Cars of Russell Bros. Pan Pacific Circus are side-tracked for winter maintenance near California winter quarters — *Circus World Museum.*

The observation car on Tim McCoy's Real Wild West was #40, the *Cheyenne*, Tim McCoy's private car. It included two staterooms, bedroom, living room, dining room, kitchen, and three shower-baths — *Circus World Museum.*

Below: This was the line-up of coaches on the 101 Ranch Real Wild West Show — *Authors' Collection. Left:* Nondescript sleepers of Golden Bros. Circus in 1924 are sidetracked alongside the wooden flatcars — *Authors' Collection.*

Above: Pride of the little Cook & Barrett's Shows was coach #7, the *Toronto*, in 1905 — *Circus World Museum. Left:* A little on the garish side, even among circus cars, was this coach of the Welsh Bros. Shows in 1900 — *Circus World Museum.*

Right: This sleeper of the Walter L. Main Circus stands high on the sidetrack in winter quarters in 1909 — *Circus World Museum.* *Above:* An observation car brings up the rear of the Al G. Barnes Circus — *William Woodcock Collection.*

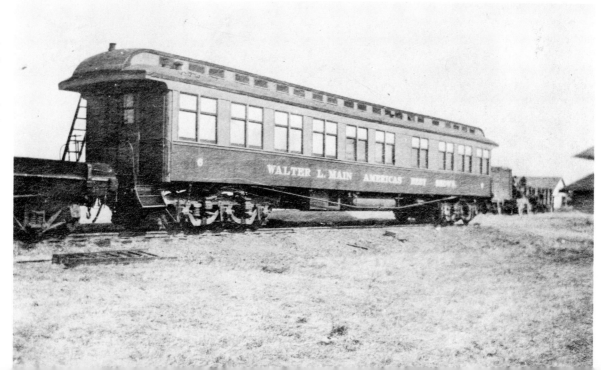

Below: The *Naomi* was part of the outfit bearing the unlikely name of Prairie Lillie & Nebraska Bill's Wild West Show in 1912 — *Authors' Collection. Left:* The combination car served Arthur Bros. Circus as a sleeper in 1945, when a postwar boom put both circus and railroad equipment in short supply. It's seen at Waukesha, Wisconsin, in July — *Authors' Photo.*

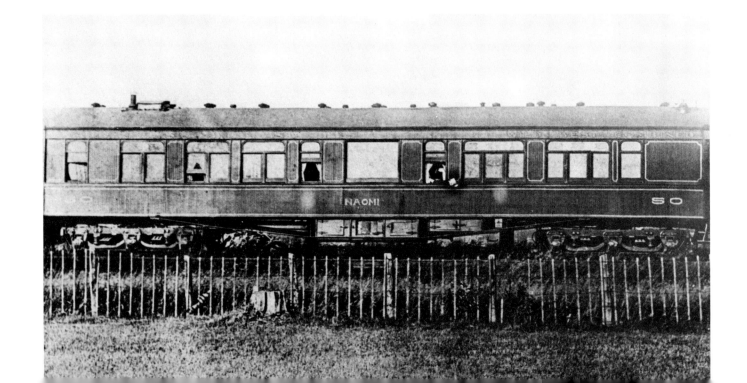

Below: Ornate iron work decorated the vestibules on cars of the Arlington & Beckmann Real Wild West in 1912. British Columbian mountains rise in the background — *Circus World Museum.* *Right:* More elaborate painting than usual marked the four coaches of Robbins Bros. Circus in 1938. Usually the last car on the train was reserved for the show owner or principal star — in this case, Jess Adkins and Hoot Gibson — *Jim McRoberts Collection.*

Above: By 1950, Ringling Bros. and Barnum & Bailey had painted its coaches silver with red trim. Inside, no evidence remained that these had once been army hospital cars. Overhead are the trolley wires of Pacific Electric at Los Angeles — *Circus World Museum.* *Left:* Midgets and giants constituted more than material for publicity shots. With circus sleepers there had to be an oversized berth for the giant and scaled-down facilities for the little people — *Authors' Collection.*

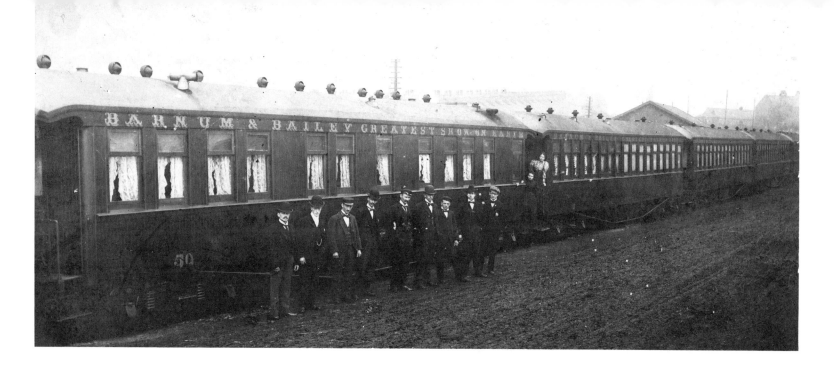

Right: Performers frequently personalized their berths on the show train by the addition of photographs, knick-knacks, and, in this case, wallpaper and lace curtains — *Circus World Museum. Above:* Car 50 was one of the eight sleepers built in England for Barnum & Bailey's five-year tour of Europe. Seen here in Germany during 1900, the cars later were repainted to take the Buffalo Bill Show on its European travels — *Circus World Museum.*

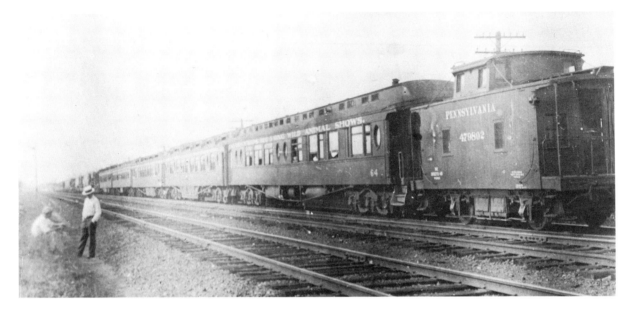

A Pennsylvania caboose with only four wheels is coupled to the owner's private car on the train of Christy Bros. Circus in 1925. Despite the presence of coaches, show trains always moved in freight service and therefore included cabooses. Since coaches were at the rear of the train, this resulted in the oddity of a caboose coupled to a passenger car — *Circus World Museum.*

The Clyde Beatty Circus started with cars from the Beckmann & Gerity carnival and replaced some with old Ringling sleepers. With four cars, one was assigned to staff, one to working men; Number 63 housed the private car, band, bosses, and ticket sellers, while 62 was the performers' car — *Gene Baxter Photo.*

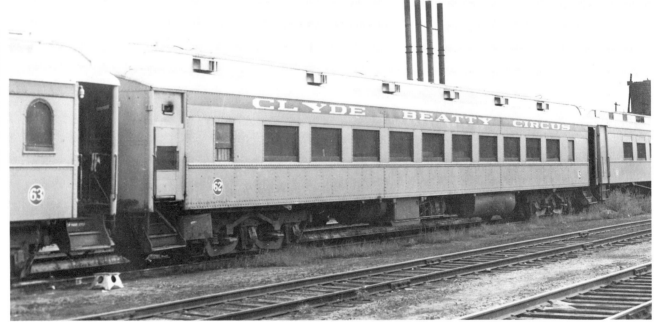

Above: The Barnes-Sells-Floto outfit included two observation cars among its eight sleepers in 1937 — *Gene Baxter Photo. Left:* Hotchkiss, Blue & Company in 1921 placed this advertisement in *The Billboard* to solicit circus car orders: "Why risk being turned down in interchange?" it asked. And indeed, circuses did have a problem in keeping up with car maintenance as well as continual development in brakes, bearings, and other car-building aspects — *Circus World Museum.*

143

Householders at Racine, Wisconsin, had new neighbors when the Great Wallace Show's sleepers were side-tracked in the neighborhood for one day in 1898 — *Chalmer Condon.*

They called it the "White Show" because nearly everything on the Sells-Floto Circus, even the flatcars and a coach named *Cody*, were painted white — *Authors' Collection.*

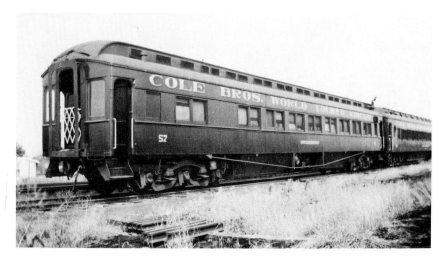

Big, blocky lettering left no doubt about the identity of these cars as the Ranch show made its 1927 campaign — *Authors' Collection*.

Circuses were one of the last strongholds for the private railroad car, and show owners prided themselves on the fittings for their homes on wheels. Zack Terrell, owner of Cole Bros. Circus, always called his car the *Owensboro* in honor of his hometown in Kentucky. An observation car #56 was the latest *Owensboro* (used in the late 1940s). It replaced an earlier *Owensboro*, #57, photographed in 1942. Sometimes, Terrell's car was green, while other coaches on the train were red — *Tedd Meyer, Gene Baxter, Circus World Museum*.

The engineer smiles proudly from the cab of Southern Pacific's oil-fired 1766, which is coupled to the Cole Bros. Circus train and Zack Terrell's *Owensboro*. Hopefully, all is going well with the show's railroading because that's the gaffer himself, Zack Terrell, striding alongside his private car — *Circus World Museum.*

Seen on the John Robinson Circus of the 1920s, Car 100, the *California*, was the private car of Jerry Mugivan, principal owner of the American Circus Corporation — *Woodcock Collection.*

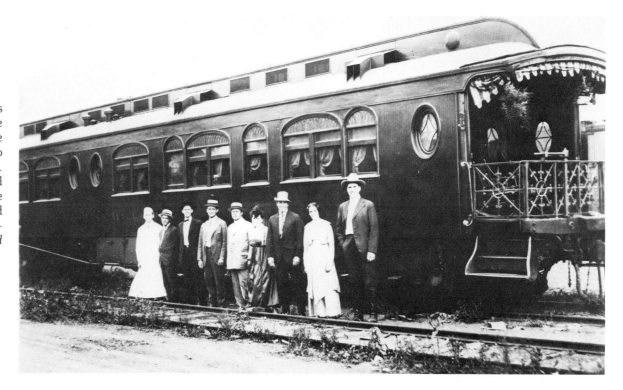

Heavyweight champion Jess Willard's own name was on the side of this private car when he was the owner of the Buffalo Bill-Jess Willard Show in 1917. Jess himself stands at the right end of the smiling group. Neither the smiles nor the private car lasted for long; the show collapsed in financial failure — *Circus World Museum.*

When Jack Tavlin operated Cole Bros. Circus in 1949, the private car was the *Saratoga Springs.* Inside, the *Saratoga Springs* was neatly outfitted with tailored couches and venetian blinds. The equine theme of the curtains and prints pointed up the interest in horses held by Tavlin's backers and owners of the car — *F. Beverly Kelley Collection.*

Above: Painted alongside of the observation platform was the quotation,

"And the night shall be filled with music,
And the cares that infest the day
Shall fold their tents like the Arabs,
And silently steal away."

— *F. Beverly Kelley Collection. Left:* Number 84, the private observation car of Charles Ringling, graces the end of the circus train at Freeport, Illinois, in 1921 — *Karl K. Knecht Collection.*

James A. Bailey's private car, #90, included a stateroom, kitchen, dining room, bathroom, and office. The car was pictured in 1897 — *Authors' Collection.*

Mr. Charley bought a new private car in 1923 and named it the *Caledonia.* It was eighty-five feet long and, like its predecessor, numbered 84. Builders' photographs show the exterior, the dining room, and a bedroom on board the *Caledonia* before the Ringlings took possession. The car saw many years of service on the circus. In recent years it has been at an off-track location near the Sarasota, Florida, airport where Art Concello, former Ringling Circus manager, has three private cars under a pole shed — *Edwin B. Luce Collection.*

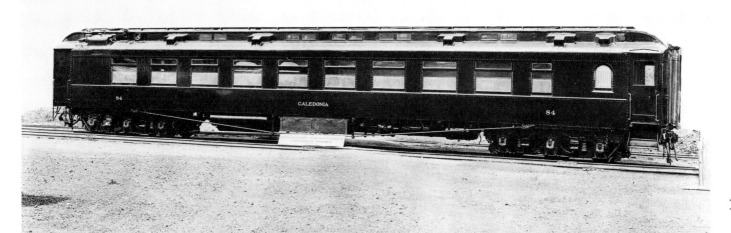

Dining room and living room of the
*Caledonia, 1923 — Edwin B. Luce
Collection.*

Sleeping compartment of the *Caledonia, 1923 — Edwin B. Luce Collection.*

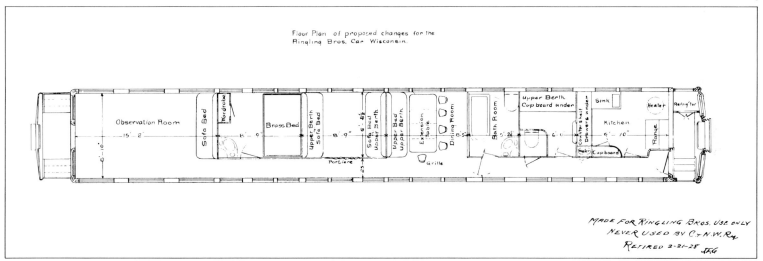

Floor Plan of proposed changes for the
Ringling Bros. Car Wisconsin.

MADE FOR RINGLING BROS. USE ONLY
NEVER USED BY C.&N.W.Ry.
RETIRED 2-21-28 J.F.G.

Another Ringling private car, the *Wisconsin,* was built by the Chicago & North Western Railway. This drawing was made in connection with proposed changes in the layout. The car was retired in 1928 — *Circus World Museum.*

Left and right: Most famous of all circus private cars was the *Jomar,* a contraction of the names of John and Mable Ringling. John lived the high life of many private car owners, cavorted with railroad presidents, and took the car on many private excursions away from the circus. Later, it was the circus home of his nephew, John Ringling North, and others of the family. Inside, the car had a comfortably fitted living room and a well-set table. The china carried the name of the car. Pictured at the show's Sarasota winter quarters in its later days, the *Jomar* was inhabited by circus employees. Later it was stored at Venice, Florida, winter quarters, where it was vandalized. Cleaned up and equipped with a new roof, the car was moved in 1973 to the Port Tampa yards of the Seaboard Coast Line, where it was stored with other obsolete circus cars — *F. Beverly Kelley Collection.*

All nine coaches used by the Tim McCoy Wild West Show of 1938 are shown in this photograph. Each car is named after an Indian tribe. The *Cheyenne* in the foreground was the private car of owner Col. Tim McCoy — *Circus World Museum.*

The Pie Car

To call it a diner was a little ostentatious; labeling it a social center was far too academic. A club car? Maybe. Circus people, however, arrived at the lowest common denominator and called it simply the pie car.

This was where the show's personnel gathered after the night performance for visiting, for food and drink, and perhaps for a game of cards or dice. Its operation was let out as a concession in many cases, run by the show in others. Typically, a circus devoted a half or a full car of its limited train space to pie car purposes. The biggest shows had a pie car in each section of their trains, and medium-sized circuses might well have half of one car for working men and half of another for performers and staff. In each there was a short-order food operation; some had a bar and the game.

In only rare instances was the pie car intended for feeding the people their main meals. Normally, that was done by the cookhouse under canvas, and those meals were free, while pie car fare came at a price. An exception was the seven-car Harris Nickel Plate Shows, a turn-of-the-century circus that had no cookhouse and fed its people on the train three times a day. The Harris horse opera was small enough to do this. Two-car shows usually fed on the cars also, but not until the space was cleared of whatever circus cargo was packed there for the jump.

When a show faced an extra long run, the cookhouse made up dukies—free box lunches—for distribution on the train en route. Still, the pie car was sure to get volume business as the bored show people whiled away long hours on the slow train.

Today the two Ringling Bros. and Barnum & Bailey trains each have a pie car—Number 45 on the Red unit and Number 151 on the Blue. These prove to be exceptions to the historical rule, for these are in fact dining cars in which a large portion of the show's people eat most of their meals. But they also operate on the old pie car format; short orders are served from early breakfast to midnight snack. And the cars are the neighborhood gathering places when the show is en route or where troupers relax after a night performance.

Part of every show train was the pie car. The Great Patterson Shows called it a diner, but it's a safe bet that all of the employees referred to it only as the pie car — *Circus World Museum.*

This was the interior of a Ringling pie car in 1902 — *Albert Conover Collection.*

156

Firewood, cleaning buckets, and supplies clutter the ornate vestibule of the Ringling pie car in 1902 — *Albert Conover Collection.*

Caviar sur Canape

Bisque of Oyster   Consomme en Tassie

Chow-Chow   Celery   Stuffed Olives

Baked Red Snapper a la Joinville

Pommes au Natural

Boiled Leg of Mutton, Bretonne

Fillet of Beef a la Jardiniere

Escalloped Oysters, Coney Island Style

Souffle a l'Orange

Roast Ribs of Prime Beef au Jus

Stuffed Young Turkey, Cranberry Jelly

Potatoes, Boiled or Mashed

Asparagus in Cream

Carrots and Peas

Candied Yams

Lobster Salad   Lettuce, Sauce Mayonnaise

English Plum Pudding, Brandy Sauce

Vanilla Ice Cream   Assorted Cake

Boston Cream Puffs

Lemon Meringue Pie   Hot Mince Pie

Fruit

Cheese   Crackers

Coffee   Tea   Cocoa

On the Ringling dining cars of 1903 you could celebrate the end of the season with a menu that featured red snapper, fillet of beef, escalloped oysters, lobster salad, plum pudding, and other delicacies — *Authors' Collection.*

157

Modern pie cars on the current editions of Ringling Bros. and Barnum & Bailey Circus are pleasant rolling restaurants where circus people congregate for dining and socializing — *Jim McRoberts*.

Show Moves

A circus came to life even as the show train rocked and rattled through the night. In the predawn hours most of the responsibility lay with the railroad and its crew in getting the show over the road. At this point the show was as dormant as it ever would be, but there still was action.

Traditionally, one man was riding shotgun in the ticket wagon to guard the receipts of the prior night's show. Other watchmen were alert to potential problems ranging from fire and accident to ailing animals or hoboes. While most people slept, some left the confines of the hot coaches for the comparative comfort of the flatcars—not so soft, but cooler and more pleasant on fresh summer mornings.

In advance of the scheduled arrival time, a man moved along the top of the stockcars and pulled the chains which opened mangers to the baggage stock inside. Another man wended his way along the flats to the cookhouse boiler wagon and stoked up the fire; starting then meant that breakfast could be ready sooner when the wagon reached the distant showgrounds.

Waiting at the depot or the yard office of the day's show town was the twenty-four-hour man, last in the series of circus advance agents and so named because he traveled just twenty-four hours ahead of the show. He was checking then on the progress of the train. On the prior day he had telegraphed the circus trainmaster with loading instructions for today's town. A principal point was the direction the wagons should be facing when they arrived at today's sidetrack. Instructions would have read, "Poles to engine" or "Poles to caboose," and referred not to the center poles for the big top, but rather to the wagon poles or tongues. It may have been necessary during the move to find a wye and turn the train around so that it would be positioned correctly on arrival. Even Coup hadn't figured a good way to unload backwards.

Now that the show train eased into the yards, the twenty-four-hour man swung aboard to be sure that the bosses and crews were awake. If it was not yet dawn, they grumbled about having to "get up in a tunnel."

What transpired in the ensuing hour or two was a process little changed through all the years of railroad circusing. Whether the 1870s or the 1970s, whether a 10-car show or a 100-car show, it was the same process, and it fairly bristled with the organization and efficiency for which circuses always had been renowned.

Ringling called its first section the flying squadron. Whether on a big show with more than one section or on the usual one-train circus, the flatcars were loaded so that the wagons needed first on the lot were first to come off of the cars. Wagons were positioned in a predetermined sequence according to lengths so as to achieve maximum use of all flatcar space. A seventy-foot flatcar should carry seventy feet of wagons, or close to it.

The concept by which the first needed was the first off is paired nicely with the loading principle that the first available is the first loaded at night. Handily, the two requirements were compatible.

Supper was served about 4:30 p.m., so the cookhouse could be loaded onto the train even before the night performance started. Since baggage stock was back at work, the stable tents could be loaded, too. No need for the calliope on the lot any longer, so it was also sent to the train early.

By the time the night show started, the menagerie had served its purpose, so it was loaded. It was an old axiom of circus going that when you came out after the show things looked so different you'd be momentarily lost; that was because the menagerie had been dismantled in the meantime. One couldn't plan to look at the animals on the way home.

Right from the first, the 1872 Barnum show alerted the public to this: "The animal cages will be closed for the evening at 8 p.m. o'clock in order to prepare for loading the three immense trains required for transportation of this Great World's Fair." Every railroad circus since had loaded the menagerie as soon as the night show got underway.

Throughout the night, everything was loaded as quickly as it had served its purpose on the lot. By the time the performance was over, most of the show had been taken to the train. If the electrical generator wagon had to be kept for lighting the lot until the last minute, no harm was done; it was the last thing needed tomorrow anyway. Often, the power plant was literally the last thing on and off the train, and the last thing on and off the lot.

Ringling-Barnum's loading order of 1955 followed such a pattern. The first wagon carried the dining tent; the first four flats carried the range wagons, cookhouse supplies, dishwasher wagons, and the rest of the dining department. The next couple of cars carried the sideshow—it was taken down as soon as the night show started in this case, but often it was kept in action for the blow-off—the end of the night show.

Next came three flats with animals and spec wagons—first of the menagerie items and things pertaining to the early part of the performance. In sequence then came four flatcars with the cages, another with the ticket wagons, and another three with more spec floats aboard. That completed the first section.

Loaded second but moving third was the section that included eleven flats, each with two thirty-five-foot seat wagons which could not be loaded until after the night show. They comprised the seats and also contained a wide assortment of equipment including wardrobe, performers' trunks, and props for the show. These could be loaded before the tent came down and had to wait for the tent to go up in the new town; hence, the switch in loading and arrival sequence.

The second section to arrive carried the big top—canvas, poles, rigging, stakes—and a lot of trucks and tractors. In it, too, were concession wagons, ring stock equipment, and the bandwagon, all of which were used late in the old town and new town alike. On the last flatcar was the big top power plant.

Nearly every loading order reflected the basic sequence in which equipment was needed at the showgrounds—cookhouse, menagerie, sideshow, big top, seats, rigging, props, wardrobe, lights.

Even in the earliest times, some shows found it necessary to reposition certain cuts of cars within the train after it was loaded. This switching process became almost universal when circuses replaced baggage horses with tractors. The horses, coming to and from side door stockcars, were available at any time. But tractors had to go on the flats. If a Cat were loaded early for use in the morning, it was out of action for the rest of the night's loading. It wasn't practical for shows to carry dual sets of trucks and tractors, so typically the last flat was loaded with such motive power, and then a switch engine set that car at the head end of the train for use in the morning.

With the Clyde Beatty Circus there were nine flats, operated in three cuts. The loading sequence was Cars 55-57-56-59-58, Car 53, and Cars 51-54-52. But for unloading it was Cars 51-54-52, Car 53, and Cars 55-57-56-59-58.

Flats 51 and 52 were loading flats or runs cars—those equipped with runs, snubbing posts, and extra reinforcement at one end of each. Regardless of whether the train was loaded poles to engine or poles to caboose, one of these flats always was in the proper place for loading and unloading. Flats 57 and 59 were seventy-foot models and were located in the train so as to be in the same relative position, regardless of the switching. In this way, wagons assigned to them would fit. The others were seventy-two-foot Warren flats. The longest cut carried equipment that could be loaded first but wasn't needed first. The cookhouse and big top canvas were on Cars 51 and 53. Poles, stakes, tractors, and lights were on Cars 54 and 52.

An incoming show train was shunted to a sidetrack at the crossing. In show terminology, the crossing was that special one at which the show would be unloaded. While the train was still moving, the crossing could be identified by the crowd waiting there. If the townspeople were out in such numbers as to overflow the street and railroad area, some showmen called it a straw house crossing—borrowing the phrase "straw house" from its usual reference to an overflow crowd in the big top. If the crossing had sidetracks to permit simultaneous unloading of two cuts, it was dubbed a double-barrelled crossing. Sometimes a train was split in the middle to use two facing runs, with the crossing between them. In such a case, the flats had been loaded part poles to caboose and part poles to engine.

Working with the railroad's train crew, the circus trainmaster paced off twenty-eight feet from the crossing to designate where the first flat should be spotted. Then he gathered about him the circus train crew to set the runs. Circus train crewmen were called razorbacks. The term had nothing to do with Arkansas hogs, but originated instead with the use of cross cages. These were smaller wagons which could be placed crosswise on the flats to save loading

space. They were lifted physically and turned ninety degrees. In this process the circus trainmaster gave the order: "Raise your backs"—razorbacks.

To a railroader, runs are trips—those events that happen between DEPARTS and ARRIVES. But to a circus man, trips are moves or jumps. And the runs are the ramps that carry wagons from flatcar to street. In another general usage, the runs were the whole loading area, roughly synonymous with the crossing.

Circusing polarized around two places each day—the lot for the performance and the runs for the transportation, the trouping. The performance always was the reason for the whole effort. But often the matter of merely existing, living, and getting on with it put the emphasis on the runs and the railroading. Morning progress at the runs determined how soon breakfast could be served. Good progress at the runs at night meant an early start for the next town—a good night's rest.

In full command at the runs was the circus trainmaster, who worked closely with the boss hostler or the tractor boss. Phillip Anthony McGrath, trainmaster for Ringling Bros. and Barnum & Bailey in the late 1940s and with various shows for thirty years, explained his job very simply: "Get it loaded, get it unloaded, get it on the lot." That was what it was all about.

A division superintendent on the Pennsylvania Railroad called his terminal supervisor to ask if the unloading of the Ringling circus were progressing and if Trainmaster McGrath were satisfied. "He's satisfied all right, or he'd be in here snarling at me," came the reply. "Silence is a compliment in his language."

Harold Ingram was a circus trainmaster on several shows, large and small. As a youngster he joined out as poler on the Campbell Bros. Circus. He continued with Ringling Bros. World's Greatest Shows and in 1912 became poler for Hagenbeck-Wallace. He was on the train crew with Sells-Floto in 1919. Night after night the show was running late, not leaving town until 2:30 a.m. because of slow loading. Presumably, that's why the management changed trainmasters, and Ingram got the call. On his first night in command it was pouring down rain—poor circus weather—but he got the show loaded by 11:30 p.m. The railroad moved it out, stranding twenty-three performers who had become accustomed to the later departures.

Ingram once explained that loading a circus train was the same regardless of size or year:

With the flats spotted for the move-out, the first job was to place the thirty-foot runs. They were pulled from the flatcar deck by a train team or by the train crew. Runs were supported by a set of six jacks of graduated size. Then the trainmaster called for the first wagons. Since each was of a different length, they had to be loaded in the right sequence so that all would fit on the tightly loaded train.

When a wagon with a hitch of perhaps eight horses came from the lot and entered the crossing, an assistant with a practiced eye set a chock at a rear wheel at the correct moment. The team would then swing the wagon around and line it up squarely with the runs. A catcher set another chock under a wheel to stop the wagon. This was called "spotting the crossing."

The long-string hitch was moved away, and a poler moved to his spot in front of the wagon. A pull-up team swung into position, and a hook-rope boy put his hook into the front corner bull ring on the wagon. Two blasts on the trainmaster's whistle and the pull-up team earned its name; with the poler guiding it, the wagon was towed up the runs and onto the flat by the team, which moved on the ground alongside the flats. A man skidded a chock along behind a wagon wheel to stop any roll-back if a rope should fail. Once the wagon was up on the deck, he brought it to a halt. A deck poler took over from the runs poler, and the pull-over team replaced the pull-up team to move the wagon down the flats and over the cross-over plates to its proper spot on the train.

The back end crew—two front chockers, two wheelers, and two rear chockers—waited for the next step

in the process. The wagon pole pin was lifted, and the pole was pulled from the running gear and dropped to the deck. The wagon rolled on, straddling its pole and steered by the wheelers who manhandled the front wheels for the final twelve feet. Chocks were placed on the flatcar deck, and the wagon was rolled into them and up their sloping faces. This drove the chock spurs into the deck. A blast from the back end foreman's whistle stopped the pull-over team. Before the front wheels began to roll back down the chock faces, the back chockers went into action. They slammed home their chocks, while the backward roll of the wagon set these spurs. The wagon was thus secured front and back. The crew awaited the next wagon, which another pull-over team probably had close at hand.

As the final wagon was loaded on each flat, the crew flip-flopped the cross-over plates. One was turned to the forward flat and one to the rear flat so that regardless of later switching, each car would have the needed two cross-over plates. If two plates had been flipped to one flat, the crew would sometimes come up short.

In loading, the pull-up team used a direct pull with small or medium wagons. But heavier loads called for using a snatch block. This was a single block and tackle arrangement; from a ring in the middle of the flat, a rope ran back over the runs, then around the pulley and back to the lead bars of the pull-up team. With the pulley hooked to the wagon, the team could handle the heavier loads.

The most dangerous job on any railroad circus was that of the poler. If a wagon wheel hit a stone, cinder, or gunnel while he was guiding it along the flat, the eleven- and one-half-foot pole could snap to one side or the other. One way it could break his legs; the other way it yanked him headlong off the flat. A big show might have ten or fifteen polers, since several could be required at once. Some were deck polers to take wagons over the flats. Others were chute polers to guide wagons toward and over the runs.

Unloading the show train was a similar process.

Polers set the cross-over plates in position between

each pair of flats. The back end crew loosened the chocks. Each wagon was used to tow the wagon pole out from under the next wagon. In this process, a ring on the end of a five-foot rope was looped over the gooseneck on the pole, and the other end of the rope was tied with a quick-release loop to the forward wagon. When the latter had moved the pole far enough, the train crewman gave a tug to free the rope. The forward wagon went on; crewmen lifted the pole and placed it on the remaining wagon.

Just before the pull-over team got the wagon to the end of the flats, a hook rope was popped into the bull ring on a rear corner of the wagon. That rope went to the snubber, who worked alongside of and midpoint with the first flat or runs car. If the roadbed wasn't high enough there, he placed a board under the car, hooking it under the far rail and running it over the near rail, lever fashion. He stood on the elevated end. The hook-rope man, working on the car deck, had a small platform to attach to the sill or gunnel, and he could stand on it as wagons rolled past him.

The snubber manned an all-important braking system. Each runs car had either one or two snubbing posts—a steel post or spools attached to the side of the car. The snubber either wrapped his rope around a single post or looped it figure-eight fashion around twin posts. The hook-rope man attached the far end of the rope to the wagon. The snubber let out enough rope to allow the wagon to roll down the runs. At the right moment, he pulled down on his end of the rope, tightening it around the post and halting the wagon that was some sixty-five feet away. The snubber could stop the feed-out and halt the wagon earlier if there were an emergency or problem.

While the wagon rolled down the runs under control of the snubber, the pull-over team's hook-rope was detached from the front ring, and the team wheeled around to go for another wagon. As soon as the rear wheels of the wagon cleared the runs and rested on the street, the snubber halted it; his hook-rope boy unhooked and brought the rope back up the runs to meet the next wagon.

A man from the crossing gang climbed aboard the wagon to operate its foot or hand brakes. Another hooked a pull-away team to the wagon by slipping a four-inch ring, on the end of its thirty-inch chain, over the gooseneck on the end of the wagon pole. The team then moved the wagon out of the crossing and down the street, where it would be out of the way of the train crew and soon would be picked up by the team and driver that would take it to the lot.

The whole process was a matter of coordinated team work, an application of tonnage, powerful horseflesh, and some fundamental devices of physics. In this dangerous game, proud men moved the shows with dedication and dispatch.

This system with horses prevailed from 1872 until the 1940s. Ringling replaced its horses with elephants in 1939 and with tractors and trucks soon after. Cole Bros. kept eight or ten baggage horses for use as train teams through 1950, as did Dailey Bros. The Clyde Beatty Circus had train teams in 1951.

The modified system oriented to trucks and tractors continued most of the old ways and picked up some modifications. The cuts of cars, the runs, crossing, cross-over plates, and poles to caboose or engine all remained unchanged. Ed Lester, a show train buff turned pro, detailed the process when tractors were used by Ringling Bros. and Barnum & Bailey Circus:

New-styled poles were hinged to fold upward against the front of the wagons. Two polers swung the pole down into place and affixed it with a chain. Others in the crew had set the runs and pried loose the chocks. First off was Number 8, the dining tent wagon. Behind it was the D-4 Caterpillar crossing tractor, which nudged the wagon forward until it rolled down the runs. A safety chain linked the wagon to the tractor behind. Once on the street, the D-4 began its chores as crossing Cat by pulling 8 Wagon over to the side to await other power.

Meanwhile, back on the flat, the third unit was an AC

Mack water truck, which moved forward a few feet until a whistle blast stopped it. Two polers leapt behind it to reach the next wagon and place its pole. Three blasts signalled the driver to back up to couple to the wagon pole. Then, two whistle toots and he drove the combination of truck and wagon forward and down the runs. Away from the crossing, it might be stopped to add the 8 Wagon with the dining tent to the tow. It would then head for the lot. The process was repeated back on the flats as a concentration of trucks and tractors linked up with wagons and moved out. Some trucks crept forward in several short takes to allow for hooking three or four wagons to their tows. Then the whole string trailed off of the train, straight to the lot.

Soon, all of the trucks and tractors had moved, but long rows of additional wagons remained. The crossing Cat then backed up the runs, down the flats, and over the plates to reach the waiting wagons. Meanwhile, another tractor was working alongside the flats in the manner of an old pull-over team. Called a Mule, it pulled the wagon forward to allow for hooking the next one to it. It prepared the sets of wagons that the crossing Cats would take along the flats and to the street.

When the first truck returned from the lot to get another load, it picked up the wagons just unloaded by the Cat. Crewmen sounded their whistles in one's, two's, and three's to signal the drivers. Those trucks and drivers that loaded early the night before and worked first in the mornings would make the most round trips. Those loaded to the rear of the train made more trips at night, fewer in the morning unloadings.

Once a cut was unloaded, the crew knocked the jacks out from under the runs, manhandled the runs onto the deck, then threw the jacks aboard. The back end crew came forward, flipping cross-over plates as it went and kicking chocks to the center of the cars.

As other cuts and even other sections arrived, the tempo picked up. More train hands were present now. Runs were pulled; jacks were set. Now there were sufficient tractors and trucks to keep a steady flow of wagons hitting the street and heading for the showgrounds. It took about eleven minutes to unload the nine flats of the gas cut.

On the second section was 44 Wagon, the heavy load of big top quarter poles. This load was fifty feet long; together with a twenty-foot AC Mack to tow it, they filled a seventy-two-foot flat. But the next combination dwarfed them. It was another D-4 crossing Cat and 43 Wagon, itself a lengthy piece of equipment and its load the sixty-two-foot big top center poles. Together they added up to seventy-three feet of load for the seventy-two-foot Warren. But that was not all. Behind the wagon and nestled under its overhanging poles was a twelve-foot Jeep. The Cat took the monster pole wagon down the runs and eased all of its length through the crossing.

By then, three crossing Cats were at work, efficiently rolling the wagons. One tractor separated wagons for coupling; the other two hauled sets of wagons forward to cut down the distance the crossing Cats had to back up. Faster and faster, the flats were cleared.

Part of the second section and all of the third were made up of flats loaded with Ringling's seat wagons. These were thirty-five-foot monsters; each pair filled a flat. They were coupled in pairs, and with all of the show's tractors and trucks now available, the fourteen flatloads of seat wagons were hustled to the lot in short order.

As the job was done, drivers headed for the showgrounds, and the train crew turned to a gilly bus for a ride to the lot, where breakfast was awaiting them. Later in the day, the railroaders switched the cars as requested by the circus trainmaster so that they would be in position for loading at night. This might involve a transfer to another railroad and the possibility of loading at a different crossing than was used in the unloading.

Equal efficiency and ingenuity were conspicuous when the show loaded out that night. As Lester recorded, the gilly bus pulled up to the runs again at 6 p.m. and disgorged the train crew. Right behind it came the fleet of roaring tractors.

One had the crossing light plant, Wagon 130, in tow. Another brought the blacksmith wagon, others the dining wagons.

A stake was sledged into place near the crossing end of each cut, and a hollow pole holding a light cluster was slipped over each stake, then wired to the power plant. Other cables were plugged into the sockets at the side of each runs car. Circus flats were equipped with an electrical circuit along the sides; more cable spanned the distance between each pair of flats. There were six clips on the side of each flat to receive angle iron brackets to which light bulbs were affixed. Each such light was plugged into the built-in sockets. Now the train power plant roared into life, and the row of lamps provided a ribbon of light all along the cut of flats.

Meanwhile, the runs were placed again, hammered into position, blocked up with jacks, and chained to the flat.

The street crew hooked the first wagon to the crossing Cat, which moved into the crossing until it was abreast of the runs. It pivoted sharply, pulled the wagon into alignment with the runs, and pivoted again at right angles with the runs and wagon so that it could be disconnected and driven out of the way.

Six men jumped to simultaneous jobs. One set the wagon brake. One disconnected the Cat from the wagon pole. Two supported the loose pole until another could chain it into horizontal position. And another hooked a wire cable to the wagon's forward bull ring.

The cable was connected to another Cat which then moved alongside the flats, putting a strain on the cable to ease the wagon forward; two polers would heave and push until the wagon was "in the chute," or directly lined up with the runs. They continued to guide it as the tractor gave it more speed and the wagon rolled up the runs and onto the deck. Polers, hooker, and Cat all moved back to the crossing for another wagon.

With a different poler in action, that first wagon also had a D-4 Cat behind it to push it across the flats to the end of the cut. An option provided for a tractor to pull it from the side if the adjacent space was available.

At the far end was the chocking crew—a head chocker, four chockers, a pin man, brakeman, hooker, two pole men, and a Mule driver with the set-in Mule. As they received each wagon, two polers took over the guiding, and the hooker connected the Mule to the bull ring. The head chocker's whistle signalled the Mule to take the wagon to within about five feet of the end of the car (or later, the prior wagon). Two forward chocks had been placed. The brakeman released the wagon, and it was taken forward slowly until the front wheels rested against the chocks. There was a pause, then two blasts on the whistle. The driver gunned the Mule, ramming the wagon wheels against the chocks and driving the spikes into the deck. As the wagon rolled slightly up the face of the chocks, the rear chockers slammed their chocks behind the rear wheels. The Mule slacked off, and the wagon hunched backward, affixing the rear chocks and settling into its secure position.

Following that first wagon was the D-4 Cat, which pushed the wagon across the flats and which in the morning would push the wagon off the car as well. It moved against its own front chocks and rocked back against the rear ones.

Now trucks were arriving at the crossing, each with its string of one or more wagons, all arranged in the proper sequence to both fit on the flats and meet the first needs on the lot at the next town. Each driver made a wide swing to line up with runs, then went full throttle toward the runs. A hooker connected the cable to the first wagon, and the D-6 backed up, thus aiding the truck in towing the heavy wagons up the runs. With all on the deck, the D-6 was disconnected, and the truck took its tow along the cut. When the truck stopped at the far end, the pin man disconnected the wagons and truck from each other so that the individual chocking could proceed.

As each flat was filled, two men ran a chain through the rear wheels of the end wagon and fastened it to the gunnels of the flat as an added safety feature. The same pair manhandled the 200-pound cross-over plates from their bridge between flats to the deck of each flat, between the wagon wheels. The electrician pulled the light plugs and removed the light bracket as each car was loaded. At the distant crossing, the trainmaster could gauge the progress by watching darkness engulf the cars as the lights went out, leaving a shorter lighted string still to be loaded.

Once the cookhouse wagons and the stake drivers had been loaded, there was a pause in the operation. The train hands could rest until the arrival of the menagerie, and that did not happen until the night show began. Trucks coming hereafter would return to the lot for additional loads. As each approached with a set of wagons, a street man sounded a stop signal and darted in to uncouple the wagons. Another snatched the lantern from the rear wagon. The driver wheeled around, let up as the street man hooked the lantern to this truck, and then accelerated toward the lot and another load.

A D-4 Cat now backed up to the first wagon and towed it into alignment with the runs. Quickly, another D-4 brought the second wagon forward. Meanwhile, the first was taken over by a D-6, which pulled it up onto the runs but then stopped. When the second wagon was aligned, the D-6 eased the first back down the runs to permit coupling the pair. With each wagon, the six-man simultaneous operation prepared it for the runs. With the second wagon linked now, the D-6 again backed up, pulling the two wagons forward until the second one halted on the inclined runs. In a moment it would be inched backward to make contact with a third wagon. When a flatcar-load of wagons was coupled, the Cat backed up until the whole set was resting on the flat deck.

A tractor driver and poler worked in unison to pull and guide the loaded wagon string along the flats and toward the less distant spot at which the chocking crew now worked. Before they had gone very far, another set of wagons was on deck, and another tractor was hooked on to follow the first along the flats. When the flow was at a peak,

one set of wagons was in the street, one was at the runs, two were moving across the flats, and one was being chocked—all simultaneously.

When a cut was loaded, the jacks were knocked from beneath the runs, and one run was centered. The D-6 crossing Cat had a small crane with which it lifted the low end of the run. The Cat then rammed the run onto the flatcar. A Mule towed it forward to allow room for the loading of the second run. With the cookhouse cut and the cage cut then loaded, they were switched off to make up the first section. The seat cut was switched into the crossing site and runs were placed. Part of the train crew was released to accompany the first section and be available to start the whole process anew the next day.

The loading of the long seat wagons followed, and when the seat cut was complete, the switcher took it aside to await its spot as the third section. The wagon cut was loaded next. By this time, the fleet of trucks and tractors, each with its final wagons of the night, was amassing in the street. A D-4 nudged the initial wagon aboard the final section of flats—the gas cut. In quick succession, the trucks roared into place, took a wide arc to line up their wagons, and climbed the runs to take their place aboard the train.

There were two pauses in this period. One came whenever the ring stock and elephants plodded past on their way to the stockcars that were spotted nearby. The other came when the massive pole wagon came on the scene. With it, the truck was unhitched, and the D-4 slowly pivoted it into place. Care was taken to see that the overhanging poles, sixty-two feet back, were not sweeping away some utility pole, front porch, or signal box.

The crossing lights were lowered and loaded. A station wagon came down the street; a basket on its bumper contained the flares that had been retrieved from corners where they had marked the route for drivers to follow between lot and runs. The station wagon drove up the runs. A D-4 took the crossing light plant aboard; the light plant still was running, and floodlights on its roof illuminated the area until the final minute. The set-in Mule had worked its way from the far end of each cut and now it climbed the runs. Last aboard was the D-6 pull-up tractor, and its rear crane fed out a cable to pull the runs up behind it. Train hands heaved the jacks and blocking onto the runs car. The train was loaded. The bus took the crew to their coach. Other circus people also had found their way to the cars and had retired.

At the crossing there was a quiet word to the railroad crew. A lantern marked a colorful arc. Silently, the flatcars rolled away to find the rest of their section.

The circus was gone.

* * * * *

Each circus day was the same for the train crew, with the exception of the last day. That was when there was no tomorrow and the train made its home run to winter quarters.

It was over the winter that the circus was refurbished. The train, like other show property, was put into top shape to start the next year's tour. Often, new cars were added to a growing show. Cars were painted. Heavier maintenance was done.

Many circuses maintained no permanent base; they might lease winter space at a fairgrounds or in some empty warehouse. Perhaps the next winter would be spent in a different place. In each case, the show sought a location that included side trackage where no demurrage would come due and where work could be done on the cars.

The bigger shows often had permanent quarters. Barnum & Bailey went home to Bridgeport, Connecticut. Al G. Barnes was at Baldwin Park, California; Sparks Circus was at Macon, Georgia; Sells Floto at Denver; Gollmar Bros. at Baraboo, Wisconsin; Hagenbeck-Wallace at West Baden or Peru, Indiana; Forepaugh at Philadelphia; John Robinson, Cincinnati; Sells Bros., Columbus, Ohio; and Ringling Bros., at Baraboo, Wisconsin.

The Gollmar quarters were small and included no train space. Their twenty-five cars were stored on C&NW Rail-way tracks and renovated one at a time in railroad-owned buildings.

Ringling, also in Baraboo, leased land in 1889-90 on which to build trackage for their new train. Cars were refurbished by the C&NW; sometimes circus cars were repainted in empty stalls of the Division roundhouse.

More space was leased from the railroad in 1897, and in 1909 ten acres adjoining the C&NW right-of-way were acquired, and new car shops were built by the circus. The main building had three tracks running through it. It could accommodate a dozen sixty-foot cars at a time. The railroad laid tracks from the main line onto Ringling property, with switchbacks into the new buildings. Roadmaster L. C. Ryan supervised the job.

Since the circus had no locomotive, it used horsepower for moving cars. Orville Kramer recalled that teams of two or four horses were sent over, depending upon the type of car, grade, and depth of the snow. If mechanical work was needed, the car was picked up by the railroad and moved a quarter of a mile to its yards.

At Bridgeport, Barnum & Bailey's quarters were next to the New York, New Haven & Hartford, with sidetracks leading into a circus building especially for train work. Similarly, when the Combined show moved to Sarasota, Florida, it built its own yards for 100 cars and a shop for maintenance work.

Typical winter work included the redecking of flatcars, greasing of king pins, and general repair of stocks and coaches. Often, the entire train was repainted and lettered with the show's title. Usually, circus cars were taken to a nearby railroad's shops where the journals were repacked and the air brake system was blown out. New stenciling declared that the cars were ready to go.

With similar work completed in other departments, the show was set for another season, another 10,000 or 15,000 miles of railroading. The advertising car moved out first. In a couple of weeks, the runs were in place and the trainmaster's whistle cued the razorbacks and teamsters. The whole process was under way again.

Wheeling tonnage through the night is the railroad's solo part in its twenty-four-hour duet with the circus, for this is the only time in the cycle that the show is nearly dormant. With Kenosha behind it, the Chicago & North Western extra crew takes a Ringling section toward Sheboygan, Wisconsin, for August 26, 1952 — *Authors' Photo.*

Right: It's 1:30 A.M. in tiny Wales, Wisconsin (population 691), and the C&NW station agent is on duty because the railroad is handling three sections of the Ringling-Barnum circus train. It's also July 25, 1951, and the big show is en route from Milwaukee to Madison — *Authors' Photo. Below:* First into Wales is the Ringling flying squadron, or first section, the railroad's #2701 extra. Earlier at Waukesha, a second locomotive was added to push the heavy circus train up and over a severe grade. The stop at Wales is to give up the extra power. Two more sections of the show train would follow the same procedure during the night — *Authors' Photo.*

Morning sun casts a long shadow as the seven flats of Gentry Bros. Circus snake around a curve in desolate western country. Ahead are the engine and stockcars. A bandsman, Walker Morris, took the photograph from a coach in 1922 — *Authors' Collection.*

170

Opposite page, below: With white flags snapping, a C&NW locomotive pulls Ringling's second section toward Madison, Wisconsin, in 1950. The first flat in this train was the last loaded. On board is Wagon 130, the train light plant, used to illuminate the crossing the night before. The show's twenty-four-hour agent had instructed the circus trainmaster to load his cars poles to caboose — *Authors' Photo. Right, above:* Extra 1519, an EMD F-3 1500 hp diesel, totes the Clyde Beatty train of fifteen cars into Boise over the Union Pacific's Idaho division in 1953. Immediately behind the locomotive is a flat-load of cages with Beatty's performing lions and tigers — *Henry R. Griffiths, Jr. Collection. Right, below:* Four years earlier on the same Union Pacific division, this Mountain type 4-8-2 locomotive, #7855, pulled the same Clyde Beatty Circus into Burley, Idaho. The train is laid out in standard format — first the stockcar, so as to minimize the jolting of elephants and horses, then the flatcars, and finally the coaches — *Henry R. Griffiths, Jr. Collection.*

This Gentry Bros. Circus move in 1922 boasted a Union Pacific double header, leading off with Locomotive 6069 — *Walker Morris Collection*.

The Cole Bros. Circus train stretches out over a Southern Pacific trestle. Shortly after the train cleared the river, the cab-forward Locomotive 1223 ran through an open switch — *Circus World Museum*.

Above: Eight flats, each with a pair of thirty-five-foot Ringling seat wagons, tag along after a C&NW locomotive en route from Kenosha, Wisconsin, to Sheboygan in 1952. The show train is wrapped up, with a trestle on the under side and a column of smoke across the top — *Authors' Photo. Right:* Often as not, circus trains moved under slow orders since railroaders tended to be unsure of the rolling stock and its lading. Here, an NC&StL crewman picks up orders for a move out of Nashville in 1947 — *Authors' Photo.*

Show people stretch their legs alongside the show train of the Great Wallace Circus somewhere in Kansas in 1899. Then and now, stops — either unscheduled or operational — were a fact of life for show train moves — *Authors' Collection*.

Headed northward out of Chicago for Milwaukee, the third section of Ringling Bros. and Barnum & Bailey Circus moves at thirty miles per hour on the C&NW Railway. This was 1947, the first year the show had its string of twenty-five new red coaches, all eighty-five-foot steel models, purchased from war surplus — *Authors' Photo.*

A frilly little float from the spectacle is next to a rough and ready Caterpillar tractor in a typical circus contrast as the North Western wheels the show train toward Milwaukee. Already a driver is in the seat of the tractor, enjoying the morning air — *Authors' Photo.*

Locomotive 2514, flying the white flags of a special train, heads up a Ringling move on the left-handed C&NW Railway into Milwaukee from Chicago in 1947 — *Authors' Photo.*

Above: North Western's diesels 1557 and 1601 bring the remodeled Ringling train of coaches and tunnel cars into Baraboo, Wisconsin, in July 1962 — *Authors' Photo. Right:* Smoke obscures the head end as the Ringling move reaches the outskirts of Milwaukee in 1947 and the C&NW becomes four tracks wide — *Authors' Photo.*

Above: Mack trucks and pole wagons ride backwards on Thrall flatcars as the North Western moves the Ringling train toward Madison, Wisconsin, in 1950 — *Authors' Photo. Right:* Coaches come into view as more flats rumble through a cut on the North Western near Dousman en route to Madison in 1950 — *Authors' Photo.*

179

The Milwaukee Road kept Locomotive 415 busy in circus service during August 1946. First it trundled the third section across Wisconsin countryside between LaCrosse, where it played on August 20, and Madison, where it played on August 21 and 22. Then, 415 pulled duty with Ringling's first section in the move from Madison to Beloit for circus appearances on August 23 — *Authors' Photos.*

Above: While show people are looking for their town of the day, townspeople are clustered around the crossing where the show train will stop. Maybe they have waited for hours. Then suddenly a headlight cuts through the early dawn, and the circus train has arrived — *Authors' Collection.*

Iconographic Collection, State Historical Society of Wisconsin

The Thrill That Comes Once in a Lifetime: BY H. T. WEBSTER

6-24

HERE SHE COMES!

TOOT! TOOT!

4 A.M.
THE MOST EXCITING PART OF THE CIRCUS

Copyright, 1949, New York Herald Tribune Inc.

The Courier Company of Buffalo, New York, lithographed this poster in 1898 showing the arrival of the circus trains and the enormous layout of tents — *Authors' Collection*.

182

Scene at Madison, Wisconsin, in 1952. Ringling Bros. and Barnum & Bailey Circus is unloading. As the massive wagons come down the runs, scores of towners are on hand to watch the fascinating operation — *Authors' Photo.*

Townspeople crowd into the yards to greet the show train and watch the ensuing spectacle. The road engine soon will be uncoupled, and a switcher will take over — *Circus World Museum.*

Once in town, the show train often required considerable switching. Here, the Ringling Bros. World's Greatest Shows of 1918, the last season before its combination with the Barnum outfit, is jockeyed for position in the Memphis yards — *Circus World Museum.*

Above: Two styles of flatcars and a variety of cages mark the tag end of the Beatty train as the Missouri Pacific handles it in the Galveston, Texas, yards on September 27, 1956 — *W. H. B. Jones Photo. Right:* When a show transferred from one railroad to another, a critical point was whether this exchange was made before or after the unloading. Here, the Galveston Houston & Henderson Railroad has picked up the Beatty Circus train from the Missouri Pacific at Galveston in 1956, and the GH&H diesel locomotive #20 will spot the outfit for unloading — *W. H. B. Jones Photo.*

A New York Central 0-8-0 yard switcher backs a string of Ringling flatcars to an unloading crossing in Albany, New York, in the 1940s — *Gene Baxter Photo.*

A switchman on the ground signals the locomotive crew as the Tim McCoy Wild West Show train is backed into position for unloading in 1938. Overcoats on the men and a trace of snow on the ground identify this as arrival in Chicago for the show's premiere appearance — *Circus World Museum.*

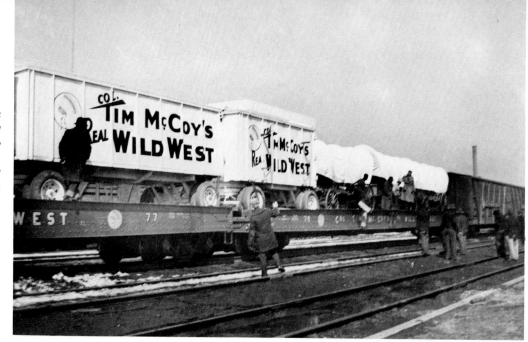

A switchman awaits his signal for spotting the heavily loaded train of Cole Bros.-Clyde Beatty Circus. This flat at the tail end of a cut is a run car, and Wagon 98 was last aboard at the previous town. Alongside the wagon wheels are the wagon poles (or tongues, to towners). Normally these would be placed under the wagons, but on a run car the runs themselves occupy that spot. The hinged door on the flat between the words "Clyde" and "Beatty" is a large compartment where crowbars, ropes, sledges, snatch blocks, and other equipment for unloading are kept. The compartment, like any similar loading space under a wagon, is known as a possum belly — *Jim McRoberts Photo.*

187

Left: During the loading and unloading procedures, Circus Trainmaster P. A. McGrath checks with the railroad engineer about the switching to be done — *Authors' Collection. Above:* A yard man hurries over to the flats that are to be spotted next. On board, the small wagons are loaded crosswise, hence their name "cross cages." These wagons were eight feet long but required only six feet of flatcar space when turned ninety degrees. By the time Cole Bros. Circus made this 1935 tour, cross cages had become a rarity — *Circus World Museum.*

The cage cut of any circus train drew the greatest attention from the town kids. Here, the Al G. Barnes Circus train is spotted at Elgin, Illinois, August 12, 1936 — *Authors' Collection.*

To showman and towner alike, it sometimes seemed that the railroad's switching was interminable. Here, an 0-6-0 switcher of the Union Pacific inches the flatcars of the Clyde Beatty Circus into position. A switchman stands atop Wagon 96, waiting for a signal to stop in the yards at Boise, Idaho, in June 1953 — *Henry R. Griffiths, Jr. Collection.*

189

A Missouri Pacific locomotive has coupled onto the coaches of the Clyde Beatty Circus to spot them at a more convenient location for circus personnel in the Galveston, Texas, yards in September 1956 — near the end of the last season for what proved to be the final tented circus to troupe by flatcar — *W. H. B. Jones Photo.*

Against a backdrop of commuter cars in the Chicago yards, an Illinois Central switcher tugs a cut of Ringling coaches to its eventual resting place for the extended run of the circus in the Windy City. Many performers would live on the cars during this 1946 visit — *Authors' Photo.*

Above: More often, the circus troupers found there was a long walk between coaches and showgrounds. Here, the personnel of the Forepaugh-Sells Circus in 1905 wends its way alongside the flats in search of the showgrounds — *P. M. McClintock Collection. Right:* With the flats spotted, it's time to get on with unloading. Here, the circus train crew pulls the runs. These long ramps are carried under the first wagons. One run has been pulled out and is being muscled into position by the show's train crew — *Circus World Museum.*

A crowd of towners clutters the area as the Hagenbeck-Wallace train crew sets the runs at Decatur, Illinois, in 1938. The crew also uncoils the required ropes. The snubbing rope is ninety feet long. Train teams work with nineteen-foot, six-inch hook ropes, placing the poler eight feet in back of the team — *Decatur Herald-Review*.

The Al G. Barnes train crew struggles with another set of runs at another town in 1936. The show's twenty-four-hour agent, having inspected the crossing earlier, arranged to have the extra planking in position before arrival of the show train — *Circus World Museum*.

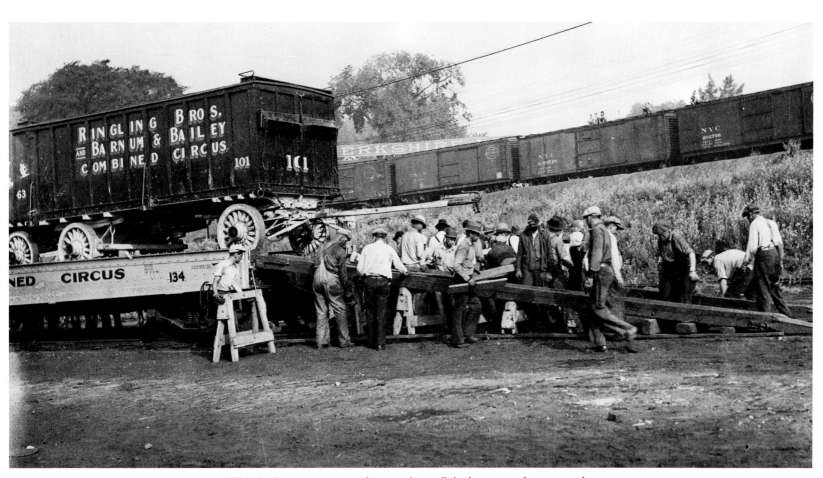

With both runs now in place and parallel, the crew places wooden jacks under them. Some men carry blocking to level the jacks. It's important to have the weight of the runs, and hence the massive wagons, distributed equally among the twelve jacks, six on each side — *Circus World Museum*.

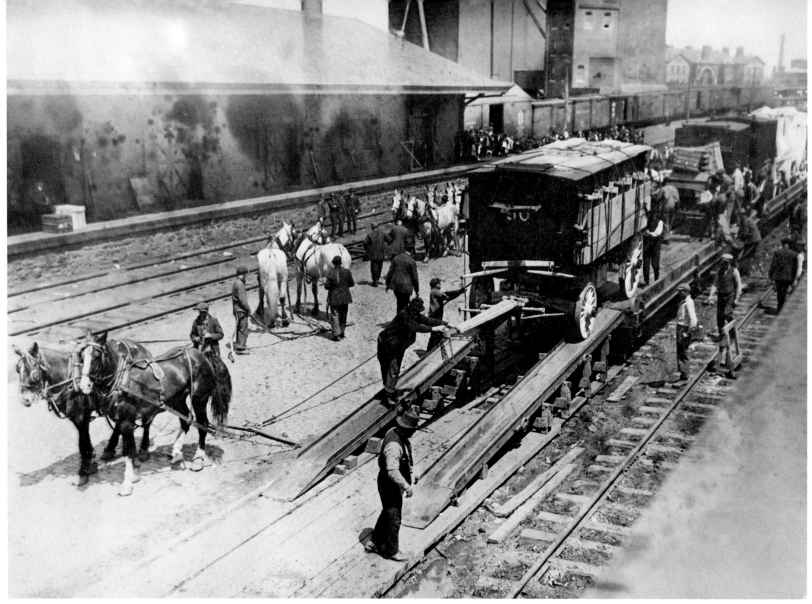

Now it's time for the first wagon to roll. In this 1908 view of Barnum & Bailey, the pull-over team at left has just stopped because the wagon hit the runs and is rolling down on its own momentum. On the runs, the poler has a firm grip on the pole to guide the wagon. The hook-rope man behind him is removing the hook from the corner bull ring by which the team had pulled the wagon. Other teams await their turns with later wagons. This is a dining department wagon with table parts lashed to the sides. On top is a supply of extra lumber — *Keeneland-Cook Collection*.

The pull-over team in this case is connected to a handy wagon brace instead of the usual bull ring on the corner. The poler, guiding the wagon on a straight course in this Barnum & Bailey scene, has one of the most dangerous jobs on the show — *Circus World Museum.*

The Sparks Railroad Circus used lighter runs than many outfits. The poler steers 41 Wagon alongside the flat, another crewman mans the snubbing post or braking device. At his feet are various tools of a circus train crew, including the long-handled implement for placing a wooden block in front of a wheel as an alternate braking system — *Circus World Museum*.

A hard-working Cole Bros. team leans into the collars to roll a cage over to the runs at Oklahoma City in 1941. Traditionally, team drivers used a hame as a convenient hook on which to hang their coats or to lash a rolled-up raincoat — *Jerry Booker Photo*.

The Ringling-Barnum circus replaced draft horses with tractors and elephants in 1939. Here, a Cat takes a cage away from the crossing after a pull-over team of elephants had moved it to the runs. Closely behind, another cage comes down. Here, the twenty-four-hour agent had installed planks and dirt to create a crossing for the circus where none had existed before — *Caterpillar Tractor Company*.

Three key men on the train crew are spotlighted in this view. At right is the poler, in the foreground is the snubber who has fixed himself a lowered platform for better footing as he mans the snubbing rope. Standing alongside the cage on a small portable platform which casts a shadow on the side of the car is the snub rope man. He will hook his rope onto the wagon as it passes and follow the wagon down the runs to the street. As long as the rope is hooked to the wagon, the man at the snubbing post can bring the wagon to a quick halt. Once the unit is on the street, the snub rope man will unhook it and walk back to his platform to await the next wagon. Behind the cage are the men who remove chocks from around the wheels and place the wagon poles in operating position. The pole of each loaded wagon is dropped to the deck to save flatcar space. It therefore has to be repositioned as each wagon takes its turn — *Chester Photo Service*.

Cross-over plates are laid between two flats to enable wagons to move across the gap. These steel plates were 30" x 48" and one-half inch thick. Wagon 141 moves across such plates as Ringling unloads at Milwaukee on July 23, 1951. It rolls from a seventy-two-footer to a seventy-foot show flat. Note the side-mounted hand brake — *Authors' Photo.*

A well-worn snubbing post attests to long seasons of service in unloading shows. The three-inch square HRS steel shank fits on the side of the flatcar; the spool is cast steel and slips over the stem. This rutted old snubbing post was used on the 101 Ranch Real Wild West Show and possibly before that on the Walter L. Main Circus. Now it still sees daily service as the Circus World Museum demonstrates how circus trains were unloaded — *Authors' Photo.*

The weight of the wagon determines the number of loops that the snubber puts around the snubbing post. When the rear wheels hit the pavement, he stops the wagon by holding back on the rope. This demonstration was photographed at the Circus World Museum — *Authors' Photo.*

Hook ropes and bull rings provided easy connection for the train team to pull the wagon from the front and also for the snub rope man to link up at the back. When the wagon cleared the runs and reached the ground, rope men would remove the hook ropes from each end — *Authors' Photo.*

Left: As this Ranch wagon rolls down the runs, the snubber lets out his line accordingly. But if anything goes wrong, he can bring things to a quick stop — *Authors' Photo. Below:* As each wagon moves, it tows the next wagon's pole out from under the wagon, where workmen can lift it. While Wagon 16 moves down the flats, the man behind it has a loose loop on a bull ring. The other end of his rope is equipped with a steel ring which is fastened to the gooseneck hardware of the wagon pole. When the pole is dragged out to the right position, he lets go of the rope, which slips out of the bull ring as Wagon 16 moves on — *Circus World Museum.*

Then the crew picks up the pole, which might weigh as much as 150 pounds, and slams it into the pole socket of its waiting wagon. A steel pin is dropped in place to hold the pole fast — *Circus World Museum*.

At left, a pull-over team, driver, and rope man head back for the next wagon. On the right, a fine pair of dapple gray Percherons moves Cage #9 over the flats — *Gene Baxter Photo*.

Right: A team of elephants provides the power as a Ringling cage is unloaded at Madison, Wisconsin, in 1941 — *Authors' Photo. Below:* Pull-over teams stepped nimbly along the rails and ties, moving wagons over the flats to the runs at the end of the string of cars — *Circus World Museum.*

Even a sharp curve in the trackage didn't hamper the circus train crew. A pull-over team takes Baggage Wagon 56 toward the runs. Another cut of cars awaits unloading while wagons already on the ground at right await the teams of four, six, or eight horses that will take them to the showgrounds. Towners watching the 1931 unloading get a bonus surprise as the circus giant walks among them on his way to the showgrounds — *John Rockwell Photo.*

The train crew of the Norris & Rowe Circus pauses for its portrait alongside the pole wagon about 1909. Since front wheels of the wagon already are on the runs, the circus men are relying on the man at the snubbing post at right to keep the heavy load from rolling away from them — *W. H. Woodcock Collection.*

This scene with Cole Bros. Circus in 1935 was duplicated as many as 200 times a year by each of hundreds of circuses which followed the same procedure from 1872 through 1956. Wagon and team, poler and runs, the system always was the same. And the process was just as intriguing to this crowd of towners as to all the others across those decades — *Circus World Museum.*

When showmen said that an outfit was "loaded like a Corporation show," they had in mind a circus loaded as heavily and compactly as this Hagenbeck-Wallace train in 1932. No flatcar space is wasted. Baggage wagons frequently utilized side racks to carry additional loads. A man reaches to the flatcar deck to get the pole which will be put into position on the #93 stake driver — *John Rockwell Photo.*

The old Campbell Bros. Circus unloaded from wooden flats in a rail yard cluttered with wooden boxcars and reefers — *Jim McRoberts Collection.*

Wagon 52 awaits the pull-away team that will take it to the side of the street. The man on the seat will manipulate the mechanical brakes. The team at left has just moved Wagon 51 onto the runs, and the snubber holds it back, waiting for the crossing to clear. The Tim McCoy Wild West Show lasted only a few weeks in 1938 — *Circus World Museum.*

Above: In an unusual procedure, two pull-over teams side by side tug simultaneously at Wagon 88 on the Al G. Barnes Circus. Usually a single team could handle even the heaviest loads on the leveled flatcar decks — *Jim McRoberts Collection. Right:* A Barnum & Bailey train crew includes the circus trainmaster in suit and heavy gloves, several men in rain gear, and one with a huge jawful of chewing tobacco — *Circus World Museum.*

Above: Six numbered center poles of the Ringling 1946 big top, plus an unnumbered spare, comprise the heavy sixty-foot load on Pole Wagon 43 as it comes down the runs at West Allis, Wisconsin — *Authors' Photo. Opposite page, above:* Wagon 26 comes down the runs for another town on the Ringling 1931 route. Awaiting their turn are other wagons on a string of flats parked on the adjacent side-track — *John Rockwell Photo. Opposite page, below:* Motive power filled an ever increasing role with flatcar circuses. Ringling's Mack 254, with a load of big top canvas, tows four massive wagons across the flats in Raleigh, North Carolina, in 1955 — *Ed Ruppert Photo.*

Left: The big top canvas crew hitches a ride with a water truck towing the big top pole wagon for the Clyde Beatty Circus at Galveston, Texas, in 1952 — *W. H. B. Jones Photo. Below:* Circus stockcars to the left of them, stockcars to the right of them, and flatcars in between, Ringling rolling stock seems to fill these freight yards during the unloading process in 1936 — *Gene Baxter Photo.*

Typically, an experienced train team handling wagons on the Hagenbeck-Wallace 1922 outfit straddles a rail of the adjacent track as it carries out its pull-over duties — *Circus World Museum*.

In this 1941 view of Cole Bros. Circus, Cook-house Wagon 20, first in line, somehow missed the runs. In this kind of a mishap, the poler stands in great risk of being yanked one way or knocked the other. Many polers were seriously injured as wagon wheels went out of control and swung the pole violently — *William White Collection*.

Throngs of people continually watched the unloading process of every railroad circus. Here, a gang of canvasmen, perched atop the big top truck, stare back at the towners — *Circus World Museum*.

A diesel switcher purrs gently while it waits for its next assignment in the Ringling unloading process on Illinois Central tracks adjacent to the Outer Drive in Chicago. Beyond, an AC Mack, just off the flats, will tow the next wagon across the busy expressway to the Soldier Field showgrounds for Ringling in 1946 — *Authors' Photo*.

A cut of cages already is spotted, and a train crew is placing the runs, while a railroader signals his engineman from atop a baggage wagon on another cut of cars. Towners at Albany, New York, watch the action as Ringling moves into town in 1945 — *Gene Baxter Photo*.

Sometimes yard facilities and crossings allow for two cuts of cars to be unloaded simultaneously. The luxury of three simultaneous operations was rare and speeded the unloading process. Mack #234 comes down the runs with a Caterpillar that has doughnut tires suitable for maneuvering over railroad iron and ties — *Authors' Collection*.

The Chicago, Milwaukee, St. Paul & Pacific Locomotive 425 idles in the crossing as crewmen confer. Alongside, Ringling tractors unload flats at Beloit, Wisconsin, in 1946. In the foreground are neatly coiled ropes and precisely aligned jacks, indicating that another set of runs was operated there earlier and will return. The flats have been switched to storage tracks to make room for another section of the circus train — *Author's Photo.*

Opposite Page: While unloading proceeds with the second section, the Maine Central's Locomotive 671 wheels into Lewiston, Maine, and pauses at the crossing with the Ringling-Barnum third section, made up almost entirely of coaches for performing and staff personnel — *Maine Central Railroad. Right:* Cars from Ringling's first section have been unloaded, and now ICRR's diesel switcher 9155 arrives on the scene with the second section — *Authors' Photo.*

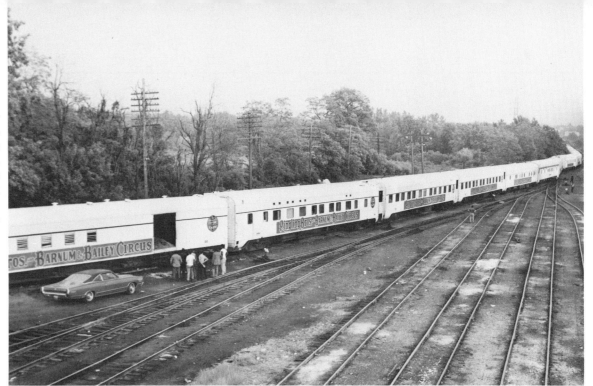

Whether the train is received loaded or unloaded is an important distinction to railroads handling a circus. Here, cars of the Ringling Bros. and Barnum & Bailey Blue unit are switched from the Penn Central to the Delaware and Hudson at Schenectady, New York, after they have been unloaded — *Gene Baxter Photo.*

Engine 5019 handles the chores as Ringling cars make the transfer at Schenectady — *Gene Baxter Photo.*

Usually first to be loaded were the wagons with cookhouse equipment, such as Wagon #1 on the Ringling runs at West Allis, Wisconsin, in 1950. In the foreground is the small light plant used to power lights for the loading area later that night. Traditionally, train light plants were numbered to correspond with the hour the crew expected to complete the loading process — *Authors' Photo*.

Loading Order for
Hagenbeck-Wallace Circus
1923
Showing the grouping of wagons into the 14 flatcar loads.

Wagon No.	Wagon Type	Wagon Length	Wagon No.	Wagon Type	Wagon Length	Wagon No.	Wagon Type	Wagon Length
34	Cook House	13'	43	Property	14'6"	8	Cage	16'6"
33	Steam Wagon	14'9"	1	Tractor	15'9"	1	Cage	16'6"
36	Stake Driver	14'	2	Tractor	15'9"	19	Cage	16'6"
40	Sprinkler	12'	27	Tableau	19'	7	Cage	9'
32	Cook House	16'7"				99	Dog Wagon	12'6"
		70'6"			65'			71'
37	Stable Wagon	16'9"	56	Pole Wagon	40'	14	Tableau	13'6"
39	Menagerie Spool	26'		Auto Truck	15'	31	Air Calliope	10'
21	Menagerie Tableau	13'	52	Property	14'6"	16	Cage	16'6"
41	Ticket Wagon	12'			69'6"	49	Seat Wagon	30'
		67'9"						70'
20	Tableau	17'	103	Light Plant	17'	51	Seat Wagon	30'
38	Side Show	20'	104	Light Plant	17'	48	Seat Wagon	20'
35	Sprinkler	12'	55	Stake and Chain	12'6"	50	Seat Wagon	20'
26	Tableau	19'	22	Tableau	17'			70'
		68'			63'6"			
53	Big Top Spool	26'6"	9	Hipp Den	18'6"	47	Seat Wagon	30'
23	Snake Den	14'6"	6	Cage	15'6"	46	Seat Wagon	20'
54	Big Top Spool	26'6"	2	Cage	17'	44	Seat Wagon	20'
		67'6"	10	Steam Calliope	20'			70'
42	Property	20'10"			71'			
25	Tableau	19'	18	Cage	14'6"			
45	Seat Wagon	30'	5	Cage	15'			
		69'10"	11	Cage	13'			
			17	Cage	15'			
			50	Cage	13'			
					70'6"			

Train Details and Loading Order
Robbins Bros. Circus 1938
Jess Adkins & Zack Terrell, Owners
Winterquarters, Rochester, Indiana

Advance Car #2		Combo., sleeper, diner & baggage
Stock #30		12 Bulls
Stock #31		30 Draft horses
Stock #33		24 Ring stock, 10 ponies & 1 zebra
Stock #35		8 Ponies, 3 camels, 1 donkey & 16 draft horses
Sleeper #51		Sleeper
Sleeper #54		Privilege car
Sleeper #57		Sleeper
Sleeper #59		Sleeper
Flat #43	82	Canvas wagon
	30	Red ticket wagon
	46	Sideshow baggage wagon
	32	Concesssion wagon, tableau in parade, 14'
	84	India tableau, 16'
Flat #41	71	Menagerie canvas wagon
	72	Air calliope
	12	Cage, cross, lion & tiger
	87	Big top canvas wagon, 16'
	83	Horse top canvas wagon
	88	Blacksmith shop wagon
Flat #42	80	Big top poles & stringers wagon, poles 40'; wagon 28'
	—	Small tractor

	—	Truck, Mack, water wagon body, 11'
	50	Light plant
Flat #44	20	Cookhouse baggage wagon, 19'
	21	Steam boiler wagon, 12'
	89	Stake driver, 13'
	18	Cage, cross, lion & leopard
	16	Cage, lions
	14	Cage, tigers
Flat #45	15	Cage, kangaroo & bear
	31	Steam calliope
	86	Ring curbs wagon & big top canvas
	73	Seat wagon, 16'
	61	Props wagon
Flat #46	—	United States bandwagon, 18'
	41	France tableau; reserve tickets wagon
	70	Belgium tableau, 16'
	81	Great Britain tableau, 18'

30	Pieces of equipment carried on show
1	Advance car
4	Stock cars
4	Sleepers
6	Flatcars
15	Car Show

(*See* Appendix for additional loading orders.)

Loading a show train is a reversal of the familiar process. Here, a train team on the Ringling show in 1915 takes the parade wagon *Russia* up the runs. Two men pole the heavy vehicle — *Circus World Museum.*

On particularly heavy wagons, some circuses used a snatch block to ease the load for the pull-up team. It acted as a single block. One end of the rope was fastened to a ring at the middle of the car. It went through the pulley block and down to the team. Here, the pulley is visible at the front of the wagon. A poler maneuvers the wheels into alignment for moving onto the flat — *Circus World Museum.*

Most of the Al G. Barnes-Sells Floto Circus has been loaded in this scene, and the pole wagon will just about complete the job. The workman in the foreground has a handle chock. If a rope should snap and the wagon roll backwards, he would slam the chock under the wheel to stop the wagon. He also assists in getting wagons squared with the runs by chocking a rear wheel as the wagon is swung around and headed into position to hit the runs — *Circus World Museum.*

As a wagon is pulled near its resting spot during the loading process, it is stopped long enough for the crew to pull the wagon pole and drop it to the deck. Without the pole for guiding, men were assigned to each front wheel for the final steering. When the train team again moved the wagon, the wheelers steered it into the chocks. The force of the wagon wheels pressed the chock spikes into the wooden deck. At the instant the wheels rolled upward on the forward chocks, men jammed two chocks behind the rear wheels. As the wagon rolled backwards slightly, it rammed the rear chock spikes into place, thus securing the wagon for its coming trip. This was the Barnes-Sells Floto Circus in California — *Circus World Museum.*

A Campbell Bros. cage is loaded, while others wait beyond the runs and a team approaches with another wagon at right. Usually, shows were loaded at night. This daytime scene probably indicates that the circus played a matinee-only in this small Kansas town of 1912 and perhaps is loading now for a longer run than usual — *Circus World Museum.*

Every wagon on the train had chocks front and back. In addition, wagons at the end of a flatcar were chained around the wheel as an extra safety precaution. This 1950 Ringling seat wagon shows a new model pole which is hinged upward into loading position. Such poles were usable after horses were replaced by trucks and tractors — *Authors' Photo.*

Some passengers were more reluctant than others. Here, a bronco resists entering a stockcar of Tim McCoy's Wild West Show in 1938 — *Circus World Museum.*

Opposite page, lower right: Last to be loaded on most shows was the light plant, since after it was gone, everything was dark. The generator wagon is last on the end flat of the ten-car Cole Bros. Circus at Douglas, Arizona, April 11, 1930. This outfit was separate from the much bigger Cole Bros. Circus which was organized five years later — *Circus World Museum. Right:* A portable ramp is used for loading ring stock into circus cars. After Ringling completed this loading in Milwaukee in 1953, the ramp was disassembled, and the parts were stowed in the slotted space under the car — *Authors' Photo.*

Right: These elephants load easily, knowing that hay will be waiting for them inside their familiar stockcar — *Circus World Museum. Below:* Most of the loading took place at night. Here, a giraffe wagon moves up the Ringling runs in the dead of a 1952 summer night in Beloit, Wisconsin — *Authors' Photo.*

The glare of lights picks out the familiar silhouette of the show train and illuminates the Ringling-Barnum title as the loaded flats stand poised, ready for the next run. Here, the Ringling train is ready to roll at Milwaukee in 1953. Behind it is the Chicago & North Western depot tower — *Authors' Photo.*

OFFICIAL ROUTE BOOK

Season 1923

Gentry Bros.
Famous Shows

COMBINED WITH

Jas. Patterson's
Wild Animal Circus
(INCORPORATED)

JAS. PATTERSON
President and General Manager

PERMANENT ADDRESS and WINTER QUARTERS,

PAOLA - - KANSAS

Circuses often printed route books as annual diaries. The Gentry-Patterson booklet of 1923 had a few observations about the railroads used during the tour. The jumps described averaged 22.1 miles per hour on the New York Central, 5.1 on the Pennsylvania, 21.9 on the Monon, and 25.5 on the Southern — *Authors' Collection.*

'Mrs. Matlock and Daisy Williams were strong opening numbers with their swinging ladder act.

The baggage stock, under Chauncey Jacobs, and ring stock under William Carpenter, and his assistant, Charles Jackson, were kept in the best of shape all season, and their fine appearance on the streets was mentioned by newspapers all along the route.

Mrs. Patterson was forced to leave the show and return home to Paola, later entering Grace Hospital, at Kansas City, where she was operated on. Last reports from the bedside were that she was on the road to recovery.

Mr. Patterson left the show at Warren, Arkansas, in response to an urgent message, calling him to the hospital, at Kansas City, where his wife was very ill.

Where are you going to winter, folk?

Write.

Don't forget that Paola is the home of the Gentry Bros.-Jas. Patterson Circus. Every merchant and citizen of this thriving little city is pulling for the success of this show. Whenever possible, visit the stores of Paola.

Messrs. Patterson, Adkins, Dobson, Beach and Dean were entertained at a "Wonder Banquet" by John Manning, while the show was at Monroe, La. For further particulars regarding this affair, inquire of Jack.

Viola Brainard left the show at Eagle Lake, upon receipt of word that Mrs. Patterson had suffered a relapse.

W. A. Adkins, one of the valued Billboard correspondents, who makes his home at Elgin, Ill., was a visitor several times while the show was near his home. W. A. is a dyed-in-the-wool circus fan, and is a welcome visitor on any show lot.

TOTAL SHOWS	177
TOTAL WEEKS	29 and 1 Day
TOTAL SHOWS MISSED	8
TOTAL PARADES MISSED	9
WHOLE DAYS MISSED	3
TOTAL MILEAGE OF SEASON	8930

A five-day stand was made at Sedalia, Mo., as feature attraction of the Missouri State Fair, August 20th to 24th.

Four-day stand at LaFayette, Ind., as feature attraction at Tippecanoe County Fair.

Clinton, Ind., Kirksville, Mo., and Rosenberg Tex., were the only three towns where no shows were given. Clinton was played later in the season.

The show traversed Indiana three times and Missouri twice during the season.

—18—

HOW THE RAILROADS HANDLED THE SHOW.

New York Central Lines made a good run from Ashtabula to Norwalk, both Ohio, 118 miles, in 5 hours and 20 minutes.

Pennsylvania Lines made the poorest run of the season in the move from Coatesville to Media, both Pennsylvania, 11 hours and 15 minutes for 58 miles.

The run from LaFayette, Ind., to Salem, Ind., 168 miles was covered in 7 hours and 40 minutes, by the Monon Route.

A record run was made from Huntingburg, Ind., to Tell City, Ind., by the Southern Railway. Show was not loaded until 6:30 a. m., due to wet grounds. Arrived at Oakland City, a distance of 68 miles, in 2 hours and 40 minutes.

The Missouri Pacific handled the show over more mileage than any other road—nearly 1200 miles.

The Wabash had the smallest mileage, 22 miles.

The Pennsylvania Lines and B. & O. each handled the show over 900 miles.

The season mileage of 8930 miles, was traveled over 22 different railroad systems.

—19—

Weary and worn from another long season, the show train finally rattles into winter quarters. Here, the Al G. Barnes Circus arrives at its Baldwin Park, California, home on December 6, 1927 — *Circus World Museum.*

Then the circus crew begins the maintenance work for the next tour. Stockcars of the Barnes Circus are being renovated at winter quarters in 1936. Roofs are repaired, rotted sills replaced, new ramps made, and cars repainted and lettered for the coming tour — *Circus World Museum.*

Workmen repair a steel plate under a flatcar at Ringling's winter quarters in Sarasota, Florida, while Trainmaster P. A. McGrath supervises at left — *Authors' Collection.*

Barnes coaches get a new coat of paint at winter quarters in 1936 — *Circus World Museum.*

Sometimes repairs were necessary en route. In 1954 this Clyde Beatty Circus flat was equipped with a new set of trucks by the Burlington Railroad — *Joseph Fleming Photo.*

Ringling's winter quarters railroad operation grew rapidly. By 1909 its trackage took this configuration around its repair shops between the North Western main line and the Baraboo River at Baraboo, Wisconsin — *Authors' Collection.*

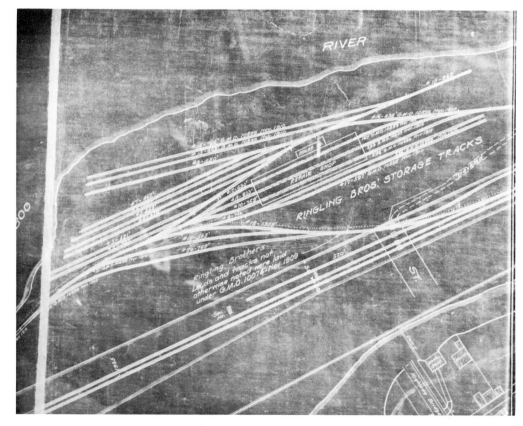

Often, local railroad facilities were made available to circuses for maintenance of circus cars. When the young Ringling brothers bought their first train in spring 1890, the Chicago & North Western Railway completed maintenance work and billed the show for these items, ranging from six sets of trucks at $480 to 24 cents for minor hardware. A $160 credit was allowed for scrap metal. A month later, the road charged the circus another $186 for additional hardware services performed just before the circus left quarters on May 4, 1890 on its maiden railroad junket. Note that labor was charged at a rate of twenty cents per hour — *Circus World Museum.*

A four-horse team was hitched to a stringer wagon for removing linen and bedding from the coaches of the Ringling train in its winter quarter car shops in 1915. The train shed still stands, now part of the Circus World Museum complex and once again housing circus railroad rolling stock — *Steve Albasing Photo.*

In 1962 the circus came back to Baraboo for another rest. By this time, however, the circus had forsaken tents in favor of arenas and therefore could troupe most of the year. Instead of taking winter off, the show pulled into Baraboo for a two-week summer lay-off. Here, the modern train stops alongside the large Baraboo depot, once busy as a division point but now abandoned. It was near this spot on the North Western that the old Ringling show loaded its trains to start the year's tour each season — *Authors' Photo.*

An 1881 print depicts the scene at the winter quarters of the Barnum, Bailey & Hutchinson Circus alongside the New York, New Haven & Hartford Railroad. The car repair shops comprised a major part of the show's home base — *Authors' Collection.*

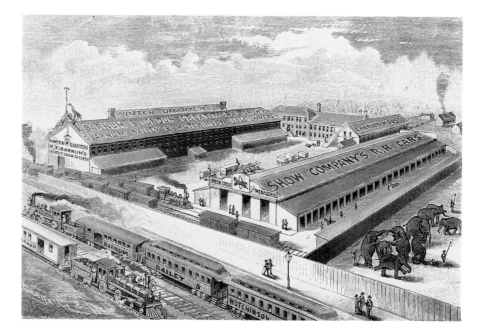

After the 1918 season, the heretofore separate Ringling and Barnum shows were combined into a single outfit at the Bridgeport, Connecticut, quarters. Seen here in the 1920s, beyond the old parade wagon and trucks at center, is a mass of circus coaches and stockcars. At the right, Car 102 is a Barnum & Bailey stockcar. Beyond it, and behind the Lehigh Valley boxcar, is a Ringling wagon. In the shops at left, the show undertook major maintenance of its rolling stock each winter — *Barnum Museum.*

Even if it is necessary to move a cut of flatcars, there may be no cause to wait for a switch engine. Elephant power moved these cars of the Clyde Beatty Circus at Louisville, Kentucky, in 1948, while a razorback manned the hand brake. It appears that the first spotting of the cars was unsatisfactory, so the runs were dismantled, and the elephants were called into action — *John Van Matre Collection.*

From 1926, the Ringling-Barnum circus maintained winter quarters and car shops at Sarasota, Florida. Replaced by newer equipment, old coaches were utilized as shops, offices, and bunk rooms at the winter quarters. But in 1960, that site was cleared for a housing development, and the circus moved elsewhere. Majestic old coaches with mahogany and brass fittings were put to the torch — *Authors' Photo.*

Excursions

The circus train itself was likely to be followed in rapid order by a whole bevy of additional trains—excursions bringing people from the surrounding countryside to see the great goings-on. These special passenger trains began arriving in town just after the show trains, and they were likely to continue until parade time.

It was the era of multitudinous passenger service on the railroads. People were accustomed to coming into the nearest city by train, doing their business, and going home via a local later in the day. For circus day, the whole schedule was ballooned.

From the time of Coup's first excursions in 1871 until the onslaught of automobiles, circuses dispatched an excursion agent to each city in advance of the performance date. His duty was to set up the excursions which railroads of the area would operate. The circus supplied thousands of heralds, or handbills, to ballyhoo the excursions and announce the schedules.

The little Dode Fisk Circus of 1910 sent this letter to each station agent on the lines serving any town it played:

"As per agreement with your General Passenger Agent, we herewith send you a package of small bills and several large pictorial hangers. The small bills kindly have distributed in your vicinity, and hang the large ones up in your waiting room.

"As this advertising matter is of equal importance to us

and to your road, you will please treat it as 'Railroad Advertising Matter.'

"You will find herewith attached a special free ticket for yourself and lady to our Famous Shows, and also an admission ticket for one boy, who you will please have distribute the bills in your vicinity.

"We thank you for what you may do in this regard, and trust your station will make a good showing on this excursion."

Hopefully, the station agent would festoon his depot with the lithographs, find a neighborhood lad to distribute the excursion heralds, sell a lot of tickets, and join the party on the train.

Villagers and farmers who had been reading the heralds and gazing at the three-sheets on their barns and shops went down to the depot for the bargain rail tickets. Sometimes they could even buy their circus tickets right in their hometown railroad stations. Going to the circus was a gala event; friends and neighbors would be on the train, too, and everyone would be in a holiday mood.

At each station for the run of up to thirty or forty miles, more people got on the train. Extra cars were added. Sometimes there were extra sections.

A decade after he introduced the excursion idea with the Barnum show, Coup was trouping a different circus under his own name. Its excursion heralds for the Tioga &

Elmira State Line Railroad of 1881 declared: "Take a Holiday, enjoy the ride and see the Largest Show in the World . . . Morning trains will arrive in season for excursionists to witness the Grand Spectacular Street Pageant at 11 o'clock A.M."

And the New York, Ontario & Western Railway's southern division superintendent, C. H. Hopkins, circulated this letter in May 1916:

"All Concerned:

"On account of Barnum & Bailey Circus at Kingston, [the] following special train will be run:

"Friday, May 19th Train consisting of combined car and number of vestibuled coaches required will leave Summitville 7:55 A.M. as 1st No. 409, making stops at all intermediate stations to Kingston.

"Returning train will leave Kingston at 6:00 P.M., making all stops to Summitville.

"Ticket agents have been authorized to sell regular excursion tickets for this service. Acknowledge receipt."

And, indeed, the people did turn out in great numbers.

When Ringling Bros. Circus played Decatur, Illinois, on August 6, 1910, railroads, street cars, and interurbans reported record traffic. Steam roads alone brought in 3,411 people. Some trains arrived with even the baggage cars jammed with people. The electric Illinois Terminal System utilized forty-six cars and brought 4,000 people. The city street cars handled an estimated 30,000 fares. To handle this business, they used all of the Decatur trolleys and brought in extra street cars from other towns.

On a season's basis, excursions represented a sizeable addition to the show's business, as well as bonus traffic for the railroads. For the 1896 tour, Barnum & Bailey calculated that its excursion agents made contracts with 130 different railroads that carried 800,000 circus customers. The next year involved 125 railroads and 896,000 people, it claimed.

Of course, no excursion agent could afford to leave any stone unturned. In 1888, Barnum & Bailey played Madison, Wisconsin, on August 1 and Janesville, Wisconsin, thirty-five miles away, on August 2. Yet an excursion train ran from Janesville to Madison on the first day—just in case someone couldn't make it otherwise.

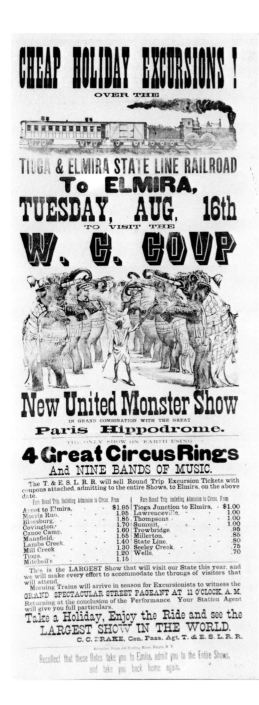

Left: Credit for the development of the circus excursion goes to W. C. Coup, who brought passenger trains into the circus scene even before he perfected the railroad circus. Ten years after he developed excursions for the Barnum show, Coup's own circus was using this ad which typically combined circus advertising with a railroad timetable to show the T & ESL fares from surrounding communities on circus day — *Authors' Collection. Above:* Excursion business was so important that big shows set up special departments to arrange them. This is the letterhead used by the Ringling excursion department in 1896. The agent in charge was Edward Arlington, who later would operate several shows of his own — *Circus World Museum.*

Left, above: Promotion of railroad excursions was a major factor in show advertising. The Buffalo Bill show, along with certain other major outfits, assigned one advertising car and its crew the special task of promoting excursions. This is the Buffalo Bill excursion car in a builder's photograph — *Denver Public Library. Left, below:* One of Barnum & Bailey's 1889 lithographic posters pushing excursions also featured a scene of the show train on the Union Pacific's "loop line" between Denver and Leadville, Colorado — *Circus World Museum.*

EXCURSION TICKET

1893

RINGLING BROS' SHOWS

ADMIT ONE.

ISSUED BY THE

CHICAGO & NORTH·WESTERN RAILWAY

W.A. THRALL, Gen'l. Passenger Agt.

Railroads and circuses frequently cooperated in the excursion business to the extent of issuing combination tickets and even printing and selling tickets for the other party. This is the original 1893 art work for tickets printed by the Chicago & North Western Railway. At that time, a person could buy railroad tickets and circus tickets all in the convenience of his local depot — *Circus World Museum.*

This departure in poster art featured a huge locomotive wheel to combine the themes of circus performances and railroad travel. Barnum & Bailey used the poster in 1893 — *Circus World Museum.*

239

Above: The 1901 courier for the Walter L. Main Circus included prominent attention to the promotion of excursions as well as art work depicting the show's railroad status — *Authors' Collection.* *Right:* The Ringling excursion car put out these heralds for the Denver engagement in 1900 to publicize the Colorado Road's excursion trains and fares. Tickets were good on the regular trains. The railroad's special rates were printed in the circus advertising — *Authors' Collection.*

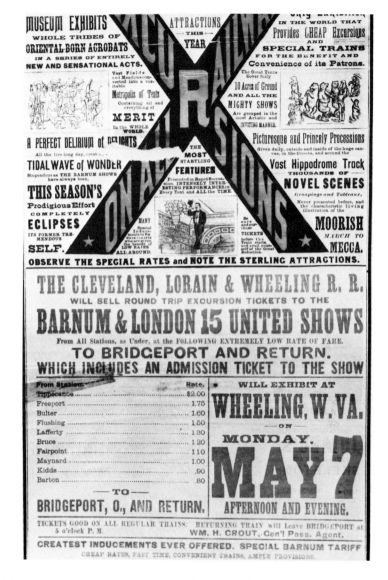

Barnum & London's 1886 excursion herald (pictured here in two segments) for the Wheeling, West Virginia, date quoted fares on the Cleveland, Lorraine & Wheeling Railroad. The show called to the attention "of our country friends" the excursions conducted on all railroads and claimed that excursion ticket holders would be admitted first to the big top. The railroads would run special trains and "sell our tickets at their depots," as Barnum's herald explained — *Circus World Museum*.

Sells Bros. lithographs stressed excursions and depicted a depot near the showgrounds where all the excursion trains could converge — *Authors' Collection.*

While some folks came by covered wagon, many others rode the numerous excursion trains converging on Barnum & London in this 1882 poster view. P. T. Barnum and his partner, Hutchinson, ride a balloon to survey the scene. Using the comic strip style of speaking in a picture, Barnum orders that all the seats be put in the big top down below because "all of his friends" are coming — *Cincinnati Art Museum.*

243

The railroads and the circuses worked closely in selling seats on coaches and seats for the show. Excursions brought trainloads of people from neighboring communities to the show town. Flyers like this 1875 example were displayed in all depots and other locations where people gathered — *Authors' Collection.*

Unusual Moves

Neither the long nor the short of it usually made any difference to a circus. Whether the jump was for ten miles or one hundred and ten, the show's procedures were the same. The people might not like the long trips, but the routine on the lot, on the train, and at the runs went unchanged.

While the first Coup railroad moves gave circuses a mobility unimagined by any prior standards, it follows that showmen would strive for even higher limits.

And they repeatedly set new dimensions on what could be done with a circus train. Since shows usually did not exhibit on Sundays, managers and show agents soon discovered that this day off was a handy time to make long jumps—leave one territory and move a substantial distance to reach a new area. So a "Sunday run" was a long trip.

This was illustrated when the 1876 Cooper & Bailey Circus took its turn at going to the West Coast. Its weekday moves usually were in the range of thirty-seven miles, forty-six miles, fifty-three miles, or perhaps even eighty miles. But successive Sundays found it moving 221 miles, 486 miles, 380 miles, 564 miles, 254 miles, and 480 miles!

Such Sunday runs were so long that a meal in the cookhouse was missed, which meant that dukies were issued—so long runs also were called "dukie runs."

For even longer jumps the circus perfected the feed and water stop. When time on the train became too prolonged, the circus planned a brief stop at a convenient station where space and sidetracks were available. Horses, and perhaps other stock, were unloaded, exercised, watered, and fed. Animal men also could feed the caged animals when necessary, but because Sunday was a usual day of fast for the menagerie, cleaning the cages and watering the animals sometimes was enough. Meanwhile, the train crew placed the runs and rolled just the cookhouse wagons off the train. This gave access to the ranges, refrigerators, and kitchen gear. The tent was omitted, but tables were set up in the railroad yards and the entire personnel of the circus was fed. Depending on the mileage yet to be covered, they might also be handed another dukie. Then everything was loaded and the show was on its way once again.

Given a dukie run or feed and water stop, a railroad circus could cover almost any mileage that presented itself. But occasionally even greater problems developed. The Sells-Floto Circus, with winter quarters in Denver, expected to open in that city and play its way toward California in the spring of 1915. But agriculture officials invoked a quarantine for hoof-and-mouth disease across most of the West. The show could not stop at intermediate towns without falling under the quarantine rules. Therefore, the forty-one cars were augmented by two water tank cars and a feed car. Then, with Buffalo Bill Cody among the troupers, the Floto Show jumped from Denver to San Bernardino, California, in one fell swoop of 1,356 miles. With the extra feed and water on board, the show was permitted to make stops and still stay aloof from the hoof-and-mouth disease quarantine.

If history was made at that time, it was nearly equalled on the thirty-one occasions that Ringling Bros. and Barnum & Bailey moved its show train from Sarasota, Florida, to New York City each spring beginning in 1927. That run totaled 1,323 miles.

The year's first trains out of Sarasota winter quarters included only the personnel, the animals, and the equipment that would be needed for the indoor stands at Madison Square Garden and the Boston Garden. In 1945, for example, the first New York section was made up of twenty flats, all painted yellow and titled in red. They carried sixty-three wagons. The second New York section included sixteen sleepers, eight stockcars, and one advance car. The latter was used on this occasion as a dukie car; feed and water stops also were to be made.

The two sections left Sarasota on the Atlantic Coast Line Railroad a little after noon on Tuesday, March 26. The next day they made a feed and water stop at Florence, South Carolina, with Willie Carr, the twenty-four-hour man, in charge of arrangements. The trains passed through Rocky Mount, North Carolina, at 7:30 P.M., March 27. On the next day they cleared Washington, D.C. at 8:30 A.M., Baltimore at 12:15 P.M., Philadelphia at 2:45 P.M., and Newark, New Jersey, at 5:45 P.M., March 28. Floated across the Hudson River to the Mott Haven yards, the flats were unloaded Friday, March 29.

While the show played New York and Boston, work was completed in Sarasota on the road show equipment. The balance of the eighty-car show then moved from Sarasota to Washington, D.C., where it rendezvoused with the two earlier sections and launched the under-canvas tour.

Surely the tallest trouping of all came in 1965 when Ringling Bros. and Barnum & Bailey took these giant steps in close succession:

Starting on June 7, moving from Toronto to Houston, 1,502 miles. Starting June 14, moving from Houston to Chicago, 1,073 miles. Starting July 5, moving from Milwaukee to Calgary, 1,643 miles. On July 15, moving from Edmonton to Portland, 1,084 miles.

Those jumps were interspersed with a couple of lesser ones and were followed soon by the 900-mile jump from Seattle to San Francisco.

Marathon runs became more frequent when the Ringling-Barnum Circus changed from tents and one-day stands to playing extended runs in principal arenas. Often it was necessary to play a city when the arena was available rather than when it was most convenient to the circus routing. So in its first twenty seasons as an arena show, the Ringling Circus made these additional jumps of 1,500 miles or more:

Toronto to Denver, 1,518 miles in 1957.
Houston to Salt Lake, 1,638 miles, Blue unit, 1969.
Vancouver to Duluth, 1,993 miles, Red unit, 1970.
San Diego to Denver, 1,552 miles, Red, 1971.
Vancouver to Winnipeg, 1,555 miles, Blue, 1971.
Las Vegas to Seattle, 1,512 miles, Red, 1972.
Vancouver to Bloomington, Minnesota, 1,919 miles, Red, 1972.
Hampton, Virginia, to Lubbock, Texas, 1,937 miles, Blue, 1973.
Vancouver to Bloomington, Minnesota, Blue, 1973.
Philadelphia to Oklahoma City, 1,641 miles, Blue, 1974.

The longest single jump, however, was that recorded by the Al G. Barnes Circus. Its 1924 tour got underway on March 15 at Santa Barbara, included a week in Los Angeles, and added Long Beach, where authorities stated that the show would not be able to leave the state because of the hoof-and-mouth disease quarantine then in effect. While the quarantine was aimed at cattle, hogs, and sheep, certain circus livestock was under the same umbrella. The Barnes show played two days instead of the scheduled one at Long Beach and then played Alhambra and Glendale and went into winter quarters at Palms, California—all in March! All the personnel was retained while the advance brigade worked frantically to find a way out of the dilemma and a territory where the show could play. For three weeks it waited.

Then Barnes made the most spectacular move in circus history. At 6 A.M. on April 20, the Barnes show train left Los Angeles on the Atchison, Topeka and Santa Fe Railroad. The quarantine extended from California to the Mississippi River, so the Barnes Show and the Santa Fe combined to put the circus down at Galesburg, Illinois. The railroad set a schedule of eight days. The show's twenty-four-hour agents jumped ahead to arrange feed and water stops and purchase provisions for the cookhouse at division points. But the Santa Fe moved the circus train on such a rapid schedule that the circus agents, using regular scheduled passenger trains, could not keep ahead of it. On April 25 the show train crossed the Mississippi, and at 4 P.M. that day it came to rest in the Galesburg yards. The Santa Fe had beaten its proposed schedule by nearly three days! The circus was beyond the reach of quarantines and on its way to a hastily contracted route through the Middle West—strange country for the Barnes title.

That long-range trouping tallied 2,058 miles.

On the short side, circuses frequently made such miniature jumps as the ten-mile run between Minneapolis and St. Paul. Even shorter were those between two stands in the same city. Cincinnati was a typical place for shows to play a day or so on one lot and then move to a second location still within the city limits.

Detroit turned up the most exaggerated example of shorthand trouping. That unique 1924 route brought the Al G. Barnes Circus to four locations in that city in five days. On Friday, May 23 it played an East Jefferson street lot. Saturday it was at Fort and Green, still in Detroit. Sunday it was at Hamtramck, the town that is surrounded by Detroit, and Monday and Tuesday found the Barnes show on the Ford lot, still in Detroit. Those jumps were as short as any circus could find.

Similarly, the Ringling Bros. and Barnum & Bailey Circus of 1953 made a miniscule eight-mile jump from Windsor, Ontario, to Detroit.

Another short run put the initiative back with the Sells Floto Circus. It was 1930 when the big show played the Chicago Coliseum then moved eighteen blocks to play the Chicago Stadium. In that extreme, extra trucks were hired to tow wagons overland, but the horses, lead stock, elephants, and people all went to the cars and rode the train to a closer siding.

The floating of circuses marks still another unusual twist of life with the railroad shows. It was necessary more often than one might suppose. Such circuses as Sparks and The Mighty Haag took railroad ships to reach Prince Edward Island. Far back in 1902, the Pan American Circus ferried across Lake Michigan and was caught in a storm. More recently and frequently, the Clyde Beatty Circus moved by ship to reach Vancouver Island. In 1946, for example, the show played Bellingham, Washington, on a Saturday, sailed on Sunday, and played Port Alberni, Courtenay, Victoria, and Nanaimo, British Columbia, during the ensuing week. On the second Sunday it returned to the mainland to play Vancouver, British Columbia. Later in the same season the Beatty Show jumped from Niagara Falls, New York, to Norfolk, Virginia, a distance of 675 miles with a couple of days en route by rail. The move was climaxed by the crossing of Chesapeake Bay. The Beatty Show repeated the process of floating to Victoria and its sister island cities in 1954 and 1955.

Not infrequently, railroad circuses were floated to various points within the metropolitan area of New York City. The New York, Ontario & Western Railroad floated the Sparks Circus from Long Island City around the tip of Manhattan to Weehawken, New Jersey, in 1912. Christy Bros. Circus was floated to Long Island, as was the Walter L. Main Circus. Inevitably, however, it was the deep harbor trips of Ringling Bros. and Barnum & Bailey that made the most of float moves. Typically, in 1952 the show moved sixteen passenger cars, five stockcars, fifteen flatcars, and one advance car via the New York, New Haven & Hartford Railroad Company. These cars were received under load from the Pennsylvania Railroad at Greenville Piers (New Jersey) float bridges on March 29 and moved to Harlem

River, New York, at a cost of $1,642. There were complications. First, the show trains were not permitted in the Hudson River tunnels, and therefore the float operation was necessary. But while the animals were not allowed in the tunnels, neither were the people allowed on the barges. So the employees of the show would cross by other means and rejoin the show in Manhattan.

There were also such problems as tide; the show had to schedule its moves so that arrivals and departures at float bridges would be compatible with tide levels for making the rail connections.

Whether it had one flat or forty, whether it moved one mile or four hundred, even if it moved by water-borne rails, the circus used the same systems in its railroading. The methods were virtually unchanged by varying conditions; there was no significant change in more than one hundred years. Time after time, the railroad circus met every challenge that was put to it.

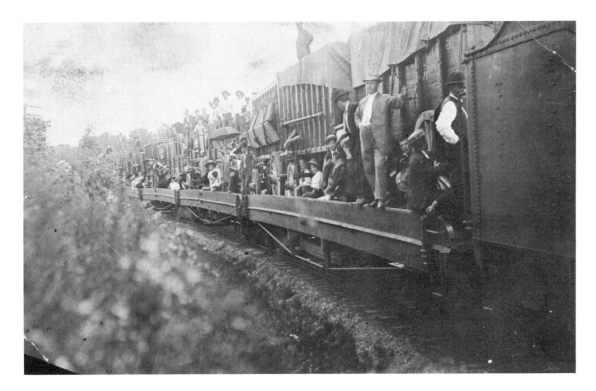

Sometimes circus people counted a long Sunday run as woeful confinement. Not so when the Ringling Bros. circus train moved from San Bernardino, California, on September 28 to Phoenix, Arizona, for Monday, September 30, 1907. Dozens of show people rode the flats in order to view the magnificent scenery on the Sunday run. Performers, not working men, this time inhabited the flats, braving locomotive soot and torrid sunshine. Someone thought to bring an umbrella — *Circus World Museum.*

During long moves, a circus train required feed and water stops for the livestock and personnel. Here, the Sells-Floto Circus train pauses at Horton, Kansas, on September 4, 1918. Both ring stock and baggage horses are being exercised and watered in the rail yards. Actually, this was an unscheduled situation. The show had expected to set up and give performances at Horton, but the showgrounds were so soft that the show was cancelled. So the circus shifted instead to the routine of a feed and water stop — *Jules A. Bourguin Photo.*

Here, the Floto cookhouse wagon comes down the runs. The cookhouse will set up a minimum operation next to the tracks in order to feed the show people. Only the first two or three wagons will be involved. After this brief stop, the wagons, stock, and people will be reloaded, and the show will jump to the next stand — *Jules Bourguin Photo.*

250

Above: The baggage stock of Ringling Bros. Circus has been unloaded for water and exercise to break up long hours in the stockcars. This picture may have been taken in 1913 when the show's schedule was interrupted by a flood that caused the cancellation of performances in four towns in Texas and Louisiana — *Circus World Museum. Left:* When Sun Bros. World Progressive Shows made this feed and water stop in 1918, the cookhouse crew set up the ranges and tables between the tracks and woodpile. The engine on the nine-car train is sidetracked beside the water tower for its own refueling — *Joseph T. Bradbury Collection.*

251

Left: The 600 miles between Portland, Oregon, and Sacramento, California, was too much to try in one jump, so the Barnum & Bailey show of 1918 made this feed and water stop at Mt. Shasta, California. Two flats were switched off to permit unloading the cookhouse wagons. Dining facilities were set up to serve a hot meal. Elsewhere, the animals would be watered, cleaned, and exercised before the show resumed its travels — *Circus World Museum. Below:* The Howe's Great London Show train was split just enough to allow movement of a single cookhouse wagon, giving access to necessary equipment for the feed and water stop. Even this brief pause of a circus train caused excitement in this little town, and a crowd gathered to watch the action. This was a marathon run from Missouri to Arizona to start the 1921 season — *Authors' Collection.*

When Ringling Bros. and Barnum & Bailey scheduled a move from St. Joseph, Missouri, to Denver, Colorado, in August 1941, the twenty-four-hour man arranged a feed and water stop at McCook, Nebraska, to break the 525-mile jump. Ring stock was tethered alongside the stockcar during the pause. Elsewhere, the camels, llamas, and zebras were unloaded, exercised, and fed. Farther down the tracks, several carloads of elephants were unloaded for similar attention, and the side panels of cage wagons were opened to permit cleaning and airing. After this sidetrack version of the interstate rest stop, the circus made the final 200 miles of its jump to Denver — *Joseph Fleming Photos.*

The use of railroad floats and ferries complicated some circus moves. Here, the cars of Christy Bros. Circus are being moved to Long Island in 1925 — *Circus World Museum*.

The barge listed markedly when the John Robinson Circus was being loaded for a float move in 1920 — *William Woodcock Collection*.

Right: Prince Edward Island presented a challenge to circuses. Here, the Sparks show is embarking from New Brunswick to play Borden, Prince Edward Island — *Authors' Collection. Below:* Half of the ten-car Gentry show is on board this railroad ferry in 1927 — *Woodcock Collection.*

Above: The Howe's Great London show is being loaded in 1921 — *William White Collection. Right:* When show trains are floated on large bodies of water, they are securely locked in place in much the same fashion that wagons are chocked to the flatcars above. If the water becomes too rough, the jacks seen on the floor are secured between the cars and the extra rail to prevent undue movement — *Authors' Photo.*

When the barge or ferry meets the dock, the two are securely clamped together to keep the rails aligned. Movements of circuses in the New York harbor had to be timed with high and low tides kept in mind — *Authors' Photo.*

1965

RINGLING BROS
AND
BARNUM & BAILEY
COMBINED SHOWS INC.

New York Office
Madison Square Garden
317 West 49th Street
New York 19, New York

OFFICIAL TOUR

General Offices and Winter Quarters
VENICE, FLORIDA

Allow Mail Enough Time to Reach Points Named Before Date Given

DATE		TOWN	STATE	LOCATION	MILES
June	2- 6	Toronto, Ontario	Canada	Maple Leaf Gardens	254
June	10-13	Houston	Texas	Astrodome	1502
June	16-29	Chicago	Illinois	International Amphitheatre	1073
July	2- 4	Milwaukee	Wisconsin	Arena Auditorium	90
July	8-10	Calgary, Alberta	Canada	Calgary Stampede Corral	1643
July	12-14	Edmonton	Canada	Edmonton Gardens	194
July	16-18	Portland	Oregon	Memorial Coliseum	1084
July	20-21	Spokane	Washington	Spokane Coliseum	376
July	22-25	Seattle	Washington	Seattle Center	309
July	30				
Aug.	1	San Francisco	California	Cow Palace	900
Aug.	2- 5	Oakland	California	Municipal Auditorium	30
Aug.	6- 8	San Francisco	California	Cow Palace	30

Courtesy Authors' Collection

Disasters

With all of the action around a circus, accidents and difficulties are bound to occur. It is logical to think first of injury to daring performers, and that does happen. But on the lot, in the big top, at the runs, and on the jumps, there are enough opportunities for trouble that even on the best organized circuses something can go wrong. The greatest concern is for those catastrophes that jeopardize the existence of the whole show. A severe storm can threaten a blow-down and leave the show immobile in the mud—old showmen called it "Jonah's bad luck." Particularly in years gone by, the threat of pestilence—either genuine or rumored by rivals to tie up competition—could bring a show to a halt. Riot and turmoil in the dimensions of a "clem" or "Hey, Rube" once were commonplace with circuses.

Even in recent times shows have been affected by tumult, such as when the Ringling show was on the fringe of the Watts riots in Los Angeles.

But there were several calamities peculiar to railroad circuses. Each problem not only threatened instant damage to the show, but raised the hazard of losing a performance or, worse, falling behind the tight, demanding schedule. Murphy's Law states that if something can go wrong, it will. In response, the circus law insists, "Keep up with the paper," which is another way of saying "The show must go on." This refers not only to performances, but also implies that the show is a roving entity that cannot afford to be stopped. To "keep up with the paper" means that a circus has to arrive in town when the dated posters say it will. The surprising fact is that of all the projected thousands of circus days, only a smidgin have been lost, thanks to the determination of circus people and the basic reliability of railroad transportation.

Nevertheless, the circuses could and did have some serious problems.

Apparently no circus was caught in the Great Chicago Fire of October 7, 1871, but on the same day, when raging forest fires wiped out Peshtigo, Wisconsin, the P. A. Older Circus was stamping out sparks and battling flying embers nearby as its show train made a run for it and escaped to show another day. No circus was inundated at the Johnstown flood, but Professor Gentry's Dog & Pony Show left town just one day earlier.

Stockcars and advance cars seemed to be particularly vulnerable to fire. The Al G. Barnes Circus in 1924 lost its bill car to a fire at Massillon, Ohio, and lost thirty-six performing horses in a stockcar fire en route in California that October. Three out of four elephants were lost when a stockcar caught fire while the Coop & Lent Circus was traveling in Ohio during May 1917. The Van Amburgh Circus of 1906 came to a panic stop somewhere in Tennessee on April 18 to battle a fire in two stockcars. That tragedy took the lives of twenty draft horses, six ring horses, a yak, three camels, two elk, a water buffalo, a llama, and one elephant. At St. Catharines, Ontario, in 1912, the elephant car of The Mighty Haag Circus was shaken by an explosion, but no animals were in the car at the time.

Ringling Bros., being among the biggest shows, sustained some of the greatest losses. In Arkansas in 1898 the wagon carrying the sacred white elephant caught fire, and the featured animal died a few days later. Ringling Bros. Circus lost forty-three empty cars in a fire at the Cleveland, Ohio, yards on May 25 and 26, 1914, and then it accomplished the impossible by rapidly assembling enough substitute equipment to keep up with its paper.

The Campbell Bros. Circus had a particularly bad series. In 1902 a train fire at La Junta, Colorado, caused $7,000 in damages. In 1903 a chandelier wagon exploded and sprayed gasoline over the train. The resulting fire cost $10,000. On May 1, 1904 at Pawnee City, Oklahoma, the second stand of the season, the stockcar burned and killed three elephants, four camels, two sacred cows, and one bear.

Sparks' advertising car went up in smoke during the spring of 1919 and took with it a full load of advertising materials. The car had just stopped at winter quarters to replenish its supply of paper. The crew had worked at loading until midnight, but all was lost in a matter of hours, and the men had to load a substitute car.

Floods along the Ohio River caused the Ringling show to lose its first and second road stands of the 1913 season and wildcat on a circuitous route that sought out dry land and stable bridges by which it could reach Clarksburg, West Virginia, and then proceed on the balance of its tour.

Two years later Gollmar Bros. Circus played Bonesteel, South Dakota, on a rainy May 24 and continued as scheduled into the Rosebud Indian Reservation, where it played Dallas, South Dakota, on May 25. By then it had rained for forty hours and much of the territory was flooded. The 122-mile jump on the Chicago & North Western to Plainview, Nebraska, was out of the question. The

best that could be done was to stop again at Bonesteel. There the loaded train was sidetracked and there it sat, stranded, for more than a week. What seemed to be a lark at the outset soon became a crisis. The circus cookhouse set up shop behind a friendly restaurant, but soon supplies of food for towners and show people ran short. A circus cowboy named Ken Maynard helped in the roundup of a few cattle on the high land. There was also a shortage of feed for local and circus horses, elephants, and other stock. The show people rented the Bonesteel Opera House and devised a home-talent show to fill the long hours. Finally, one of the Gollmar brothers induced a local man to try reaching the outside world by dinghy. He made it, and Gollmar then turned to the Chicago & North Western for assistance. Some hours later, a bold train crew brought a locomotive through the flooded area, coupled it onto the circus train, and inched its way back through the flood. At Niobrara, Nebraska, they gave a wildcat performance, and on June 4, at Worthington, Minnesota, Gollmar caught up again with its paper.

The year 1909 was big for holdups of circus trains. Any right-thinking circus would not be out and about on January 2, but on that night the 101 Ranch Wild West show train was en route near Fort Worth, Texas. Thieves broke into the ticket wagon and escaped with $15,000. It was neither long after nor far away that the Yankee Robinson Circus got the same treatment. On October 31 the show was rolling along between Rison and Fordyce, Arkansas, when two men boarded the train, forced their way to the private car, beat the show treasurer into unconsciousness, and took $6,000 from the safe before jumping off of the train.

The greatest disasters to strike circus trains were wrecks—the collisions and derailments. There have been more than 150, perhaps 200, notable wrecks of circus trains; no compilation lists them all. Often they didn't cost the circus more than a performance or one day. W. F. (Doc) Palmer reflected the usual situation and attitude when he wrote about his Palmer Bros. Circus of 1921: "We had quite a bad little wreck going into Hot Springs [South Dakota], but we were able to give a night's performance and we got $1,500."

A twenty-seven-car section of the John Robinson Circus of 1887 was wrecked in St. Louis, freeing many animals in the Union Station yards. The 101 Ranch Wild West of 1912 lost several parade wagons, including the calliope, in a November railroad wreck. A hippopotamus escaped in a Sells Bros. wreck at Birmingham, Pennsylvania, in 1878. A narrow tunnel in Virginia scraped the cross cages off of the W. W. Cole train in 1885. A trestle weakened by floodwaters caused a wreck of the Ringling Bros. Circus near Washington, Kansas, in 1892 with the loss of two men, twenty-six horses, and four cars. Near Saskatoon, Saskatchewan, the Norris & Rowe Circus of 1906 derailed five flatcars and lost fifteen wagons, among them a den in which six sea lions were crushed. There were additional smash-ups of the Sparks Circus at Quebec City, Quebec, in 1928; Al G. Barnes Circus at Canaan, New Brunswick, in 1930; Ringling Bros. and Barnum & Bailey at Charlotte, North Carolina, in 1932; Cole Bros. at Battle Creek, Michigan, in 1937; Robbins Bros. Circus at Johnstown, Pennsylvania, in 1938; and perhaps the last circus train wreck of any consequence—that of the Clyde Beatty Circus at Hubbard, Nebraska, on July 8, 1947.

One of the big disasters came when the Walter L. Main circus train jumped the track near Tyronne, Pennsylvania, on Decoration Day 1893 and splayed the whole works across a field. Five men died. All of the flats and stocks were wrecked. Fifty-two horses were killed, and sixteen cages were cracked open, freeing such animals as two tigers, three lions, and a panther.

Sometimes show train wrecks came in rapid sequence. Take the S. H. Barrett Railroad Show of 1884, for example, which sustained wrecks on April 10, April 19, April 30, May 3, and July 2.

The Cook & Whitby Circus of 1892 was wrecked on July 7 and again on July 8. That show was owned by Ben Wallace, whose Great Wallace Circus and Hagenbeck-Wallace Circus experienced some of the worst railroad wrecks in circus history. Before their combination, the Carl Hagenbeck Wild Animal Show had wrecks at Gonzales, Texas, Tiger Creek, Arkansas, and in Old Mexico, while the Great Wallace Circus had a smash-up at Shelbyville, Illinois, in 1903.

The combined Hagenbeck-Wallace Circus had similar wrecks at Big Rapids, Michigan, in 1907; St. Paul, Minnesota, in 1908; Ann Arbor, Michigan, in 1917; Mason City, Iowa, in 1927; and Somerset, Pennsylvania, in 1936.

Hagenbeck-Wallace's most appalling wreck was the major disaster of 1918, easily the worst crash in circus history, publicized widely at the time and listed in the almanacs ever since. In this incident, the Hagenbeck-Wallace first section stopped near Ivanhoe, Indiana, and was rammed from the rear by an empty troop train. Fire broke out in five coaches, killing many working men and a number of performers. The death count reached sixty-eight, and 127 were injured.

Another serious wreck came to the Great Wallace Circus on Friday, August 7, 1903. It was 3:45 A.M. A car checker and a yard foreman of the Grand Trunk Western Railroad at Durand, Michigan, watched as the twenty-two-car first section of the Great Wallace Circus stopped for coal and water at the depot on the eastbound track on the main line. Suddenly, the stillness was pierced by sharp blasts from another locomotive. Its engineer was whistling for hand brakes. His train carried the second section of the Great Wallace Circus and was only one quarter of a mile away when he realized that he had no air in the brake system. The second locomotive crashed into the caboose and the adjacent bunk car of the first section before it tipped over into a ditch. Twenty-six men, among them two railroad officials and the circus trainmaster, all of whom were in the caboose, died in one of the most disastrous train wrecks in Michigan history. Nine men died in the car ahead of the first section caboose, six men perished in the car behind the

261

second section locomotive, and eight others died of injuries later. Twelve other cars in both sections were demolished, parade wagons and cages were broken up, and horses, camels, dogs, and an elephant were killed. Terrified draft horses galloped through town.

The circus lost performances that day and the next but caught up to its billing on Monday at Bay City, Michigan. Most of the circus casualties were department heads and bosses. Upon hearing the news, the Barnum & Bailey Circus dispatched its assistant bosses to help get the Wallace show back on its feet. This sort of assistance to competitors was typical of the circus business whenever disaster struck.

At the Durand wreck, the engineer and fireman of the second locomotive had jumped clear and were not hurt. At the inquest the engineer testified that when he saw the signals set against him, he had attempted to set the brakes but had no air. He was approaching at thirty-five to forty miles per hour and testified that the air was okay at Charlotte, where the circus had played on the previous day, and at Lansing, where he had stopped for water. But he admitted that he had not checked his air gauge at Lansing. The inquest brought out the fact that the engineer had lapped the brake valve to reduce the speed of the circus train while it was crossing over from one track to another at Lansing. A crucial error came when he forgot to put the brake valve back into the release, or running, position. Consequently, when he needed braking power he had insufficient air pressure in the train line.

Near Bismarck, North Dakota, in 1907, the Northern Pacific Railroad dumped the Gollmar Circus train into a ditch. Great physical damage was done to wagons and stockcars, and numerous horses were killed. The railroad appeared to be at fault, and Gollmar Bros. prepared to press its claims. However, their first cousins, the Ringlings, telegraphed to urge that they not seek any damages. The Ringlings were fearful that the railroad would, if sued, refuse to carry any circus in the future. So the Gollmars negotiated a settlement by which the Northern Pacific paid only $600 for horses and rebuilt five stockcars.

The Buffalo Bill Show experienced a wreck in 1896 under odd circumstances. The first section stalled on a hill in Wisconsin so the train was divided in half, and the engine moved on with the forward cars only. The second section was flagged routinely as it approached the halted portion of the first train.

The second engine was then uncoupled from that train and used to push the remainder of the first section up the hill. But that first engine was coming back for the stalled cars. Circus cars were crunched between the two locomotives. Five flats were abandoned in the ditch. Seven wagons were demolished. Four coaches were damaged, but no one was injured seriously.

Shocking as wrecks were to people, animals, and equipment, circus trains could make quicker recoveries than most. Using its elephant power, a circus could sometimes correct lesser derailings on its own before a railroad wreck crew could arrive. Even in bad situations, there was instant help to be had from circus manpower, generators, blacksmiths or welders, the cookhouse if need be, and tractors, all of which already were on the scene. The self-sufficient circus was able to get back on the road in minimum time, thanks in part, too, to the old adage that "the show must go on."

Something went wrong with the trestle over Tiger Creek in Arkansas. Four flatcars and sixteen wagons of the Carl Hagenbeck Wild Animal Circus went into the ditch. Iron railroad wheels and circus sunburst wheels took to the air in uncommon position. Circus trains sustained their share of railroad wrecks and other disasters — *Circus World Museum.*

263

Left: As the Campbell Bros. Circus entered the yards at Babcock, Wisconsin, on August 16, 1910, another train crashed into it at a junction and split the elephant car in half — *Circus World Museum. Below:* Because of the tremendously high death toll, the 1918 wreck of the Hagenbeck-Wallace show is considered the worst in circus history. The engine pictured here headed up an empty troop train, ran red signals, and plowed into the rear of the circus train which was stopped in the process of transferring from one road to another — *Circus World Museum.*

Sells-Floto flats plowed up the tracks in Colorado in 1919 — *Circus World Museum.*

When the St. Louis-San Francisco Locomotive 1249 got off the rails, its abrupt stop jackknifed two stockcars filled with horses. This wreck occurred in 1919 as the Ringling Bros. and Barnum & Bailey train was en route to Okmulgee, Oklahoma — *Authors' Collection.*

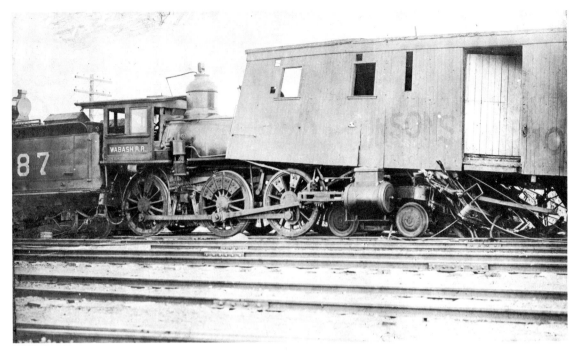

Wabash Engine 87, a 4-6-0, sliced the end sill and deck out of this stockcar of the John Robinson Ten Big Shows of 1903 — *Circus World Museum.*

The Gollmar Bros. Circus train of 1915 is up high and dry. But it can't go anywhere because of the floods surrounding it in North Dakota. After being stranded several days, the show owner and a railroader inched a locomotive through the water to get help — *Circus World Museum.*

Fire was another scourge of circus trains. Here, the pie car of the 101 Ranch Real Wild West goes up in flames in 1924 — *Circus World Museum.*

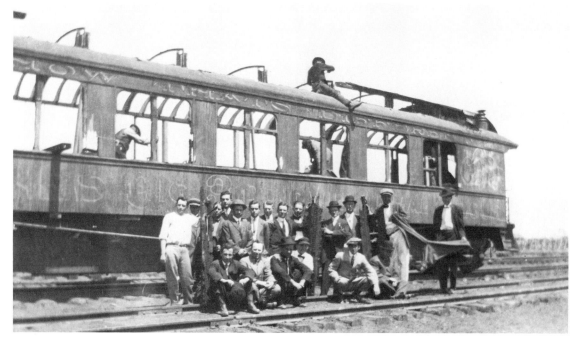

Still another fire on the Al G. Barnes Circus train occurred on May 27, 1914 at Glendive, Montana. A passing Northern Pacific locomotive showered sparks on the roof of the car, which was sidetracked in view of the circus showgrounds. Performers who lived in this car stood helplessly by and watched their belongings go up in flames. To commemorate the occasion, troupers posed alongside the gutted car and held charred remnants, including, for some reason, a pair of pants — *Circus World Museum.*

267

Left: While Ringling Bros. World's Greatest Shows played Cleveland May 25 and 26, 1914, a lumberyard fire spread to the nearby sidetracked circus cars and ruined forty-three flats and stockcars. The outfit borrowed cars from its sister show, Barnum & Bailey, and elsewhere, and managed to continue its tour with a minimum of lost time — *Circus World Museum. Below:* Expedient showmen compensated for some of show life's minor tragedies along the way. The rear wheels of a Sparks baggage wagon were torn away, perhaps on a muddy lot. Ingenious circus men lashed a timber to each side of the wagon so it could be loaded. This picture was taken the next morning as the crippled wagon was coming down the runs in the new town. Before the day was out, the circus repaired the undercarriage and had the wagon back in action — *Circus World Museum.*

A faulty journal caused this smash-up of Cole Bros. circus train on the Northern Pacific Railway near Little Falls, Minnesota, on July 27, 1945. Five flats loaded with wagons were involved in the wreck. In a few days the circus was rolling again — *Both Photos: Circus World Museum.*

Both photos, this page and opposite: Another highly publicized circus train wreck occurred July 20, 1930 as the Canadian National took the Al G. Barnes Circus from Newcastle toward Monckton, New Brunswick. Fifteen miles short of its destination, a flatcar jumped the track alongside Canaan Station. In all, eight cars piled up, ripping tracks, smashing coal bunkers, and wiping out various railroad shanties. Circus coaches, flatcars, and heavy wagons were spewed along the right-of-way. The circus mobilized its own facilities to start salvage and rescue work almost immediately. The Canadian National dispatched railroad crane #50113 to lift flats and heavy circus wagons. At Monckton, the circus set up temporary shops for its blacksmith, carpenters, and others to rebuild wagons. Other substitute equipment was rushed from Peru, Indiana, winter quarters. After seven days of concentrated reconstruction, the show was ready to roll again — *Circus World Museum.*

Both photos, this page and opposite: At Redding, California, in 1946, an engine pushing a Cole Bros. elephant car split a switch. The stockcar caught the corner of a flat loaded with cages of tigers and lions, tipping both cars on their sides. To get the elephants out, torches were used to cut a hole through the car roof. Inside, the car leg chains had to be cut to release the elephants. Cars and animals were hosed down while the torch was being used. At right, with a flashlight in his pocket, is elephant superintendent Bill Woodcock looking after the welfare of his trapped charges. All turned out well. The railroad furnished the circus an eighty-foot baggage car while the elephant car was being repaired. The cages and flatcar were righted with minimum damage — *Noyelles Burkhart Collection.*

272

273

Left: Disaster was narrowly averted, thanks to quick action by railroaders, when a flatcar on the first section of the Ringling show split a switch in 1956. The train was halted before any major damage occurred — *Circus World Museum. Opposite page:* In another notorious circus wreck, the Walter L. Main circus train was scattered over the countryside four miles west of Tyrone, Pennsylvania, when it jumped Pennsylvania Railroad tracks. The circus was en route from Houtzdale to Lewistown, Pennsylvania, for May 30 performances. On reaching a long down grade with a severe curve at the bottom, the engineer of locomotive 1500 realized he had inadequate braking power. When the engine hit the curve, all the flatcars rolled over the thirty-foot embankment, breaking loose from the engine. A combination car left the tracks but was yanked sideways and became a buffer to stop the three coaches. All three stockcars, loaded with horses and elephants, followed the flats and rolled over the embankment. Five men were killed and twelve injured. Sixteen cages broke open, and animals either were killed or they escaped. Sixty-nine out of 130 horses were killed or had to be shot. The Pennsylvania Railroad provided replacement cars and assisted in the repair. In ten days the circus was back together and putting on a performance at Tyrone. Investigation revealed that a second locomotive had been requested for the move so as to add braking power on the steep grade, but the request had been denied. The train was hitting forty miles an hour on the curve at the bottom of the hill — *Circus World Museum.*

May 30 1893.

WALTER L. MAHN'S ALL NEW MONSTER SHOWS.

Current show trains aren't immune from accidents. Ringling's 500 Car on the Red unit was sideswiped in 1976 at Selkirk, New York, with this result — *Gene Baxter*.

Two-Car Shows

In a world that boasted of bigness and measured its trains at sixty, eighty, even one hundred cars; in a setting where hugeness was the only significant dimension, where size was paramount, there came to be an array of amazing miniature marvels.

Each was as illusionary as a magician's hat, for out of such a tiny container came wonders in unbelievable quantities. It looked big, it talked big, but it trouped on just two railroad cars. The one really big thing about it was its claim to being a railroad show.

The two-car circus was an entirely different operation than its relative, the flatcar show. A two-car show usually had just that many railroad cars. But since "two-car show" was the name given to a whole class of shows by circus people, it might also have a single car or three cars, even five, and operate in the same fashion.

The basic difference came in its railroading. Where the standard railroad circus made special moves on its own schedule with a system locomotive and crew assigned to it, the two-car show usually moved on regularly scheduled trains. Its consist typically included a coach and a baggage car. Two-car shows were moved quite often in regular passenger service, coupled to the tag end of local passenger trains. But if a passenger train wasn't available, a regular freight would do. These miniature shows comprised a subculture of circus business, living in a separate world of tank towns, branch lines, and mixed trains.

Two-car shows moved in passenger service rather than freight, and the roads acted as common carriers, not private, in such moves.

"Railroads transporting private cars of theatrical companies have not been held private carriers since the act took place." So stated the Interstate Commerce Commission.

It is clear, too, that the two-car shows would have to be classed the same as the rest of the train in which they moved and that the tickets they bought for the move would be governed by ICC rules and rate setting.

On board, the two cars were overloaded and overcrowded. Equipment was double-decked and dual purpose. People doubled in brass. It was a maximum of circus concentrated in a minimum of railroading.

But those two cars gave each such tiny show the valued privilege of proclaiming the coming of a railroad circus. That in itself gave the outfit size and stature.

Basic to the operation of two-car circuses was the standard railroad passenger provision that anyone buying a specified number of first class tickets—usually twenty-five—was entitled to a baggage car as well. On the strength of that provision many shows of all kinds transported people in one car and freight in another, all for the price of the people alone. With two-car circuses that owned rolling stock, the railroads operated in the same way: buy enough tickets and they would move the two cars.

Of course, this led to the ultimate confrontation between conductor and cut-rate showmen. After the conductor made his usual pass through the regular cars to check tickets, he came to what normally was the end of his train only to face the chaos of a two-car circus. Entering the coach, he sought the owner and the specified number of tickets. But he also was charged by the road with the duty of counting people. The show would have purchased the minimum required tickets for making the move but often enough had on its payroll more people than the tickets covered. While many conscientious showmen would have paid the proper fare, the lore of two-car shows is replete with tales of short-money shows which stashed extra people into possum bellies, odd compartments, and especially the baggage car, until the conductor had gone.

Moving via scheduled passenger trains provided plenty of conflict between available railroad timetables and traditional circusing schedules. There just might not be a train to get the two-car show into town of an early morning. If it was a two-line move, the show cars might be set out at a junction by one train to await the arrival of another. By the time a two-car show reached its next stand, it might be nearly noon. But after all, the reality of this circus was its compact size, and it could be in the air and ready to go in shorter time than other shows required.

The two-car outfits often utilized showgrounds right at the railroad crossing or near the depot. Often as not, the space was rented from the railroad. Such a circus, using a generic term of show business, stated that it was "playing railroad lots," which were in contrast to showgrounds played by bigger circuses elsewhere in town.

It all began in the 1880s with a whole class of shows called "Ten-Cent circuses." It picked up speed in the 1890s when small circuses discovered railroads and found that a baggage car carried as much show plunder as a fair number of wagons in an overland circus. In the 1890s, show business was peppered with so-called "pavilion" shows, a name that alluded to the smaller round tops in which the performance was given. Circus men soon dubbed them "two-car shows," and that designation stuck within the profession.

At the outset, pavilion show operators decorated and painted their two cars in the same flamboyant style as the bigger flatcar shows. However, in time, the more knowledgeable among two-car showmen chose to paint their cars in a color scheme like green and black. They omitted the art work and left off the title. This new approach came with the concept that townspeople sometimes scoffed at any circus arriving with only two cars. It was better if this circus slipped into town unnoticed, its rolling stock sitting on the sidetrack without identification. Let the townspeople see the tents, the midway, and the parade before they adjudged the show.

If the cars were unpainted and the entrance banner to the side show not too specific, the identity of the circus was spelled out only in the posters, newspaper advertising, and other printing. Thus, the show was free to change its name on short notice. There was good economic reason for doing so. Printers of lithographic posters often produced huge supplies of paper for a larger circus only to have that show go broke before the stock of paper was exhausted. Two-car showmen discovered that they could buy this imprinted paper at bargain rates, so they changed the name of their show to that on the paper. Thus, there was a short-lived Hugo Bros. Circus, and a few years later a two-car show operated under the same name. There were big shows by the name of Campbell and Cole and Sanger, and in each case a subsequent two-car show took the name to use up the remaining paper. When his source of bargain posters was gone, the two-car showman could change his show title again.

A two-car show might be populated with as many as seventy-five people, though it operated well with half that number. There was a band of eight or ten plus several performers, a few working men, and a scattering of trainers, side show people, ticket sellers, a cook, a treasurer, clowns, and the owner. Since much doubling in brass occurred, one might find the sword swallower as the pony trainer at a later time, the sideshow magician as a big show circus clown.

Every two-car show was framed differently, but on the

lot there might be a forty- or fifty-foot side show top with an appropriate banner line in front. Lacking an office wagon, this circus sold big show tickets from a folding ticket box. The midway also included·a lemonade stand, balloon vendor, and the marquee leading to the big show. There was no menagerie tent. Any cages with wild animals were exhibited in the sideshow or wheeled into the big top when it was time for their charges to perform. Traditional circus seating was used—the blue general admission bleachers and a few lengths of star-back reserves. Wrapping it up was an eighty-foot round top and one, two, or three middle pieces depending upon the number of rings and stages used in the performance.

The program might include an act by the trainer with a cage full of lions. There was bound to be a heavy helping of pony acts, including individual trained animals, pony drills of six or eight head, hippodrome races, and tableau acts with other animals. Trained dogs were in profusion, along with some monkeys and goats. A camel was nearly inevitable on a two-car show. Most of these marvels had an elephant, but when the animal grew too large the owner traded it off for a smaller one that didn't take up too much room and still cleared the door to the baggage car. In the performance, too, were a few acrobats and aerialists, although two-car shows would fuss with only a minimum of aerial rigging.

Almost all of the outfits in the two-car class trouped as gilly shows. This meant that they either hired local wagons or trucks to carry the show from train to lot or carried their own gilly wagon—a skeletal frame on four wagon wheels. If there were two gilly wagons, the crew could load one while the show's single team hauled the other to and from the showgrounds. When the circus was loaded, the gilly wagon's wheels were dismounted, and all the spindly parts of the wagon were stuffed into the last remaining space on the baggage car. Some two-car shows carried a single team of work horses, others carried four light horses which were used first with gilly wagons, then as a four-horse team on a

bandwagon, and finally as a liberty act in the big show.

Some two-car shows had bandwagons, and in many cases they corralled enough show equipment to present a creditable parade. Included was the band, perhaps a lion cage, and smaller dens with monkeys or birds. Performers rode on trained horses. The pony act was split up to draw cages. There might be clown carts, the camel, and the elephant. One two-car show capped its parade with a calliope on a Model-T truck, but by that time it had exceeded the capacity of its railroad cars, and the Model-T was driven overland.

Exceptions to the gilly show format were those several circuses that utilized tunnel cars. In these cases the baggage car, sometimes of extra length, had end doors. The show would affix runs and load low-cut baggage wagons and cages end-to-end in the tunnel car. Upon arrival in the next town, these wagons would be unloaded in a fashion similar to that of flatcar circuses, and teams would take them to the showgrounds. The circuses operated by Floyd and Howard King in the early 1920s utilized three, four, and five cars, including tunnel cars. The Sparks Old Virginia Shows had three cars at the turn of the century—a coach, an overladen flatcar, and an overlength tunnel car. An almost identical seventy-six-foot baggage car was on Busby Bros. Circus of 1902 and the Cook Bros. Circus of 1906.

A good number of circuses that reached major proportion or played significant roles in circus history began as two-car shows. Among these were Christy Bros., Gentry Bros., and Rhoda Royal. Still others began as wagon shows and shifted to the two-car format, among them the Mollie Bailey Show. The John H. Sparks Circus began on wagons, shifted to two-car operation, and grew into the flatcar classification.

The greatest name among two-car showmen was that of Jones—J. Augustus Jones and his brother, Elmer Jones. They operated a whole fleet of two-car shows, sometimes several in a single season, and occasionally interspersed a bigger show among them. The J. Augustus Jones All-New

Model Plate Railroad Shows of 1902 had three cars and seventy people. In 1904 they had the Jones Model Plate Railroad Shows and the Jones New Empire Show, each on two cars. The Jones & Adams New Century Railroad Shows of 1906 boasted of its own electric light plant. The Jones brothers also had Cole & Rogers Circus during the same year. The West & Wells Circus, as well as the King & Tucker Circus, the Parks & Banks Circus, and the Stone & Murray Circus, were two-car operations in the Jones stable. There was the Great Eastern Hippodrome Show of 1918, Rice Bros. Circus of 1920, and Wheeler Bros. All New Shows in 1921. Elmer Jones went to western Canada in 1913 with two seventy-foot circus cars, twenty-eight people, fifteen ponies, twelve dogs, a camel, and an elephant. The Jones brothers' 1918 Hugo Bros. Circus had a sleeper with two staterooms, a washroom, kitchen, and berths. Working men slept in the ninety-foot baggage car. The show made $60,000 in Canada and closed early because of the flu epidemic. The three-car Cole & Rogers Circus of 1928 had two camels, two elephants, four baggage horses, about twenty-four ponies, several small cages, a bandwagon, and a gilly wagon.

Two-car outfits were high grass shows, playing the sticks and making every corner of the country, but they thrived in certain territory. The mountains of Tennessee and Virginia were two-car country. These shows were constantly to be found on the coal roads of Kentucky and West Virginia. The Dakotas were happy hunting grounds for two-car shows, and in the sparsely settled provinces of western Canada the two-car shows fairly stumbled over each other as they followed the wheat harvest.

What began in the 1880s reached a peak about the time of World War I. At that time railroad rates, the coming of automobiles, and the gradual elimination of local passenger trains spelled out the doom of two-car circuses. Only Elmer Jones stuck it out to the middle 1930s. His outfit played New York state in June 1934 and then made a lengthy tour of Canada. When the two cars were switched back to a United States line, the show was stopped because of faulty rail equipment. The cars were bad-ordered. That left only Cooper Bros. Circus. As the last of the two-car shows, it played Canadian towns all season. After that Elmer Jones called it quits; the two-car circus was a thing of the past.

Opposite page, above: The end door is wide open and gilly wagons are parked at the two side doors as the lone baggage car of Cole Bros. Circus gives forth the makings of its 1924 edition. Presently that Model-T pick-up will tow another load to the lot. No need to call attention to smallness by painting the show's title on the cars. Only the initiated would know that CBS stood for Cole Bros. Shows. And despite its number, that blistered old coach completes the consist. Even counting the two cars on Elmer Jones' other outfit, Cooper Bros. Circus, there was no way they could muster enough cars to utilize seven numbers. Two-car shows were the little giants of circus business, trouping unbelievable quantities of show property in minimum rolling stock — *Joseph Fleming Collection. Opposite page, below:* Mixed in with freight cars, the Col. George W. Hall Trained Wild Animal Circus is trundled through the mountains of western Canada. This was a 1916 show operated on two cars by William P. (Low Grass) Campbell. The baggage car was 100 feet long and the coach 80 feet. There were seventy-five people on the show. Two-car shows moved in regular passenger trains or along with usual freight trains. Only rarely did they make special moves by themselves — *Circus World Museum.*

This intriguing car was the rolling stock for Teets Bros. Palmetto Shows, a trick that played crossroads and junction towns in Kentucky and Tennessee for nearly fifty years (but not sixty-five). They carried four ponies, two draft horses, and a knocked-down gilly wagon. The picture was taken about 1900 — *Harry Armstrong Collection.*

A battered old coach with a new side door has been converted to baggage purposes. Coupled to another coach, they comprise the Backman & Tinsch Two-Car Circus of 1920 — *Authors' Collection.*

These two cars made up the Busby Bros. Circus, Museum & Trained Animal Exhibit, a two-car outfit in 1900. Wagons were rolled through the end doors of the extra-length baggage car. One of the acrobats on this show was a performer destined to fame in the movies, Joe E. Brown — *Circus World Museum*.

The Skerbeck family of Dorchester, Wisconsin, trouped a show on this unmarked car in 1904 — *Circus World Museum.*

Sometimes Buckskin Ben's Wild West was off on its own, but here it has signed on as part of the Greater Sheesley Shows. Therefore, its two cars were attached to the carnival train — *Walker Morris Collection.*

Moving in passenger service, two-car shows bought a minimum of twenty-five first-class passenger tickets. This entitled them not only to move the passengers and their car, but also to move the baggage car. The system also was used for other show cars. This ticket issued by the New York Central for passage between Cleveland and Peru, Indiana, in February 1937, is stamped on the back to indicate that a baggage car was included. Apparently this is one of the tickets purchased to transport the Terrell Jacobs wild animal act from the Cleveland Grotto Circus back to the Peru winter quarters — *Authors' Collection.*

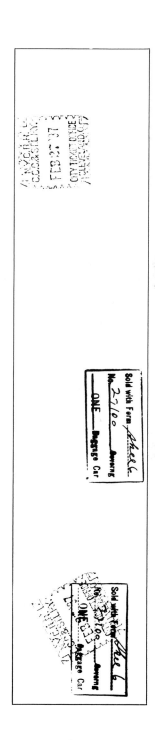

The two-car format was so popular that printers of stock advertising materials offered showmen such art as this. The view of cars, luckily numbered 7 and 11, and tent could be used by two-car circuses or by such other two-car enterprises as Uncle Tom's Cabin shows, minstrel shows, tent theaters, and even early tented movie outfits — *Circus World Museum*

Modern Moves

John Ringling North in mid-season 1956 ordered his circus home and declared that its days as a tented show were ended. At the Sarasota winter quarters he sidetracked the seventy-nine cars and with it the eighty-five-year tradition for circus tents and circus trains.

But Ringling Bros. and Barnum & Bailey was still in business. Thereafter, it played modern arenas instead of tents and switched to the transportation format identified with indoor circuses. For several years Polack Bros. Circus, Hamid-Morton Circus, and other winter shows had been travelling by a combination of motor truck and baggage car. Now each act or family had its own truck and house trailer for overland transportation. The show-owned equipment, primarily elephants, moved by baggage car in regular passenger service. Single performers, mainly clowns, rode on passenger trains with tickets that the circus bought to move the baggage car. It was an adaptation of the old two-car format. It was the system used as well by scores of theatrical companies, orchestras, operas, and principal vaudeville acts.

Starting in 1957 Ringling Bros. and Barnum & Bailey transported its indoor circus on nine semitrailers, other assorted trucks, and three railroad cars. The latter were the showmen's favorite—balloon-top baggage cars from the Pennsylvania Railroad. They were seventy feet, nine inches long and nine feet, one inch wide with a load capacity of 50,000 pounds. Equipped with roller bearings, they moved in regularly scheduled passenger trains. These cars bore names that reflected their show business assignment. Car 6090 was the *Tannhaeuser* and carried Ringling horses. Car 6084, the *Mozart,* and Car 6094, the *Edwin Booth,* carried Ringling elephants.

The Ringling circus discovered that this system was not without problems. On occasion the baggage cars and performers missed passenger train connections. Performers driving overland were delayed by breakdowns and weather and sometimes got lost. The cost of truck operations surged upwards. The system was used for the seasons of 1957, '58, and '59.

Then circus manager Art Concello and his assistant, Lloyd Morgan Sr. sought a new way. They had been selling off the old circus flats and stockcars, but there was no market for the coaches. Working with what they already had on hand, Concello and Morgan reworked fifteen of the American Car & Foundry coaches which the circus had bought from the Army Medical Corps and used through 1956. In 1960 Ringling Bros. and Barnum & Bailey again was a full-fledged railroad circus, but with a difference. Since it no longer carried tents and seats and generators and a cookhouse and all the other equipment that once was necessary to make it self-sufficient, the show no longer needed eighty or ninety cars. The new show carried only the people, the paraphernalia and the animals essential to the performance. This was a fifteen-car show which, from the outside, looked like as many coaches. In actuality there were eight refurbished coaches, one elephant car, one ring stock car, and four tunnel cars.

Concello and Morgan found that the interior of the cars could be converted readily to carry elephants and horses. It took more effort and help from ACF to devise the tunnel cars. The interiors were removed and the ends were taken off. With cross-over plates, wagons could be rolled the full length of the tunnel created by the four cars. Ringling Bros. and Barnum & Bailey designed and built new wagons with dimensions that utilized the maximum amount of car space. An interior system of cable and pulleys with a power unit on one car pulled the circus wagons into the tunnel cars. A ten-kilowatt light plant on Car 20 supplied power for the tunnel and stockcars. Two forty-kilowatt light plants furnished power for the coaches. Arrangements were made to heat the coaches because in its new routing the circus would be playing all winter and experiencing temperatures below freezing. The new wagons were seven feet high and seven feet wide. Most of them were sixteen feet long, and all moved on dual wheels with twelve- or sixteen-inch pneumatic tires. The new rigging wagon was twenty-four feet long. There were two rubber mat wagons, one twenty-seven feet long, the other nineteen and one-half feet in length. Together they carried 130 pieces of rubber matting, which served as a protective flooring on which the performance was given in each arena. These three largest wagons were equipped with three wheels on each corner, partly because of the weight and partly to insure a continued mobility, even in the case of tire failure. A flat tire on a wagon in a tunnel car would be nearly inaccessible and could cause damaging delay.

Proud with its new train, the Ringling circus set out again with new spirit. No longer was it limited to the low speed limits of old. Now it was cleared for up to seventy-nine miles an hour and for regular passenger service. While at the outset it was expected that the train would move as a part of regular passenger trains on occasion, in actuality this happened only rarely, if at all. From the first, all of the jumps were made as special moves.

Despite its innovations, its inventiveness, and initiative, the Ringling circus train really was not a new development. It was in fact a simple extension of the old two-car circus system. The two-car shows had tunnel cars, perhaps only one. They had coaches, perhaps only one. They carried animals in baggage cars, perhaps only one. The Ringling show now used the same tried and true formula on a grander scale.

Ringling's Cars 30 and 31 each carried ten elephants and included a room with twelve bunks at one end. A zebra and guanaco also traveled in these cars. Car 32 carried twenty-three horses, five ponies, and three burros. One end was fitted out as a fine stateroom for Dr. J. Y. Henderson, the circus veterinarian. The tunnel cars were numbers 20, 21, 22, and 23. The first was a runs car. Together these units carried four tractors, fourteen wagons, one carriage, six floats, and a big cage wagon, plus eight smaller cages that were loaded two abreast.

For this operation Concello was executive director, Harold (Tuffy) Genders was general manager, Charlie Smith was superintendent of transportation, and Deacon Blanchfield was trainmaster.

Ringling's return to full rail operation was highly successful. The show recovered its old spirit, and its financial picture improved immensely. The train was expanded to twenty-five cars, carrying a correspondingly bigger circus. Then in 1968 it was sold by the Ringling family to a new combination headed by Irvin Feld, a Washington, D. C. showman who had been active in the promotion of Ringling dates for a decade and who had great ideas for expanding the show.

The first and biggest step in his program came in 1969 when the circus fielded an entirely new second unit on twenty railroad cars. The established show was identified as the Red unit, and it continued on twenty-five cars. The new Blue unit moved on cars from the Penn Central's Twentieth Century Limited and the Rock Island's Rocket, which by then had been discontinued. It had a single tunnel car and four brand new piggyback flats. For twelve seasons there had been no flatcar circus train. Now Ringling not only continued the tradition of tunnel cars, but also revived the heritage of open flatcars. In 1970 both units moved on twenty-five cars, and the other unit was altered to make room for flatcars. The Red unit had three tunnel cars, four stocks, and four piggyback flats. The Blue unit had two tunnel cars, four stockcars, and five piggyback flats. Each unit included fourteen coaches.

The growth pattern continued in 1971 when the two shows were increased to thirty cars each, made up of three tunnel cars, four stocks, five piggyback flats, and eighteen coaches. There was still another development in the next season. Lloyd Morgan Sr., general manager of the Blue show, incorporated a two-level rack car of his own design. Cages of wild animals were on the lower level; automobiles of circus executives and stars were carried on the upper level.

Thus, in 1973 the Blue train had one tunnel car, four stockcars, one rack car, five piggyback cars, and nineteen coaches. The Red unit reflected additional growth with a consist of thirty-two cars, including two tunnel cars, four stockcars, five piggyback flats, one new rack car, and twenty coaches. The show's piggyback flats, constructed by the American Car & Foundry Company, were eighty-nine feet and four inches long, and cost about $25,000 each.

In early 1972 Ringling Bros. and Barnum & Bailey purchased thirty cars from the Union Pacific Railroad, including sixteen coaches in the 5400 series and fourteen baggage cars also just out of streamliner service. They were shipped to winter quarters at Venice, Florida, where circus crews converted the cars into a complete new train for the Red unit that went into use in 1973. The retired show train, made up of cars which had given the circus a quarter cen-

tury of fine service, were held under twenty-four-hour security at the Port Tampa yards of the Seaboard Coastline for further use at Ringling Bros. and Barnum & Bailey's Circus World, a gigantic 600-acre circus theme park in central Florida.

The 1973 season marked another departure in circus railroading. Since time immemorial, probably back to that first move made by William Cameron Coup out of New Brunswick, New Jersey, in 1872, circuses had to pay cash on the barrelhead for each railroad stint at the time of the move. Only a few instances of circus moves on credit have been recorded. One such move was made by Gentry Bros. Dog & Pony Show about 1908. Another was made by the Col. Tim McCoy Real Wild West Show during its death throes in 1938. For every other circus move through 1972, a century of circus railroading, some railroad agent had to keep the office open or pound through the yards at midnight to find the right show executive. And on each of those hundred years of show nights, every circus had to prepay the cost of the move in currency, not check. With the 1973 season, the Ringling Circus and the railroads started a new plan. Robert Maio, Ringling's railroad contracting agent, proposed it, and the railroads eagerly accepted it. Now invoices are sent to the show's Washington, D. C. headquarters, and transportation fees are paid monthly in the normal business fashion by which billings are handled.

As railroad circusing moved into its second century, Ringling Bros. and Barnum & Bailey Circus was moving on sixty-two cars, a total almost identical with the consist of that pioneer Barnum Show of 1872. Both the differences and the similarities were multitudinous. Diesel replaced steam. Electricity replaced kerosene. Aluminum replaced iron. But coaches and stockcars were much alike. Flatcars were little changed, and their runs and cross-over plates were the same. On board were clowns and elephants and wild animals and aerialists and trainers and all the rest required then and now to present that fabulous entertainment called the circus. In ensuing seasons the two units continued to grow and prosper. The future was bright for Ringling railroading, and there was a promise of even more new units in future seasons.

* * * * *

Reconstitution of the Ringling-Barnum Circus is well illustrated by the make-up of its railroad trains over a period of slightly more than twenty years.

In 1956, operating as a tented attraction, the show carried its own seats, poles, canvas, cookhouse, power plants, and all the other equipment to make it nearly self-sufficient. It moved on seventy-nine cars. But this traditional circus came to a halt that season.

Thereafter, it operated in arenas, carrying only those things that contributed directly to the massive performance. It started modestly in difficult times, but the growth has been constant and often spectacular—especially in 1969 when it fielded an all-new duplicate circus, nearly doubling itself.

Together, the two units comprised nearly as many railroad cars and certainly more total performance than it had under the older format. Here is how it grew:

REVIVAL OF RINGLING AS A RAILROAD CIRCUS
From the Close of the Tented Show in 1956

Season	Coaches	Stocks	Flats	Tunnels	Racks	Total
1956	24	8	47	—	—	79
1957	—	3	—	—	—	3
1958	—	3	—	—	—	3
1959	—	3	—	—	—	3
1960	8	3	—	4	—	15
1961	8	3	—	4	—	15
1962	8	3	—	4	—	15
1963	8	3	—	4	—	15
1964	10	4	—	5	—	19
1965	13	4	—	5	—	22
1966	14	4	—	6	—	24
1967	13	4	—	6	—	23
1968	14	4	—	7	—	25
1969						
Red	14	4	—	7	—	25
Blue	11	4	4	1	—	20
						45
1970						
Red	14	4	4	3	—	25
Blue	14	4	5	2	—	25
						50
1971						
Red	18	4	5	3	—	30
Blue	18	4	5	3	—	30
						60
1972						
Red	18	4	5	2	1	30
Blue	19	4	5	1	1	30
						60
1973						
Red	20	4	5	2	1	32
Blue	19	4	5	1	1	30
						62
1974						
Red	20	4	7	2	1	34
Blue	20	5	7	1	1	34
						68
1975						
Red	19	5	7	2	1	34
Blue	20	5	7	1	1	34
						68
1976						
Red	21	5	7	2	1	36
Blue	20	6	7	2	1	36
						72
1977						
Red	21	5	7	2	1	36
Blue	23	4	7	2	1	37
						73
1978						
Red	22	5	7	2	1	37
Blue	23	4	8	2	1	38
						73

Sturdy caretaker of the tradition for railroad shows, Ringling Bros. and Barnum & Bailey Circus operated two major, modern show trains in the late 1970s, utilizing more than seventy cars in all. This is the Red unit on Penn Central tracks at Troy, New York, in 1976. Twenty years before, the picture was less favorable — *Gene Baxter Photo.*

Both photos: Ringling-Barnum coaches snake through the countryside at Troy, New York, in 1976, and long strings of piggyback flatcars carry on the century-old tradition and processes of the railroad circus — *Gene Baxter Photo.*

Watching a circus load up at night is part of being a boy, and some small part of those boys still runs off to join the show. These trackside superintendents are on duty at Troy, New York, in 1977 — *Gene Baxter Photo.*

Few townspeople are present to watch when the engagement is over and the circus goes back to its train. Circusing is an around-the-clock operation — *Gene Baxter Photo.*

Tail lights and floodlights blur the scene as two wardrobe wagons are nuzzled up to a tunnel car. Ringling-Barnum is loading out at Troy, New York, in 1977 — *Gene Baxter Photo.*

During the last three years of the Fifties, the Ringling circus held on to its status as a railroad show by the slim margin of these three Pennsylvania baggage cars, leased to carry show horses and elephants while other circus property moved by semitrailer. The baggage cars, especially designed for transporting show equipment, were seventy feet, nine inches long and nine feet, one inch wide inside. While representing a latter-day circus operation, these were an historical throwback to the days of two-car gilly shows — *Authors' Photo.*

Lloyd Morgan, Sr., half-century veteran of the Ringling Bros. and Barnum & Bailey Circus, first converted the old train of tenting days into the new fifteen-car tunnel show in 1959, utilizing the concept originated by Art Concello, general manager of the circus. Later, Morgan converted Rock Island Rocket baggage cars and Twentieth Century Limited Pullmans into an all-new show train for the Ringling Blue unit, for which he was to be general manager. Morgan also updated the two Ringling circus trains in subsequent seasons as newer equipment was brought into use. He is shown here inspecting historic circus wagons and flatcars at the Circus World Museum — *Authors' Photo.*

Ringling executives decided that trains comprised the only way to troupe. So while their interim outfit moved about by semis and baggage cars, activity burst forth at the railroad yards and winter circus quarters at Sarasota, Florida. This was the scene as the show gutted its old sleepers and rebuilt them to carry wagons, elephants, and horses as well as circus personnel. At the center is a tunnel car and beyond it, to the right, is an older private car from the heyday of the railroad show. Here, certain of the former army hospital cars take on their third form as tunnel cars and stockcars for the circus — *Authors' Photo.*

All else might change, but it is still the Greatest Show on Earth — *Authors' Photo.*

It was back to the high iron for the big show. Here, Ringlings' fifteen-car train moves over Chicago & North Western tracks at Milwaukee in 1960 — *Authors' Collection.*

Trainmasters on the 1978 show trains included Charlie Smith, popular veteran with the Ringling Bros. and Barnum & Bailey Red unit. He began trouping with a medicine show, later went with the Dailey Bros. Circus, saw a season or so with the Clyde Beatty show, and came to Ringling in the fateful season of 1956. He saw the show increase its railroad operation from three baggage cars to trains of thirty-seven and thirty-eight cars each. Here, Smith surveys the scene from the runs in Union Pacific yards at Seattle in 1977 — *Authors' Photo.*

Circus trainmaster Charlie Smith mans one of the show's leased Clark tractors to unload Wagon 25 and incidentally demonstrate the technique of tunnel car operation. It utilizes the traditional runs and end-loading concept of flatcar circuses but makes use of tunnel cars equipped for passenger car service. Jacks under these runs were equipped with telescoping legs that could be adjusted to fit terrain in varying crossing conditions — *Authors' Photo*

Tunnel cars gave a clear shot for towing wagons on and off. A cable visible at the center of the deck was used for pulling wagons into the cars and assisting in the unloading — *Authors' Photo.*

Slim tolerances for wagons in tunnel cars made it necessary to stabilize adjacent cars so that the decks would remain even and wagons could roll freely from car to car. This was a problem not faced when the circus used flatcars that were not only open on top, but also were equipped with less responsive spring action. With tunnel cars, a loaded unit might be several inches below the deck of an adjacent unloaded car — *Authors' Photo.*

Right: Tunnel cars or not, Ringling continued the old flatcar system of cross-over plates for hauling wagons from car to car. Hand brakes had to be placed out of the way for both circus and railroad procedures — *Authors' Photo. Above:* Some wagons of the first Ringling tunnel train were narrow enough to be loaded two abreast. Here, a Clark tractor (equipped with a portable welding outfit) tows not only a string of tiger cages shrouded in canvas, but also the sections that make up the arena in which the tigers later will perform — *Authors' Photo.*

Former circus coaches became side door Pullmans for high-strung ring stock such as this dapple gray, which is being loaded aboard 32 Car in 1960 — *Authors' Photo.*

Regardless of the nature of the rolling stock, a circus train soon takes on its own familiar appearance. In this photo, picketed horses munch hay and a groom relaxes with his newspaper at the ramp — *Authors' Photo.*

Early evening sees lights turned on in Milwaukee's high-rise skyline and in the coaches of the new-style Ringling train, which pauses under the old train shed of the C&NW depot — *Authors' Photo.*

Success of the modern Ringling operation encouraged the show to duplicate the entire system when it created an all-new second circus in 1969. Once again the winter quarters became the scene of much work on rail cars. But this time the circus had purchased coaches from the New York Central and baggage cars from the CRI&P Railway — *Authors' Photo.*

New brake shoes and springs are among the items of railroad hardware stockpiled at trackside during the conversion of Rock Island equipment to Ringling use — *Authors' Photo.*

The pride of the new train for Ringlings' Blue unit was the *Hickory Creek,* a private car utilized by general manager Lloyd Morgan, Sr. Earlier, *Hickory Creek* had been the tail end car of one unit of the Twentieth Century Limited. Here the circus has retained the old Pullman name but already has added the Greatest Show on Earth herald at the forward end and a Ringling-Barnum circus logo where once there was the identifying drum of the prestigious Century — *Authors' Photo.*

With the creation of a second show in 1969, Ringling completed a cycle by adding piggyback flatcars. Here, Ringling wagons and tractor grace the deck of eighty-nine-foot "pigs." Wagons on the new Blue unit had been used earlier on a European unit and would not have fit into tunnel cars — *Authors' Photo.*

Here, the cross-over plates are so sophisticated as to include hinges, but the basic circus operation remains unchanged with the show's utilization of piggyback flats — *Authors' Photo.*

Finished and ready to roll, the Ringling cars were white, with the title painted in red and yellow. At this time, the Blue unit joined its sister Red outfit, thus doubling the number of circus trains on American rails — *Authors' Photo.*

While the circus traveled once again in freight service and invariably by special move, the new version nevertheless was equipped for much faster operation. Steel wheels, air brakes, and other operations meeting passenger service standards were used by the circus — *Authors' Photo.*

Perfection and modification continued. Here the show makes use of a set of jacks designed to rest, not on the ties and roadbed, but on the rails. This system assures the circus of consistent measurements day after day. Logical as the system seems now, circus men had tried it fifty years earlier and rejected it. In the earlier case, the 101 Ranch Real Wild West Show had wooden jacks that spanned the rails and sat on top of them like those pictured here, but the plan was deemed impractical. Circus train crews of that era went back to jacks that were blocked up from the roadbed. Now a tractor operator with Ringling's Blue unit wheels the 17 Wagon from piggyback flat to crossing via the modernized runs — *Authors' Photo.*

It's new and yet it's old. Here the Ringling Blue unit is unloaded at St. Petersburg, Florida, in January 1970, the first time the circus was unloaded during its Centennial seasons. The tractor, runs, flats, and wagons all are new, and yet each traces its heritage to the earliest days of circus railroad operation — *Authors' Photo.*

Still the modernization goes on. In 1972 the Ringling show modified one of its piggyback cars to serve as a doubledeck rack car. On top would be the private automobiles of show executives and circus stars. On the lower deck were cages of trained tigers. Sliding panels allowed ventilation and protection in winter, a feature needed now that the circus traveled virtually year around — *Authors' Photo.*

New sets of wheels were lined up for installation at circus winter quarters in Venice, Florida. Each pair is stencilled with the identifying word "circus" — *Authors' Photo.*

Utilizing former Union Pacific cars, the new rolling stock of the Ringling Red unit included five light plants such as this 300 kilowatt unit mounted just above the six-wheel trucks of 46 Car — *Authors' Collection.*

Handling the details of railroad transportation of both the Red and Blue trains of the Ringling circus operation was Robert Maio (on the ground). He moved in advance of both trains to confirm railroad contracts and arrangements. Here he checks the layout at Tucson, Arizona, with Jim Koch, trainmaster of the Southern Pacific railroad — *David R. L. Titus Photo.*

Left: Operation of show trains requires constant maintenance. This possum-belly on a Ringling car in Venice quarters includes a supply of heavy washers used under coil springs of railroad trucks, as well as spare coupler parts and draw bars — *Authors' Photo. Below:* A new coat of white enamel is applied to the cars of Ringlings' Blue unit at Venice winter quarters in January 1974 — *Authors' Photo.*

Life aboard the circus train can be very comfortable. Here, lion trainer Wolfgang Holtzmeyer and his daughter, Silvana, enjoy the comforts of their stateroom. The appointments are a blend inspired in part by the circus, in part by European origins, and — at least in the case of the television — by a competing entertainment institution — *Ringling Bros. and Barnum & Bailey.*

Part of life on the circus train still centers on the pie car. Performers and others meet here for meals and socializing. After performances and while the train is en route, the pie car hums with activity — *Ringling Bros. and Barnum & Bailey.*

Official symbol of the United States Bicentennial helps decorate this coach in the Ringling Bros. and Barnum & Bailey circus train for the 1975-76 Bicentennial edition — *Ringling Bros. and Barnum & Bailey.*

Modified and modernized, the circus continues its long affiliation with the nation's railroads. Here, in February 1975, the train of the Blue show moves from Venice winter quarters to Lakeland, Florida, where it will launch a new season in a new arena. Locomotive 330 is at the head end as the SCL RR moves the train over its main line from Tampa to Lakeland — *Authors' Photo.*

Above: Sidetracked to unload in the Lakeland yards of the Seaboard Coast Line, the combination of tunnel car and piggyback flats gives the circus train its traditional appearance — *Authors' Photo. Right:* End-of-the-rack car displays not only the high-riding automobile and the lower deck of tandem tiger cages, but also an array of high-rise runs in folded traveling position and combination cross-over plates and runs below — *Authors' Photo.*

With the switching accomplished and the runs in place, a Ringling truck wheels out the 15 and 16 Wagons to launch another season of trouping by rail — *Authors' Photo.*

Cars of the Ringling Bros. and Barnum & Bailey circus train stretch out along sidetracks in the Kansas City yards of the Frisco line in the 1960s — *Jim McRoberts Photo.*

Originally army hospital cars and then passenger coaches for the Ringling flatcar circus, this rolling stock now serves as side-door Pullmans for show horses. Similar cars quarter the circus elephants. This was the unloading scene at Kansas City in 1964 — *Jim McRoberts.*

AT & SF Extra 4019 North climbs out of Colorado Springs, Colorado, in August 1976. It's one and the same as the Red unit of the Ringling circus en route between Albuquerque, New Mexico, and Salt Lake City, Utah — *Robert R. Harmen Photo.*

On its first run of the 1978 season, the Ringling Red unit rolls into Lakeland, Florida. The Seaboard Coast Line Railroad has brought the show from Venice, Florida, site of its winter quarters and opening stand — *Authors' Photo*.

Aboard a Show Train

To pinpoint the smooth interrelationship between a railroad and the Ringling Circus in a modern-day move, one of the authors (C. P. Fox), who had an opportunity to ride the Red Show train of Ringling Bros. and Barnum & Bailey from Salt Lake City to Denver in fall 1977, detailed the following narrative:

The finest performers from many nations are taking their bows. Here, beautiful caparisoned horses prance, and there, a seemingly endless line of ponderous elephants forms a long mount. The arena is filled with glorious spectacle — the finale of Ringling Bros. and Barnum & Bailey Circus. Ten thousand people in the audience stand and cheer and clap.

A long blast of the ringmaster's whistle brings the show to a close. "This concludes our performance of the Greatest Show on Earth," he says. "May all your days be circus days!"

It is the end. And yet, it is just the beginning.

Because the performance is over — the last of a six-day stand at the Salt Palace in Salt Lake City — it is time for the other half of circusing to start. Now the part that has been dormant for six days springs to life in a continuation of the century-plus duet by railroads and circuses. The show is about to move.

Actually, the process had started during the performance. The circus trainmaster, Charley Smith, had ordered motive power from the Denver & Rio Grande Railroad to be ready exactly six hours from the starting time of the final performance. In that interval, the circus will perform and load. During that show, as the need for each item is completed, the equipment will be loaded. Props for the tiger act, the jugglers' ten pins, the acrobats' teeterboard — all will be loaded in the designated wagons. As show girls finish with each production number, those costumes will be returned to cases that will roll at once into wagons.

Even as the audience is still leaving, great activity builds up at the Salt Palace. Tractors brings wagons. Men lower rigging to the floor. The blocks and falls are carefully laid out, then coiled, bagged, and loaded into 35 Wagon. Rubber floor mats are loaded onto 26 and 27 Wagons. Electrical equipment goes back into 21 Wagon. Each and every piece is loaded into the same box and the same wagon each time the show moves. Wagon 30 is packed with equipment from the horse department. If 22 Wagon rolls by, the circus bosses know that it carries the elephant blankets. As each load is completed, the wagon is coupled to others, and the set is towed to the railroad siding, where the thirty-eight cars are spotted. The circus trainmaster has been in touch with the railroad crew that will be handling the train on the trip from Salt Lake City to Denver. Cars are spotted in proper relation to the street crossing to give adequate room for loading. Horse cars and elephant cars are placed so that the animals can get aboard. The show's trainmaster, anticipating unloading plans, loads all wagons poles to caboose. The circus train crew has set up the runs. The cross-over plates link the cars. Light poles are strung along the flats, anticipating the night's work.

First loaded are staff automobiles, placed on the top level of the rack car. The lower deck is for the tiger cages, which will arrive soon, since the cats were the first act in the performance.

There is a lull at the crossing until the distant performance ends at 10:30 P.M. But then activity steps up at the train. The horses and elephants arrive. Strings of from two to six wagons, drawn by tractors or Jeeps, come into view. The personnel bus has been shuttling performers and workers from the building to the train. Inside the Salt Palace, the final wagons, loaded with rubber flooring and ring mats, are ready. There is one last check for anything left behind, and then the building is cleared. Outside, the streets are cluttered with circus vehicles and a crowd of towners that has come to watch. The wagons are loaded onto flatcars.

At 1:30 A.M. October 4, the circus trainmaster advises the railroad men that the show train is secure and ready to roll. The road dispatcher is so advised. Aboard the caboose on a nearby track, the conductor and brakeman confer by radio with the engineer. The motive power begins to make up the train. The horse cars — 32 and 33 — and the elephant cars — 30 and 31 — are at the head end, followed by the long string of coaches. Then come the flatcars with the wagons and finally the tunnel cars with the tigers and leopards. Once the train is made up, the brake system is pumped up with air and checked. The circus train — three-quarters of a mile of mysterious load — is now in the capable hands of the Denver & Rio Grande Western Railroad. This is the Red unit of Ringling Bros. and Barnum & Bailey. But now it takes on railroad designations as well, and a series of numbers becomes significant. The show outfit is designated as Train Number 108. Motive power is one SD45 diesel locomotive, two GP35s, and one GP30. These four giants provide the massive total of 9,750 horsepower that will contend with 612 mountainous miles between Salt Lake and Denver. The train crew knows its business. The men are aware of rules, clearances, signals, sidings, operating instructions, speed restrictions, train orders, zone speeds, and other details to help make this a safe trip.

The brakeman allows that this is the first circus train that he has worked, and he looks forward to the trip. The conductor brags that back in the early '30s he handled the Hagenbeck-Wallace Trained Wild Animal Circus. Their radios interrupt as the engineer reports that his maximum speed is restricted to fifty-five miles per hour. They check again with the circus trainmaster in Number 40 Car. Then almost imperceptibly the train begins to move. It is exactly 4 A.M.

The circus train heads southeasterly out of Salt Lake City and disappears into the night. Townspeople at the runs see the red marker lights of the caboose disappear into the dark. Ringling Bros. and Barnum & Bailey Circus is on the move.

Just thirty-five minutes out, the train passes over a DED and the signal flashes purple. The train immediately slows and stops. DED means Dragging Equipment Detector, and something is hanging from the train. After a radio conversation with the engineer, the caboose crew starts forward, the conductor on the left side, the brakeman on the right. With their electric lanterns, they search the underside of the circus cars. About ten cars up from the caboose, the brakeman finds the trouble. A hasp on the door of a possum belly had broken, allowing the door to swing down. The problem is fixed quickly; at 4:50 A.M. the train is on its way again.

It is gliding through Provo, Utah, at 5:45 A.M., when the station agent comments to the engineer on the radio, "That's a nice looking train you have there. How are your lions and tigers? Be careful, buddy, don't pet them."

Back comes the reply: "This train handles beautifully. Great equipment. And don't worry about the tigers; they are at the back end of the train."

At 6:40 A.M. the churning locomotives take their heavy load over Soldier's Summit, Utah, where briefly the railroad is five tracks wide. Two westbound freights are waiting for the Ringling special to clear so that they can head out.

As each signal along the right-of-way is passed, the caboose crew confirms what it saw, a verification to the engine crew that all is well and functioning properly. At Helper, Utah, there is a ten-minute stop for a crew change. This will occur three times before the run is completed. It is 7:45 A.M.

By 9:45 A.M. the train rolls over the bridge spanning the Green River, and in another hour the show train crosses the state line. There is no fancy information booth to announce it, only word from the conductor who says with a smile that "Ringling Bros. is in Colorado and Barnum & Bailey in Utah."

A feed and water stop had been arranged at Grand Junction, Colorado, where the train slips into the yards at

11:20 A.M., twenty minutes ahead of the scheduled time. The train will be here for an hour. Upon approaching Grand Junction, the circus trainmaster had notified his management and department heads, so as the train came to a stop, circus workmen swarmed out of the cars to take care of their assigned chores. The train crew walks along both sides of the flatcars to check tie-down chains and to see whether any vehicle has shifted. Men of the wild animal department give each tiger and leopard fresh water and check to be sure that all is well. Men of the elephant and horse departments check their animals and supply fresh water, fill the hay bags for horses, and give the elephants new hay.

Along the trackside is a very regular-looking assemblage of people, dressed in combinations of blue jeans, shorts, blouses, dungarees, T-shirts, and sweatshirts. They hardly appear to be those special people — the spangled performers from around the world who appear in the Greatest Show on Earth. Here, along the railroad tracks in western Colorado, they are just nice people, exercising dogs, throwing stones into a creek, playing catch, or conversing. It is a pleasant break in the long train ride, and the hour passes rapidly.

The train crew and circus trainmaster exchange radio conversations; they need two minutes more. When the circus boss nods, the engineer gives two blasts on the locomotive horn. Performers and working men climb aboard to resume the routine of life aboard a circus train, with card games, writing, sewing, reading, and perhaps going to the pie car for lunch.

The Denver & Rio Grande Western tracks now skirt the Colorado River and cut through more beautiful country. As the long cars move through canyons and around sweeping curves, the circus people enjoy the magnificent scenery.

Frequently, the track parallels an interstate highway. The motorists are startled and pleased to see the silver cars with twenty-four-inch red letters identifying the circus train. Truck drivers give blasts of their horns in response to waves from circus people in the vestibules of the railroad cars.

Automobiles loaded with vacationing families speed ahead of the train so that they can pull over and allow all to jump out, cameras in hand, to watch the unexpected show train.

All afternoon the cars glide through the magnificent landscape. Around this curve a hillside is decorated in bright yellow fall colors of aspen trees. Around that canyon, one looks down upon the rushing waters that tumble and splash among gigantic boulders. The train moves through Grand Valley, Rifle, and Glenwood Springs, after which the tracks turn north for a few miles, then curve eastward again. The Colorado River continues its splashing flow as if to escort the tracks and train. After all, *it* was here first, the railroad builders only followed as best as they could the route which the river cut through this country thousands of years before. But the railroad then made changes; the tracks slash through mountainsides, first in deep cuts and then in tunnels. The locomotives at the head end of the circus train purr along consistently even when the long train is negotiating a gigantic S-curve through this rugged country. Whenever the train comes to a stretch of welded track, it seems to float along; the clickety-clack is missing.

By 4:30 P.M., just over twelve hours out of Salt Lake City, the train passes through Troublesome Flat. Twelve miles farther east is Sulphur Springs. Townspeople, caught by surprise at seeing the silver cars, at first just stare, then smile and finally wave. The same pattern had been seen at each town along the way — American Fork, Thistle, Wellington, Solitude, Sphinx, Silt, Grizzly, Fox Junction.

At Sulphur Springs the track turns generally south, curving this way and that way as it winds through the Rocky Mountains. At Winter Park the route again turns east, and the train is suddenly upon the west portal of the world-famous Moffat Tunnel. The circus trainmaster had radioed prior warning to all department heads. Now the circus train plunges into the sudden darkness of the six-and-one-half-mile artery through the massive rock formations. Speed is restricted to forty miles per hour. The tunnel is well ventilated and equipped with twenty-one telephone stations from which the train dispatcher could be advised of any emergency or need to stop deep in the bowels of the mountain. While in the Moffat Tunnel, the circus train crosses — or passes under — the Continental Divide.

Now the circus train is only fifty miles from Denver, but the going is slow because of the rough terrain. It is 8:30 P.M. before the outskirts of Denver come into view. The train rolls over a railroad car scale on the main line. As the diesels move the train over the scales at about five miles per hour, each car is weighed without stopping. The total weight of the circus, including people, equipment, elephants, and everything, is an astounding 2,730 tons, or nearly 5,500,000 pounds.

By 9:30 P.M. the train is well into the Denver yards. There are "greeting committees" at each crossing — kids of all ages standing or sitting on automobiles or in grandpa's arms or clinging to the grab irons of neighboring boxcars. They smile and wave at the circus folk and some in their excitement wave at the flatcar loads of wagons. Denverites are out to meet Ringling Bros. and Barnum & Bailey Circus.

At 9:45 P.M. the silver train rolls to a stop, 17:45 hours and 612 miles from Salt Lake City. The four throbbing road locomotives are uncoupled. A yard switcher takes their place and eases the train around a 180-degree curve, which brings it into the north marshalling yards and onto the tracks of the Burlington Northern Railroad. There, Burlington Northern switchers take over and begin spotting the cars on the siding for unloading. By 10:30 P.M. all cars are spotted, electrical connections made, animals watered, trash bags placed at the ends of each coach, and pedestal steps set on the ground at each vestibule. The show folks settle into a familiar routine at their new Denver home.

There is time to spare, so unloading is postponed until 7 A.M. October 5, when the trainmaster signals and action starts. Two blasts on a whistle prompt a tractor driver to move ahead. One blast means "stop." Three is the signal to back up. Soon wagons move off the flats and onto the streets. A mile away at the Denver Coliseum, the performance director and his assistant assign the dressing areas, clowns in one place and show girls in another. The permanent dressing rooms of the building are assigned to key performers, and their names are taped to doors. At 8:30 A.M. Number 25 Wagon rolls into the empty coliseum, and men unload the aerial rigging. From 35 Wagon come the ropes and falls and cables so carefully coiled at Salt Lake City. Other wagons roll through the big doors. Number 26 and 27 bring the rubber flooring. Eighteen has rigging and props, and 21 Wagon contains the electrical equipment. More and more wagons are spotted in and around the coliseum. Sixty horses clatter down the cement driveway to the waiting picket line. The circus purchasing agent is checking on deliveries of meat and hay. The elephant crew sweeps out its assigned space.

It is an easy day, with no afternoon performance. By 2:00 P.M. all of the circus is ready, but the only action is around the animals and out in the rings, where a teeterboard troupe is practicing. Now the coliseum is busy and warm. Horses are knee deep in straw. The distinctive odor of elephants permeates the building. Occasionally, the tigers roar. There are ropes and wagons and props everywhere.

At 6:30 P.M. early-bird patrons begin to arrive at the coliseum, and at 7:15 P.M. the clowns tumble out to entertain the waiting thousands. It's going to be a straw house. Almost 9,000 people, every last seat filled with a human being waiting for that exciting moment. And it comes at 7:30 P.M. There is a blast of the ringmaster's whistle, and he begins. "Ladies and Gentlemen, children of all ages. . . ."

It's the start of another performance.

And it's the end of the other phase of circusing — that transformation, the trouping, the move from one stand to another.

All photographs this section: Ringling Bros. and Barnum & Bailey Red Show traveling the Denver and Rio Grande Western between Salt Lake City and Denver, 1977 — *Authors' Photos.*

Outgrowths

It isn't only that circus railroading has been around for a century. There is more to the matter than some 500 million car-miles of circus moves. For, in fact, nearly every other kind of show business also took to tracks.

Certainly, other kinds of shows and show people would have traveled by train whether circuses had blazed the trail or not. It was inevitable; everything that moved went by rail, and the multifacets of show business were no exception.

The result was some of the most unique and colorful equipment ever to ride the rails. There are two categories of additional rail shows to consider. One class is patterned after the two-car circus. The other duplicates the format of flatcar circuses.

I

In the age of vaudeville and upstairs opera houses there were as many actors as traveling salesmen on the local passenger trains. A great deal of fiction recalled them as a destitute troupe on the depot platform, left stranded by an absconding manager. Neither the stranded nor the prosperous among them is the topic of this discussion. They rode the standard coaches, carried gladstones, and checked a few trunks and diamond drops. With less show property and smaller casts, they traveled lighter.

Apart were their fellow show people who operated their own railroad rolling stock—the so-called car shows. These performers functioned in the same fashion as two-car circuses. For some, a private Pullman was enough. For others, a coach was set aside for the cast and a baggage car for the props. Sometimes even more cars were used. The performers bought their own cars and moved in passenger service, buying enough tickets to entitle them to move the baggage car as well as the coach.

Among the car shows were Shakespearean companies, melodrama troupes, big illusion expositions of famous magicians, many minstrel shows, "Uncle Tom's Cabin" companies, burlesque, opera, symphonies, famous theatrical personalities, medicine shows, vaudeville features, and every other sort of wandering troubadors and thespians.

Comprising a whole branch of show business were the proliferate companies presenting "Uncle Tom's Cabin." They came in all varieties—crossroads companies, big city productions, hall shows, tent shows, wagon shows, and railroad shows.

One of the first to take to a car of its own was Sutton's "Uncle Tom's Cabin" Company of 1888. Already it was into the dodge of giving the conductor enough tickets to earn the baggage car and hiding the excess population. Its stowaways were stashed behind the cage of bloodhounds which were used in the play.

In the 1890s, "Uncle Tom's Cabin" shows were numerous, and many of them, like circuses, were so-called pavilion shows, using tents for theaters and traveling in two or three cars of their own. The Ed F. Davis UTC company headed west, but the railroads declined to move its eighty-foot baggage car for fear it couldn't make the clearances. In 1893 the Sutton show became the first "Tom" show to reach California, and in all it logged 10,942 miles on the season.

Many showmen changed readily from operating circuses to running "Tom" shows. Among them were Andrew Downie, the Welsh brothers, Leon W. Washburn, and Tom Hargreaves. Circus man Al Martin became one of the biggest operators in UTC business, starting in 1895. His custom-built baggage car included theater-style grooves built in to hold scenery flats while in transit.

In 1902 there were sixteen "Uncle Tom's Cabin" companies. One of the biggest in the business was Stetson's Big Double Spectacular Uncle Tom's Cabin Company, which operated four units in 1904. When this quartet of shows combined to play the Star Theater in New York, the production boasted of fifty-six ponies, twenty-five bloodhounds, twenty chariots, eight donkeys, and eight carloads of scenery.

Whether as hall shows playing theaters and upstairs opera houses or as tent shows with circus-style tents, seats, and parade wagons, most "Tom" shows were railroad outfits.

A separate retinue were the railroad minstrel shows. Arising out of circuses of the 1830s, minstrels at one time were the most popular of the different types of amusement. A pioneer was Edwin P. Christy, whose successor, a circus sideshow dancer named George Harrington, operated as George Christy and the Christy Minstrels. Many of the great names in legitimate theater got their start in minstrel shows.

This form of show business also functioned both as a hall show and tent show, and most minstrel shows traveled by rail, often in their own cars. Among those active in 1903, for example, were Frank Adam's Minstrels, Billy Clark's Minstrels, Lew Dockstader's, Al G. Fields', Hi Henry's, Haverley's, Richards & Pringle's Minstrels, and Vogel's Minstrels. Twenty principal companies would be en route in the typical season.

At the turn of the century, Shreveport, Louisiana's minstrel fare was not out of the ordinary. A. G. Allen's Big Original New Orleans Colored Minstrels with eighty people and two bands arrived there in 1899 on two cars and performed under canvas near Union Depot. Mahara's Minstrel Carnival, with fifty black artists, ten ponies, forty trick dogs, Professor William Handy's Band, and a noon parade, was in Shreveport that Christmas. It was followed quickly by the combination of Richards & Pringle's Minstrels and Rusko & Holland Minstrel Show, which stopped at the Grand Opera House in January 1900. It boasted fifty-five stars, two bands, and a drum corps, all aboard their special train of Pullmans. Then came the Black Patti Troubadors' Greatest Colored Show on Earth, with Black Patti and Thirty Ebony Ecstacies at the Grand Opera House later in 1900.

The Vogel, Coburn, and Van Arnam minstrel outfits had one car each. Among the biggest and best on tour was the Cohan & Harris Minstrel Show, which toured two seasons and then sold out to Honey Boy Evans, another of the better known minstrel names.

The famous Al G. Field Minstrel Show moved on a dining-baggage combination car called the *Southland* and a sleeper called the *Dan Emmett*, named for the composer of "Dixie." Emmett also had been a star of the Field show in 1895. When the Field show ceased operations, the cars were sold in 1928 to F. S. Wolcott's Rabbit Foot Minstrel Show. The Rabbit Foot and another minstrel outfit called

"Silas Green from New Orleans," both made up entirely of black performers, continued as railroad outfits longer than any, although the Rabbit Foot moved on trucks by the time of its demise in the 1950s.

The fleet of shows roaming the nation's rail network also included the bigger acts in vaudeville—Powers' Elephants, Fink's Mules, Woodward's Seals, Singer's Midgets, and many more. Theatrical companies presenting "Ten Nights in a Bar Room," "East Lynne," Gilbert & Sullivan, or Shakespeare existed in all sizes and traveled as car shows. Medicine shows readily found their way to rails, and the biggest among them, the Kickapoo Indian Medicine Company, fielded up to two dozen units at a time, each on its own railroad car.

In 1905 more than 300 theatrical troupes worked out of New York, while another 100 or so trouped out of Chicago. By and large, these were separate from the standard med shows, rep shows, UTC shows, minstrels, and vaude attractions. Nearly all of them used some combination of coaches and baggage cars, and nearly all of them moved as extra cars in regular passenger trains.

Many car shows stayed in a chosen territory. Pioneering in the Southeast at the turn of the century with a ten-cent vaudeville show was James Adams, with a tent theater and two railroad cars. Second in that territory was Jethro Almond, who acquired his first railroad car in 1904, soon added a second, and continued for sixteen years with an outfit that included trained animals, vaudeville acts, and newfangled movies—all under canvas, all on two cars. Almond later recalled that 310 railroad cars were operated by the one- and two-car shows. In 1915 show owners formed an association and protested that the railroads had increased rates by a range of from 76 percent to 240 percent. Their complaints continued after World War I.

These rates and the availability of trucks were principal factors in knocking out car shows, but perhaps the greatest factor was the added attraction presented by Almond—the movies. In any case, one calculation shows that theatrical road companies—just one measure of the status of car shows—numbered 327 in 1905, 124 in 1915, 75 in 1925, and 22 in 1935. In that span of years, J. Augustus Jones and then his brother, Elmer, operated those two-car circuses along with such dandies as the Frank Money Dramatic Company and the Georgia Smart Set Minstrels. By 1936 their last show had faded from the field. Most of the other car shows had disappeared as well.

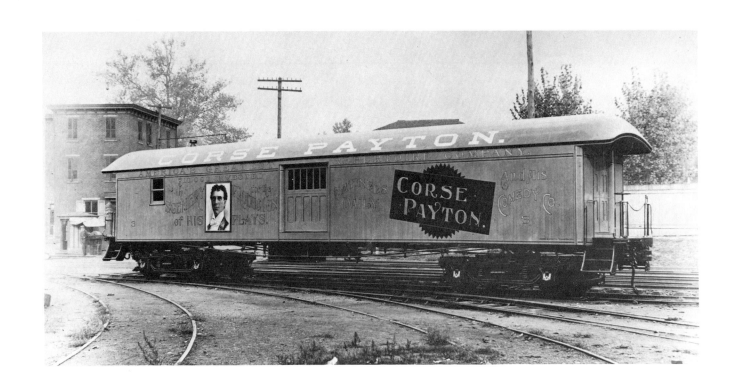

A copycat among dog and pony shows, Sipe & Blake duplicated the Gentry operation even to buying this car from the same Ohio Falls builder — *Authors' Collection.*

Opposite page, above: Corse Payton billed himself as "America's Best Bad Actor" and the "Worst Actor in the World," but he was so successful with his comedies that he used gold coins for coat buttons and his wife wore fifty-two different gowns in each week's productions. Moreover, Payton had his own railroad cars. Jackson & Sharp of Wilmington, Delaware, built this baggage car for scenery and costumes — *Delaware Division of Historical & Cultural Affairs, Department of State. Opposite page, below:* Before he toured a tent show on more cars, Prof. H. B. Gentry played theaters with his dogs and ponies. His special car was built in the 1880s by the Ohio Falls Car Manufacturing Company, Jeffersonville, Indiana— *Authors' Collection. Right:* For more than twenty years Jethro Almond toured the Southeast with two-car shows, exhibiting pioneer movies and vaudeville. Later he operated a motorized circus — *Orlo Rahn Collection.*

Above and opposite page, above: Al W. Martin turned from circus gambling to "Uncle Tom's Cabin" and bought these cars from the Jackson & Sharp plant at Wilmington, Delaware, later part of the American Car & Foundry Company — *Delaware Division of Historical & Cultural Affairs, Department of State.*

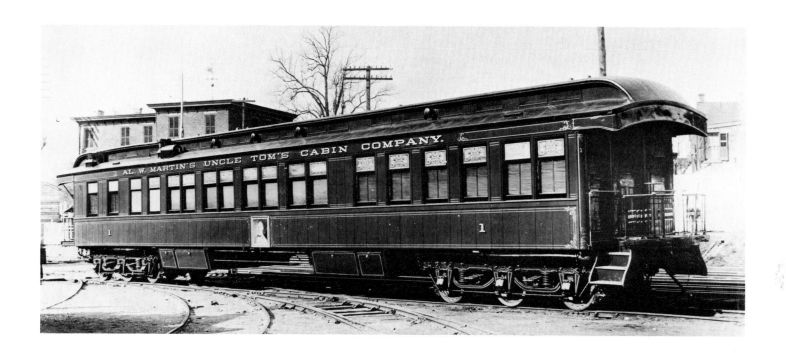

After minstrels disappeared elsewhere, two outfits continued with black casts in southern black communities. One was "Silas Green From New Orleans," operated by a car-show veteran who learned the business from the Skerbecks — *Woodcock Collection.*

Above: The other was F. S. Wolcott's Rabbit Foot Show. In 1934 it was aboard two cars bought from the famous Al G. Fields Minstrels in 1928. The sleeper, *Dan Emmett,* was named for the composer of "Dixie." The *Southland* was a diner-baggage combination — *Woodcock Collection.*

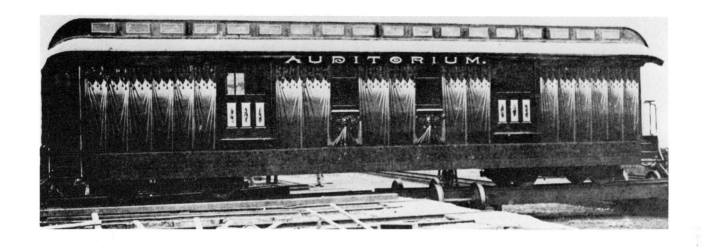

Opposite page, below; this page; and the following page: The man who started it all, W. C. Coup, made several comeback attempts with circuses and once with a five-car museum outfit. The people lived on this car. Another was called the "Auditorium Car," while still others were full of museum displays. The cars were built for Coup by the St. Charles Company — *Smithsonian Institution.*

"Uncle Tom's Cabin" shows were so numerous that they were a whole branch of show business by themselves. Many of them used the two-car system perfected by circuses. Typical was the Terry "UTC" company of 1915, lined up alongside its cars and ready to make parade at Moline, Illinois, with the entire company. There was a ten-piece band, an eight-piece band, a black drum corps, Jubilee singers, a pony carriage for Eva, two cages of bloodhounds, and more — *Authors' Collection.*

The Kickapoo Indian Medicine Co. operated as many as twenty-five units like this one, Number 17. Each had six Indians, three specialty performers, a lecturer, and sometimes such extras as a fireworks display or balloon ascension. In each town they set up a stage and six tepees and gave a show to draw a crowd. Then the "lecturer" orated about aches and pains, all preliminary to his pitching such cure-alls as Kickapoo Buffalo Salve and Indian Worm Killer — *Authors' Collection.*

Left: The Pacific Whaling Company was made up of showmen who did all of their whaling aboard railroad cars containing stuffed whales. Here, one of the five units moves into its Chicago location on temporary tracks. The custom-built rail car unfolded to create the show place. Long lines of customers stood in the shadow of the Wrigley Building and Tribune Tower to see the whale. Business was phenomenal. Another unit in New York outdrew Admiral Byrd's Antarctica exhibition — *Authors' Collection. Above:* Stetson's "Uncle Tom's Cabin" Company of 1895 had an overlong unit that was mostly baggage car but part flatcar to carry the steam calliope. Simon Legree and the rest lived on the other car — *Authors' Collection.*

Temporary trackage was used by night crews to place the whale show's car in place near Chicago's Michigan Avenue, between the river and Tribune Tower — *Authors' Collection.*

II

Relying heavily on baggage car moves was the Redpath Chautauqua System of White Plains, New York, one of the numerous lecture and concert bureaus which adopted the name and concept of the movement that originated and continues at Chautauqua, New York.

They used system cars and paid a per-mile charge in place of buying specified numbers of first-class tickets for the cars.

Chautauqua was a combination of cultural music, educational lectures, and grass roots entertainment sprinkled with a generous religious influence. The original program was founded more than a century ago. Entertainers, educators, statesmen, and principal speakers on every sort of political and social issue still share Chautauqua platforms.

Before the turn of the century and well into the 1920s, independent commercial enterprises took the Chautauqua

idea to nearly every community in the country. The programs were given in tents at parks, fairgrounds, or bible campgrounds, continued for a week in each town, and won great popular support and approval. The Redpath Chautauqua System was one of the major operators. It moved eight units aboard baggage cars in a 1918 circuit and corresponded with the New York, Ontario & Western Railway about its moves:

Redpath president, Crawford A. Peffer, to G. L. Robinson, general passenger agent, NYO&W Ry, June 12, 1918:

"Enclosed please find a schedule which shows our requirements for baggage cars for the shipment of our Chautauqua equipment for our New York and New England Circuit for the coming summer . . . We have checked the movements which originate on your line and will ask you to kindly instruct the proper persons in your organization to furnish us with Railroad Schedule and issue the necessary orders for the baggage cars to be placed as required."

General passenger agent to Redpath president, June 24, 1918:

"The movements over this line are as follows: July 25th, Hamilton to Herkimer; July 26th, Norwich to Oneida; July 27, Walton to Fulton . . . This will tie up three baggage cars at our very busiest season. Is there not some way that you can spread this service so that it will only be necessary to use one baggage car?"

Redpath to NYO&W Ry, June 25, 1918:

". . . We wish to advise you that it will be necessary to have a baggage car for each of the three moves on the dates specified . . . ."

General passenger agent to Redpath president, July 5, 1918:

". . . Conditions will not permit the use of three baggage cars that will be necessary to cover the movements on dates shown above. All of our baggage cars are in use in our regular train service daily, and our resources are taxed to the limit in taking care of the movement of baggage for our summer travel, which is at its heaviest during the latter part of July. In addition, we have a very large movement of peas and lettuce by express from the northern part of New York state to New York City at that time, and we are sorely tried to provide for this foodstuff service in addition to our regular business.

"I trust you will appreciate that conditions entirely beyond our control render it impractical to give you the full service you request. If you can make necessary changes in dates that will enable us to handle these movements with one baggage car, we will be very glad to hear from you further as to details."

Redpath president to NYO&W Ry general passenger agent, July 6, 1918:

". . . By a glance at the enclosed complete schedule for our Chautauquas for this season, you will see that it would be impossible to change the opening date on any Chautauqua, as it would disarrange the whole system and disorganize and throw into endless confusion the schedule of nearly 100 speakers, entertainers, and concert attractions which move from place to place on daily Chautauqua programs.

"Perhaps you do not understand that the Chautauqua equipments for Hamilton, Norwich, and Walton comprise three different equipments or units.

"However, since you can only make one baggage car available, here we think is the solution. Use that car for the movement of Equipment No. 6 on July 25th from Hamilton to Herkimer and get the same car to Walton for the afternoon of July 26 so that it can be loaded that night and move on the 27th from Walton to Fulton; then provide a forty-foot furniture car with end doors for the movement of equipment from Norwich to Oneida on July 26th.

"Other roads have used furniture cars for the movement of Chautauqua equipment in cases of emergency and have attached the same to passenger trains. While I understand that this is irregular, the necessity of the movement of Chautauqua equipment on the schedule, we understand, has been thought to justify the action."

NYO&W Ry general passenger agent to Redpath president, July 10, 1918:

"On taking this matter up with our General Manager, he states that it would be impossible for us to use furniture cars in our passenger train service and that he will use every effort to furnish the service that you desire, but that the same cannot be guaranteed."

NYO&W general manager to superintendent, July 12, 1918:

"The Redpath Chautauqua requests a sixty-foot baggage car for movement: July 25th, Hamilton to

Herkimer; July 26th, Norwich to Oneida; July 27th, Walton to Fulton.

"If these baggage cars can be furnished without detriment to our regular service, or the food products moving from the Northern Division, we should furnish.

"I would like Mr. Hartigan to try and get a foreign baggage car for the movement, Hamilton to Herkimer. If you cannot furnish the equipment, please notify me and we will try to get it."

In a maze of dates and towns, the Redpath Chautauqua System maneuvered baggage cars to bring its strange combination of education and entertainment to the populace. This was the 1918 schedule — *Authors' Collection.*

1918 SCHEDULE
REDPATH CHAUTAUQUA SYSTEM

CRAWFORD A. PEFFER, Manager   WHITE PLAINS, N. Y.

Itinerary

1.	Niagara Falls, N. Y.	June 24	25	26	27	28	29
2.	Ransomville, N. Y.	June 25	26	27	28	29	July 1
3.	Lyndonville, N. Y.	June 26	27	28	29	July 1	2
4.	Williamson, N. Y.	June 27	28	29	July 1	2	3
6.	Newark, N. Y.	June 28	29	July 1	2	3	4
5.	Brockport, N. Y.	June 29	July 1	2	3	4	5
7.	Albion, N. Y.	July 1	2	3	4	5	6
8.	Akron, N. Y.	July 2	3	4	5	6	8
1.	Batavia, N. Y.	July 3	4	5	6	8	9
2.	Attica, N. Y.	July 4	5	6	8	9	10
3.	Arcade, N. Y.	July 5	6	8	9	10	11
4.	Perry, N. Y.	July 6	8	9	10	11	12
5.	Honeoye Falls, N. Y.	July 8	9	10	11	12	13
6.	Geneseo, N. Y.	July 9	10	11	12	13	15
7.	Canandaigua, N. Y.	July 10	11	12	13	15	16
8.	Naples, N. Y.	July 11	12	13	15	16	17
1.	Ovid, N. Y.	July 12	13	15	16	17	18
2.	Clifton Springs, N. Y.	July 13	15	16	17	18	19
3.	Moravia, N. Y.	July 15	16	17	18	19	20
4.	Cortland, N. Y.	July 16	17	18	19	20	22
5.	Cazenovia, N. Y.	July 17	18	19	20	22	23
6.	Hamilton, N. Y.	July 18	19	20	22	23	24
7.	Norwich, N. Y.	July 19	20	22	23	24	25
8.	Walton, N. Y.	July 20	22	23	24	25	26
1.	Oneonta, N. Y.	July 22	23	24	25	26	27
2.	Cobleskill, N. Y.	July 23	24	25	26	27	29
3.	Cooperstown, N. Y.	July 24	25	26	27	29	30
4.	Fort Plain, N. Y.	July 25	26	27	29	30	31
5.	Dolgeville, N. Y.	July 26	27	29	30	31	Aug. 1
6.	Herkimer, N. Y.	July 27	29	30	31	Aug. 1	2
7.	Oneida, N. Y.	July 29	30	31	Aug. 1	2	3
8.	Fulton, N. Y.	July 30	31	Aug. 1	2	3	5
1.	Wolcott, N. Y.	July 31	Aug. 1	2	3	5	6
2.	Oswego, N. Y.	Aug. 1	2	3	5	6	7
3.	Camden, N. Y.	Aug. 2	3	5	6	7	8
4.	Adams, N. Y.	Aug. 3	5	6	7	8	9
5.	Carthage, N. Y.	Aug. 5	6	7	8	9	10
6.	Antwerp, N. Y.	Aug. 6	7	8	9	10	12
7.	Gouverneur, N. Y.	Aug. 7	8	9	10	12	13
8.	Ogdensburg, N. Y.	Aug. 8	9	10	12	13	14
1.	Potsdam, N. Y.	Aug. 9	10	12	13	14	15
2.	Massena, N. Y.	Aug. 10	12	13	14	15	16
3.	Malone, N. Y.	Aug. 12	13	14	15	16	17
4.	Plattsburg, N. Y.	Aug. 13	14	15	16	17	19
5.	Burlington, Vt.	Aug. 14	15	16	17	19	20
6.	Montpelier, Vt.	Aug. 15	16	17	19	20	21
7.	Lancaster, N. H.	Aug. 16	17	19	20	21	22
8.	North Conway, N. H.	Aug. 17	19	20	21	22	23
1.	Berlin, N. H.	Aug. 19	20	21	22	23	24
2.	Newport, Vt.	Aug. 20	21	22	23	24	26
3.	Lyndonville, Vt.	Aug. 21	22	23	24	26	27
4.	Hardwick, Vt.	Aug. 22	23	24	26	27	28
5.	Woodsville, N. H.	Aug. 23	24	26	27	28	29
6.	Laconia, N. H.	Aug. 24	26	27	28	29	30
7.	Kennebunk, Me.	Aug. 26	27	28	29	30	31
8.	Rumford, Me.	Aug. 27	28	29	30	31	Sept. 2
1.	Farmington, Me.	Aug. 28	29	30	31	Sept. 2	3
2.	Skowhegan, Me.	Aug. 29	30	31	Sept. 2	3	4
3.	Waterville, Me.	Aug. 30	31	Sept. 2	3	4	5
4.	Auburn, Me.	Aug. 31	Sept. 2	3	4	5	6

III

While the private Pullmans and the car shows mostly disappeared, by no means had show business forsaken rails. A latter-day phase of the business was wrapped up pretty tightly with a fleet of forty-two special cars—the balloon-top baggage cars of the Pennsylvania Railroad. Built specifically for show usage, these cars were the Showman's Friend. Of course, shows moved in ordinary baggage cars of other railroads as well; second choice were the nine end-door baggage cars of the Santa Fe, numbered between 1890 and 1899. But the far-and-away favorites were the Pennsy's balloon-top baggage cars.

Numbered 6055 through 6099, these cars were named for operas, composers, actors, and other features of the concert and theatrical world. They were spacious, thanks to the balloon tops, and easier to load with awkward and bulky show property, thanks to the end doors. Probably their biggest users were the legitimate theater companies—Broadway musicals and dramas which toured the principal cities. But legit was not the only user. Whenever a symphony orchestra, an opera company, a magician, or any other kind of show company decided to tour, its agent called for Pennsy balloon-top baggage cars in appropriate number.

As usual, the companies bought twenty-five first-class tickets to earn both a baggage car and a passenger car. When show personnel moved by different means, an unaccompanied baggage car required twenty-five fares. However, a second one cost only fifteen fares.

In theory, there was a limit of two baggage cars to any one user in this service. But a showman who needed more had only to create a second name for the rest of his troupe. Thus, if his company had a repertoire of several grand operas, he could get two cars for the "Aida" company, another pair for "Madame Butterfly," more for the "Faust" unit. Then all moved together as the single opera company.

Theatrical companies over the years have been gilly shows, although many probably never heard the term. They moved in baggage cars and, having no other transport of their own, hired local wagons or trucks to shuttle the gear from train to theater and back. Circuses started it; many others followed suit. All cities with sufficient theatrical activity developed theatrical transfer companies, whose field it was to gilly show property from team track to stage door. Few survive today. But even now, current union requirements for legit shows often include car loaders—the people who transfer theatrical freight. Once they had worked in the baggage cars. In the absence of railroad moves, car loaders now move the trunks, scenery, and props to the tailgate of the semitrailer so that stage hands can take over from there.

Starting in 1936, a new category of baggage car users came on the show scene. These were the ice shows. They sought the balloon-top cars, paid with first-class tickets, and followed the system derived from two-car circuses. Among them were Sonja Henie's Hollywood Ice Revue, Shipstads & Johnson's Ice Follies, John H. Harris' Ice Capades, and Morris Chalfen's Holiday on Ice. Usually they required about four baggage cars and a number of system Pullmans.

Veterans of those baggage car moves recall that the Pennsy cars were difficult to get and equally difficult to keep. Legit shows tried to "steal" them away from the ice shows while the cars were sidetracked during an engagement. To prevent such incursions, railroad friends would bad-order the cars, so would-be takers stayed away. However, when the ice show was ready to go again, the tags came off and the switcher tied on.

The cars were equipped with nonstandard bronze bushings, which meant that sustaining a hot box could spell doom for a show on its way to another engagement just hours away. There was no time for sidetracking the car and awaiting parts. As a result, Ice Capades carried its own supply of bushings for instant use in case of trouble.

By the 1950s it had become increasingly tough to move baggage car shows. Two agents who faced the problems were Al Butler, advance man for "Annie Get Your

Gun," "South Pacific," and "My Fair Lady," among others, and Bob Hickey, of Ice Follies. Both were former circus agents. Each noted that fewer regular passenger trains existed, that survivors frequently lacked diners for show people, and that the railroads were reluctant to spoil the appearance of name trains by the addition of several foreign-road Pullmans and a string of Pennsylvania baggage cars.

By 1960 the Ringling-Barnum train featured a string of open-ended tunnel cars in which circus wagons were lined up. Wagons were towed out of the cars and all of the way to the inside of the arenas by tractor. The need for car loaders was eliminated. Efficiency was enhanced.

Most ice shows were quick to see the advantages of this method. Although Ice Follies stayed with the old system of loose loads in system baggage cars, Holiday on Ice and Ice Capades changed to the Ringling system.

Holiday moved first. It bought three baggage cars from the Pennsylvania—not balloon tops, but more modern, lightweight units. It arranged for Ringling people to convert these and equip them with wagons. Soon thereafter, Ice Capades changed, too. But it bought Pennsylvania balloon-top cars. One unit of Ice Capades was equipped with four cars in 1963; the other obtained three cars a year later. In the cases of ice shows, no passenger cars were acquired. Unlike the circus, the ice shows relied on each railroad to furnish coaches or Pullmans as needed; their people lived in hotels rather than on the train. When Ice Capades acquired those Pennsy cars, it also bought a new supply of bronze bushings to keep the cars running on schedule.

But the time came when those cars were bad-ordered for real. In Chicago one of the three blue Ice Capades cars on the West company was tagged and the others were threatened; the old balloon tops had come to the end of the line. A friend on the Santa Fe reported that modern stainless steel baggage cars of the style recently used on the Super Chiefs were stored and available in Iowa. Ice Capades bought three at that time and four the next season for the East company. The Santa Fe shops converted the cars, knocking out the ends and fitting them as tunnel cars for the ice show's wagons.

To identify its cars, Ice Capades first used its initials, IC, until notified that another distinguished operator of rail equipment already claimed them—Illinois Central. So the ice show cars were identified as ICAP 105 through ICAP 111. When contracting for rail moves, the show told the roads that its cars were "ICAP 105 through 107 (formerly Santa Fe 3462, 3463, and 3466)" on one unit and "ICAP 108 through 111 (formerly Santa Fe 3457, 3459, 3461, and 3464)" on the other, according to Dick Palmer, general manager of the show.

Ice show cars still were moved on tickets when the railroad involved was one continuing its passenger service independent of Amtrak. On the Southern Railway, for example, thirty first-class tickets still got you a free baggage car. If the cars were unaccompanied by passengers, the second car required fifteen fares. In the 1970s the show moved its people by the best available methods—sometimes by air or bus and sometimes by rail.

The original ice show moves were in cars of Pennsy colors. With its own cars, the show lettered its title boldly across the sides. The stainless steel Santa Fe cars were fitted with nameplates to proclaim only modestly the name of the show.

Then Amtrak came into the scene. First, it replaced the old ticket system with prosaic dollar-per-mile rates. Then it took the same objections which the roads had voiced earlier about the appearance of their trains. It asked Ice Capades to conform. Thus, like the two-car circuses which painted rolling stock a standard green to meld into the scene, Ice Capades painted its baggage cars in bright Amtrak design to match the color scheme of the trains in which they rode.

There were other problems that could not be overcome—sky-high costs, limited schedules, and uncertain arrival times. So, reluctantly, Ice Capades gave up railroading. In April 1977, as its season came to a close, the show bought trucks and sold off its seven tunnel cars. That left Ringling's twin trains and two carnivals as about the last of show business on rails.

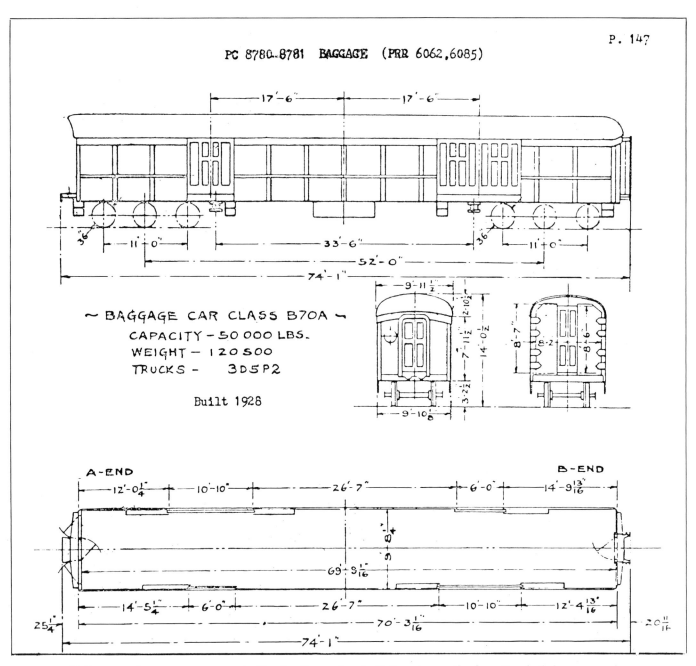

Balloon-top baggage cars operated by the Pennsylvania Railroad were the favorite of all showmen who operated baggage car shows — *Penn Central Railroad*.

Three former Pennsy balloon-top baggage cars are lined up like circus flats or tunnel cars, and the Illinois Central switcher stands by as a poler and a Jeep work a show wagon over the IC's piggyback ramp at Champaign, Illinois — *University of Illinois.*

Ice shows used theatrical baggage cars and traditional rail moves for the first twenty years of their existence. After years with leased cars, Ice Capades bought these balloon-top baggage cars from the Pennsylvania Railroad. Trunks, crates, scenery, and props were stowed inside, then shuttled to and from arenas by local trucks — *Ice Capades.*

One Ice Capades train made use of ex-dining cars that had been converted to tunnel cars and contained the circus-style wagons which transported the show's Eastern unit — *Ice Capades.*

Opposite page, all photos: As another generation of show railroading, Ice Capades bought former Santa Fe Chief baggage cars and converted them into tunnel cars. Familiar systems and equipment are visible. The ice show continued to transport two units on cars like these until 1977 — *Ice Capades.*

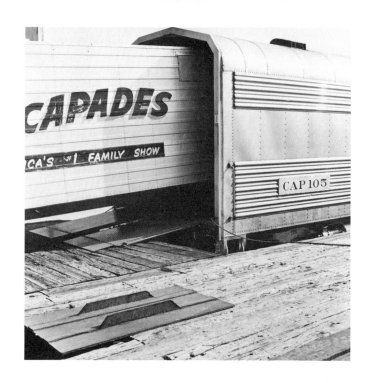

NATIONAL RAILROAD PASSENGER CORP.

CENTRAL REGION

TRANSPORTATION NOTICE

CHICAGO: January 29, 1974
FILE: TN-C-G059

PARTY.................ICE CAPADES 33rd EDITION WEST

ITINERARY............BAGGAGE CARS: ICAP 105-106-107 AND HEATER CAR.

AR.	GRAND FORKS	BN FREIGHT	APPROX 9:00AM	WED.	JAN.	30
LV.	GRAND FORKS	#8		11:40PM	WED.	JAN.	30
AR.	MINNEAPOLIS	#8		6:30AM	THU.	JAN.	31
LV.	MINNEAPOLIS	#8		7:00AM	MON.	FEB.	4
AR.	CHICAGO	#8		2:50PM	MON.	FEB.	4
LV.	CHICAGO	#59		6:10PM	MON.	FEB.	4
AR.	CHAMPAIGN	#59		8:30PM	MON.	FEB.	4

INSTRUCTIONS.........THREE (3) ICE CAPADES CARS ICAP 105-106 and 107 ALONG WITH
BN HEATER CAR TO ARRIVE MINNEAPOLIS #8 JAN. 30. HEATER
CAR TO BE DROPPED AT MINNEAPOLIS AND THREE (3) ICE CAP-
ADES CARS TO CONTINUE ON #8 FEB.4 TO CHICAGO. CARS TO
BE POSITIONED IN TRAIN SO AS TO FACILITATE UNLOADING.
IMMEDIATELY UPON ARRIVAL AT MINNEAPOLIS CARS ARE TO BE
SPOTTED FOR UNLOADING AT STUB 11 (OLD GN TEAM TRACK)
½ MILE WEST OF STATION IN MINNEAPOLIS.

IN AS MUCH AS SHOW WILL OPEN IN ST. PAUL ON JAN.31st
IT IS ESSENTIAL THAT THESE CARS BE HANDLED AS EXPED-
ITIOUSLY AS POSSIBLE, WITH SPECIAL HANDLING TO BE ARRANGED
IF TRAIN #8 SHOULD BE EXCESSIVELY LATE ON ARRIVAL GRAND
FORKS.

MR. ED PIERCE, ICE CAPADES MANAGER, WILL HANDLE
DETAILS CONCERNING BONDING.   BALANCE OF ROUTING NOT
AS YET CONFIRMED. WILL ADVISE AS SOON AS IT BECOMES
AVAILABLE.

EVERY EFFORT WILL BE MADE TO MAKE CONNECTION FROM
#8 TO #59 FEB. 4th. ALL CONCERNED PLEASE WATCH TO PRO-
TECT THIS CONNECTION IF AT ALL POSSIBLE.

F. E. RIZZUTO
Regional Manager-Service

MET OR ASSISTED BY:_____

COMMENTS:_____

_____

_____

IV

In the matter of transport, no enterprise was closer to the flatcar circus than the carnival. When they got to a town, circuses were quite different from carnivals. But en route they were one and the same. Carnivals duplicated the circus system, and at the outset of their history they leaped directly into an era of big railroad shows.

The carnival is a relative newcomer to the show scene. While independent operators took rides and shows and games to early fairs and soldiers' reunions, the idea of their forming into organized midways was a long time in coming. The Chicago World's Fair of 1893 gave them the word and concept of *Midway*, but it still took a while to get underway. A premature carnival train moved in 1895 on seven flats and six boxcars, but apparently it used few, if any, wagons.

Soon carnival showmen learned circus ways and adapted them to carnival needs. With the Gaskill-Munday show of 1898, carnival business really got underway. By 1903 there were twenty-two carnivals, and all traveled by rail. C. W. Parker not only operated a twenty-six-car show and used a steam tractor for loading it, but he also manufactured rides, show fronts, wagons, and even railroad cars for sale or lease to other showmen. By 1907 he was operating four shows with a total of eighty-three cars. Principal titles of that time included the Great Patterson Shows, Con T. Kennedy Shows, Johnny J. Jones Shows, the Barkoot Shows, Dodson's World's Fair Shows, the Sheesley Shows, and the outstanding outfits of Wortham & Allen.

In its first stage, the carnival consisted primarily of midway shows—plantation, or minstrel shows; girl shows that derived from the Chicago fair's Little Egypt; exhibits of human oddities; monkey shows; snake displays; wrestling contests; haunted houses and fun houses; glass houses or mirror mazes; and others.

They also had concessions and games—shooting galleries, pitch-til-you-win, number wheels, bingo, and such midway classics as the high-striker (swing the mallet to ring the bell) and the African dip (hit the target with a baseball and dump the clown into the water).

At first there were only a few midway rides—the Ferris Wheel, Merry-Go-Round, and Giant Swings. But as time went by, more rides were invented; among them were the Whip, Caterpillar, Dodgem, and Tilt-a-Whirl. Ultimately, rides dominated the business, and progressively fewer shows were available. Since these were spotted at the rear of a midway to dress up the far end, they became known as back-end shows.

Carnival names in the 1920s included the Rubin & Cherry Shows, the Brundage Show, Zeidman & Pollie Shows, Beckmann & Gerety Shows, Morris & Castle Shows, West's World Wonder Shows, and the Royal American Shows. In the early 1920s, one typical small carnival was the N. J. Lapp Shows. It operated on ten flats, two coaches, and a baggage-coach combination. The latter carried draft horses, and the flatcars carried these loads:

Flat No.	Description	Wagons, Numbers, Loads
#30	Semi-steel 50'	Dengler Boat Swing 14' Fun House 14' Barrel Roll
#36	Wooden flat 45'	Oriental front wagon Wagon #9 1 power unit
#40	Semi-steel 62'	Jenny Wagons #25, #26, #27
#41	Semi-steel 62'	Whip Ride Wagons #30, #31, #32
#42	Semi-steel 62'	#33 Whip, #1 Office Wagon #67 Pit Show, #68 Snake Show
#44	Semi-steel 62'	Eli Wheel & power unit Wagons #20, #21, & #22
#45	Semi-steel 62'	#60 Water Circus, #7 Mechanical City, #71 Oriental, #6 Wild West

#50	Semi-steel 58'	#35 & #36 Drome, #50 Hot Dog #66 Pet Show & Power Plant
#51	Semi-steel 58'	Concessions #15, #5, #8
#25	Semi-steel 45'	#9 Cookhouse, #3 Utility & #37
#31	Semi-steel 50'	#65 Athletic Show, #109 Monkey Speedway, #100 Single-O

"Jenny" is a carnival term for Merry-Go-Round. The "Eli Wheel" was a Ferris Wheel, manufactured by the Eli Bridge Company. A "Single-O" was a sideshow exhibiting a single attraction, as opposed to a "Ten-In-One," which might have that many or more freaks.

A firm caste system allowed little crossover of people between circuses and carnivals, but equipment was a different story. Carnivals bought circus railroad cars. They bought wagons in some cases, but the loads were so different that it proved better to build new wagons for specific purposes. Flatcars in particular were in demand and were readily turned from circus to carnival use without modification.

C. A. Wortham, for example, bought part of the Buffalo Bill train and all of the cars of the Mighty Haag Railroad Circus. The Hennies Bros. Shows bought ten flats from Tim McCoy's Wild West. Flats from Sells Floto and Hagenbeck-Wallace were sold to the Art Lewis carnival, which, in turn, sold them to the Strates Shows. Foley & Burk Shows had some flats from the Buck Jones Wild West. The Royal American Shows purchased a large string of Ringling flats in 1960. Cars from West's World Wonder Shows went to Dailey Bros. Circus, then via a middle man to the Metropolitan carnival, which later was sold to the Royal American. The Mighty Sheesley Shows in 1930 purchased a new train of Warren flats and sold them in the 1940s to the Cetlin & Wilson carnival.

By 1959 seven carnivals still traveled by rail. They included Cetlin & Wilson, thirty-five cars; Foley & Burk, ten; James E. Strates, fifty; Olson Shows, thirty; Royal American, seventy; and World of Mirth, fifty. All of these shows owned their equipment. The World's Finest Shows in Canada had thirty-five system cars.

Carnivals traditionally played each town for a week. In the spring there were "still dates," which were either played on their own or under the auspices of a local sponsor. In the late summer and fall they played state and county fairs. Carnival trains usually moved only on Sundays, the idle time between engagements. But in the 1950s, still dates virtually disappeared, and fairs broke out of the one-week format in order to include more than one weekend in their run. So carnivals had to change their scheduling, too.

In many cases, carnival trains were composed almost entirely of flatcars. Since a circus moved every night, its people lived on the train and required coach space. But moving once a week or less, carnival people lived in hotels and needed less spacious train quarters. As a result, they had fewer coaches.

Well before circuses abandoned draft horses for work purposes, carnivals had turned to tractors, which decreased the need for stockcars. In recent decades, a carnival might have only one stockcar and use it as a rolling warehouse for plaster novelties, prize glassware, give-away blankets, and other merchandise that would be given as prizes at the concession stands.

In 1953 the Royal American had nineteen coaches, two stockcars, and thirty-eight flats. In the next season it bought the Cavalcade of Amusements train of thirty cars. The Olson Shows of 1958 had twenty-five flats, four coaches, and a boxcar.

The James E. Strates Shows bought fourteen new eighty-five-foot piggyback railroad cars in 1968 to begin the trend away from the old Warrens and Mount Vernons. Soon Strates ordered more; in 1972 he announced full conversion to piggyback flats for his fifty-car show. His train had been caught in a flood at Wilkes Barre, Pennsylvania, in 1972, damaging many of the coaches. So Strates further updated his train by acquiring seven Erie-Lackawana coaches as replacements.

The world's largest carnival is the Royal American

Shows, which had ninety cars in 1972. Section 1 had thirty-seven flats, two boxcars (former stocks), one pie car, and seven sleepers. Section 2 had twenty flats, two boxcars, two private cars, one entertainment car, one diner, and seventeen sleepers. C. J. Sedlmayr, Jr., president and general manager of Royal American, annually indicated the sequence in which the 160 wagons and trucks were needed on the lot. Then Ed Lester would develop the train loading order.

Intricacies of the task are pointed up by the fact that the wagons came in seven or more lengths, ranging from twenty-two to forty-one feet, yet flatcar space was utilized to a maximum. In 1953 the average seventy-two-foot flat had sixty-four feet of wagons. In 1962 it was sixty-nine feet, and by 1964 it was seventy-one feet.

Here is the loading order for the fifty-seven flats when the Royal American Shows left its Tampa winter quarters for the 1972 tour:

Royal American Shows
1972 Train Loading List

Wagon No.	Contents
18	Truck & Tractor Shop
AC12	Tip Top air compressor
420	IBM Machines
38	Press Office
33	Front Gate
146	Rest Rooms
161	Showers Wagon
126	Dodgem cars
122	Mother Goose show
37	Dodgem cars
200	Galaxi quarters

115	Electrical stock
61	Concession supplies
435	Concession stock
24	Concession trunks
82	Concession canvas
23	Concession lumber
22	Galaxi flash
31	Pitch joints
106	Grab joint
62	Matterhorn tubs
M4	German mule
334	Myra illusion show
55	Flash coaster cars
201	Richie concessions
370	Stevens concessions
171	Richie concessions
100	Flash coaster flash
80	Flash coaster iron
114	Sky Diver platforms
90	Kiddieland organ
156	Round-up ride
26	M-G-R horses
150	Sky Diver tubs
77	Spider tubs
88	Galaxi cars
104	Pirate Ship
151	Gorilla illusion show
86	Wax show
84	Kid Swamp Buggies ride
43	Barrel of Fun House
87	Kid Boat ride
160	Kid Motorcycle ride
32	Kid Astronaut ride
RC12	Astronaut ride center

19 Kid Snowmobile ride
68 Kiddieland & art dept
93 Derby Racer

121 Kid Bus ride
111 House of Infinity
TD10 Tire dolly

79 Motordrome equipment
101 Saturn Six ride

20 Roll-O-Plane ride
181 Outhouse Inn

46 Sky Fighter & Kid Tanks rides
143 Zipper ride

63 Kid Auto & Kid Wheel rides
186 Glass House

52 Tilt-A-Whirl tubs
191 Tilt-A-Whirl plates
45 Scrambler ride

112 Flash coaster iron
139 Tip Top ride

40 Spider iron
154 Rok-N-Rol ride

89 Motordrome equipment
166 Turbo tubs

190 Motordrome equipment
176 Turbo center

56 Motordrome frame
136 Trabant ride

96 Office department equipment
210 Motordrome wall
134 Bonnie & Clyde show

51 Arcade machines
221 Arcade machines

71 Shop equipment

211 Whip tubs & flash

83 M-G-R flash
131 Dodgem plates

48 Rotor lights
94 Shop supplies
16 M-G-R center
21 M-G-R sweeps

65 Left Space Wheel
75 Right Space Wheel

28 Rotor flash
240 Rotor center

34 Presidential office
54 Galaxi track

47 Arcade tent
140 Alpine Avalanche Slide

A14 Tower/power plant
B14 Tower/power plant
91 Matterhorn flash

C14 Tower/power plant
D14 Tower/power plant
42 Toboggan tower

118 Electrical shop
E14 Tower/power plant
57 Toboggan track

120 Matterhorn sweeps
124 Matterhorn center
CT24 Toboggan crane truck

50 Electrical supplies
F14 Tower/power plant
137 Giant Wheel sweeps

T22 Train department service truck
G14 Tower/power plant
135 Dodgem building

M5 German mule
64 Machine shop
85 Space Wheel center

T16 Porter department truck
H14 Tower/power plant
250 Sky Diver center

ST43 Space Wheels semi set
C4 D4 Caterpillar
66 D6 bulldozer wagon

T27 Concession department truck
J14 Tower/power plant
400 Concession department office

T19 Tire truck
78 Spare wagon
128 Whip plates

E15 Electrical department Scout
ST55 Giant Wheel semi set

T17A Lot sanitation truck
235 Pony ride
P18 Train department pickup truck

T20 Water truck
K14 Tower/power plant
237 Giant Wheel tower

M3 Case mule
T18 Water truck
440 Main office

C6 D4 Caterpillar
142 Paratrooper ride
S15 Shop department Scout
W13 Welding unit

S17 Staff car
CT21 Truck department crane truck
234 Torture show

M1 Case mule
12 Train department shop
C5 D4 Caterpillar
M2 Case mule
B19 Cat "950" bucket

C2 D4 Caterpillar
(runs)
C3 D4 Caterpillar

All of this equipment was unloaded, set up, torn down, and reloaded eleven times in the course of the six-month tour. The show's 1960 route involved 8,239 miles on twelve railroads. Typically, on the closing night of a fair in western Canada the midway was jammed with customers for the rides, shows, and joints until midnight. Meanwhile, showmen prepared for the tear-down. As a signal, the general manager pulled the lights on one of the towers.

Then about 400 men began the giant job of dismantling and loading.

As various loads were ready, each tractor took enough wagons in a single string to fill one flatcar. At the runs the process was the same as with circuses. There were crossing Cats, pull-over tractors, cross-over plates, runs cars, and polers. It was just like a circus, just like W. C. Coup and all those showmen since him.

Above: The carnival business took so much of its inspiration from the circus that much of the public couldn't tell one from the other. Nowhere was this more true than in the railroading. Hennies Bros. carnival rode Warren flatcars — *Art Speltz Collection. Left:* A great name among carnivals, the Rubin & Cherry Shows used baggage cars and gilly wagons in two-car circus fashion about 1919 — *Albert Conover Collection.*

Right: The early Rubin & Cherry Shows tied down its wagons by bringing heavy ropes under the cars and then up to the bull rings on the wagons, an unusual move apparently to minimize sway — *Albert Conover Collection.* *Above:* Dodson's World's Fair Shows, like several carnivals, used wooden flats some time after most circuses had switched to steel. But carnivals turned to tractors and to wagons with steel wheels and rubber tires long before circuses did — *Art Speltz Collection.*

The biggest carnival was the Royal American Shows, which used up to ninety cars, many of them the former Ringling-Barnum rolling stock. In 1976 it used about eighty cars to reach its string of engagements at major state fairs — *The Milwaukee Journal.*

Both photos: Immaculate roadbed, trimmed right-of-way, and a neatly loaded show train make for a pretty picture as the Royal American Shows rides the Milwaukee Road en route to Portage, Wisconsin, in 1961 — *Authors' Photos.*

353

Season's Route
Royal American Shows
1960

Tampa to Memphis	ACL to Birmingham IC to Memphis	1147 miles
Memphis to St. Louis	Frisco	305 miles
St. Louis to Davenport	CBQ	269 miles
Davenport to Winnipeg	CBQ to St. Paul GN to Winnipeg	796 miles
Winnipeg to Brandon	CP	133 miles
Brandon to Calgary	CP	698 miles
Calgary to Edmonton	CN	232 miles
Edmonton to Saskatoon	CN	331 miles
Saskatoon to Regina	CN	162 miles
Regina to Ft. William	CP	775 miles
Ft. William to Superior, Wis.	CN to Ft. Francis DW&P to Duluth GN to Superior	405 miles
Superior to St. Paul	GN	156 miles
St. Paul to Topeka	CRI&P	546 miles
Topeka to Hutchinson, Kan.	CRI&P	155 miles
Hutchinson to Oklahoma City	CRI&P	329 miles
Oklahoma City to Little Rock	CRI&P	355 miles
Little Rock to Jackson, Miss.	Mo. Pac. to Tallulah IC to Jackson	258 miles
Jackson to Shreveport	IC	217 miles
Shreveport to Tampa Winterquarters	IC to Meridan SO to Selma WRA to Montgomery ACL to Tampa	970 miles

The Strates Show traded new piggyback flats for its veteran circus-style cars and continued as a major railroad carnival. This was the scene as the train passed through Albany, New York, in 1971 — *Gene Baxter Photo.*

Right: In 1969 the Strates Shows played eastern fairs, using circus cars and circus systems. But already it was switching over to piggyback flatcars. And it upgraded its passenger cars by purchases from railroads after a flood damaged its earlier cars — *Authors' Photo. Below:* To handle extra-long wagons, the James E. Strates carnival removes one set of trucks from an old Warren flat, which links a standard pair of runs and its modern piggyback flats to give a more gentle slope — *Authors' Photo.*

Strates equipped its Warren run cars with hydraulic jacks and tanks on the underside. Power takeoff on a tractor activates the hydraulic system, which lifts the flatcar high enough to permit rolling the trucks out from under it — *Authors' Photo.*

The detached truck is rolled out of the way, and unloading progresses. Strates trainmen are enthusiastic about the system, which occasionally has been approximated by earlier shows. But some other contemporary rail showmen see little need to go to the effort, and they note that there is no place to put the truck on a split crossing with facing sets of runs — *Authors' Photo.*

Above: Another eastern carnival of long standing, the World of Mirth Shows rolled on cars that came from circuses. Its Mt. Vernon flats had been on Sparks, Hagenbeck-Wallace, and other shows. The oddity at the left is a cut-down stockcar once used on Tim McCoy's Wild West. After the World of Mirth failed, most of its flatcars were acquired by the Circus World Museum — *Art Speltz Collection. Left:* The popular Johnny J. Jones carnival featured its train in a lithograph for advertising the 1946 season — *Authors' Collection.*

Right: Pennsy's electric power hauls the Endy Bros. carnival through Frankford Junction, Pennsylvania, in 1936. Wooden flats still were in use — *Gene Baxter Photo. Below:* The Goodman Wonder Show was another well-known title prior to World War II. It had a long string of wooden flats in 1936 — *Gene Baxter Photo.*

Above: Much show train lore is wrapped up in this move by the Lawrence Carr carnival on the Bangor & Aroostook Railroad in 1970. The carnival normally moved by highway trucks, but the jump from Maine into Quebec was too long. So, like the earliest wagon circuses, it rented a train. And the railroad, lacking the cars itself, got them from a piggyback leasing firm. The cars, of course, were piggyback derivatives of the original circus idea. And loading was according to good circus practice — *Bangor & Aroostook Railroad. Right:* A working boss, Charley Guttermuth is trainmaster of the Royal American Shows and another of the veterans active in 1978. He had been with the Royal since 1964 and earlier was with the train crews of the Strates, Cetlin & Wilson and World of Mirth carnivals and the Cole Bros., Robbins Bros., and Clyde Beatty circuses. Here, he changes out a set of wheels that is below gauge. Behind him is a Warren flat from the carnival train — *Authors' Photo.*

Otto (Stoney) Stonecypher had handled the train for the James E. Strates Shows for twenty-five seasons and continued as one of the veteran trainmasters active in 1978. The Warren flats used as run cars on the Strates show came either from the Johnny J. Jones carnival or the Sells Floto Circus. Stonecypher's crew painted the nicknames of departed fellow workers on the sides of flats as memorials — *Authors' Photo.*

A nostalgic outgrowth of circus railroading was the eye-popping train conceived and developed by the Circus World Museum of Baraboo, Wisconsin, the likes of which neither the show world nor railroading has ever seen. This re-creation of old-time procedures was a fitting culmination of the first century of circus railroading.

The Circus World Museum, under the direction of Charles Philip Fox, combed the country for a decade in a concentrated effort to locate and assemble antique circus equipment. In the collection are about 100 elaborate bandwagons, ornate cages, colorful tableaux, and gaudy calliopes from old-time circuses.

The museum displays railroad cars from many shows. There are more than forty veterans of show service, including Warren and Mount Vernon flats, coaches, stockcars, and advertising cars from such venerable establishments as Sparks, Cole Bros., John Robinson, Clyde Beatty, and Hagenbeck-Wallace circuses. There are cars that carried the names of the great carnivals and such wild west shows as Tim McCoy's and the 101 Ranch. Some are fixed exhibits at the lively museum.

But more of the cars comprise the ready-to-troupe show train with its array of authentic circus parade wagons.

Under the auspices of the Jos. Schlitz Brewing Company, these wagons were brought annually to Milwaukee for the Schlitz Circus Parade, heart of the company's "Old Milwaukee Days" civic celebration on the Fourth of July.

The first parade took place in 1963, and after the second such presentation the enormity of the task of trucking the wagons 125 miles by highway from Baraboo to Milwaukee became overpowering. Late in the summer of 1964 the World of Mirth carnival folded, and Fox suggested to Robert A. Uihlein, then president of Schlitz, that the circus parade wagons be brought to Milwaukee by train in the same manner that circuses had functioned. The World of Mirth flats were acquired.

So the 1965 event included not only the street parade, but also the circus train. Sixteen cars were in the first year's run. By 1972 there were twenty-nine cars—two stocks, twenty-two flats, and five coaches, including converted Milwaukee Road baggage cars now used as open-sided observation cars to carry guests.

The museum train had as many cars as most of the famous circuses in history. On board were accumulated parade vehicles in greater number and glory than any single circus ever had. The train was operated in exactly the same way that regular circuses once functioned. There were train teams, runs, polers, cross-over plates, and snubbing posts. No modern improvements were allowed, no changes from the circus way.

The train originally was moved entirely by the Chicago & North Western Railway. In later years it rolled on C&NW to Madison, where it transferred to tracks of the Chicago, Milwaukee, St. Paul & Pacific. The Milwaukee Road then took it to the Mitchell street yards on the Milwaukee lakefront where, at an interchange, the North Western took over again and spotted the train for unloading.

The train and its cargo were valued at $2 million, and they got careful handling and great consideration from both railroads. Besides the circus cars, the outfit included three more passenger cars. The Santa Fe contributed Diner 1407, built in 1925, eighty-three feet long and seating thirty-six people. Two more came from Pullman. A sleeper and buffet-lounge, once the *Dover Bay*, has six double bedrooms and a lounge that seats fourteen. The sleeper-lounge formerly named *Monte Baldo* has ten open berth sections and a fourteen-seat lounge, plus a classic observation platform.

In some seasons steam power was used and at other times standard road diesels pulled the colorful train while tens of thousands of people lined the right-of-way to see the circus consist and hear the steam calliope. After each parade in Milwaukee, the train was reloaded and returned to the museum at Baraboo. Nine times this majestic train made its way to Milwaukee.

Now the circus train is sidetracked at the Circus World Museum, poised to troupe again. The cars and the parade wagons can be seen by museum visitors. The museum management, like true circus people, maintains active plans and preparations for the train to roll again.

The circus train is lettered to honor many of the great names from the era of railroad circusing. In some cases, each side of a flatcar carries a different historic title. In all cases, the museum has used authentic phraseology, typography, and coloration for each of the shows.

Those flatcars herald Christy Bros.' Big 5-Ring Wild Animal Circus and Gollmar Bros. Enormous New Shows; also included are John Robinson's Ten Big Shows Combined, Gentry Bros. Famous Shows United, and the 101 Ranch Real Wild West. Many of the familiar titles flash by— Sells Bros., Al G. Barnes, Robbins Bros., Adam Forepaugh, Buffalo Bill, Walter L. Main, Sparks, Cole, Beatty and Haag.

Some of the titles on museum cars carry more significance when one recalls the heritage and tradition of circus railroading. On one car is the Barnum & Bailey Greatest Show on Earth title, saluting the roles played by P. T. Barnum and James A. Bailey. Another carries the name of W. W. Cole's Great New York & New Orleans Zoological & Equestrian Exposition, bringing to mind the outfit's pioneer junket to the west coast on new rails. Another flatcar is painted with the title of Ringling Bros. and Barnum & Bailey, the biggest show that ever trouped.

Perhaps most notable is the silver and maroon lettering on one side of Flatcar 56, a yellow seventy-two-foot Warren. It reads: W. C. Coup New United Monster Shows. All who look upon that car might well recall the man who turned dreams into action and demonstrated that there could be such a thing as a big railroad circus.

DETAILS of the 29 CAR CIRCUS TRAIN of the CIRCUS WORLD MUSEUM, Baraboo, Wisconsin

as run for the Schlitz Old Milwaukee Days Special on JUNE 28, 1973

#44 Elephant Car 70' (all steel) —both sides "James E. Strates Shows Wild Animal Menagerie" with art and lesser works. Basic orange with multi color trim.

#49 Stock Car 72' (wood) —one side "Sells Bros. Millionaire Confederation of Stupendous Railroad Shows" orange; white & green letters & trim
—one side "Hagenbeck-Wallace Circus" orange with white letters.

50 Flat Car 70' (Mt. Vernon) —both sides "Al G. Barnes Circus" orange; silver letters/green outline. (RUN CAR)

#51 Flat Car 70' (Mt. Vernon) —both sides "Christy Bros. Big 5 Ring Wild Animal Circus" orange; black letters. (RUN CAR)

#52 Flat Car 72' (Warren) both sides "Gollmar Bros. Enormous New Shows" red; white letters/light and dark blue shading.

#53 Flat Car 72' (Warren) —both sides "Ringling Bros. and Barnum & Bailey Circus" silver; red letters/white outline.

#54 Flat Car 70' (Mt. Vernon) —both sides "The Great Sells-Floto Shows Consolidated" white; red letters/white outline, blue outline. (RUN CAR)

#55 Flat Car 72' (Warren) —both sides "John Robinson 10 Big Shows Combined" orange; white letters/blue outline.

#56 Flat Car 72' (Warren) —one side "Gentry Bros. Famous Shows Combined" yellow; green letters.
—one side "W. C. Coup New United Monster Shows" yellow; silver letters/maroon outline.

#57 Flat Car 72' (Warren) —one side "101 Ranch Real Wild West" orange; purple letters/white outline & black inside shading.
—one side "Robbins Bros. Circus with Hoot Gibson The Screen's Most Popular Western Star" orange; red letters/white shading.

#58 Flat Car 72' (Warren) —one side "Burr Robbins New Consolidated Railroad Shows" red; silver letters/shaded light blue.
—one side "Ringling Bros. World's Greatest Show" red; white letters.

#59 Flat Car 72' (Warren) —one side "The Great Adam Forepaugh & Sells Bros. Shows United" silver; blue letters/ shaded white, light blue outline.
—one side "Buffalo Bill's Wild West & Pawnee Bill's Great Far East" silver; green letters.

#60 Flat Car 72' (Warren) —one side "Walter L. Main All New Monster Shows" yellow; blue letters.
—one side "Barnum & Bailey Greatest Show On Earth" yellow; red letters/black outline.

#61 Flat Car 70' (Warren) —one side "Sparks Circus" orange; white letters. (RUN CAR)
—one side "Cole Bros. Circus with Clyde Beatty & Ken Maynard" silver; red letters/silver shade, blue-green outline.

#62 Flat Car 70' (Mt. Vernon) —one side "Clyde Beatty Circus" silver; red letters/shaded blue.
—one side "Sun Bros. World's Progressive Shows" silver; yellow letters/red outline.

#63 Flat Car 70' (Mt. Vernon) —one side "The Mighty Haag Shows" orange; white letters/blue outline. (RUN CAR)
—one side "W. W. Cole's Great New York & New Orleans Zoological & Equestrian Exposition" orange; silver letters/shaded red.

#64 Flat Car 70' (Mt. Vernon)	—one side "The Greater Norris & Rowe Show" red; yellow letters/orange outline. —one side "Howe's Great London Circus with Van Amburgh's Trained Wild Animals" red; white letters/gold outline.
#65 Flat Car 70' (Mt. Vernon)	—one side "W. H. Harris New Nickel Plate Shows" blue; orange letters/white outline. (RUN CAR) —one side "Yankee Robinson 3 Ring Circus" blue; orange letters/shaded white.
#66 Flat Car 70' (cut-down stock)	—both sides "Circus World Museum Baraboo, Wisconsin" silver; red letters/white outline.
#67 Flat Car 70' (Warren)	—both sides "Royal American Shows" silver; red letters/black outline. Plus special scroll trim.
#68 Flat Car 70' (Warren)	both sides "Buffalo Bill's Wild West *and Congress of* Rough Riders of the World" silver; red letters/white outline (*reversed*).
#69 Flat Car 70' (Warren)	—both sides "Hagenbeck-Wallace Circus" silver; orange letters/blue outline.
#75 Flat Car 70' (Warren)	—both sides "Foley & Burk Shows" silver; yellow letters/orange shading in blue insert flat oval.
#244 Flat Car 70' (Warren)	—both sides "Royal American Shows" silver; red letters/black outline. Plus special scroll trim.
#43 Coach 65' (converted baggage car) "The Dorchester"	—both sides "Circus World Museum, Baraboo, Wisconsin" plus other lesser wording—red; mixed colors and artwork.
#45 Coach 65' (converted baggage car) "The Wonewoc"	—both sides "Circus World Museum, Baraboo, Wisconsin" plus other lesser wording—white; mixed colors and artwork.
#46 Pullman Observation Car 80'	—"The Baraboo", various Schlitz, CWM and Wisconsin promotional slogans—blue.
#47 Pullman Compartment Car 80'	—"The Delavan", various Schlitz, CWM and Wisconsin promotional slogans—white.
#48 Santa Fe Dining Car 80'	—"The Janesville", various Schlitz, CWM and Wisconsin promotional slogans—red.

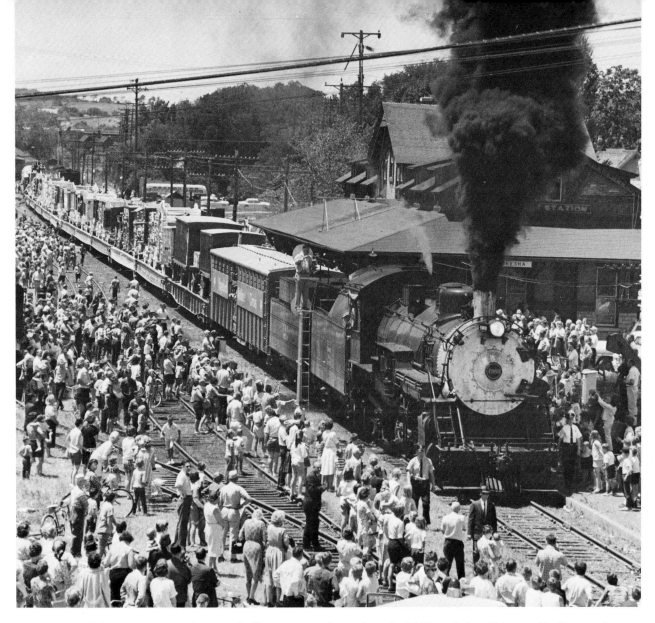

It could be any time in the past half-century, at least, but it's 1965 and the Chicago, Burlington & Quincy's steam engine, 4960, eases the Circus World Museum's parade train before an admiring throng along North Western right-of-way in Waukesha, Wisconsin, en route to the Fourth of July parade sponsored by Schlitz in Milwaukee. A second tender was used since there were no water stops on the run — *Circus World Museum.*

The move began earlier at Baraboo Yards, where the museum's collection of antique circus wagons was loaded on old circus flats. Southern Railway's engine 4501 made up the train at dawn in the 1972 move, then headed for Milwaukee and the celebration — *Circus World Museum*.

The 125-mile route was lined with spectators during each of the nine times that the Schlitz Brewing Company sponsored the train. The old bandwagons, cages, and calliopes appeared in eleven annual parades, glamorous with bands and eight-horse hitches, just as they had done for decades with the big circuses — *Circus World Museum*.

Upon arrival at the Milwaukee lakefront, the show train was unloaded. Every step was authentic. Flatcars, train teams, polers, snubbing posts, and cross-over plates — all were used exactly as they had been on circus trains for a century. The wagons, cars, and horses returned to the museum at Baraboo, where they continue to give daily demonstrations of how circus trains were operated — *Circus World Museum.*

Appendix

A Railroad's Circus Correspondence

NYO&W Ry, File 14

The general superintendent of the 700-mile New York, Ontario & Western Railway Company maintained File 14, Movement Circus Trains, and filled it with the correspondence generated by the small and medium-sized circuses that wanted to play central New York and northeastern Pennsylvania. The contents give a vivid picture of how railroaders regarded the circus and how circus moves were handled.

The oldest item in the file is a Special Rate Notice, dated July 3, 1895 covering the proposed moves of the Hunting's Great New York Shows to a half dozen towns on the NYO&W. It established a $100 charge for moving the fourteen-car train. But on July 18 the general superintendent wrote to his inspector:

"I presume likely you will shed tears when you read the attached notice of cancellation . . ." It seems that the Hunting show changed its route when Ringling Bros. Circus got into the territory first. A substitute contract called for only one move on the line. And the railroaders rejoiced.

The following are excerpts from similar correspondence in File 14:

Traffic manager to superintendent, April 5, 1909:

"The Howard Damon Circus have been after us for some time to quote rates on our line.

"Their outfit consists of two stockcars, three flatcars, one diner, and one sleeper, a total of seven cars with one advance car. We have declined to handle them during the period covered by our summer timetable. They now ask us for quotations covering the movement in the early part of

June before our summer timetable goes into effect and threaten if we do not given them figures, they will take the matter up with the Interstate Commerce Commission . . . Is there any objection to moving them before the summer timetable? We will exact from them as high a rate as the Almighty or the Interstate Commerce Commission will permit."

General superintendent to traffic manager, April 6, 1909:

". . . If this circus train consists of only seven cars and one advance car, I think we would have no difficulty in handling it at that time of the year.

"An outfit of this kind is likely to have very poor equipment and the law is now so specific and strict in relation to defective safety appliances, there is always more or less risk in handling these circus trains, and I do not think as a general rule the company has ever received any profit or net money in moving them. Rates generally per car are so much less than the ordinary freight rates and there is an expense of switching and practically a continuous engine service in moving, unloading, and loading these trains while on the line.

"I presume the Interstate Commerce Commission would not require the Company to handle this class of freight and passengers at less rate than any other. I noticed some time ago that the Lackawanna Company had refused to handle circus trains altogether."

General passenger agent to general superintendent, June 17, 1909:

"Howes Circus will show at Norwich Monday July 26. They have one advance car, four coaches, three stockcars, five flatcars, and one boxcar. There are 12 people traveling in the advance and about 150 with the circus. They wish to make a trip over our line but I informed them that that was impossible on account of our lack of siding. However, they wish to go from Norwich to the Delaware & Hudson RR and desire to know if we can move them from Norwich to Sidney on the night of July 26. Kindly advise whether we shall contract for this business or whether you prefer to have us decline the same."

Superintendent to general superintendent, June 19, 1909:

". . . We can handle the Howes Circus train of 13 cars, Norwich to Sidney, on the night of July 26, without any troubles I think."

General superintendent to superintendent, July 8, 1910:

"Referring to the movement of the Mighty Haag Shows . . . we are quite short of power and likely to be throughout the summer and I do not think we should undertake this kind of special service which hardly pays for the expense and risk of handling. As you know the equipment of these show trains generally is in very poor condition and there is considerable risk in handling and loading and unloading."

General passenger agent to general superintendent, April 20, 1911:

"We have contracted with the manager of California Frank's Show for (eight movements, May 24-June 2). Cars to be delivered to West Shore RR at Cornwall.

"We have also received application from the manager of the Haag Circus for the movement of his circus which consists of 12 cars and one advance car between (ten points, June 2-13). Before making any contract, will you kindly advise me if you can take care of these movements."

General superintendent to general passenger agent, April 21, 1911:

"I do not think we should try to handle Haag Circus as we are handling other circuses at the same time and should not in any event try to make Monticello. To handle train to that point account heavy grade would require at least three engines."

General superintendent to superintendent, May 11, 1911:

"The traffic department advise that they have contracted with California Frank's Wild West Show, Inc., consisting of four flatcars, three stockcars, three coaches, and one advertising car . . . On the afternoon of May 23, cars will be delivered to us, empty, at Sidney by the D&H Co. Cars are to be loaded on our tracks at Sidney. At East Branch cars are to be delivered to the D&H RR, being returned to us the following day . . . The agreement is made with the understanding that each of the above mentioned cars is equipped with automatic couplers and air brakes as provided by law. The advertising car will make the same movement as the show, two weeks in advance of the show, and it is to be hauled on such trains and at such times as most convenient to the railway company. At Port Jervis, the cars will be delivered, empty, to the Erie RR."

General passenger agent to general superintendent, May 16, 1911.

"I am enclosing herewith copy of agreement made with the Mighty Haag Show for movements over this line. We have for the last five years refused to carry any circus during the summer months, telling them it was impossible for us to take care of them but saying that if they would move over the line before the summer timetable went into effect we would be glad to take care of them.

"This year the manager of the Mighty Haag Show called at this office and said that he would like movements over this road in the spring, and there did not seem to be any way to get out of it, and we, therefore, made the enclosed contract." The price was $135.50 per move.

General passenger agent to general superintendent, May 26, 1911:

"I am enclosing herewith copy of new agreement made with the Mighty Haag Shows . . . You will note that they have changed their route, omitting Delhi and showing at Hancock instead on June 14. Also they desire to be moved from Middletown to Cornwall and delivered to the West Shore Railroad on June 18. The amount to be collected for each movement has also been changed to $116 . . ."

General passenger agent to general superintendent, June 2, 1911:

"The Cole & Johnson show, consisting of one passenger coach, two baggage cars and one advance car, all to be carried on our regular trains, have applied at this office for (13 movements) . . . The charge for moving the coach and two baggage cars will be $50 for each movement, and $25 for each movement of the advertising car . . ."

General superintendent to general passenger agent, June 6, 1911:

". . . I think we will be able to handle passenger coach and two baggage cars on our regular trains on the dates mentioned in your letter, and if you will kindly advise movement of the advance car, we will handle that on regular trains . . ."

General passenger agent to general superintendent, February 26, 1912:

"L. E. Cooke, representing Buffalo Bill's Wild West Show, called at this office today in relation to movement of the company from Scranton, Pa., to Middletown, N.Y., on April 25. There will be 47 cars and three advertising cars in advance. Mr. Cooke advises there is no other way that he can make the jump from Scranton to Middletown except over our line and requests me to take the matter up with you. We can probably charge him about $1,000 for the jump."

General superintendent to general passenger agent, February 27, 1912:

". . . I don't think we should accept this show train. We haven't track facilities adjacent to the highways at Middletown where this number of cars could be unloaded or stored, and I don't think we should take the risk of running the circus train over the Scranton division. We certainly could not afford to handle it for $1,000 . . ."

General passenger agent to general superintendent, May 3, 1912:

"I am enclosing herewith copy of agreement made with the Rice Bros. Show for movements over our line from May 7 to May 19, inclusive. You agreed to loan this company 60-foot baggage car, which please have placed at Cornwall on Sunday, May 5, for loading. This company will occupy their own sleeper which should be moved with baggage car as shown on enclosed schedules in agreement. Special movement should be made, leaving about 1 a.m. or earlier as soon as cars are loaded . . ."

Traffic manager to general superintendent, May 4, 1912:

"Ringling Bros. asked us to move their circus from Norwich to Rome on Wednesday, June 5. Their show consists of 85 cars made up as follows: 16 coaches, 6 box cars, 19 stock cars, 41 flats, and three advance cars. I told them that our yard room at Norwich and Rome was limited, but that if we could receive this circus loaded from the DL&W at Norwich and deliver it to the New York Central loaded at Rome, I would take the matter up with you. Their representative stated that he thought he could make that arrangement with the DL&W and the New York Central. As we will probably not be moving any coal at that time and have engines at Norwich to spare, it seems to me that we could afford to handle the traffic."

General superintendent to traffic manager, May 6, 1912:

". . . Our yard tracks at Rome will be in such condition due to the Barge Canal work as to prevent us handling, and it would also be impossible to load these cars at Norwich yards."

Traffic manager to general superintendent, May 6, 1912:

"DL&W advises that it is impossible for them to deliver cars to us loaded but that they will deliver cars to us empty at Norwich for loading on our tracks. Have we sufficient side trackage at Norwich so this can be done?"

Traffic manager to general superintendent, May 10, 1912:

". . . Lackawanna advises account of track facilities at Norwich it would be impossible for them to load circus and deliver to us loaded. Any switch we have near Norwich, say within two or three miles, would be agreeable to Ringling Bros. for loading. They state that New York Central will accept cars at Rome loaded from our line. DL&W have agreed to unload at Norwich but have not sufficient track room to load. Ringling Bros. are in difficulties over the matter and I would like very much to help them."

Rome superintendent to general superintendent, May 8, 1912:

". . . It would be impossible for us to handle this show at Rome, account limited room and inadequate facilities."

General superintendent to traffic manager, May 10, 1912:

"We have not track facilities at Norwich yard to load the 85 circus cars and would not attempt to handle this circus."

General superintendent to superintendent, May 10, 1912:

". . . It is possible that the Traffic Department may insist on our taking it at Norwich and loading it up, and if so, it will be necessary to move out of Norwich all of the cars on the sidings north of Main Street and I suppose on the east side south of Main street, to some other switch or station. If this was done, do you think it would be possible to load up those 85 cars? I suppose the coaches could be loaded up at any point and got out ahead of the other cars."

Superintendent to general superintendent, May 11, 1912:

". . . I think we can arrange the matter of loading the show at Norwich without much trouble by clearing the cars off the sidings north of the station, and we could also move it to Rome, but it would be absolutely out of the question for us to unload at that city. If arrangements can be made with the New York Central to receive the loaded cars immediately upon arrival at Rome and unload on their tracks, I think we can handle the business satisfactorily. The show consists of 82 cars, three of the 85 being advertising cars which move in advance of the show. The coaches usually run on the second or third section of the train and can be loaded up very readily." (Ringling Bros. played the towns, thanks to the NYO&W traffic manager's insistence, which, in turn, must have been generated by the circus agent.)

General freight agent to general superintendent, July 18, 1912:

"I am enclosing herewith copy of agreement made with the Sparks Show for movements on our line from August 4 to August 16 inclusive. The advertising car will be floated from Long Island City on Saturday morning, July 20, and when received at Weehawken please move by first convenient train to Port Jervis . . . The circus train proper will be floated from Long Island City on the morning of Sunday, August 4, which please arrange to move by special train from Weehawken to Port Jervis early as possible."

General passenger agent to general superintendent, June 30, 1913:

"I am enclosing herewith copy of agreement made with the Sanger's Great European Shows for movements over our line from July 18 to July 22. Advertising car will be delivered to our line at Sidney from the Delaware & Hudson Company about July 3 and should make the same movements as the circus, as desired by the advertising crew."

General passenger agent to general superintendent, July 23, 1913:

"I am enclosing herewith copy of our agreement with the manager of the Frank A. Robbins Circus for movements over our line from August 5 to August 12 inclusive. Advertising car will be delivered to our line at Middletown from the New York, Susquehanna & Western . . ."

Assistant general passenger agent to general superintendent, May 13, 1914:

"Mr. Edward Arlington, proprietor of the 101 Ranch, has requested us to name rates on the transportation of his show, 35 cars . . . Will you kindly advise if our facilities will allow us to take care of this business?"

General superintendent to assistant general passenger agent, May 18, 1914:

"It wil be impractical to handle a show train of 35 cars, either to unload or load them at either of the yards mentioned, during the summer. The only tracks we have at Fulton which would be convenient for this purpose are located in the street, and at Fulton we have only one main track from Broadway to the Canal Branch, the new siding."

Superintendent to general superintendent, June 22, 1914:

". . . Relative to movement of the 101 Ranch Show, 32 cars and three advance cars, on July 22, Norwich to Fulton, we are to receive them from the DL&W at Norwich, where they show on the 21st. It will be loaded about midnight and delivered to the NYC at Fulton on the morning of the 22nd. We will move this show in two trains and with good luck should have them in Fulton by 7 a.m."

Assistant general passenger agent to general superintendent, July 10, 1914:

"Referring to your acknowledgement of contract covering movement of Frank A. Robbins Circus, contract should read, floatage charge of $91.00 from Long Island City to Weehawken, and $185.00, Weehawken to Ellenville, making total charge $276.00."

Assistant general passenger agent to general superintendent, July 15, 1914:

"I am enclosing herewith copy of contract made with the 101 Ranch Wild West Show, Miller Bros. & Arlington, Prop'rs. for movement over our line from Norwich, NY to Fulton, NY on the morning of July 22."

Superintendent to general superintendent and claim agent, August 7, 1914:

"Following from Agent Fitzgerald at Roscoe . . . Pick up while switching struck the Haag Show Advertising Car quite hard, upsetting desk and threw manager Victor Stout down on floor, injuring his back slightly. Says he will advise you in a.m. if anything serious develops. No damage done to car."

General passenger agent to general superintendent, August 10, 1914:

"Enclosed you will find contract covering the movement of the Mighty Haag show over our line from August 16 to 22, inclusive . . ."

Superintendent to all concerned, May 9, 1916:

"Arrangements have been made for movement of LaTena's Wild Animal Circus over our line as follows:

"Receive the empty cars from the DL&W at Norwich on the morning of May 24, 1916, for movement from Norwich to Oneida about 1:00 a.m. May 25 and deliver cars empty to the NYC at Oneida.

"The show will consist of 6 flatcars, 3 stockcars, 4 passenger coaches, and 1 advertising car two weeks in advance. It is understood that each of the above mentioned cars is equipped as provided by law.

"Mr. Daley will please arrange to furnish a Class I engine in first class condition for this service. Yardmaster at Norwich will arrange to receive the empty cars from the DL&W and place them for loading as may be arranged later."

Superintendent to all concerned, June 12, 1916:

"The Coop & Lent Circus, consisting of 10 flatcars, four stockcars, five passenger coaches and one advertising car about two weeks in advance will move over our line . . . The Show company is to pay this Company in advance the sum of $160 for each run . . ."

General passenger agent to general superintendent, August 8, 1916:

"Enclosed please find copy of contract made with the

Cook & Wilson's Wild Animal Circus for movement over our line as follows:

"Receive cars empty from the Delaware & Hudson RR at Sidney, N.Y., on the morning of August 9 for movement as follows:

"Sidney N.Y. to Walton, N.Y. about 1:00 a.m. August 10.

"Walton, N.Y. to Carbondale, Pa., about 1:00 a.m. August 11 and deliver cars empty to the Delaware & Hudson Co.

"Advertising car has already been moved over our line. Copy of tariff covering above movement is enclosed."

General passenger agent to general superintendent, May 17, 1917:

"We have entered into contract with the John Robinson's Ten Big Shows Company, consisting of 20 flatcars, 12 stockcars, 11 passenger coaches, 2 advertising cars, for movement over our line . . . Cars will be received empty from the Ulster & Delaware Railroad at Kingston . . ."

General passenger agent to general superintendent, June 4, 1917:

". . . Mr. E. C. Knupp, general agent of the circus, advises that his agreement with the Ulster & Delaware is as follows: 'We will agree to move the cars of the John Robinson Circus Company, consisting of 43 cars and two advance cars, the former to be delivered empty by West Shore RR all in one train for movement to NYO&W tracks at Kingston for the sum of $100.00 including setting over cars in sections to transfer tracks at O&W interchange track, provided the O&W engine will be on hand prepared to take the cars without delay from the U&D tracks.'"

General passenger agent to general superintendent, June 4, 1917:

"We have contracted with Sun Bros. Circus, consisting of 4 flatcars, 2 stockcars, 2 passenger coaches and advertising car . . ."

General passenger agent to general superintendent, June 11, 1917:

"In relation to movement of Sun Bros. Circus . . . Mr. H. A. Mann, their general agent, advises that it will be impossible for the show to play as outlined, and I will be glad if you will cancel any instructions you have issued concerning above movement . . ."

General passenger agent to general superintendent, June 25, 1917:

"We have been requested by the manager of Sun Bros. Circus to move their show, consisting of 1 advertising car, 2 passenger coaches, 2 stockcars and 4 flatcars, as follows:

"Circus equipment will be floated from Long Island City to Weehawken, Monday morning, July 23, for movement to Ellenville, where they desire to show, July 23.

"Ellenville to Liberty, where they will exhibit, July 24

"Liberty to Walton, where they will exhibit, July 25

"Walton to Sidney, where they will exhibit, July 26 where cars are to be delivered empty to the Delaware & Hudson. Should the Delaware & Hudson not be in position to accept them at Sidney, they desire to move on the 27th to Earlsville, where cars will be delivered loaded to West Shore for further movement. . . ."

New York Committee of Executives to presidents, February 13, 1918:

"The director general has advised that provided circuses confine their engagements during the coming season to territories not within the congestion region, no objection will be found to their being moved as usual, subject to the stipulation that, if necessary to relieve freight congestion or to aid war activities, contracts for their transportation may be cancelled . . ."

General passenger agent to general superintendent, May 22, 1918:

"I am enclosing herewith a copy of our agreement made with John Robinson's Circus . . ."

USRA director general, NYO&W to federal manager, May 20, 1919:

"We have a request from the John Robinson Circus . . . The show consists of 14 flatcars, 7 stockcars, 7 sleepers and 2 advertising cars."

USRA-NYO&W and Sells Floto Circus, June 10, 1919:

". . . The Railroad agrees that it will transport the show . . . Subject, however, to the condition that on the dates named, no troops, enlisted men for the army, or government property or supplies are being moved or required by federal authorities to be moved, over the line . . . In such case, however, the first party will endeavor to transport the show and property above specific if considered practical by the railroad authorities . . . The show shall consist of 14 flatcars, 7 stockcars, 7 coaches and 2 advertising cars."

General passenger agent to general manager, May 17, 1920:

"We have contracted for the movement of the Walter L. Main Shows, consisting of 9 flatcars, 4 stockcars, 5 coaches and 2 advertising cars, over our line . . ."

General manager to general passenger agent, April 5, 1920:

"I assume that in this movement, they will want us to furnish parking space and unloading facilities for this circus and there is question in my mind whether or not the inconvenience to which we would be put in furnishing this space would more than offset the revenues which we would receive. Will you kindly advise me how much revenue we would receive . . ."

General passenger agent to general manager, April 8, 1920:

"Charge for each movement would be $220. If it is going to be inconvenient to take care of them, we can very easily refuse to accept the business."

General manager to general passenger agent, April 10, 1920:

"At a number of points it will be of such inconvenience to us and it will require the use of a special engine to load and unload the train that I think that after we pay the expense of our train crews and the other expenses of this operation that there will not be enough left to compensate us for the inconvenience. I would suggest that you refuse the business."

NYO&W RR and Walter L. Main Circus, May 14, 1920:

". . . The party of the second part agrees to pay to the party of the first part, in advance, the sum of $290 for each movement . . ."

Superintendent to all concerned, July 14, 1920:

"Please arrange for the following movement of Howes Great London Show, consisting of 6 flatcars, 4 stockcars, and 4 coaches:

"Tuesday, July 20, receive cars empty from U&D RR at Kingston.

"Wednesday, July 21, Kingston to Middletown, leaving about 1 a.m.

"Thursday, July 22, Middletown to Liberty, leaving about 1 a.m.

"Friday, July 23, Liberty to Scranton (Park Place), leaving about 1 a.m. and cars will be delivered loaded to DL&W RR at Scranton (Park Place). A charge of $205 is to be made for each run plus 3% war tax, must be paid in advance."

Superintendent to all concerned, May 20, 1921:

"Please arrange for the following movement of Sparks Shows (Circus), consisting of 6 flatcars, 4 stockcars, 4 coaches and 1 advertising car . . . The charge for each movement will be $285.50, plus 3% war tax."

General manager to traffic manager, June 21, 1921:

". . . I think the best thing to do hereafter would be not to book any show movements to Carbondale, unless they are willing to unload and load at points where it is not necessary to use the main track."

General passenger agent to general manager, February 1, 1922:

"A representative of John Robinson's Circus called in relation to movement of their show, which consists of 14 flats, 7 stockcars, and 8 sleepers, 1 advance car . . ."

Superintendent to general manager, February 9, 1922:

". . . While Friday July 21 will undoubtedly be a heavy passenger day, still we should be able to handle this train."

General manager to general passenger agent, February 11, 1922:

". . . While Friday, July 21, will probably be a pretty busy day, we can probably move the circus from Liberty to Walton. They however will have to adjust their loading at Liberty in accordance with our facilities."

Superintendent to all concerned, May 5, 1921:

"We have contracted for the movement of the Sparks Circus . . ."

General manager to general passenger agent, June 16, 1922:

"Mr. Ballinger of the Sparks show was in today and we have agreed to the following schedule:

"We will receive the empty cars at Kingston during the day, July 11 and will move them over our line to show at Ellenville on the 12th, Middletown on the 13th, Liberty on the 14th, Carbondale on the 15th, Walton on the 17th and Oneida on the 18th . . ."

Lessons for a Budding Show Agent

Theatrical railroading made easy! In 1911 there were enough jobs as advance agents for shows that a correspondence school put out a course in how to do it. Lesson Two told how to handle the railroading:

THE HAMILTON-HAVRE BUREAU
LETTER OF INSTRUCTION
No. 2.
"THEATRICAL RAILROADING"
Copyright 1911.

Before the days of the Interstate Commerce Commission theatrical railroading was almost one of the fine arts. Those were the days that the best agent was the fellow who could turn the neatest tricks with the railroads—all his other accomplishments were secondary. When the government permitted each railroad to make its own rates and cut them as it desired, there was the livliest competition between rival lines for the transportation of theatrical companies. Old-time agents took advantage of this competition and worked the railroads to a finish. It was a feather in an agent's cap to move his company from point to point cheaper than the other fellow, and the size of his salary check was largely influenced by the success he achieved in this particular.

But with the passage of the Interstate Commerce Laws, all this was changed. These laws established *fixed* rates for various classes of service between different points. There is no more *rate-cutting* and the agent of to day need not worry lest some other agent is getting the better of him on the movement of a company. This fact removes one of the greatest obstacles to success in the press-agent's profession reducing as it does the railroading feature from the *hardest* to the *simplest* of the press-agent's duties.

. . . .

In our first letter we explained that in all probability the movement of your company out of New York or Chicago (or wherever launched) would be arranged by the home office. Usually these arrangements include the first few towns. This information will be given you when you receive your contracts. So your railroading experience, in all probability, will begin when the arrangements made by the home office expire. If, however, it *should happen* that you are asked to arrange for the *first movement* of the company do not be alarmed. The instructions given herewith will apply quite as well to the initial movement as any other.

One much traveled path for shows out of New York is over the New York, New Haven & Hartford railroad, touching towns like Stamford, New Haven, New London,

Providence and so on into Boston. Let's assume that your show has been sent over this route and that the railroading as far as Boston has been arranged by the home office. You arrive in Boston a week or ten days ahead of your show and you find a letter enclosing contracts for the next two weeks. Your route may be like this:

Monday night, Dec. 11—Worcester, Mass.
Tuesday night, Dec. 12—Springfield, Mass.
Wednesday night, Dec. 13—Albany, N.Y.
Thursday night, Dec. 14—Utica, N.Y.
Friday night, Dec. 15—Syracuse, N.Y.
Saturday, mat. & night, Dec. 16, Rochester, N.Y.

And from Rochester into Buffalo for a week's stand.

Consulting your railroad map, you will find that your towns are on the New York Central. Go, therefore, to the *city ticket office* of the New York Central in Boston and inquire for the *city passenger agent*. This official, or one of his assistants, will wait on you. The conversation will run something like this:

You:— "I am the agent of "The Slim Princess" Company. I want to arrange a little movement over your line."

He:— "All right, sir. (He secures memorandum form) How many will there be?"

You:— "Sixty people. We require two sixty-foot baggage cars."

He:— "Can't you make fifty-foot do?"

You:— "Can't possibly do it. Must be sixty."

He:— "Very well. Will arrange it. Now then, what's your towns?"

You will submit your route as given above. He will also want to know your name and the name of the man back-with-the-show. With this information the city passenger agent will prepare your *itinerary*. This *itinerary* will give the time of the departure of your company from Boston, the time of arrival in Worcester; departure from there and arrival at Springfield, and so on throughout the week. It will tell the time your baggage cars will be placed on the siding ready for loading after the show in each town; it will give the per capita rate of fare and *every other necessary detail of information*. Two copies of this itinerary will be furnished you, one of which you will keep and the other you will send with your advice sheet to the manager back with the show.

. . . .

Of course this movement we have just described is a very simple one. The towns lay along the same road. Suppose that after Albany, instead of Utica you play Binghamton. Look at the map. Binghamton is on the Delaware and Hudson. So when you arrived at Albany you would go to the city passenger agent of the Delaware and Hudson and arrange your Binghamton jump in the manner precisely as described.

In the event that there are two or more lines between points select the one that will give you the most convenient service. The rates will be the same (except in a rare number of cases where the Interstate Commerce Commission has made a "differential" rate, because one line is so much superior to another. This is seldom encountered and applies only on long jumps. When you do encounter a "differential" you will use your best judgment or confer with your home office as to the proper line to use.)

. . . .

In letter No. 1 we cautioned you repeatedly against *asking questions*. We did this because we don't want anyone about the home office to get the impression that you are *green in the business*. But this advice doesn't apply to your railroading. *Ask all the questions that may occur to you* concerning the movement of your company. The railroad agents will be glad to answer them and if you *do ask foolish questions* occasionally it will not matter, for the railroad men are not paying your salary and you need not care what their opinions are.

Over most railway systems a party ticket of twenty-five fares will entitle a theatrical company to the *free* use of a baggage car. Under twenty-five fares, baggage cars are charged for *extra*. The charge for a baggage car is usually fifteen cents a mile. *Sometimes it is profitable in moving a small company to pay more fares than you really require in order to get your baggage car free.*

Let's figure this out. Suppose you have an hundred mile jump with a dramatic company. The ticket fare is 2-cents a mile or $2.00 per capita. The baggage car would cost you $15.00, equivalent to 7-1/2 fares. Now it will be apparent that if you have eighteen people in your company it would be cheaper to pay for twenty-five and get the baggage car free. (Eighteen fares at $2.00 would be $36.00 and adding $15.00 for car would be $51.00 as against $50.00 figured on the 25 ticket plan.)

You will find that on any jump the "split" comes along about seventeen or eighteen. So if your company is about that size, always figure out whether it will be cheaper to buy the actual number of fares and *pay* for your baggage car or buy *twenty-five* and get your car *free*. On the same ratio a company of fifty will entitle you to two cars, a company of seventy-five to three, etc.

Very often a railroad agent, in order to get your haul will find some vaudeville players, or other travelers, who are going to move at the same time your show does and to the same destination. These fares can be included in your party ticket and so save any extra fares that you would otherwise be called upon to pay on account of your car.

Naturally railroad men will want to give you a small baggage car and you will have to insist on a sixty-foot car, if your scenery and trunks demand it. Your stage carpenter will *always* specify a big car, because he can load it easier. But nine times out of ten a show that calls for a sixty-foot car can be packed in a fifty-foot car if the stage crew uses a little diligence and ingenuity. *So in a pinch* you are not taking very much of a chance if you permit the railroad to specify the smaller car, when larger ones are *really unavailable*. Stuff crowded out of a special baggage car can always be checked on the regular baggage cars.

If you are playing one-night stands you should arrange to leave each city between 10 A.M., and 2 P.M. There is no reason to linger in the city where you played last night. *Get out early as you can, being reasonably considerate of your company's comfort.* The sooner you get to your next town the more advertising you receive. *Never take a chance on the last train between two cities. Something always happens.* Get in your next stand by 3 or 4 o'clock in the afternoon at the very latest. Of course, if you have arranged for a matinee, you must arrange for your company to get in before noon.

It is the usual thing for your baggage car, which is always loaded immediately after the last performance, to be taken to your next town on the *"first train after loading."* That's the way it's noted in the itinerary. Sometimes in making a bad jump it is necessary to have your stage crew move on this same train, in order to get things in readiness for the performance in the next town, while the company follows at a more convenient hour. When this occurs the railroad will issue what is known as a *SPLIT TICKET*.

In eastern territory railroads do *not* figure the advance agent as a one of the party of twenty-five necessary to secure the baggage car. So he buys his ticket separately and charges the same on his expense account; or he may take a ticket from the ticket-agent and give him a receipt for same, allowing the manager with the show to pay for it when he comes along. In certain western territory the agent's fare is figured in with the twenty-five. All agents of first class companies are permitted to use Pullmans on long journeys and to charge the Pullman fares in on their expense accounts. (Expense accounts will be taken up in detail in another letter.)

POSTSCRIPT.

By exercising ordinary common-sense there is little

chance that you will make any mistakes in this department of your work. Everybody has traveled and knows how to use railroad maps and time tables and there is in every town a city passenger man for every line, whose business it is to give you every bit of information and assistance that you require. You will find that these railroad fellows, when competition is keen, will seek you out at your hotel or theatre, in an effort to have you use their respective lines. Do not decide hastily but give each of them a chance to be heard. Finally select the line that:

(a) has a train at the best hour.
(b) makes the best time.
(c) Arrives at depot most convenient to theatre.
(d) provides best accommodations for company (as special day coach; special chair car, etc.)
(e) supplies required length baggage cars.

You will find, of course, that no one line possesses *all* the advantages, so it will be in the last analysis up to your *own judgment.*

Make-up of the Ringling Bros. and Barnum & Bailey Circus Train, 1932

First Section, "The Flying Squadron"

Stockcars
10—Baggage Horses
11—Baggage Horses
12—Baggage Horses

Flatcars—Wagon Number, Load and Length
109-   12, Baggage Stock Trappings, 18'
    105, Lot Layout, 16'
    107, Stake Driver, 12'
    136, Mack Truck, 20'

110-   6, Commissary, 20'
    46, Concession Dept., 16'
    108, Stake Driver, 12'
    2, Steam Boiler Cookhouse, 16'

111-   7, Cookhouse Baggage, Meat, 18'
    10, Baggage Canvas, 20'6"
    102, Water Wagon, 11'
    9, Blacksmith Shop, 18'

112-   11, Baggage Stock Poles and Rigging, 20'
    Station Wagon auto
    128, Mack Truck, 18'
    5, Cookhouse Baggage, Dishes, etc., 18'

113-   8, Cookhouse Canvas and Poles, 20'
    103, Water Wagon, 11'8"
    106, Stake Driver, 12'
    4, Cookhouse Baggage, Dishes, etc., 18'

114-   3, Cookhouse Ranges, 16'
      1, Cookhouse Water Wagon, 15'
   132, Mack Tractor
    14, Menagerie Canvas, 21'

115- 15, Menagerie Poles, 42' Poles, 30'
   104, Water Wagon, 11'
    13, Menagerie Stake and Chain, 16'

Cage Cut

101- 69, Cage, Hyenas, 16'
    71, Cage, Tigers, 15'
    67, Tableau Cage Wagon, Nilgai, 14'
    88, Cage, Hippo, 20'

102- 87, Tableau Cage, Gemsbok and Brindle
       Gnu, 14'
       Dragon Spec Float
    83, Tableau Cage, Kangaroo, 14'
    85, Tableau Cage, Tapir, 14'
    76, Tableau Cage, Stork and Crane, 14'

103- 97, Giraffe Van, 16'
    96, Giraffe Van, 16'
    92, Giraffe Van, 16'
    89, Cage, Monkeys, 15'

104- 79, Cage, Chimpanzee and Orangutang, 18'
    73, Cage, Tigers, 16'
    80, Cage, Puma and Black Leopards, 14'
    84, Cage, Brown Bears, 18'

105- 121, Yellow Ticket Wagon, 18'
    78, Cage, Rhinoceros, 16'
    74, Cage, Rhinoceros, 16'
    70, Cage, Tigers, 16'

108- 90, Tableau Cage, Reedsbuck and Audad, 14'
    91, Tableau Cage, Porcupines, 14'
    95, Cage, Leopards, 14'
    53, Props, 22'

Coaches

70—Connecticut
71—Indiana
72—Minnesota
73—Michigan

Second Section

Stockcars

13—Baggage Stock
14—Baggage Stock
15—Baggage Stock
16—Baggage Stock
17—Baggage Stock

Flatcars — Wagon Number, Load and Length

116- 119, Side Show, Panel Front Wagon, 20'
   120, Side Show, Panel Front Wagon, 20'
   115, Side Show, Canvas

117-   36, Performers' Rigging, 15'
   123, Red Ticket Wagon, 18'
      Mack Side Show Bus
   135, Mack Tractor, 16'

118- 202, Midway Lunch Stand, 18'
   111, Midway and Menagerie Light Plant, 16'
    40, Big Top Sidepoles and Rigging, 17'3"
   133, Mack Tractor, 18'

119- 114, Light Dept., 16'
    64, Wardrobe Dept., 16'
   116, Side Show Trunks, 18'
   200, Baggage Wagon for Auto, 18'

120-   57, Props, 22'
    37, Big Top Canvas, 21'
    42, Big Top Canvas, 21'

121- 39, Big Top Stake and Chain, 16'
141, Baggage Wagon for Auto, 19'
137, Mack Tractor, 18'
129, Mack Tractor, 16'

122- 58, Props, 26'
49, Ring Stock Poles and Canvas, 20'6"
125, Trunks, 16'

123- 50, Backyard Stake and Chain, 16'
30, Carpenter Shop and Ring Curbs, 15'
38, Big Top Stake and Chain, 16'
112, Big Top Lighting Plant, 16'

124- 113, Light Dept., 16'
110, Backyard Light Plant, 16'
45, Big Top Quarter Poles (33'6" poles), 32'

125- 44, Big Top Blue Quarter Poles (41' poles),
35'-38'
134, Mack Tractor, 16'

126- 43, Big Top Center Poles (55' poles), 40'
1220, Train Light Plant, 12'

Coaches

74—Illinois
75—Florida
76—Wisconsin
77—Nebraska
78—Maryland
79—Alabama

Third Section

Stockcars

18—Baggage Horses
19—Baggage Horses

20—Baggage Horses
32—Supplies and Storage
33—Supplies and Storage

Flatcar — Wagon Number, Load and Length

140- 101, Wardrobe Dept., 18'
63, Wardrobe Dept., 16'
Spec. Float
94, Cage, Sea Lions, 16'

139- 201, Concession Dept., 18'
61, Trunks, 17'
23, Bibleback Seats, 14'
93, Cage, Sea Lions, 16'

138- 41, Props, 17'
Ford Auto
24, Bibleback Seats, 14'
20, Long Side Grandstand Chairs, 19'

137- 65, Wardrobe Dept. Trunks, 17'
Funny Ford Clown Taxi
Zacchinis' Cannon Truck
122, White Ticket Wagon, 18'

136- 25, Bibleback Seats, 14'
Spec Float
35, Extra Red Seats, 15'
99, Dog Wagon with Section on Rear, 18'

135- 51, Trunks, 19'
17, Blue Seat Planks, 13'6"
16, Blue Seat Planks, 13'6"
142, Short Side Grandstand Chairs, 21'

134- 56, Wild West Wardrobe and Props, 16'
27, Bibleback Chairs, 14'
26, Bibleback Chairs, 14'
54, Stages, 21'

133- 118, Band Top and Wardrobe, 16'
55, Props, 18'

48, Ring Stock Trappings, 16'
59, Trunks, 18'8"

132- 21, Bibleback Seats, 14'
    52, Trunks and Props, 14'
    22, Bibleback Seats, 14'
  143, Short Side Grandstand Chairs, 21'

131- 34, Grandstand Seat Stringers
      (38' stringers), 32'6"
    19, Long Side Grandstand Chairs, 19'

130- 153, Ring Curbs and Stage Sills, 20'
    29, Seat Jacks, ½ Blue and ½ Long Side, 20'
    28, Seat Jacks, ½ Blue and ½ Long Side, 20'

129- 33, Blue Seat Stringers (35' stringers), 30'
    32, Blue Seat Stringers (35' stringers), 30'

128- 18, Long Side Grandstand Chairs, 19'
  100, Amplifier, 12'
   66, Trunks, 18'
   60, Trunks, 18'8"

127- 31, Grandstand Seat Stringers
      (38' stringers), 32'6"
  139, Seat Jacks, Short Side Grandstand, 20'

Coaches

94—Atlanta
95—New Orleans
96—Portland
97—Pittsburgh

Fourth Section

Stockcars

21—Ring Stock (Performing Horses)
22—Ring Stock
23—Ring Stock
24—Ring Stock

25—Ring Stock
26—Lead Stock (Camels, Zebras, etc.)
27—Lead Stock
28—Elephants
29—Elephants
30—Elephants

Coaches

81—Louisville
82—Des Moines
83—St. Louis
84—Cleveland
85—New York
86—Worcester
88—Los Angeles
89—Seattle
90—Washington
91—San Antonio
100—Jomar, John Ringling's Private Car

Advance Cars

1—Advertising Car
2—Advertising Car

Totals

40 Flatcars
23 Stockcars
25 Coaches
 2 Advance Cars
_____

90-Car Circus

Third Section is loaded second. Second Section is loaded third. In the Second Section, Flatcar 126, with big top center poles, is loaded last but then is switched to the head end of that cut of flatcars so as to be in necessary sequence for arrival at the next show grounds.

1971 Route, Ringling Bros. and Barnum & Bailey, Blue Unit

Dates	Cities	Railroads	Miles	Hours
Feb. 22-24	Venice, Fla.	SCL	165	4
Feb. 26-28	Orlando, Fla.	SCL to Atlanta		
		So. to Knoxville	695	22
Mar. 3-7	Knoxville, Tenn.	So. Ry.	317	16
Mar. 9-10	Macon, Ga.	SCL	445	12
Mar. 12-14	Fayetteville, NC	SCL to Richmond		
		C&O to Charleston	579	19
Mar. 17-21	Charleston, W. Va.	C&O to Potomac Yds		
		Penn Cent to unload	387	15
Mar. 24-Apr. 18	Washington, D.C.	Load on PC. Transfer.		
		So. Ry. to Birmingham	799	36
Apr. 21-25	Birmingham, Ala.	Transfer empty to L&N		
		L&N to Montgomery	97	5
Apr. 27-28	Montgomery, Ala.	L&N to New Orleans		
		SoPac to Lafayette	479	18
Apr. 30-May 2	Lafayette, La.	SoPac to New Orleans		
		IC to Jackson	304	10
May 4-5	Jackson, Miss.	IC	190	5
May 7-9	Baton Rouge, La.	IC to Meridian		
		Sou to Bristol		
		N&W to Roanoke	974	44
May 12-15	Roanoke, Va.	N&W to Hagerstown		
		PC to New York	801	37
May 18-31	New York, N.Y.	PC to Washington		
		RF&P to Richmond		
		C&O to Hampton	486	34
June 3-6	Hampton, Va.	C&O to Richmond		
		Sou to Meridian		
		IC to Monroe	1164	58
June 11-13	Monroe, La.	IC to Shreveport		
		T&P to Sweetwater		
		SF to Lubbock	624	23
June 15-16	Lubbock, Texas	Santa Fe	121	4
June 18-20	Amarillo, Texas	SF to Sweetwater		
		T&P to Abilene	162	6

June 22-23	Abilene, Texas	T&P	499	20
June 25-28	Tulsa, Okla.	T&P to Ft. Worth		
		MoPac to Houston	654	24
June 30-July 11	Houston, Texas	SP to Shreveport		
		HB&T track rental	232	10
July 13-14	Shreveport, La.	SL-SW to Memphis		
		L&N to Louisville	775	30
July 16-18	Louisville, Ky.	L&N to E. St. Louis		
		TRRA at St. Louis		
		MoPac to Kansas City	557	23
July 21-25	Kansas City, Mo.	SL-SW	484	17
July 29-Aug. 1	Memphis, Tenn.	SL-SW to Kansas City		
		CRI&P to Des Moines	705	27
Aug. 5-8	Des Moines, Ia.	CRI&P	180	8
Aug. 10-11	Waterloo, Ia.	CRI&P	370	15
Aug. 13-15	Lincoln, Neb.	UP	1082	27
Aug. 18-23	Salt Lake City	UP	439	12
Aug. 27-29	Butte, Mont.	BN	377	11
Aug. 31-Sept. 1	Spokane, Wash.	SIR to Eastport, Ida.		
		CPR to Edmonton	657	30
Sept. 3-5	Edmonston, Alta.	CN to Brownsville		
		BN to Seattle	914	28
Sept. 8-13	Seattle, Wash.	BN	185	5
Sept. 15-19	Portland, Ore.	BN	347	10
Sept. 22-26	Vancouver, BC	CN	1555	48
Sept. 30-Oct. 4	Winnipeg, Man.	BN to St. Paul		
		CMStP&P, Bloomington	465	20
Oct. 6-10	Bloomington, Minn.	CMStP&P to St. Paul		
		BN to Duluth	162	9
Oct. 12-13	Duluth, Minn.	CMStP&P	481	14
Oct. 15-18	Milwaukee, Wis.	CMStP&P	83	3
Oct. 19-20	Madison, Wis.	CMStP&P to Savanna		
		BN to Omaha	519	16
Oct. 22-25	Omaha, Neb.	BN to Chicago		
		PC to Indianapolis	672	24
Oct. 28-31	Indianapolis	PC	303	16
Nov. 2-7	Detroit	PC	164	12
Nov. 9-15	Cleveland	PC	661	24
Nov. 18-21	New Haven, Conn.	PC to Washington		
		RF&P to Richmond		
		SCL to Venice	1310	61

9 Months	45 Cities	75 RR/Moves	23,627 Miles

Ringling Bros. & Barnum & Bailey
Train Make-Up List
Mid 1950s

FOURTH SECTION—Total 14

COACHES

60
58
62
64
66

JOMAR

93
65
84
57
61
59
55
56

This section is ready to leave any time after the Third Section pulls out.

Check with Bennie Mathis our Train Master for any other details or information you desire.

In case of emergency contact:

1st Sec.—L. Morgan   Car 38
2nd Sec.—F. McClosky   Car 41
3rd Sec.—W. E. Lawson   Car 49
4th Sec.—A. Concello   Car 66

RINGLING BROS. & BARNUM & BAILEY COMBINED SHOWS, INC.

TRAIN MAKE-UP LIST

FIRST SECTION—Total 22

FLATS	STORE CARS
Cage Cut	19
121 Run Car	32
146	**COACHES**
148	37
139	38
119	39
128	40
117	
109 Run Car	

Cookhouse Cut
101 Run Car
149
129
137
132
124
144
108 Run Car

This section starts to load at approximately 5:30 p.m.

Usually loaded and ready to leave town at 10:30 p.m.

Always check with our Train Master Bennie Mathis for any late changes.

SECOND SECTION

FLATS	FLATS
Gas Cut	Wagon Cut
140 Run Car	116 Run Car
145	102
131	106
112	R.B.X. 8
138	R.B.X. 7
125	103
114	100
143	105
115 Run Car	104
	133 Run Car

STOCK CAR #30

COACHES

41
42
43
44
45
47
46

This section is usually loaded and ready to leave town at 2:00 a.m.

THIRD SECTION—Total 26

FLATS	FLATS
120 Run Car	127 Run Car
113	135
136	147
110	141
118	122
123	130
111	R.B.X. 10
134 Run Car	R.B.X. 9
	126 Run Car

RINGSTOCK STOCK CARS	ELEPHANT STOCK CARS
20	28
21	29
22	**COACHES**
24	48
25	49

This section is always loaded as soon as the First Section pulls out but doesn't leave until after the Second Section pulls out.

THE THIRD SECTION IS LOADED AFTER THE FIRST BUT DOES NOT LEAVE TOWN UNTIL AFTER THE SECOND SECTION HAS LEFT.

Clyde Beatty Circus, 1951

Flats	Wagons
#55	2—Cage
	3—Cage
	6&7—Cages
	8&9—Cages
	4—Cage

This is the loading order. After loading, flats 51, 54 and 52 are switched forward, and flat 53 is coupled behind #52. Then remainder of the train is coupled behind #53.

#57	5—Cage
	80—Arena
	98—Chairs
	44—Red Ticket

#56	81—Props
	82—Trunks
	83—Band
	97—Chairs
	45—White Ticket

#59	84—Wardrobe-Ring Stock
	80—Concessions
	-—Midway Diner
	39—Automobile

#58	93—Planks
	94—Planks
	95—Jacks
	92—Stringers

#53	30—Cookhouse
	46—Menagerie
	41—Annex
	85—

#51	31—Cookhouse
	21—Truck with boom
	90—Canvas
	99—Empty

#54	23—Truck, water
	91—Poles
	38—Train lights
	24—Tractor

#52	41—Lights
	22—Truck, stake driver
	96—Stake & Chain
	25—Tractor
	43—Light plant

Unloading order, then, is: #51-54-52-53-55-57-56-59-58.

Flats #51 and #52 are loading flats, equipped with runs, snubbing posts and with extra reinforcement at one end of each. Regardless of whether train is loaded poles to engine or caboose, one of these flats always is at the proper place for loading and unloading.

Flats 57 and 59 are 70 ft. models. They are located in train so as to be in the same relative position regardless of how flats are switched.

Flat 57 is a Mt. Vernon. All others are Warren type, except one, which is a Keith but has the same appearance as a Warren.

Train also includes five sleepers and two stock cars, making a total of 15 cars.

One stock car carried 6 elephants.

The other has 14 ring, and 4 baggage horses and 10 ponies. Both stocks are lightly loaded. Double-deck end for ponies is not used.

Postscript

After this book was prepared, the following information on a new railroad circus became available.

T.P.
C.P.F.
September 1978

Even at the end of the 1970s, an all-new railroad circus was being built. A part of the Ringling organization, the new show was to open in February 1979 as the International Circus Festival of Monte Carlo Spectacular, featuring talent from the annual world circus competition sponsored by Prince Rainier in Monaco. Among the cars being refitted for the new show were Pullmans *Green Pine* and *Whispering Pine* from the Louisville & Nashville Railroad — *Authors' Photo.*

Also earmarked for the Monaco circus were three of these four cars on the Ringling shop track at Venice, Florida. Nearest is the former RF&P RR's *King William.* In the distance are the ex-NYNH&H RR 2075, *Monument Beach,* and the former Union Pacific Baggage Car 6320. In charge of all such work for Ringling was Neal Simpson, assistant vice-president for transportation. He also handles all contracts with scores of railroads that move Ringling's Red and Blue units over their rails. John Bridges is train repair superintendent. In July 1978 the new train was expected to have ten cars; by September, plans called for a fifteen-car circus — *Authors' Photo.*

Index

Adkins, Jess, 139
Adam Forpaugh Circus, 2, 21, 22, 23, 24, 41, 62, 77, 86, 88, 91, 167, 363
A. G. Allen's Big Original New Orleans Colored Minstrels, 324
Al G. Barnes Circus, 7, 26, 28, 41, 63, 89, 97, 98, 114, 137, 167, 189, 192, 207, 227, 228, 246, 247, 259, 261, 267, 270, 362, 363
Al G. Barnes-Sells Floto Circus, 43, 50, 89, 124, 143, 221
Al G. Fields Minstrels, 324, 330
Al. G. Kelly-Miller Bros. Circus, 29
Albany, NY, 3
American Car & Foundry, 287, 288, 289, 328
American Circus Corp., 28, 97, 146, 205
American Locomotive Co., 45, 49
Amtrak, 339
Apache, RR Car, 131
Arapahoe, RR Car, 130
Arlington & Beckmann's Real Wild West, 139
Arlington, Edward, 237, 373
Arms Palace Horse Car Co., 118
Art Lewis Carnival, 346
Arthur Bros. Circus, 29, 43, 112, 138
Association of American Railroads, 39
Atchison, Topeka & Santa Fe RR, 24, 39, 40, 49, 247, 314, 338, 339, 342, 361, 364
Atlantic Coast Line RR, 246, 354
Austin Bros. Circus, 29

B. E. Wallace Circus, 24, 33, 96
(See also Great Wallace Circus)

Backman & Tinsch Two Car Circus, 282
Bailey, James A., 23, 24, 25, 86, 88, 149, 362
Baldwin Park, Calif., 167, 227
Bangor & Aroostook RR, 360
Baraboo, WI, 24, 98, 167, 178, 229, 232, 361, 363, 366, 367
Baraboo, RR Car, 364
Barkoot Shows, 345
Barney & Smith Co., 23
Barnum, P. T., 16, 18, 19, 21, 23, 24, 32, 130, 243, 362
Barnum's—*see* P. T. Barnum's World's Fair
P. T. Barnum's Museum Menagerie & Circus
Barnum & Bailey Greatest Show on Earth, 25, 26, 30, 41, 61, 69, 72, 76, 88, 102, 120, 141, 167, 182, 184, 194, 195, 207, 233, 236, 238, 239, 252, 262, 268, 362, 363
Barnum Bailey & Hutchinson Circus, 233
Barnum & London Circus, 23, 24, 32, 77, 241, 243
Beatty, Clyde, 107
Beckmann & Gerety Carnival, 108, 142, 345
Ben, RR Car, 130
Benton, Steamboat, 15
Beveridge's Montana Wildest West Show, 84
Bill Hames Carnival, 98
Billy Clark's Minstrels, 324
Blackfoot, RR Car, 131
Black Patti Troubadors, 324
Blanchfield, David (Deacon), 288

Boston Garden, 29, 246
Boudinot, F. A. (Babe), 85
Bridgeport, Conn., 167, 233
Bridges, John, 386
Brown, Joe E., 283
Brundage Show, 345
Buck, Frank, 131
Buck Jones Wild West Show, 28, 346
Buckskin Ben Show, 26, 284
Buffalo Bill, *see* William F. Cody
Buffalo Bill's Wild West Show, 25, 84, 97, 130, 141, 238, 262, 346, 362, 364, 370
Buffalo Bill-Jess Willard Show, 147
Buffalo Bill-Pawnee Bill Show, 26, 363
Bulgar & Cheney Show, 26
Burlington Northern RR, 319
Burr Robbins Circus, 33, 363
Burte, Le Jeune, 2
Busby Bros. Circus, 279, 283
Butch, RR Car, 130
Butler, Al, 338

C. A. Wortham Shows, 346
C. S. Noyes Crescent City Circus, 5
Caddo, RR Car, 130
Caledonia, RR Car, 131, 149, 150
California Frank's Show, 26, 369
California, RR Car, 146
Calliope, 1, 23, 75, 261
Campbell, Bailey & Hutchinson Circus, 28
Campbell Bros. Circus, 26, 161, 206, 222, 260, 264, 278
Campbell, William P. (Low Grass), 280
Canadian National Ry., 34, 270, 354

Canadian Pacific Ry., 354
Cardiff Giant, 16
Carl Hagenbeck Wild Animal Show, 261, 263
Carr, Willie, 246
Castello, Dan, 15, 16, 18, 19
Caterpillar Tractor, 163, 164, 165, 166, 167, 176, 197, 213, 349
Cavalcade of Amusements, 346
Central Pacific RR, 5, 22, 23, 24
Central Vermont Ry., 133
Cetlin & Wilson Shows, 313, 346
Chalfen, Morris, 338
Chambers, Wash, 2
Chautauqua, 325, 335, 326, 336
Cheyenne, RR Car, 130, 131, 134
Chicago & North Western Ry., 40, 43, 46, 78, 90, 151, 167, 168, 169, 171, 173, 175, 176, 177, 178, 179, 225, 229, 230, 232, 239, 260, 296, 301, 362, 365
Chicago Burlington & Quincy RR, 47, 229, 354, 365
Chicago Coliseum, 247
Chicago, Indianapolis & Louisville Ry., 226
Chicago, Milwaukee, St. Paul & Pacific RR, 45, 180, 215, 353, 362
Chicago, Rock Island & Pacific RR, 39, 72, 289, 301, 302, 354
Chicago, St. Paul Minneapolis & Omaha Ry., 43
Chicago World's Fair, 345
Christy Bros. Circus, 26, 28, 97, 98, 142, 247, 253, 279, 362, 363
Christy, Edwin P., 324
Christy, George W., 324
Christy's Minstrels, 324
Cincinnati, Ohio, 167

387

Circus World Museum, 85, 89, 98, 198, 199, 294, 358, 361, 362, 363, 364, 365
Cleveland, RR Car, 130
Cleveland Grotto Circus, 285
Cleveland, Lorraine & Wheeling RR, 241
Clyde Beatty Circus, 29, 60, 108, 130, 132, 142, 160, 163, 171, 185, 189, 190, 210, 229, 234, 247, 261, 297, 313, 361, 362, 363
Coburn Minstrels, 324
Cody, RR Car, 144
Cody, William F., 25, 88, 130, 245
Cohan & Harris Minstrel Show, 324
Cole Bros. Circus, 28, 29, 30, 41, 66, 80, 86, 93, 95, 97, 98, 107, 109, 112, 128, 130, 131, 145, 146, 147, 163, 172, 187, 188, 196, 204, 211, 223, 261, 269, 272, 278, 280, 313, 361, 362, 363
Cole & Johnson Show, 26, 370
Cole & Rice Circus, 26
Cole & Rogers Circus, 26, 280
Cole, William Washington, 22, 24
Comanche, RR Car, 130
Con T. Kennedy Shows, 345
Concello, Art, 149, 287, 288, 294
Connecticut, RR Car, 130, 379
Continental Divide, 319
Cook & Barrett's Shows, 136
Cook & Whitby Circus, 261
Cook & Wilson's Wild Animal Circus, 373
Cook Bros. Circus, 279
Cooke, L. E., 370
Coop & Lent Circus, 259, 372
Cooper & Bailey Circus, 23, 245
Cooper Bros. Circus, 280
Coup, William Cameron, 14, 15, 16, 17, 18, 19, 20, 21, 22, 31, 40, 97, 102, 129, 159, 235, 237, 245, 289, 331, 349
Cummins Wild West Show, 25
Dailey Bros. Circus, 29, 70, 130, 133, 163, 297, 346
Dakota, RR Car, 130
Dan Castello Circus, 5, 13, 16, 18
Dan Emmett, RR Car, 324, 330

Dan Rice Circus, 4
Davenport, Ben, 130
DED, Dragging Equipment Detector, 317
Delavan, WI, 15
Dalavan, RR Car, 364
Delaware & Hudson RR, 216, 369, 371, 373, 376
Delaware, Lackawanna & Western RR, 368, 370, 371, 372, 374
Dempsey, Jack, 131
Den Stone's Original Railroad Circus, 2, 3, 9
Denver, CO, 167, 245, 253
Denver & Rio Grande Western RR, 316, 317, 318, 320
Denver Post, 82
Detroit & Mackinaw RR, 82
Dixie, RR Car, 130
Dode Fisk Circus, 235
Dodson's World's Fair Shows, 345, 351
Dolly Vardon, 22
Dorchester, RR Car, 364
Dot, Admiral, 16
Dover Bay, RR Car, 362
Downie, Andrew, 36, 130, 324
Downie Bros. Circus, 28
Downie & Wheeler Circus, 26, 130
Dukies, 155, 245
Duluth, South Shore & Atlantic Ry., 43
Duluth, Winnipeg & Pacific Ry., 354

Ed. F. Davis Uncle Tom's Cabin Show, 324
Edwin Booth, RR Car, 287
El Dorado Elf, 16
Elephants, 1, 3, 5, 30, 34, 42, 115, 116, 117, 127, 128, 163, 171, 197, 202, 224, 234, 262, 264, 272, 274, 279, 289, 294, 295, 314, 316, 318, 325, 363
Eli Bridge Co., 346
Endy Bros. Carnival, 359
Erie RR, 49, 369
Erie-Lackawanna Ry., 346
Eva, RR Car, 130
Evanston, RR Car, 130
Excursions, 16, 19, 235, 243

F. S. Wolcott's Rabbit Foot Minstrels, 324
Famous Robinson Shows, 26, 28
Feld, Irvin, 288
Fiji Cannibals, 16, 19
Fink's Mules, 325
Florence Nightengale, RR Car, 131
Frank Money Dramatic Co., 325
Florida, RR Car, 130, 167
Foley & Burk Shows, 346, 364
Forepaugh, Adam, 21, 22, 25, 32
Forepaugh & Sells Bros. United Circus, 25, 26, 83, 191, 363
Frank Adams Minstrels, 324
Frank A. Robbins, Circus, 26, 41, 82, 371, 372
Galveston, Houston & Henderson RR, 185
Gaskill-Munday Show, 345
Genders, Tuffy (Harold), 129, 288
Gentry Bros. Shows, 26, 28, 61, 98, 121, 170, 172, 255, 259, 279, 289, 327, 362, 363
Gentry-Patterson Circus, 28, 226
George W. Hall (Col.) Trained Wild Animal Circus, 280
Georgia, RR Car, 130
Georgia Smart Set Minstrels, 325
Gibson, Hoot, 139
Gillette, Mrs. L. C., 81
Giraffe, 16, 19, 42, 379
Golden Bros. Circus, 28, 56, 135
Goliath, 116
Gollmar Bros. Circus, 26, 28, 43, 80, 81, 100, 167, 260, 262, 266, 362, 363
Goodman Wonder Show, 359
Goold & Sons, James, 3
Goshen, Colonel, 16
Grand Trunk Western Ry., 261
Great Eastern Circus, 19, 21
Great Eastern Hippodrome Show, 280
Great Forepaugh Show, 21, 22 (*See also* Adam Forepaugh Circus)
Great Northern Ry., 65, 354
Great Patterson Shows, 156, 345
Great Railroad Combination Circus, 5
Great Wallace Circus, 24, 87, 103, 144, 174, 261, 262

Great Western Railroad Circus, 2
Greater Sheesley Shows, 284
Green Bay & Western RR, 43
Green Pine, RR Car, 386
Gulf, Colorado and Santa Fe Ry., 74
Guttermuth, Charley, 360

Hagenbeck-Wallace Circus, 26, 28, 29, 41, 43, 60, 63, 87, 97, 98, 101, 110, 119, 122, 131, 161, 167, 192, 205, 211, 261, 317, 346, 358, 361, 363, 364
Hagenbeck-Wallace Forepaugh Sells Combined Shows, 87
Haight & Chambers Circus, 4
Hamid-Morton Circus, 287
Handy, Prof. William, 324
Hargreaves, Tom, 324
Harrington, George, 324
Harris, John H., 338
Haverley's Minstrels, 324
Henie, Sonja, 338
Hemmings, Cooper & Whitby Circus, 4, 5
Hemmings, Richard, 4
Henderson, Dr. J. Y., 288
Hennies Bros. Shows, 346, 350
Heritage Bros. Circus, 28, 43
Hi Henry's Minstrels, 324
Hickey, Bob, 339
Hickory Creek, RR Car, 302
Hippotheatron, 19
Holiday on Ice, 338, 339
Hollywood Ice Revue, 338
Honey Boy Evans Minstrels, 324
Hopper, Arthur, 77
Hotchkiss, Blue & Co., 143
Howard Damon Circus, 368
Howes & Robinson, 4
Howes Great London Show, 2, 23, 26, 28, 105, 252, 256, 364, 369, 374
Howes, Seth B., 3, 15
Hugo Bros. Circus, 278, 280
Hunting's Great New York Shows, 368
Hutchinson, James L., 243
Hyatt Railroad Circus, 4

Ice Capades, 338, 339, 341, 342
Ice Follies, 338, 339

Illinois Central System, 68, 190, 212, 215, 339, 341, 354
Illinois Terminal RR, 236
Indiana, RR Car, 379
Indian Pete's Show, 26
Ingram, Harold, 161, 162
International Circus Festival of Monte Carlo Spectacular, 386
Interstate Commerce Commission, 36, 39, 40, 49, 55, 56, 73, 77, 102, 277, 368, 375, 376

J. Augustus Jones All-New Model Plate Railroad Shows, 279
J. W. Warner & Co. Great Pacific Combination, 22
Jackson & Sharpe Co., 327, 328
Jacobs, Terrell, 285
Janesville, RR Car, 364
James Adams Show, 325
James E. Strates Shows, 313, 346, 355, 356, 357, 363
James Masterson Show, 26
Jeep, 164, 316, 341
Jethro Almond Show, 325, 327
John H. Sparks Circus, 81, 279 (*See also* Sparks Circus)
John Robinson Circus, 21, 23, 24, 26, 28, 41, 43, 64, 77, 89, 92, 97, 123, 146, 167, 254, 261, 266, 361, 362, 363, 373, 374
Johnny J. Jones Shows, 313, 345, 358
Jomar, RR Car, 131, 153
Jones and Adams New Century Railroad Shows, 280
Jones Bros. Shows, 26, 132
Jones, Elmer, 279, 280, 325
Jones, J. Augustus, 132, 179, 280, 325
Jones New Empire Show; 280
Jumbo, 24, 34

Keith Car Co., 98, 113
Kickapoo Indian Medicine Company, 325, 333
King, Floyd, 279
King, Howard, 279
King Bros. Circus, 28
King Bros. & Cristiani Circus, 28

King & Tucker Circus, 26, 280
King William, RR Car, 386
Kit Carson Show, 26
Koch, Jim, 307
Kramer, Orville, 167

La Mothe Mfg. Co., 32
La Tena's Wild Animal Circus, 372
Larkin, Frank, 95
La Tena, RR Car, 130
La Tena Circus, 43
Lawrence Carr Carnival, 360
Lee Bros. Circus, 28
Lehigh Valley RR, 233
Lent, Lewis B., 4, 11, 15, 19, 21
Lent's Circus, 21
Lester, Ed, 163, 164, 347
Lew Dockstader's Minstrels, 324
Loretto, RR Car, 131
Louisiana, RR Car, 130
Louisville & Nashville RR (L&N), 43, 49, 54, 57, 386
Luria Steel & Trading Co., 98

M. L. Clark Circus, 27
Mabie Circus, 15
Mack Truck, 101, 164, 179, 208, 212, 213, 378, 379
Macon, Georgia, 41, 167
Madigan, Henry, 2
Madigan, Myers & Barton's RR Circus & Amphitheatre, 2
Madison Square Garden, 29, 246
Maginley, Ben, 13
Mahara's Minstrels, 324
Maine Central RR, 215
Maio, Robert, 289, 307
Malaya, RR Car, 131
Mann, H. A., 373
Martin, Al W., 324, 328
Maynard, Ken, 260
Menagerie, 1, 3, 5, 160, 379
Metropolitan Carnival, 346
Michigan Central RR, 90
Michigan, RR Car, 379
Midway, 345
Mighty Haag Show, 26, 27, 43, 130, 247, 260, 346, 362, 363, 369, 370, 372
Miller Bros., 92, 372

Minnesota, RR Car, 379
Missouri Car & Foundry Co., 24
Missouri Kansas & Texas RR (Katy), 39
Missouri Pacific RR (MoPac), 43, 55, 56, 73, 185, 190, 354
Mix, Tom, 116
Moffat Tunnel, 318, 319
Mollie Bailey Circus, 26, 279
Montana, RR Car, 130
Monte Baldo, RR Car, 362
Monte Carlo Circus, 386
Montgomery Queen Circus, 26
Monument Beach, RR Car, 386
Morgan, Lloyd Sr., 287, 288, 289, 294, 302
Morris & Castle Shows, 345
Morris, Walker, 170
Mt. Vernon, IL, 97
Mt. Vernon Car Mfg. Co., 97, 98, 101, 105, 106, 107, 113, 114, 115, 123, 127, 346, 358, 361, 363, 364
Mozart, RR Car, 287
Mugivan, Jerry, 77, 123, 146
Myers, Madigan & Barton's RR Circus, 9
McCoy, Col. Tim, 130, 131, 134
McGrath, Phillip Anthony, 161, 188, 228

N. J. Lapp Shows, 345
Naomi, RR Car, 138
Nashville, Chattanooga & St. Louis Ry., 173
Navajo, RR Car, 130
New York Central RR, 40, 42, 43, 70, 186, 226, 285, 301, 370, 371, 372, 376
New York, New Haven & Hartford RR, 167, 233, 247, 375, 386
New York, Ontario & Western Ry., 236, 247, 335, 336, 368, 371, 373, 374
New York, Susquehanna & Western RR, 372
Nichols, H. F., 2
Norfolk & Western Ry., 7
Norma, RR Car, 130

Norris & Rowe Circus, 41, 43, 81, 204, 261, 364
North, Henry Ringling, 44
North, John Ringling, 153, 287
Northern Pacific Ry., 72, 117, 262, 267, 269

O'Brien, Pogey, 19
Ohio Falls Car Mfg. Co., 327
Old Milwaukee Days, 361
Older, Pardon A., 19
Olinza, Madame, 2
Olson Shows, 346
101 Ranch Wild West Shows, 26, 28, 77, 92, 98, 114, 135, 145, 198, 200, 260, 261, 267, 305, 361, 362, 363, 372
Orton Family, 27, 80
Osage, RR Car, 130
Owensboro, RR Car, 130, 131, 145, 146

P. A. Older Circus, 259
P. T. Barnum's Great World's Fair, 18, 19, 41, 160, 235, 237, 289
P. T. Barnum's Museum, Menagerie & Circus, 15, 16, 17, 18, 77, 160
Pacific Electric Ry., 46, 140
Palace Cars, 18, 23, 24, 77
Palestine Giant, 16
Palmer, W. F., 260
Palmer Bros. Circus, 260
Palmer, Dick, 339
Pan American Circus, 247
Parades, 1, 3, 4, 18, 19, 23, 279
Parker, C. W., 345
Parker & Watts Circus, 28
Parks & Banks Circus, 280
Pawah, 116
Pawnee, RR Car, 131
Pawnee Bill Show, 25
Payton, Corse, 327
Peffer, Crawford A., 335
Penn Central RR, 40, 216, 289, 291
Pennsylvania Railroad, 16, 40, 68, 69, 142, 161, 226, 247, 274, 287, 294, 338, 339, 340, 341, 359
Peru, IND, 24, 167, 270, 285
Philadelphia, PA, 167
Polock Bros. Circus, 287

Potter Three Link Drawbar Couplers, 24

Powers Elephants, 325

Prairie Lillie & Nebraska Bill's Wild West Show, 138

Prince Rainier, 386

Promontory Point, 5

Pullman, 75, 78, 79, 129, 130, 294, 300, 302, 314, 323, 324, 338, 339, 361, 377

Railroad Circus & Crystal Amphitheatre, 2, 3, 9

Railway Guides, 40

Redpath Chautauqua System, 325, 335, 336, 337

Rentz Show, 83

Revolving Temple of Juno, 19

Reynold's Great Railroad Shows, 54

Rhoda Royal Circus, 28, 57, 279

Rice Bros. Circus, 280, 370

Richard & Pringle's Minstrels, 324

Richmond, Fredericksburg & Potomac RR, 386

Ringling Bros. Circus, 24, 25, 26, 41, 62, 91, 156, 157, 161, 167, 184, 230, 231, 232, 233, 236, 237, 240, 248, 251, 260, 261, 262, 268, 363, 368, 370, 371

Ringling Bros. and Barnum & Bailey Combined Shows, 3, 7, 27, 28, 29, 40, 41, 42, 43, 44, 46, 55, 58, 68, 78, 79, 85, 89, 90, 94, 95, 98, 99, 103, 105, 106, 107, 109, 113, 116, 117, 121, 123, 126, 129, 130, 131, 132, 140, 142, 149, 155, 158, 159, 160, 161, 163, 164, 167, 168, 169, 173, 175, 177, 178, 179, 180, 190, 197, 198, 202, 208, 210, 212, 213, 215, 216, 217, 220, 222, 223, 224, 225, 228, 229, 232, 233, 234, 246, 247, 253, 259, 261, 265, 274, 276, 287, 288, 289, 290, 291, 292, 294, 295, 296, 297, 299, 301, 302, 303, 304, 305, 306, 307, 308, 310, 313, 314, 315, 316, 317, 318, 319, 320, 339, 346, 352, 362, 363, 379, 382, 383

Ringling Bros. and Barnum & Bailey Circus World, 289

Ringling, Charles, 131, 148, 149

Ringling Family, 288

Ringling, John, 28, 39, 40, 70, 131, 153

Ringling, Mable, 131, 153

Ringling, Robert, 130

Road-Railer, 3

Robbins & Co. Circus, 22

Robbins Bros. Circus, 28, 53, 77, 87, 97, 109, 139, 261, 313, 362, 363

Robinson, G. L., 335

Robinson, Yankee, 15, 26, 28

Rock Island Rocket, 289, 294

Royal American Shows, 98, 313, 345, 346, 347, 352, 353, 354, 364

Rubin & Cherry Shows, 345, 350, 351

Rusko & Holland Minstrels, 324

Russell Bros. Circus, 29, 51, 134

Ryan, C. L., 167

S. H. Barrett Railroad Show, 261

St. Charles Co., 331

St. Louis-San Francisco RR (Frisco), 39, 40, 265, 313, 354

Sanger's Great European Circus, 26, 28, 120, 278, 371

Sarasota, RR Car, 130, 131

Sarasota, FLA, 167, 228, 234, 246, 287, 295

Saratoga Springs, RR Car, 147

Schwab, Charles M., 131

S. F. & N. P. RR, 23

Schlitz Circus Parade, 361

Schlitz Brewing Co., 361, 364, 365, 366

Script, 44

Seaboard Air Line RR, 58

Seaboard Coast Line RR, 153, 289, 310, 311, 315

Sedlmayr, C. J., Jr., 347

Seils-Sterling Circus, 8

Sells Bros. Circus, 24, 91, 167, 242, 261, 362, 363

Sells Floto Circus, 26, 28, 43, 64, 82, 97, 98, 104, 108, 116, 118, 124, 130, 144, 161, 167, 245, 247, 249, 250, 265, 313, 346, 363, 374

Settlemire, W. A., 98

Sheesley Shows, 345, 346

Shipstads & Johnson, 338

Shreveport, RR Car, 130

Siamese Twins, 16

Sig Sautelle Circus, 26

Silas Green From New Orleans, 325, 329

Simpson, Neal, 386

Singer's Midgets, 325

Sipe & Blake Dog & Pony Show, 327

Skerbeck Family Shows, 284, 329

Smith, Charlie, 288, 297, 316

Southern Ry., 226, 339, 354, 366

Southern Pacific RR, 22, 24, 51, 172, 307

Southland, RR Car, 324, 330

Spalding, Dr. Gilbert, 2, 3

Spalding and Rogers Circus, 2, 3, 4, 11

Sparks, Charles, 28

Sparks Circus, 26, 28, 29, 41, 64, 73, 77, 85, 97, 110, 127, 167, 196, 247, 255, 260, 261, 268, 358, 361, 362, 363, 371, 374, 375 (*See also* John H. Sparks Circus)

Steamboats, 2, 3, 4

Stetson's Uncle Tom's Cabin Company, 324

Stone, Den, 2

Stone & Madigan Circus, 2

Stone & Murray Circus, 280

Stonecypher, Otto (Stoney), 361

Stout, Victor, 372

Stratton, Sherwood, 15

Sun Bros. Circus, 26, 43, 93, 251, 363, 373

Sunday Run, 245

Super Chief, 339

Sutton's Uncle Tom's Cabin Show, 324

Tannhaeuser, RR Car, 287

Tavlin, Jack, 147

Teets Bros. Palmetto Shows, 282

Temple, Harry, 96

Terrell, Zack, 130, 145, 146

Terry's Uncle Tom's Cabin Co., 333

Thrall Car Co., 98, 113, 179

Thumb, Tom, 15

Tiger Bill's Show, 26

Tim McCoy's (Col.) Wild West Show, 28, 98, 125, 130, 131, 134, 154, 187, 206, 223, 289, 346, 358, 361

Tioga & Elmira State Line RR, 235, 237

Tom Mix Circus, 28

Toronto, RR Car, 136

Track Gauge, 3

Twentieth Century Limited, 289, 294, 302

Uihlein, Robert A., 361

Ulster & Delaware RR, 373, 374

Uncle Tom's Cabin Shows, 286, 323, 324, 325, 328, 333

Union Pacific RR, 5, 7, 13, 22, 23, 24, 47, 67, 171, 172, 189, 238, 289, 297, 307

United States Rolling Stock Co., 28

Van Amburgh Circus, 259

Van Amburgh Menagerie, 2, 24

Van Arnam Minstrels, 324

Van Orden, Wessell T. B., Jr., 2

Venice, FLA, 289, 306, 308, 310

Venice Transportation Co., 28, 98, 104

Vogel's Minstrels, 324

W. C. Coup New United Monster Shows, 362, 363

W. H. Coulton Shows, 26

W. H. Harris Nickel Plate Shows, 155, 364

W. W. Cole New York & New Orleans Circus, 22, 23, 24, 25, 40, 261, 362, 363

Wabash Ry., 66, 68, 266

Wagner, Sleeping Car, 18, 21, 24

Wallace, Ben, 261

Wallace Bros. Circus, 28

Walter L. Main Circus, 25, 28, 59, 98, 137, 198, 240, 247, 261, 274, 362, 363, 374

Warren, PA, 97

Warren Tank Car Co., 29, 97, 98, 100, 101, 106, 108, 109, 112, 113, 115, 116, 161, 164, 313, 346, 350, 355, 361, 363, 364

Washburn, Leon W., 324
Welsh Bros. Show, 26, 136, 324
West & Wells Circus, 280
West Baden, IND, 167
West Shore RR, 369, 370, 373
West's World Wonder Shows, 345, 346
Western Railway of Alabama, 354
Western Trunk Line Committee, 52
Westinghouse Air Brakes, 24
Whale Shows, 112, 116
Wheeler Bros. All New Shows, 280
Wheeler Bros. Circus, 43
Whispering Pine, RR Car, 386
Whitby's Metropolitan Railroad Circus, 4
Willard, Jess, 147
Wisconsin, RR Car, 130, 151
Wonewoc, RR Car, 364
Woodcock, Bill, 272
Woodword's Seals, 325
World Bros. Circus, 28
World of Mirth Shows, 313, 346, 358, 361
World's Finest Shows, 346
Wortham & Allen Shows, 345

Yankee Robinson Circus, 15, 28, 260, 364
Young Buffalo Wild West, 26

Zeidman & Pollie Shows, 345
Zouane, 19

The Circus Moves By Rail *was set in Souvenir type by B. Vader Phototypesetting of Fort Collins, Colorado. Pruett Press/O'Hara, Inc. of Boulder, Colorado, printed the book on seventy-pound White Shorewood Suede Offset stock. Roswell Bookbinding of Phoenix, Arizona, furnished the edition binding. Book design by Dianne Kedro; dust jacket design by Jim Kifer.*